POLITICAL ARGUMENT

California Series on Social Choice and Political Economy

EDITED BY BRIAN BARRY, ROBERT H. BATES, AND SAMUEL L. POPKIN

POLITICAL ARGUMENT

A Reissue with a New Introduction

Brian Barry

UNIVERSITY OF CALIFORNIA PRESS
Berkeley   Los Angeles

University of California Press
Berkeley and Los Angeles, California

© 1965, 1990 Brian Barry

Printed in Great Britain

Library of Congress Cataloging-in-Publication Data

Barry, Brian M.
    Political argument : a reissue with a new introduction / Brian
Barry.
      p.   cm.
    Reprint. Originally published: New York : Humanities Press, 1965.
    Includes bibliographical references and index.
    ISBN 0-520-07049-6. — ISBN 0-520-07051-8 (pbk.)
    1. Political science.   I. Title.
JA66.B34   1990
320—0020   90-50356
                                                         CIP

To J.H.B.

CONTENTS

ANALYTICAL CONTENTS

ACKNOWLEDGEMENTS

IN the six years that have elapsed since I began this book I have received so much assistance that I sometimes wonder if I am entitled even to claim the usual credit for my mistakes, let alone anything more. My first thanks must go to my graduate study Supervisor, Professor H. L. A. Hart. During my first two years after graduating he read and criticised, always in a wonderfully detailed and constructive way, the enormous quantities of ill-written and inchoate material which I brought to him. Since then, too, he has given valuable advice on successive drafts of the manuscript, which has greatly improved its final state. During the first two years I was supported financially by the British taxpayer: I can only hope that he has at last got something of use out of it. In 1960–61 I held the Lloyd-Muirhead Fellowship in Social Philosophy at Birmingham University and on two occasions was allowed to subject my colleagues there to some of the ideas I was working on at the time. Then in 1961–62 the Rockefeller Foundation awarded me a grant under its Program for Research in Legal and Political Philosophy and Harvard University elected me to an honorary Research Fellowship. Among the many benefits provided by that year, I must single out the opportunity it gave me for discussion with Professors John Rawls, E. C. Banfield and T. C. Schelling. My two D.Phil. examiners, Mr P. F. Strawson and Mr John Plamenatz, both made very helpful criticisms at the *viva voce* examination and in addition Mr Plamenatz was kind enough to copy out his notes and send them to me. At many points their criticisms were so clearly well taken that I have simply met or evaded them as best I can without specific mention. However, in a few places I have wanted to stick up for what I said against Mr Plamenatz's criticisms and there I have quoted the criticism from him with attribution. Finally, I should like to express my real gratitude to Miss Diana Marshallsay, Assistant Librarian in the

xvii

Social Sciences faculty at Southampton University, for preparing the Index and helping with the Bibliography.

Southampton, 1965

The dedicatee of *Political Argument*, Joanna Barry, and I were married in 1960, so the book played a large part in the early years of our life together. Although our paths have separated in recent years, and she is now living a very different kind of life as a member of a contemplative order in the Anglican diocese of Milwaukee, I know that she will be pleased to see the book back in print.

There is one new acknowledgement, which goes to the unknown student who stole the copy of *Political Argument* belonging to one of the editors of the California Series in Political Economy, Robert Bates. With the well-honed reactions of a rational choice theorist, Bates immediately recognised that if a book has theft value it must also have sale value, and initiated the process that led to this reissue under the current imprints.

Bloomsbury, 1990

POLITICAL ARGUMENT
AFTER TWENTY-FIVE YEARS
An Introduction to the Reissue

I. HOW *POLITICAL ARGUMENT* HAPPENED

Political Argument was first published in 1965. It has been out of print for some time in Britain and was never really in print in the United States: after the initial shipment of a few hundred copies was exhausted, buying a copy required a combination of persistence and luck. As a further barrier to the book's circulation, it was never issued in paperback, while the price for the hardback edition rose from a (pre-decimal) two pounds ten shillings to a large multiple of that. I am glad that all these shortcomings are now being remedied by this reissue.

With the exception of two additional paragraphs in the Acknowledgements and the correction of one error,[1] the text here is exactly the same as in the 1965 printing. (The Index has, however, been revamped and incorporates references to this Introduction.) There are obvious economic advantages in not resetting the book, but there are two considerations favouring a straightforward reprint which would have much weight even if expense were no object. The first is that in its first quarter century *Political Argument* has attracted a steady stream of citation and critical commentary—which is, indeed, the justification for reprinting it

[1] In the original version, the upper right cell in Figure 4 on page 248 read 'Measure fails' and had utility entries appropriate to that outcome. Since the cell is defined by both groups voting for the measure, this obviously made no sense at all. I discovered this blunder myself about ten years ago when I had assigned the chapter for a class and had to reread it. Nobody had ever pointed out the error to me. Since I know plenty of people who would have been happy to do so if they had spotted it, I hope this means that the text is so persuasive as to render the figures redundant.

at all. I shall say something later (in Sections 3 and 4) about the book's reception and the fate in the hands of others of those ideas in it that have caught on. The relevant point is, however, that rewriting the book at this stage would at the least throw off the page references in the existing literature and at the most make it impossible to tie up the old criticisms with the new text.

That kind of inconvenience might be accepted if revision were a feasible proposition. But it is not—and this is the decisive consideration—because the intellectual world into which *Political Argument* was born has vanished. It can be reconstructed, and indeed it will be my object in Section 2 to do just that. But there is no point in trying to update something that is as much a creature of a particular time as was *Political Argument*. As well try to turn a PVC miniskirt into a jogging suit.

If this is all true, however, it invites the question: why not write a new version instead of reissuing the old one? I answer that the question is based upon a misconception. I am in fact currently engaged in doing exactly that. The first volume of a trilogy on social justice (each volume of which will be a good deal longer than *Political Argument*) was published in 1989.[2] The trouble is that, as this suggests, on my present rather grandiose idea of the scale required to do the job properly, redoing the whole of *Political Argument* would take me well into my dotage (which I sometimes feel is creeping up already when attacked by graduate students as obnoxious as I was at their age). It would be a bit too simple-minded to say that the three volumes of my projected treatise correspond to Chapter VI of *Political Argument* so that redoing the whole thing would need thirty volumes. Nevertheless, it is certainly correct to say that the scope of *Political Argument* is very much wider, though in another sense it is less ambitious.

I shall attempt an overall assessment from my present vantage point in the last section of this Introduction (Section 5). The next section (2), will be devoted to the task of reconstructing the intellectual world within which *Political Argument* was conceived. Sections 3 and 4 will take up some of the central ideas, follow their

---

[2] *Theories of Justice*, Volume 1 in *A Treatise on Social Justice*, has the same publishers as this reprint of *Political Argument*. Volume 2, *The Possibility of Justice*, is due out in 1991. Volume 3 will be entitled *The Just Society* and will be concerned with concrete applications within and between countries.

their subsequent fate, and offer comments and, in some cases, revisions. As a means of providing a background to that, let me begin by saying something about the way in which the book came to be written.

Political Argument began life as my Ph.D. (or, as it is called at Oxford, D.Phil.) dissertation, in which form it was entitled *The Language of Political Argument*. (The significance of this will become apparent in Section 2.) When I began work on it I had no real idea of what I wanted to do, except that it should be theoretical in a constructive and analytical way rather than being about what somebody else had said. An immediate problem that arose, given this vaguely-defined but strongly-held ambition, was to find a sympathetic supervisor. A few years ago (at which point Oxford University fell on hard times) an aspiring graduate student had a choice of five people who did this kind of political theory, all of whom were of world class, and even now there are three.[3] It will help to set the scene if I say that in 1958 there was nobody in Oxford whose interests corresponded to mine. (The Professor and Reader were Isaiah Berlin and John Plamenatz respectively, both of whom were primarily concerned with the history of political thought.)

By sheer serendipity I acquired H. L. A. Hart, recently installed as Professor of Jurisprudence, as my supervisor. The way this happened was as follows. The Queen's College, where I studied philosophy, politics and economics as an undergraduate, had (like most colleges with a strong PPE student body) a society whose purpose was to invite speakers once or twice a term. (Ours was called the Bentham Society, in commemoration of one of the college's illustrious—if critical—products.) During the last term before I graduated, Hart gave a talk to this society. I cannot now recall the subject, but I do well remember the impact it had on me. He seemed to me someone noticeably more clear-headed than anyone I had come across before—a judgement that I have found no reason for revising subsequently.[4] In the October following my graduation, then, I turned up on Hart's doorstep and asked

---

[3] 'World class' means 'liable to be offered a senior post by a major American university'.

[4] The reader who wonders why I had not already become aware of Hart's reputation should bear in mind that in 1958 *The Concept of Law* (Oxford, 1961) still lay in the future.

him to take me on. For whatever reason (and I suspect my path may have been smoothed by his wife Jenifer having chaired the board of examiners for PPE), he acceded to my request.

I began by improving my education as a theorist. At Hart's instigation I read the work of Kelsen, Renner and such Scandinavian realists as Hägerstrom and Alf Ross. This inspired me to write some extremely lengthy and elaborate disquisitions on types of social decision procedure and their interrelations which (although I never looked at them again) were, I suppose, the remote ancestors of Chapter V.

Sociological theory appeared to me another lacuna, and when I put this to Hart he pointed me towards Talcott Parsons, whose existing œuvre, though it had not in 1958 swelled to its later proportions, was sufficiently bulky to hold me up for a couple of months. In the end, as may be verified from the index, I made use only of Parsons's first (and best-written) book, *The Structure of Social Action*, most significantly for the point that societies create wants as well as satisfying them. I did, however, get a better return on my investment (and a measure of revenge for suffering through Parsons's prose) in my second book.[5]

By the spring of 1959, I had concluded that I was not interested in producing a general theory of social decision procedures and even less interested in contributing to the theory of society as envisaged by Parsons (and it should be borne in mind that at that time sociological theory was virtually synonymous with Parsonian theory). I therefore pursued a new direction and, over the following year or so, I wrote a dissertation-length manuscript about evaluative language, an enormously compressed version of which constitutes Chapter II of *Political Argument*. The original target of this (though his name nowhere appears in the chapter) was R. M. Hare, whose idea that words had 'descriptive' and 'evaluative' meanings (with the evaluation stuck on rather like a rosette to a marrow in a vegetable show) seemed to me hopelessly shallow, as deployed by him and even more by epigoni in Oxford and elsewhere. As will be seen, I seized on the initial statement of H. P. Grice's theory of meaning to provide the framework for my analysis. It served my purposes well. The analysis still seems to me

---

[5] *Sociologists, Economists and Democracy* (London, 1970; reprinted Chicago, 1978, 1988).

to stand up, as far as it goes, though the Gricean theory has been much developed and elaborated in the years since.

I think that what I had at this point would probably have passed muster as a doctoral dissertation. It certainly had all the hallmarks of contemporary 'linguistic analysis' (see below, Section 2). That is to say, it had hundreds of examples, minutely distinguished with a fanatical attention to 'ordinary usage'. The general line of argument is faithfully preserved in Chapter II: that it distorts our understanding of evaluative language to take as typical a word like 'good' which is, indeed, stuck on like a rosette, and that the normal case is one where the evaluation arises from the descriptive meaning.

The trouble with the manuscript was, precisely, that it was possible to boil it down into the length of a chapter. Although the examples had been useful in suggesting problems and giving me some confidence in my answers, I could see no reason for inflicting them on anybody else. Examiners, of course, don't count—it's their job to be bored—but by this time my aspirations, vague in all other respects, had assumed definite form in one direction. I wanted to write a book that would, with luck, double as a dissertation rather than a dissertation that might, with luck, be transformed into a book.

Leaving on one side my manuscript about the meaning of evaluative words in general, I therefore shifted my attention to the process of evaluation itself, and in the course of the next eighteen months wrote a draft of what became the substantive core of *Political Argument*: Chapters V through XIII, preceded by a skeletal version of Chapter III.

As with my foray into the theory of meaning, the impetus for this second extended exercise was dissatisfaction with an existing theory. (This pattern was to continue: I would say that it is only since the mid-1970s that I have written things inspired by a programme of my own rather than, overtly or covertly, taking as my starting point the inadequacies of some current set of ideas.) In this case the irritant was a book published in 1959 by two English philosophers, Stanley Benn and Richard Peters, and entitled *Social Principles and the Democratic State*.[6]

[6] All references in this text unsupported by publishing information may be found in the Bibliography. Other works are provided with publishing information at their first appearance. *Social Principles and the Democratic State*, may,

This book was crucial in providing both a model and a target. It provided a model in that it talked about the meanings of concepts used in political evaluation: it had chapters on freedom and on justice, for example. It provided a target in that it reduced all principles to a bland mush described by the authors as 'a cautious Utilitarianism which takes full account of the principle of impartiality'.[7] If the object of Benn and Peters was to show that all political principles could be reconciled with one another within a framework that allegedly fused the insights of Bentham and Kant, mine should be to demonstrate that different principles conflicted at the ground-floor level.

In this aim I have no doubt that I drew support from Isaiah Berlin's inaugural lecture as Chichele Professor of Social and Political Theory, published in 1958, 'Two Concepts of Liberty'.[8] Although I did not like (and still do not like) his distinction between two concepts of liberty, I did approve of his defence of the notion that there is an irreducible plurality of values (see below, Section 3.B). There really are, Berlin insisted, different values all of which have a valid claim on us, and in some circumstances we shall have to choose between pursuing one and pursing another. If there is one thing that ties *Political Argument* together (a big 'if', perhaps), it is the attempt to see what happens when that idea is followed through seriously in the analysis of political principles.

The academic year 1960–1 was spent as a research fellow in the Philosophy department of the University of Birmingham. Although my state studentship had another year to run, I had had enough of Oxford after five years. (I later returned for spells of four and then three years, suggesting that my tolerance has declined steadily.) The Birmingham department was small but distinguished: in fact all of its members went to chairs within a very few years. It was salutary to discover that the sort of philosophy done in Oxford was not the only sort, and this no doubt strengthened my inclination to make the move discernible

---

[7] Ibid., Preface (unnumbered prelims).

[8] The most convenient source is now Isaiah Berlin, *Four Essays on Liberty* (Oxford, 1968).

---

incidentally, be recognized by American readers under the title *Principles of Political Thought* (New York, 1964). Perhaps the publishers thought the original title had a dangerously socialistic sound to it.

in *Political Argument* away from concern with language and towards more substantive concerns.

In the course of the academic year, I was given the opportunity (recorded in the Acknowledgements) of trying out two bits of the dissertation (one on desert and one on interests, I seem to recall) on my colleagues in the department. This was useful but of more value still was the chance to subject an adult education class to ten substantial chunks of it. My research fellowship paid the same as the bottom of the university teaching scale, £800 a year. This sounds very little now and it was not a lot then, so I was responsive to the suggestion (made through a member of the department) that in return for some modest fee I should put on an adult education course. Looking back, I am amazed that anyone trusted me with such an assignment, since even now I am sure I would be quite a big risk. I am even more amazed that, after an initial shakeout, a dozen or so citizens of Birmingham turned out each week through the winter of 1962 to hear and discuss draft chapters of my dissertation, written, towards the end of the course, in the week preceding the meeting. Presumably the members of the class who kept coming must have felt they were getting something out of it; I certainly learned a lot about exposition from their reactions, and I should like belatedly to raise my hat to them for persevering through this wildly inappropriate course of adult education lectures.

The scene now shifts to the United States, where during the academic year 1961–2 I held a research fellowship awarded by the Rockefeller Foundation, which I believe was really supposed to be postdoctoral. This was not tied to any particular location, and I chose to take it up in Cambridge, Massachusetts, primarily because John Rawls was there. He was, in fact, based at that time at the Massachusetts Institute of Technology, though he moved to his present position at Harvard University at the end of the academic year. *A Theory of Justice* was, of course, still a decade in the future, though there already existed a draft (corresponding, though in briefer compass, to Parts I and II of *A Theory of Justice*) which I was given a copy of. We had two or three stimulating and encouraging conversations in the course of the year, for which I am grateful. As far as I recall, however, he did not read any dissertation drafts (nor did I expect him to) and I think it is fair to say that the dissertation would have finished up much the same if I had simply read 'Two Concepts of Rules' and 'Justice as Fairness' and stayed in England.

There were other ways, however, in which spending the year in Cambridge did make a difference to the final form of the dissertation, as well as having a more lasting effect on the direction of my interests, and these arose from my association with Harvard University. When Herbert Hart knew of my plans, he wrote to C. J. Friedrich, who (I discovered later) held Hart in very high regard, asking if he could do something for me while I was in Cambridge. Acquiring as a patron Friedrich, one of the most august figures in the extremely hierarchical Government department at Harvard, proved absolutely crucial. He arranged for me to be given a Research Fellowship which, again, should normally have been reserved for people who already had a doctorate. Although non-stipendiary, this allowed me to attend any courses I chose, gave me the run of the Widener library with borrowing privileges and threw in membership of the Harvard Faculty Club. Only a very wealthy institution could afford such generosity (the LSE would charge a hefty research fee in return for less), but it is perfectly easy to be rich without being generous. The facilities that Harvard provided made all the difference, and I am happy to have the chance to express my gratitude here.

In effect, I had the position of a graduate student, but with no restrictions on the courses I could take and no need to write term papers or worry about grades. I naturally gravitated towards my *de facto* if not *de jure* peers, the graduate students in the Government department. Doing a doctorate in Oxford (or indeed anywhere in Britain) is a lonely business. Since there is no coursework, there is nothing to do except hole up and start writing. The contrast between the Oxford scene and the common room at the top of the Littauer Center was almost overwhelming. Over coffee, brown-bag lunches, and then yet more coffee, the students and sometimes faculty argued with one another continuously and energetically, about politics, political science, and everything else under the sun. (It should be recalled that the year contained the launching of Sputnik and the Cuban Missile Crisis.) By the end of my time in Cambridge I felt that I had acquired more or less by osmosis an education in American political science as well as some ideas about the characteristic thought-processes of Americans.

All of this no doubt had some diffuse effect on the dissertation and some of my thoughts about the distinctiveness of American political culture come out in IV.6 and Note G in *Political Argument*. (Chapter VI was drafted on the way home aboard a cargo ship bound from Wilmington, NC, to Avonmouth.) A much more direct influence on the final form of the dissertation (and hence of *Political Argument*) can be attributed to some of the Harvard courses I sat in on. Two made minor though specific contributions. An excellent course on legal interpretation given by Paul Freund underlies the discussion of 'neutral principles' in relation to the prohibition of segregation on pages 124–6, while the unattributed reference to Samuel Beer at the end of Note U came out of a seminar on British politics.

Two other courses, however, had a much larger influence and between them generated almost a fifth of the book (Chapters XIV and XV and Notes Q–Z) that would not otherwise have existed. One was an introduction to game theory by Thomas Schelling which covered much the same ground as his recently published book *The Strategy of Conflict* but started even further back and also went further into applications.[9] The other was a course entitled 'Political Economizing' given by Edward Banfield. Banfield, a very bright and strongly opinionated conservative, had a unique teaching method. He would talk for about twenty minutes on the subject of the week's reading, baiting his mainly liberally-inclined audience into an almost uncontrollable frenzy of indignation. The rest of the time was devoted to gladiatorial combat, with Banfield single-handedly fending off the enraged students—with, I must say, great skill and resourcefulness, spicing his responses with a sardonic wit that was highly effective against liberal bluster. This was very unlike the home life of our own dear Oxford, where the only form of partisanship regarded as acceptable in an academic setting was dogmatic belief in the virtue of the dead centre (i.e. the right wing of the Labour party).

As new to me as the method of the course was the matter. Nowadays such a course would be labelled 'Public Choice', but in 1962 there was scarcely a self-conscious literature. There were Arrow's

---

[9] Among the materials distributed for the course was Robin Farquharson's then unpublished D.Phil. dissertation (1958) on strategic voting. This is the work referred to in Appendix C, page 294, as the 'unpublished study of voting' by 'Farquarson' [*sic*]. It was eventually published as *Theory of Voting* (New Haven, 1969).

book and Vickrey's article (see Bibliography), but not the burgeoning field of social choice; there was Downs but not all the later formal work on party competition; and cost-benefit analysis was still at an embryonic stage with the work of Hitch and McKean. The 'Virginia School' of political economy had not yet become the well-oiled machine of its later years, but more of the shape of things to come was already visible, since James Buchanan and Gordon Tullock had just published *The Calculus of Consent*.

We got to *The Calculus of Consent* about two-thirds of the way through the semester, and thereafter my appearances became rather sporadic as I churned out a twenty thousand word critique of the book. With a good deal of recasting, this in due course became the last two chapters of *Political Argument*. Although they take off from *The Calculus of Consent*, I am inclined to think that these two chapters are actually the most original in the book. However, coming at the end of a work of political philosophy they have, perhaps inevitably, failed to make an impact within the public choice fraternity (an appropriate term, incidentally, for an almost exclusively male group).

The rest of the story can be told quite quickly. The following academic year was spent at the University of Keele, in North Staffordshire, where the dissertation was finished, and submitted in June 1963. I do not believe that the university contributed anything except a light teaching load which enabled me to spend most of the time at home working on successive revisions. My wife and I were living at this time in an urban village called Penkhull from which one could look down over the potbanks of Stoke-on-Trent. The village boasted a congenial pub, described in the *Good Pub Guide* for 1989 as 'what the 1940s should have been like, but sadly never really were'. Here we repaired to celebrate in rough cider the completion of the dissertation—three times, before it really was finished. (I find that this pattern of false dawns has been an enduring phenomenon, though I'm afraid that over the years the celebratory tipple has moved on to supermarket champagne.)

The published version is not greatly different from the dissertation. I pulled out some of the more lengthy and digressive footnotes, turning them into additional notes at the end (the dissertation had only five), and at the same time I added some new material in the notes at the end, mainly to deal with detailed objections put forward by John Plamenatz, who was one of the D.Phil. examiners. That is all. Nowadays there would presumably be readers' reports that would call for revision, but the editorial process then was rather more informal than that. Bernard Williams, as Assistant Editor of the Routledge and Kegan Paul 'International Library of Philosophy and Scientific Method', recommended publication, I signed a contract, and that was that. I did as a matter of fact press Williams for comments but his only remark (delivered over tea at some philosophy conference) was that the ideas put forward on pages 60–1 seemed to him to bear the hallmarks of the sort of misplaced moral fastidiousness one might expect from a member of the United Nations Association. I could see his point but I did not in the event do anything about the passage in question.

2. THE CONTEXT OF *POLITICAL ARGUMENT*

The preceding narrative is not, I should like to think, altogether the artless trip down memory lane that it may appear to be. I hope that it will, first of all, prove consoling to any contemporary Ph.D. students who read it by illustrating the point—made often enough but still somehow hard to believe in one's own case—that unless a dissertation is so cut-and-dried as to be barely worth doing it is almost inevitably going to be the product of a lot of floundering around and false starts in the early stages and will continue later on to be subject to periodic bouts of rethinking its entire structure which will quite possibly produce at different times different answers to the question 'What is this thing really about?'

Following on from this general point, I believe that it is helpful in trying to make sense of *Political Argument* to think of it as being made up of three main strata, each laid down at a different time. The oldest layer is the analysis of evaluative language, now worn down to a single chapter. The middle stratum is the thickest and contains the typology of principles and the discussions of particular principles. Although this might be said to be, in loose terms, 'conceptual analysis', the primary concern is with the relations between principles and with the way in which principles are deployed in disputes about public policy. When we get the latest stratum, the analysis of power-diffusing and power-concentrating constitutions in the last two chapters, we can say that the 'linguistic' framework is completely abandoned. The discussion is still about the application of political principles, since it seeks to discover the tendency of alternative constitutional forms to promote the public interest. But the analytical framework is provided by axiomatic public choice theory rather than linguistic analysis.

What this means is that in the course of reading the book one is actually tracing an intellectual odyssey that took the author far from the orthodoxy of his *alma mater*. I said a moment ago that it is quite common for someone writing a dissertation to go through several different conceptions of what it's all about. In the case of *Political Argument* there are, fairly clearly, three conceptions each of which manifests itself in a different part of the book. I think it is nevertheless pulled together by the thick middle layer. Sympathetically viewed, anyway, the book is a substantive discussion of political principles guided by a typology, which is preceded by some general material on evaluation with special reference to evaluative language, and followed by a venture into the analysis of the institutional implications of political principles. It is, I must confess, also possible to view the degree of integration less sympathetically, and one person who did so was my second D.Phil. examiner, Peter Strawson, who concluded his questions with the remark, 'You do realise that the only thing holding this together is the binding?'. (Fortunately, he apparently did not regard this as an insuperable objection.)

In the rest of this section, I want to set *Political Argument* in its historical context. This will involve some intellectual archeology, and a certain amount of the spadework for this has already been done in the previous section. Quentin Skinner, John Pocock, and their associates have made us familiar with the idea that

> the meaning of a past text—establishing which is of course an essential preliminary to any critical analysis—cannot be determined simply through a close reading (or series of readings) using modern standards of interpretation. For the meanings carried by key terms, and the logic of arguments used, will depend upon the intellectual milieu in which the text was produced. Thus we need to understand the context of ideas and arguments within which the text was written —what Pocock would call a 'language' of political thought, or Skinner an 'ideology'—to give a proper account of the literal meaning of the text itself. Beyond that, Skinner in particular has argued that to

understand a text we must grasp not only its meaning, but also the author's intentions in writing it. Again, this requires us to identify with some precision the political context in which the work appeared: for instance the positions the author took himself to be rebutting, or the assumptions regarded as commonplace on which he relied.[10]

It may at first sight seem that this is unnecessarily heavy artillery to wheel out for a book no more than a quarter of a century old. In fact, though, the assumptions about political philosophy prevalent in the early 1960s are not all that much more distant from those current today than are those prevalent in the early 1690s. Moreover, the period twenty-five to thirty years ago inevitably falls into a kind of historical shadow. For most people are either too young to be in a position to remember it or too old to be able to, while at the same time it is still too recent to have been written up systematically.

How best to recapture the world of 1958, when work on *Political Argument* began? Inescapably, the starting point must be the famous, or infamous, Introduction that Peter Laslett wrote for the first *Philosophy, Politics and Society* collection, published in 1956.[11] It seems fairly clear that the initiative for the collection came from the publishers, eager to cash in on the success of the two volumes entitled *Logic and Language* which were a compendium of the most highly approved products of the 'linguistic analysis' school.[12] The Introduction is taken up with complaints about the difficulty of finding anything to include[13] and with

[10] David Miller, 'The Resurgence of Political Theory', *Political Studies* (forthcoming).

[11] See under Weldon in the Bibliography for publishing information.

[12] A. G. N. Flew (ed.), *Logic and Society* (First Series, Oxford, 1951; Second Series, Oxford, 1953). These volumes constituted a veritable *vade mecum* for the student of PPE in the mid-1950s. It is sobering to reflect that two or three of the pieces in the Laslett collection must be more often consulted now than any of those in Flew's two volumes.

[13] 'It has to be admitted that the editor's area of choice was severely limited, and in only one field, jurisprudence, has any considerable body of work been published since 1945. A survey of our philosophical periodicals for the purposes of this collection gives the impression that their editors have often included articles on political subjects merely out of a sense of their conventional duty. Their contributors, too, sometimes give the feeling that they have turned their attention to political subjects only because the curriculum of their university requires it. . . . Editorial policy has been a difficult problem, as might be expected when the task has been to draw a circle round a hole.' Laslett, p. xi.

attempts to account for the lack of suitable material. In a much-quoted sentence, Laslett summed up the situation with the words: 'For the moment, anyway, political philosophy is dead.[14] And it has to be admitted that this gloomy estimate was borne out fairly well by the contents of the book. If this was the best work that could be found in 1956 (and it probably was), then political philosophy was perhaps not dead but at the least moribund.

As for explanations of the parlous state of political philosophy, Laslett gestured half-heartedly at two possible ones—that 'politics have become too serious to be left to philosophers' and that the rise of sociology had somehow inhibited the speculations of political philosophers[15]—but then pinned the blame squarely on developments within philosophy itself.

> So striking and so complete is the difference between the philosopher's world of our own day and that of Bosanquet's time, or even of Harold Laski's, that it is really very easy to point to the culprit. The Logical Positivists did it. It was Russell and Wittgenstein, Ayer and Ryle who convinced the philosophers that they must withdraw unto themselves for a time, and re-examine their logical and linguistic apparatus. And the result of this re-examination has been radical indeed. It called into question the logical status of all ethical statements, and set up rigorous criteria of intelligibility which at one time threatened to reduce the traditional ethical systems to assemblages of nonsense. Since political philosophy is, or was, an extension of ethics, the question has been raised whether political philosophy is possible at all.[16]

Although Laslett's diagnosis has been widely quoted and is indeed often swallowed without any critical examination, I believe that it is highly questionable. To begin with, one must cast some doubt on the credentials of someone who thinks that Russell and Wittgenstein, Ayer and Ryle can all be lumped together—and all regarded as 'Logical Positivists'. Russell boxed the compass several times; Wittgenstein's life must be divided into the reign of Ludwig the First and Ludwig the Second; and Ryle would have been very unhappy to be called a logical positivist at any time. (As a fairly faithful attender at Ryle's weekly 'informal instructions' for about four years, I can say that I never once heard him worry about some

[14] Ibid., p. vii.
[15] Ibid., pp. vii–ix.
[16] Ibid., p. ix.

assertion's 'meaningfulness' according to verificationist dogma.) Out of Laslett's list of prominent philosophers, only Ayer could plausibly be presented in 1956 as a down-the-line logical positivist. In any case, it is not true to say that adherence to logical positivism ruled out the possibility of engaging in philosophical activities of a substantive kind with relevance to moral or political issues. Suppose (as C. L. Stevenson maintained in *Ethics and Language*) that someone who says 'Utility-maximizing acts are good' should be construed as saying 'I approve of utility-maximizing acts. Do so as well!' This still leaves it open to those who are prepared to accept the injunction to argue with one another about the practical implications of accepting it, and it also leaves it open to those who are disinclined to accept the injunction to point out to those who do that they are thereby committed to endorsing specific injunctions (e.g. to frame innocent people) that they might find unpalatable. And in fact even in the heyday of logical positivism arguments of exactly this kind about utilitarianism appeared regularly in the philosophical journals. If similar arguments were not carried on in relation to politics, this was not simply because nothing could in principle be said.

All this is just skirmishing, however. The main point is that 'Oxford philosophy' in 1956 was not logical positivist. (Because philosophy was a component in two of the most popular degrees, Oxford contained a large proportion of all the philosophers in the country and was without question the centre.) No doubt from far enough away—from across the English Channel, for example—logical positivism and so-called 'ordinary language' philosophy would appear as insignificant variants on the same old Anglo-Saxon positivism. (The Anglo-Saxons, of course, return the compliment by throwing together under the umbrella term 'continental philosophy' a number of warring schools.) But from closer up, the ideas of J. L. Austin and Gilbert Ryle could not easily be assimilated to those of A. J. Ayer, and there was as a matter of fact no love lost between Ayer and the other two.[17] Nor, it might be

---

[17] Austin's lectures on 'Sense and Sensibilia', which convulsed their undergraduate audiences when delivered with his impeccable timing, were an unsparing attack on Ayer's theory of knowledge; and Ryle went as far as to resign from the board of electors to an Oxford philosophy chair when Ayer was elected to it over his opposition. (Austin's lectures were published posthumously: see J. L. Austin, *Sense and Sensibilia*, ed. G. J. Warnock [Oxford, 1962].)

added, could anyone who knew their work at all well regard Austin and Ryle as interchangeable figures. That Ryle preferred to talk about 'concepts' whereas Austin insisted on talking about 'words' was only symptomatic of divergent views of the nature of the enterprise. Austin really did, it seems to me, see himself as a sort of armchair lexicographer substituting sharp wits for index cards, whereas Ryle was ultimately interested in ideas and simply saw our use of words as giving us useful clues. (As this probably prejudicial sketch will suggest, I always found Ryle's approach more congenial than Austin's.)

For the present purpose, however, I must eschew nuance and follow convention in cobbling together a composite Oxford orthodoxy, 'linguistic philosophy' or 'ordinary language philosophy'. A slightly flippant way of characterizing a serious (and, let me emphasize, salutory) movement would be to say that it was the later Wittgenstein with less *Angst* and more concern for results. It took what has been called 'the linguistic turn' by starting from the expectation that what have been held traditionally to be deep problems about the nature of reality will turn out on closer inspection to be a reflection of some linguistically-generated bemusement. So, Ryle sought in *The Concept of Mind* to exorcise the 'ghost in the machine' by showing that everything we want to say about mental activity can be said without postulating the existence of a disembodied 'mind' somehow pulling the strings of the 'body'. And Austin, in *Sense and Sensibilia*, argued that Ayer's doubts about the possibility of our knowing anything could be laid to rest by careful attention to humble words such as 'see'.

Where did this leave political philosophy? The answer is, I suggest: on the margins but not completely out in the cold. It must be on the margins because the big metaphysical game hunted by Ryle and Austin was not (it might plausibly be supposed) to be found in the territory occupied by political philosophy. No doubt, for example, in their efforts to rest political obligation on consent, social contract theorists have grievously abused the notion. But demonstrating this to everybody's satisfaction would entail, from the standpoint of mainstream philosophy, only local adjustments. It would hardly have implications on anything like the same scale as would the acceptance of Ryle's claim about mind or Austin's about perception. At the same time, however, there is nothing in the basic approach of 'linguistic philosophy' that interdicts the application of the method to politics if one happens to be interested in politics. *Political Argument* illustrates this, though it is (as I have observed) not a pure example.

If Laslett could find little contemporary work on politics by philosophers to collect in 1956, then I do not believe that the reason can be the one stated by him—that 'winter [had] set in for the political philosopher', giving rise to a 'climate' in which 'so much of the young growth of political speculation [was] blasted as it burgeoned.'[18] I am inclined to believe that the explanation is, rather, something I have already touched on: the prevalence of utilitarianism among philosophers in the 1950s and the early 1960s.

Adherence to utilitarianism makes for very boring political philosophy, because once the goal has been postulated (some version of Bentham's 'greatest happiness principle'), everything else is a matter of arguing about the most efficacious means to that end. Is there a duty to obey the law? It depends on the consequences for aggregate utility. Can governments legitimately be overthrown by force? Same answer. Is economic equality desirable? Same answer again. And so on for any question that might be asked. Now it is hard to imagine that any useful generalizations can be made about most of these means-end relationships. The only possible response in most instances would be that the answer depends on the precise circumstances of the case. And whether the appropriate answers are off-the-peg or tailor-made, the questions do not seem to be of a kind that lend themselves to treatment by philosophers. For the answers will turn on estimates of the tendency of actions, laws, constitutional arrangements and so on to conduce to or detract from the general welfare. And these seem to be matters that, to the extent that there can be said to be experts on them at all, call for the expertise of social scientists rather than that of philosophers. The revival of political philosophy therefore depended on a decline in the appeal of utilitarianism.

This connection between adherence to utilitarian doctrine and the belief that there can be no useful employment for political philosophers helps to account for the Weldon phenomenon. In his Introduction, Laslett says of T. D. Weldon's *The Vocabulary of Politics* and a specially-commissioned article in *Philosophy,*

[18] Laslett, p. ix.

Politics and Society summarizing its arguments: 'These are the only attempts known to me at a general consideration in contemporary logical terms of the conventional content of political philosophy'.[19] This judgement in fact incorporates the error about the nature of contemporary philosophical orthodoxy that, as I have pointed out, underlies Laslett's whole discussion in the Introduction.[20] For although Weldon was only four years older than Ryle (which, incidentally, made him just old enough to fight in the First World War), he does go quite a long way towards filling the bill as a logical positivist. 'To put it crudely', he wrote, traditional political philosophers 'have formulated questions to which no empirically testable answers could be given, and such questions are nonsensical.'[21] And putting it less crudely involved nothing more than adding that 'their recommendations to statesmen have frequently been shrewd and helpful'.[22]

On the penultimate page of *Political Argument*, in the course of talking about the prospects of 'analytical philosophy', I took a sideswipe at Weldon, saying that *The Vocabulary of Politics* 'in spite of its title is an application of unreconstructed logical positivist criteria of meaning to traditional thought rather than a detailed analysis' (p. 290, n. 2). This is all true but I would now suggest that the logical positivism did not entail the lack of detailed analysis, as I rather implied there. For it is quite consistent with logical positivist premises to discuss substantive recommendations ('imperatives' for Stevenson or 'prescriptions' for Hare) such as those of utilitarianism, as I have pointed out. There would therefore be room for Weldon to analyse particular principles without abandoning his view that the 'foundations' offered by the classical political theorists are worthless.

Why then did he conclude that 'only by intensive study of the facts can we reach sound appraisals' and that, when verbal

[19] Ibid., p. x.

[20] I fear that Laslett's assessment may be increasingly taken over by careless commentators as the period recedes into the past. An illustration is provided by a just-published book, *New Developments in Political Science: An International Review of Achievements and Prospects*, ed. Adrian Leftwich (Aldershot, 1990). John Horton, in his contribution 'Weight or Lightness? Political Philosophy and Its Prospects' (pp. 126–42), says of *The Vocabulary of Politics* that it is 'the prime exemplar of linguistic analysis in political philosophy' (p. 128).

[21] Weldon, *The Vocabulary of Politics*, p. 74.

[22] Ibid., pp. 74–5.

confusions are tidied away, the questions of traditional political philosophy are empirical ones, so that 'writers on political institutions and statesmen, not philosophers, are the proper people to deal with them'?[23] The best explanation is, I suggest, that Weldon was, as far as can be gathered from what he says about particular issues, more or less a utilitarian. Hence, all normative problems in politics become empirical questions—questions of means—once we have the end in view. Principles are therefore to be understood not as values such as freedom or equality, but as generalizations of dubious validity. They 'have as much and as little use in making political decisions and political appraisals as they have in fighting battles or criticizing works of art. They save time and trouble and sometimes help us to avoid elementary mistakes, but they cannot make our decisions or do our appraising for us.'[24]

A slight qualification should be made to what has been said about the implications of utilitarianism. It is possible to discuss different principles (such as freedom and equality) from a utilitarian standpoint, but the result will have to be the rather odd one that all principles have the same content. At the most, we shall be able to say that different principles draw attention to different considerations that are all ultimately significant in virtue of their contribution to the satisfaction of the utilitarian criterion. It would not be guying the book beyond permissible limits to say that this was the burden of *Social Principles and the Democratic State*.

Since it appeared in 1959, this book came too late to be mentioned by Laslett, though in the Introduction to the Second Series of *Philosophy, Politics and Society*, it is coupled with Hart's *The Concept of Law* as marking a revival of political philosophy.[25] To complete the task set by Quentin Skinner, I must conclude this discussion by returning to *Social Principles and the Democratic State*. For if I am to say what was my intention in writing the middle chapters of *Political Argument*, the most honest answer would be: to knock Benn and Peters into a cocked hat. I have to confess that I took the blandness and

---

[23] Ibid., p. 192.
[24] Ibid., p. 180.
[25] Peter Laslett and W. G. Runciman (eds), *Philosophy, Politics and Society*, Second Series (Oxford, 1962), p. viii.

general mediocrity of their book as a sort of personal affront. (I have mellowed a lot since then, or so it seems to me.) Although there is a bit of sniping from footnotes in *Political Argument* (especially on pages 48, 120 and 171), I do not see that it would be possible to reconstruct this intention from internal evidence. However, the vigour with which principles are distinguished from one another and their incompatible implications insisted on can be traced to my underlying objective of burying the 'cautious utilitarianism' espoused by Benn and Peters.

3. THREE LEADING IDEAS AND THEIR FATES

3.A. *Introduction.* The two preceding sections have been designed to set the stage for the main business of this Introduction: to trace the later careers of the ideas put forward in *Political Argument* and to comment on them from my present vantage point. I shall begin, in this section, with three ideas that can fairly be said to have entered into the currency of Anglo-American political philosophy. Although I cannot claim real originality for any of them, the formulation of them in *Political Argument* has assumed something of a canonical status. The first is the treatment of 'value pluralism' in terms of indifference curve analysis; the second is the distinction between want-regarding and ideal-regarding principles; and the third is the distinction between aggregative and distributive principles.

Pro captu lectoris habent sua fata libelli—the fate of books depends on the reader's understanding of them. Once a book is launched, the author has no more control over the use made of the ideas in it than the child who drops a twig in a stream has over its course and destination. On the whole the analysis of value pluralism and the aggregative/distributive distinction have had fairly smooth sailing, but the same cannot be said of the want-regarding/ideal-regarding distinction. I shall therefore take the unusual opportunity offered here to give it a push in the right direction.

For ease of reference, each subsection has following the title a note of the chapter and section in *Political Argument* where the major discussion of the idea occurs.

3.B. *Value Pluralism (I.2)*. Value pluralism is simply the idea that there is 'an irreducible plurality of equally basic moral principles'.[26] It thus consists in the denial of value monism, the doctrine that there is just one principle applicable to all evaluations. On the face of it, the claim made by value monism is an extremely implausible one, and I think that the only reason for its having been adhered to so tenaciously by philosophers is the fear that the only alternative is chaos.

What was distinctive about the treatment of the matter in *Political Argument* was certainly not the affirmation of value pluralism but the attempt to allay the fears of chaos by invoking the standard neoclassical economic analysis of consumer behaviour in terms of indifference curves. In earlier times economics was in effect a branch of utilitarian analysis, and it was assumed that rational choice on the part of consumers must be choice aimed at maximizing a single quantity, 'utility'. But, in the neoclassical system that I learned as an undergraduate doing PPE, rationality entailed nothing more than consistency in choice. An ideally rational consumer would have a set of surfaces in n-dimensional space (one dimension for each good), each surface connecting all combinations of goods that were equally choiceworthy.

For the simple case of two goods, this set of n-dimensional surfaces reduced to a set of curves that could be drawn on a page. These curves were called indifference curves because they connected up points representing combinations of the two goods among which the consumer was indifferent. Rational choice was then understood as a matter of picking the combination of the two goods that got the consumer on to the highest feasible indifference curve. For any consumer whose purchases were not large enough to affect the prices facing him, the 'budget constraint' would be a straight line corresponding to the relative prices of the two goods. For a society as a whole, the 'production possibility frontier' was assumed in general to be convex to the origin. Either way, the condition for getting to the highest attainable point was to pick the point of tangency between indifference curves and feasibility frontier.

It seemed to me that the same analysis could be carried over to deal with competing values, and I proposed this on pages 3–8 of

---

[26] Joel Feinberg, *Harm to Others* (New York and Oxford, 1984), p. 247, n. 12.

Political Argument. I now have two reservations about the treatment offered there. First, the example I gave of efficiency being traded off against equity is quite problematic, though it was (and is) a commonplace in the writings of economists. For, as Julian Le Grand has recently argued, it is not apparent that efficiency is a value to be traded off against others; rather, it is perhaps best thought of as referring to the best attainable trade-off.[27] And second, the account I gave seems to me defective in failing to explain systematically how indifference curves interact with the feasibility frontier to generate a chosen outcome: the point is mentioned only in the footnote at the end, on p. 8.

David Miller has recently given an exposition of the essential ideas that seems to me to avoid both pitfalls and I cannot do better than to quote it:

> Despite the allure of monism, it must be rejected. When we think seriously about a political matter, it is rarely the case that we light on some single guiding principle that alone will resolve the issue. Instead we find that we have to arbitrate between several competing values, none of which we feel inclined, on reflection, to abandon. The solution we choose will be the one that on balance gives us the most of what we value—or to put the point in a quasi-technical way, that puts us on the highest feasible indifference curve, representing our preferences as between various combinations of the values at stake. Nor can the slope of these indifference curves be deduced from some general theory. We must rely simply on our judgements about where the balance should be struck between considerations such as freedom, justice, and aggregate utility in particular cases, and try to fit these judgements into a consistent pattern.[28]

Without much doubt the best known and most influential discussion of value pluralism since *Political Argument* has been that of John Rawls in *A Theory of Justice*.[29] However, Rawls's treatment of the issue is (like much of Rawls's work) rather more

[27] Julian Le Grand, 'Equity versus Efficiency: The Elusive Trade-off', *Ethics* 100 (1990), pp. 554–68.

[28] David Miller, *Market, State, and Community: Theoretical Foundations of Market Socialism* (Oxford, 1989), p. 4. (Miller cites chapter 1 of *Political Argument* for the source of the indifference curve analysis of values.)

[29] John Rawls, *A Theory of Justice* (Cambridge, Mass., 1971), Section 7, 'Intuitionism', pp. 34–40. (*Political Argument* is cited as a source for value pluralism in n. 18, p. 34; and indifference curve analysis is used to illustrate the idea on pages 37–8, with citation of *Political Argument* in n. 19, p. 37.)

complicated than it appears at first glance and has often, I believe, been misinterpreted. Since it raises some large questions about methodology that I shall come to in Section 5, as well as bringing up unsuspected ambiguities in the notion of value pluralism, it is worth some careful attention.

Rawls frames his whole discussion not in terms of 'value pluralism' but in terms of 'intuitionism'. He begins with these words: 'I shall think of intuitionism in a more general way than is customary: namely, as the doctrine that there is an irreducible family of first principles which have to be weighed against one another by asking ourselves which balance, in our considered judgement, is the most just.'[30] Now what Rawls dubs 'intuitionism' corresponds roughly to what I have been calling 'value pluralism', but only roughly. Rawls himself says that 'perhaps it would be better if we were to speak of intuitionism in this broad sense as pluralism'. His reason for not doing so hints at the complexities ahead: he says that 'a conception of justice can be pluralistic without requiring us to weigh its principles by intuition. It may contain the requisite priority rules.'[31]

Rawls acknowledges that his use of 'intuitionism' is eccentric, since intuitionism is usually understood as a methodological or epistemological doctrine about the basis of all ethical claims. There is no necessary connection between the position one takes on intuitionism so conceived and one's position on value pluralism interpreted simply as the denial of value monism. Henry Sidgwick thought, for example, that utilitarianism (the paradigmatic monistic moral theory) might be derived from a single intuition.[32] Conversely, value pluralism need not rest on intuitionist

---

[30] Ibid., p. 34. It is, of course, misleading to define the idea by talking about competing principles that have to be balanced to arrive at a conclusion about what is *just*. Normally it would be supposed (as it is in *Political Argument*) that justice is one of the elements that should enter into a conclusion about what, all things considered, is right. Rawls, however, has an idiosyncratic concept of justice such that the principles of justice are those principles—whatever they may be—that should be the first principles (i.e. those with priority over all others) governing the basic structure of a society. Thus, utilitarianism is, for Rawls, a possible conception of justice (indeed, the main rival to his own), rather than a moral view which has no room for justice as a ground-floor principle.

[31] Ibid., p. 35.

[32] Indeed, he thought that this was the inescapable upshot of the intuitionist method. 'I am finally led to the conclusion . . . that the Intuitional method rigorously applied yields as its final result the doctrine of pure Universalistic Hedonism

foundations—a point which the case of Rawls himself illustrates, as we shall see shortly.

If we construe value pluralism as the denial of value monism (and I suggest that this is the only useful definition) then Rawls is clearly a value pluralist even with respect to justice, and he admits that there are other values as well as justice.[33] What is it, then, about his position that enables him to say he is not an intuitionist? Rawls gives two answers, which are quite different in their logical status. What unites them is that they both entail rejection of the intuitionist doctrine 'that there exist no higher-order constructive criteria for determining the proper emphasis for the competing principles of justice.'[34]

The most straightforward answer (and the one that is generally thought to be Rawls's only answer) is that his theory of justice contains 'the requisite priority rules'. There is no need for 'intuitive' balancing of principles because they come with lexicographic priority rules: the first principle, mandating equal liberties, has priority over the second part of the second principle (equal opportunity), which in turn has priority over the first part of the second principle, the so-called difference principle, which requires social and economic inequalities to be to the greatest possible benefit of the least advantaged socioeconomic group in the society.[35]

However, Rawls concedes that these priority rules hold only under favourable conditions. The 'general conception' of justice that underlies all three principles is that 'all social primary goods—liberty and opportunity, income and wealth, and the bases of self-respect—are to be distributed equally unless an

---

[33] A conception of justice, Rawls says, deals with 'the distributive aspects of the basic structure of society'. . . . A complete conception defining principles for all the virtues of the basic structure, together with their respective weights when they conflict, is more than a conception of justice; it is a social ideal' (ibid., p. 9). This talk of weighting sounds 'intuitionistic' in Rawls's sense. But it does not, on Rawls's account, contaminate the theory of justice because the lowest-ranking principle of justice, the difference principle, 'is lexically [sc. lexicographically] prior to the principle of efficiency and to that of maximizing the sum of advantages' (ibid., p. 302), and presumably other non-distributive principles.

[34] Ibid., p. 34. Once again, we should strike out the reference to justice to obtain a general definition of intuitionism.

[35] See ibid., pp. 302–3 for a formal statement.

—which it is convenient to denote by the single word, Utilitarianism.' Henry Sidgwick, *The Methods of Ethics*, pp. 406–7.

unequal distribution of any or all of these goods is to the advantage of the least favored'.[36] Thus, under less than ideal circumstances it may be 'that the opportunities of the least favored sectors of the community would be still more limited if [inequalities of opportunity] were removed'.[37] And in his discussion of the priority of liberty he says that, under conditions of real material scarcity, the only guidance that can be given here derives from the 'general conception'. 'Until the basic wants of individuals can be fulfilled, the relative urgency of their interest in liberty cannot be firmly decided in advance. It will depend on the claims of the least favored as seen from the constitutional and legislative stages.'[38] Indeed, Rawls's exposition could be very well illustrated by an indifference curve figure, since he talks about 'the marginal significance for our good of further social advantages diminish[ing] relative to the interests of liberty' as conditions improve until 'beyond some point it becomes and then remains irrational' to sacrifice any liberty for more material advantages.[39] Thus, in economists' terms, liberty is a 'superior good', which becomes more relatively valuable the more the budget constraint is relaxed.

Does this mean, then, that Rawls is only a fair-weather anti-intutionist? It would be easy to conclude so, and Rawls himself sometimes gives the impression that he thinks this too. But in his general discussion of 'the priority problem',[40] Rawls puts forward lexicographic priority only as the 'second possibility' of dealing with the problem within the framework of his theory of justice. The first possibility is more modest but becomes important once we recognize that the second possibility of lexicographic priority is very limited in potential.

What, then, is this alternative? Simply that, even if we have to be content to settle for trade-offs between principles, we may be able to avoid purely 'intuitionistic' balancing, that is to say substitution rates for which no further justification can be given. 'Thus I suppose that in the original position the parties try to reach some agreement as to how the principles of justice are to be balanced. Now part of the value of the notion of choosing principles is that

[36] Ibid., p. 303.
[37] Ibid., p. 302.
[38] Ibid., p. 543.
[39] Ibid., p. 542.
[40] Section 8, 'The Priority Problem', ibid., pp. 40–5.

the reasons which underlie their adoption in the first place may also support giving them certain weights. Since in justice as fairness the principles of justice are not thought of as self-evident, but have their justification in the fact that they would be chosen, we may find in the grounds for their acceptance some guidance or limitation as to how they are to be balanced.'[41]

The idea here is, as I understand it, that it may be possible to offer a rationale for the structure of trade-offs between competing principles. Rawls's theory of justice is a 'constructivist' theory, as he has later come to call it. We begin by constructing an 'original position', a morally privileged choosing situation, and then ask what principles would be chosen in it. Since the situation is fair, the principles chosen in it will be just: this is the basic idea of 'justice as fairness' that underlies Rawls's theory. Although it is hard to grasp its implications immediately as a practical proposal, Rawls is, it seems to me, putting forward a very suggestive notion about trade-offs. For what he is saying holds out the promise that we may be able to have value pluralism, with trade-offs rather than lexicographic priorities, yet at the same time get beyond a set of trade-offs about which nothing further can be said. I shall return to this in Section 5.

3.C. *The Want-regarding/Ideal-regarding Distinction (III.3)*. In introducing the distinction between want-regarding and ideal-regarding principles, I suggested that the decision to draw my fundamental division among principles along these lines could 'be justified only by the power of the distinction to illuminate political controversies whose foundations are at present obscure' (p. 38). I think that the distinction has proved illuminating, and underlies much contemporary discussion among political philosophers of the idea that a liberal state should be 'neutral' between 'conceptions of the good'. I shall, however, postpone discussion of that question until I have said something about the distinction itself and tried to deal with misunderstandings of it.

The first thing to get clear is that the ideals are in the eye of the beholder—the person doing the evaluating—rather than being in the people whose situation forms the subject of the evaluation. A want-regarding evaluation is one that takes account of the extent of

[41] Ibid., p. 42.

want-satisfaction and nothing else, counting all satisfied wants equally regardless of their nature. Personal or social ideals are thus treated as wants on all fours with grosser desires in the process of evaluation. An ideal-regarding evaluation, in contrast, is one that discriminates among want-satisfactions, assigning a greater value to some than to others and perhaps assigning to some a zero or even a negative value. Again, the ideals in question are those of the person doing the evaluating: the satisfaction of a want derived from a person's own ideals might be negatively valued, as Hume disdained the 'monkish virtues'.

Ideal-regarding principles are generally spoken of now as 'perfectionist', following a usage established by Rawls in *A Theory of Justice*, and indeed Rawls refers to 'ideal-regarding considerations' as the kind that the holder of a perfectionist moral theory would advance in an argument about public policy—for example, with regard to public funding for the arts.[42] However, Rawls's own discussion raises some significant questions about the interpretation of the want-regarding/ideal-regarding distinction, and reflecting on it will lead me to the modification I would now wish to make to the analysis.

Rawls asks whether his own theory of justice is a want-regarding or an ideal-regarding theory, and answers that it should be considered as an ideal-regarding theory for three reasons. One is that 'we are to encourage certain traits of character, especially a sense of justice'.[43] This certainly falls within the conception of an ideal-regarding approach as it is defined in *Political Argument*, since I say that 'someone might' as part of an ideal-regarding theory 'attribute value to . . . such things as people's tastes, characters or beliefs' (p. 40). Whether the claim is actually correct is another matter. The relevant question is whether the character trait consisting in a concern for justice has intrinsic value within Rawls's theory or whether it has only instrumental value. Justice for Rawls is a virtue only under the 'circumstances of justice', which include scarcity in relation to demands and lack of consensus on an overriding social end.[44] Suppose that these circumstances did not exist, so that the world had no use for what Hume called the 'cautious,

---

[42] Ibid., p. 331.
[43] Ibid., p. 327.
[44] Ibid., pp. 126–30; see also my *Theories of Justice*, pp. 152–63.

jealous virtue of justice'.[45] Would we have to say that the world was a poorer place for the lack of the appropriate character trait? I cannot see that there is anything in *A Theory of Justice* to force that conclusion upon us.

Rawls's second reason for saying that his theory of justice is ideal-regarding betrays a misunderstanding of the notion that seems to me instructive. He says that 'the fulfillment of desires incompatible with [the principles of justice] has no value at all'.[46] However, all this means is that the principles of justice are distributive rather than aggregative—a distinction I shall go on to discuss next. The satisfaction of wants incompatible with a just distribution, therefore, does not count as an improvement in the situation.[47] But a distributive principle is still a want-regarding principle so long as it does not discriminate among wants according to their supposed moral qualities, and this Rawls's principles of justice do not do.

On Rawls's interpretation, the only kind of want-regarding principle there can be is an aggregative principle, and Rawls as much as tells us that this is his assumption when he says his theory 'occupies an intermediate position between perfectionism and utilitarianism'.[48] This embodies a false idea of the conceptual relationships. There is not some continuum that has utilitarianism lying at one end and perfectionism at the other, with distributive principles coming somewhere in the middle. Want-regarding principles are those whose material is want-satisfaction, without regard to the object of the wants in question. But want-regarding principles can be concerned with the distribution as well as the total amount of want-satisfaction.

Rawls refers us in the same context back to an earlier section of his book, with the claim that this establishes that 'a certain ideal is embedded in the principles of justice'.[49] But this seems to me to

---

[45] See *Theories of Justice*, p. 154.

[46] Rawls, *A Theory of Justice*, p. 327.

[47] Strictly speaking, even this is not quite true. For, as I pointed out in footnote 33 above, Rawls apparently envisages the principles of justice as having lexicographic priority over others, such as that of maximizing aggregate utility. If two situations were equally just, therefore, the one with more aggregate utility would be better than the other. Thus, all that can be said is that aggregate want-satisfaction does not balance out injustice. But it does have value as a tie-breaker.

[48] Ibid., p. 327.

[49] Ibid., p. 326.

raise the same issues as his first ground for claiming that his principles of justice are ideal-regarding. Turning to the section referred to, we find a repetition of the point that there is 'no value in fulfilling' wants that are incompatible with justice but we also find a further move: that 'the social system should discourage them'.[50] However, there is no reason for saying, on Rawls's theory, that such wants are intrinsically bad. If my just income will not run to the ownership of an ocean-going yacht then perhaps it would be a good thing for the social system to discourage the widespread craving for ocean-going yachts among people whose just incomes are like mine. But this is simply because we will be frustrated by just outcomes. Those whose just incomes would enable them to afford such luxuries need not be discouraged from forming a taste for them. And as a society becomes more prosperous, the range of wants to be discouraged will presumably diminish. Once again, then, there is no real ideal-regarding conception here. What matters is want-satisfaction within the constraints set by just arrangements. All that is added here is that people will get more satisfaction if their wants can be accommodated by their just incomes, civil and political rights, and so on.

Rawls's third and final point is quite different in form from the other two. It is that 'the principles of justice do not even mention the amount or distribution of welfare but refer only to the distribution of liberties and the other primary goods'.[51] In the later jargon that has grown up around this much-discussed topic, *A Theory of Justice* is thus a 'resourcist' rather than a 'welfarist' theory.[52]

Now in *Political Argument* I in fact anticipated exactly this point. Thus, I said at the end of my discussion of the want-regarding/ideal-regarding distinction, that a distributive principle might be concerned with the distribution of resources rather than the distribution of happiness or pleasure. Anticipating by a couple of decades the recent outpourings on 'expensive tastes', I mentioned that if equality of income were taken to be an attempt at

---

[50] Ibid., p. 261.
[51] Ibid., p. 327.
[52] See Ronald Dworkin, 'What is Equality?' Part I: 'Equality of Welfare', *Philosophy & Public Affairs* 10 (1981), 185–246; Part II: 'Equality of Resources', 283–345. For a useful discussion, see G. A. Cohen, 'On the Currency of Egalitarian Justice', *Ethics* 99 (1989), 906–44.

equality of welfare, it could then be said that 'this would require paying easily pleased people less than fastidious ones'. But I concluded that there was no need to understand claims for equality of income in that way: it may simply be 'thought fair that everyone should have access to an equal value of scarce goods' (p. 43).

Equality of income is here treated as a want-regarding principle. This means that want-regarding principles must be understood as not only concerned with the actual amount on distribution of want-satisfaction but also as concerned with the amount or distribution of opportunities for want-satisfaction. My definition on page 38 of *Political Argument* in fact covered precisely this point. For want-regarding principles were defined there as 'principles which take as given the wants which people happen to have and concentrate attention entirely on the extent to which a certain policy will alter the overall amount of want-satisfaction or the way in which the policy will affect the distribution among people of opportunities for satisfying wants'. The only amendment that I would wish to make would be to remove any suggestion that all aggregative principles are welfare-regarding and all distributive principles are resource-regarding. There is, I think, a strong tendency that way but it should not be built into the definition of want-regarding principles. The general statement should simply be that want-regarding principles have as their subject-matter either want-satisfaction itself or the means to (or opportunities for) want-satisfaction.

I argued earlier on that Rawls was mistaken in positing a continuum with perfectionism (ideal-regarding principles) at one end and utilitarianism (understood as an aggregative want-regarding principle) at the other, with distributive principles somewhere in the middle. I stand by that. But at the same time I have to concede that there *is* a continuum in the following sense. Ideal-regarding principles are defined simply as the complement of want-regarding principles. But wherever we draw the cut-off point for want-regarding principles, we shall find that some ideal-regarding conceptions are only just over the line while others are further away.

I want to defend drawing the line in the place that I proposed in III.3.C. This puts pleasure and happiness over on the ideal-regarding side on the line. The rationale for this upon which I want to lay most emphasis is the first of the three listed on pages

41–2; in fact, I wish to some degree to repudiate the second and third ones to which I devoted a lot more space. The critical point, then, is this: by putting want-satisfaction (and opportunities for want-satisfaction) on one side of the line and everything else on the other side, we draw it in the one place that is, at least in principle, determinate.

Want-regarding principles are defined as those that take as their subject-matter preferences or the means of satisfying preferences. Ideal-regarding principles allow for the possibility of substituting someone else's judgement of what makes an agent better off for the agent's own view of things. (Ideal-regarding principles may do other things too, but then there is no difficulty in recognizing them.) I pointed out in the text (p. 41), that ' "happiness", in the ordinary acceptation of the word, includes considerable "ideal" elements', and that is perhaps obvious enough. But making the distinction as I have phrased it should enable me to show quite clearly that 'pleasure', conceived of as a psychological quantity, must be classified as an ideal-regarding concept. Thus, I very much want to finish writing this Introduction by the deadline for copy, but if I were to pursue pleasure there are quite a few things I could be doing instead. Anyone who judged my well-being according to the criterion of pleasure would therefore have to say that it is less than it might be, even though there is nothing I want to do more than what I am doing. Of course, the response is liable to be that, if what I really want to do most is finish the Introduction, that must hold out the greatest prospect of pleasure. But that is simply the move discussed in my third point (pages 41–2). Either pleasure is identified with want-satisfaction or it is not. If it is, then it is a constituent in want-regarding principles; if it is not, then it is a constituent in ideal-regarding principles. It has to be conceded that the effect of this is to make hedonistic utilitarianism an ideal-regarding moral theory. (This point is made implicitly in the reference to Sidgwick on page 41 of *Political Argument*.) But I do not see this as an objection. It is, I suggest, actually illuminating to point out that hedonism, taken seriously (an important qualification), is an ideal-regarding notion.

This, however, brings me to the main issue: that some ideal-regarding concepts are more ideal-regarding than others. For it has a significant bearing on some remarks that come at the beginning of Chapter VI. I say there (pp. 95–6) that ideal-regarding principles do not lend themselves to systematic analysis of the kind given to want-regarding principles in *Political Argument*. I am not sure that my reasons for saying this are very well spelt out, but the key passage occurs at the end of the discussion, when I say: 'Once you have decided that a good kind of human being would have the qualities *x*, *y* and *z* and that this is a *political* judgement then everything else connected with it is either a question of means to that end or a question of trade-offs. . . . Neither of these problems . . . allows much scope for a general discussion' (pp. 95–6). It now seems to me that in what I wrote I was focusing too narrowly on attempts to improve people's characters or elevate their tastes. If I had kept in view ideal-regarding judgements that simply give more weight to the satisfaction of some wants than others, I would have reached a less negative conclusion.

The bearing of this point on pleasure and happiness is that they are examples of ideal-regarding concepts that can (and do) enter into principles that are identical in form with want-regarding ones. We can be concerned with the aggregation and distribution of pleasure or happiness just as much as we can with the aggregation and distribution of want-satisfaction or the means to want-satisfaction. The point has further ramifications. Chapter XI is entitled 'Other Aggregative Concepts', and begins by discussing in the first section 'welfare' and 'good'. 'Welfare', I suggest, may well function as a partial want-regarding concept—that is, it may concentrate attention on strategically important aspects of want-satisfaction, but not be regarded as having independent value (pp. 187–8). But it may also, I argue, 'be used with an ideal-regarding tinge' (p. 188), since it may actually be traded off against undifferentiated want-satisfaction. Speaking about somebody's 'good' is, I maintain (pp. 189–90), normally used in ideal-regarding contexts. In spite of that, I treated 'welfare' and 'good'— quite rightly—as possible constituents of aggregative judgements. And I would now wish to add that they are also possible constituents of distributive judgements too. What this shows, though, is that what I said at the beginning of Chapter VI has to be partially retracted. Some ideal-regarding concepts can play the same kind of role in aggregative and distributive principles as is played by want-regarding concepts such as opportunity, resource, interest and preference.

I said at the beginning that I would eventually get to a controversy illuminated by the want-regarding/ideal-regarding distinction: that involved in the claim that the state should be 'neutral' between 'conceptions of the good'. I can now redeem that promise. The idea of state neutrality is in essence that the allocation of rights, opportunities, incomes and so on should not be dependent on the recipient's 'idea of the good'. This amounts to saying that ideal-regarding criteria should not be employed in political argument. Ideals, in other words, should be kept out of politics.

In *Political Argument* I called this anti-ideal-regarding position 'liberalism', though I added the cautionary remark that it was only one strand in classical liberalism (p. 62). More recently, Ronald Dworkin and Bruce Ackerman have identified the same position with liberalism, omitting the cautionary qualification.[53] And Alasdair MacIntyre has been happy to make the same identification, though his purpose is to bury liberalism rather than to praise it.[54]

In recent years the pros and cons of liberalism so defined have become the subject of a lively transatlantic debate, but there was no debate at all when I wrote IV.4-6 of *Political Argument*. What actually existed was a widespread British assumption that ideal-regarding considerations must play a part in politics and a widespread American assumption (especially among the kinds of people one was liable to come across at Harvard) that ideal-regarding considerations were out of place in politics. I simply brought these assumptions face to face and asked what might be said in favour of each if they were raised to the level of consciousness and forced to justify themselves.

Although I would not be so bold as to maintain that I invented the equation of liberalism with the anti-ideal position, I am not aware of having got it from anyone else: I think I simply distilled

[53] See Bruce Ackerman, *Social Justice and the Liberal State* (New Haven, 1980) and Ronald Dworkin, 'Liberalism', in Stuart Hampshire (ed.) *Public and Private Morality* (Cambridge, 1978), pp. 113–43; reprinted in Ronald Dworkin, *A Matter of Principle* (Cambridge, Mass., 1985), pp. 181–204. For a discussion of Ackerman and Dworkin, and also of Rawls, see my 'How Not to Defend Liberal Institutions', *British Journal of Political Science* 20 (1990), 1–14.

[54] Alasdair MacIntyre, *After Virtue* (Notre Dame, Ind., 1981), ch. 17, and *Whose Justice? Which Rationality?* (Notre Dame, Ind., 1988), ch. 17. For a critique of the second, see my review article 'The Light that Failed?' *Ethics* 100 (1989), 160–8.

it from a difference between the British and American political cultures that struck me forcibly. Nor does any predecessor occur to me now. This, however, is bound to cast doubt upon the idea insisted upon by Ackerman and Dworkin that neutrality is the historic core of liberalism. My more modest claim that it is one strand seems to me the most than can reasonably be said.

3.D. *The Aggregative/Distributive Distinction (III.4).* In contrast with the want-regarding/ideal-regarding distinction, the distinction between aggregative and distributive principles has had pretty smooth sailing. The distinction has also continued to be marked with the words that I gave to its two elements, and I think I should feel pleased that it has become a part of the common stock of ideas. No doubt its reception was aided by its being picked up by Rawls in *A Theory of Justice*, where he introduces 'the aggregative-distributive dichotomy' without attribution or explanation as if it would already be familiar to his readers.[55] The context is the indifference-curve analysis of value pluralism discussed earlier in this section, and I think that this context may have given Rawls's interpretation of the aggregative-distributive distinction an idiosyncratic turn that fortunately does not seem to have caught on.

Thus, Rawls's example of what he calls the 'aggregative-distributive dichotomy' is a conception with 'two principles: the basic structure of society is to be designed first to produce the most good in the sense of the greatest net balance of satisfaction, and second to distribute satisfactions equally'.[56] These two principles are to be brought into relation with one another intutionistically 'because no priority rule is provided for determining how [they] are to be balanced against each other'.[57] And this is illustrated with an indifference curve diagram showing 'equality' on one axis and 'total welfare' on the other.[58]

This is fair enough as an example that can be got on to the two dimensions of a sheet of paper, but Rawls later goes on to write as if 'the aggregative-distributive dichotomy' must be represented by two just principles, one aggregative and one distributive. Thus,

[55] Rawls, *A Theory of Justice*, p. 36.
[56] Ibid.
[57] Ibid., p. 37.
[58] Ibid.

he writes in the next section that 'the aggregative-distributive dich-otomy is no doubt an attractive idea, but . . . it does not factor the problem of social justice into small enough parts'.[59] However, as *Political Argument* attempts to make plain, there is in fact a whole family of distributive principles. The one that Rawls takes, the principle that want-satisfaction should be distributed equally, is one possible one but it is not even among the most popular. (Many people who accept a variety of distributive principles would give it no place at all, in either its satisfaction-regarding form or its resource-regarding analogue.) Rawls, it is surely evident, tries to get by with far fewer distinct principles than I canvassed in *Political Argument*, so I have to say that it was a bit cool to suggest that the aggregative-distributive distinction does not have an adequate conceptual richness.

Let me conclude this discussion with some tidying up. The dis-cussion of aggregative and distributive principles should be brought into line with the modification I introduced at the end of my discussion of the want-regarding/ideal-regarding distinction. That is to say, it should be made clear that distributive principles can be satisfaction-regarding as well as resource-regarding and conversely that aggregative principles can be resource-regarding as well as satisfaction-regarding.

It is, indeed, very plausible that there are real examples of all four possibilities. Thus, if we think about desert as one distribu-tive principle, and ask about, say, the basis for assessing fines on people, it seems reasonable to suggest that monetary penalties should be adjusted to the wealth of different people guilty of the same offence so that the amount of the fine will 'mean the same' to all. And this is clearly a satisfaction-regarding notion, since it requires us to go behind the distribution of resources to an im-puted distribution of want-satisfaction.

On the other side, we can find resource-regarding aggregative principles, whether they are ultimately to be regarded as plausible or not. Thus, it is sometimes suggested that we should 'maximize the total amount of freedom' in whatever society we are consider-ing. And freedom is most sensibly treated as a resource-regarding notion, dealing as it does with the range of opportunities open to people (or the barriers that close off opportunities to them) rather

---

[59] Ibid., p. 44.

than with actual want-satisfaction. We may also bear in mind the suggestion of Richard Posner, the hero of 'economic analysis of law', that the objective pursued by judges (especially in tort cases) should be 'wealth-maximization'.[60]

4. RIGHTS, DESERTS AND NEEDS

4.A. *Rights (VIII.4)*. In his book *Social Justice*,[61] David Miller identifies three components of social justice: rights, deserts and needs. Of these, rights got fairly short shrift in *Political Argument*, desert was said to be most likely on its way out as a significant factor in social evaluations, and needs were dismissed as having no independent normative force. Since Miller's view of the matter would, I believe, be quite widely shared, it seems worth subjecting these concepts to a renewed scrutiny twenty-five years later. I shall begin with rights.

There is no problem about rights that are established by a constitution or by law. To the extent that the provisions of the constitution or law are definite, they give rise to definite rights. We can also quite intelligibly speak of moral rights on a quasi-legal model, arising from promises or legitimate expectations, as when we say that someone who spends years caring for an aged relative has a moral right (as distinctive from a legal right) to inherit something. All these rights are the creature of rules or conventions.[62]

Let us lay these on one side and ask about the status of rights that are not anchored in the same way. Here we should distinguish between general assertions of rights and specific assertions of rights. General assertions are the kind contained in the American Declaration of Independence and the French Declaration of the Rights of Man and of the Citizen. In the terminology of *Political Argument*, they constitute assertions of 'fundamental equality' (pp. 119–20). The claim that everybody has equal rights is equivalent to the claim that everyone forms part of a single

[60] Richard A. Posner, *Economic Analysis of Law* (Boston, Mass., 2nd edn. 1977); *The Economics of Justice* (Cambridge, Mass., 1981). For a critique see Tom Campbell, *Justice* (London, 1988), ch. 5.

[61] David Miller, *Social Justice* (Oxford, 1978).

[62] See ibid., pp. 68–70, and H. L. A. Hart, *Essays on Bentham: Jurisprudence and Political Theory* (Oxford, 1982), pp. 83–5.

'reference group' (pp. 11–15). The establishing of a reference group is an essential preliminary to any political argument because it tells us who are the subjects of political principles. The claim that human beings are fundamentally equal is sometimes expressed by saying that everyone should be given equal consideration or everyone should be treated equally. I shall not stop to ask how such a claim might be defended.[63] The point that matters here is that, understood in this way, the idea of rights detached from an institutional setting is quite intelligible.

Specific assertions of rights are another matter. We are all familiar, of course, with claims that there exist a variety of 'natural' or 'human' rights, and the language of rights is the *lingua franca* of the United Nations: in addition to the rights enumerated in the Universal Declaration of Human Rights, the General Assembly is constantly discovering new ones, such as the right to economic development. My view is that talk about rights of this kind is perfectly intelligible, but only so long as it is understood to be *asserting* a claim but not *justifying* it. In other words, to say that people have a right to something (free speech, paid holidays, or whatever) is to say that there is some good reason for their having it, but it is not to say what that reason is.

Thus, specific 'natural' or 'human' rights are not the moral basis for demands in politics. Rather, they are demands themselves, and the justification for the demand has to be forthcoming in each case. The reasons can be, and will be, of quite different kinds. Thus, claiming a 'right to economic development' is saying that rich countries ought to help poor ones (with aid, favourable trading and licensing arrangements, and so on), and there are presumably some arguments of a distributive kind underlying such a claim. Claiming a 'right to paid holidays' is saying that governments ought to enact legislation requiring employers to provide workers

[63] There is a good deal of controversy as to the possibility of providing foundations for the assertion that human beings are fundamentally equal, in the sense that the human race forms a single reference group. On one view, this is an ultimate ethical premise so it cannot be further supported. On the opposing view, an empirical claim to the effect that almost all adult members of the human race reach a certain threshold for rationality, self-control, moral capacity, and so on, is relevant to the claim of fundamental equality. I discuss this question (and come down in favour of the second view) in the entry on 'Equality' in Lawrence Becker, ed., *Encyclopedia of Ethics* (forthcoming from Garland Press, New York and London).

with paid holidays, and this claim can again presumably be backed with distributive arguments involving an appeal to social justice. The claim of a right to free speech is a demand on governments (or constitution-makers) to provide the appropriate legal framework for a regime of free speech. This claim can be defended by invoking the value of freedom, which (as I argue in VIII.3) can in turn be derived from a variety of other considerations.

The upshot of this discussion is, then, that rights do not play a foundational role in political evaluation and justification. I am thus taking a harder line here on 'natural' or 'human' rights than that embodied in VIII.4, where I said, without further remark, that 'one of the commonest justifications of negative freedom is the claim that it is a "natural", "human" right' (p. 149). I would now wish to say that this puts things back to front. In the rest of the section, however, I went on to say that rights other than 'negative' ones must be derived from some distributive principles. I would now suggest that the same thing should be said of 'negative' rights.

4.B. *Deserts (VI.4).* In 1965, I wrote that 'in examining the concept of desert we are examining a concept which is already in decline and may eventually disappear' (p. 112). From the vantage point of the present day, it now appears that I was writing towards the end of a period (lasting from the 1930s to the 1970s) when the prestige of desert was at its lowest ebb. As late as 1976, David Miller suggested that 'the concept of desert has become less popular in recent years', but the tide was already turning and in 1988 Tom Campbell maintained that 'there has recently been a return to the idea that desert is a central feature of justice'.[64]

At any rate in the Anglo-American philosophical literature, the revival of interest in (and, generally, support for) the concept of desert is very noticeable. When I was writing *Political Argument*, the only serious philosophical treatment of desert after Sidgwick's in *The Methods of Ethics* (and the only thing to which I referred) was Joel Feinberg's essay 'Justice and Personal Desert', first published in 1963.[65] Since then, there have been many more. David

[64] Miller, *Social Justice*, p. 102; Campbell, p. 151.

[65] A more accessible source for this than the original one cited in the Bibliography is Joel Feinberg, *Doing and Deserving: Essays in the Theory of Responsibility* (Princeton, NJ, 1970), pp. 55–94. (This version includes an excellent appendix, not in the original, on 'Personal Income as Deserved'.)

Miller made desert one of the three elements of social justice in his book *Social Justice*, and has subsequently moved away from the view expressed there about its limited role under contemporary economic conditions. In a recent book, he argues that (given a just initial distribution of resources) market outcomes reflect desert.[66] In a somewhat similar vein, James Sterba, in *The Demands of Justice*, makes needs and deserts (as determined by the market) central to his conception of social justice.[67] In addition, two whole books, by Wojciech Sadurski and George Sher, have recently been devoted to the concept of desert and its practical implications.[68]

It will inevitably be pointed out that Rawls, in *A Theory of Justice*, takes a strongly anti-desert line in relation to the primary goods (in particular income) whose distribution is the subject of social justice. In the key passage, Rawls writes:

> Perhaps some will think that the person with greater natural endowments deserves those assets and the superior character that made their development possible. Because he is more worthy in this sense, he deserves the greater advantages that he could achieve with them. This view, however, is surely incorrect. It seems to be one of the fixed points of our considered judgements that no one deserves his place in the distribution of native endowments, any more than one deserves one's initial starting place in society. The assertion that a man deserves the superior character that enables him to make the effort to cultivate his abilities is equally problematic; for his character depends in large part upon fortunate family and social circumstances for which he can claim no credit. The notion of desert seems not to apply to these cases.[69]

The point that is revelant in the present context, however, is not what Rawls wrote but what the response has been. And the response since 1971 has been overwhelmingly negative. I cannot as a matter of fact think of anything that has been written defending Rawls on desert, while the standard annotated bibliography

---

[66] Miller, *Market, State, and Community*, ch. 6.

[67] James P. Sterba, in *The Demands of Justice* (Notre Dame, Ind., 1980). See also his 'Justice as Desert', *Social Theory and Practice* 3 (1974), 101–16.

[68] W. Sadurski, *Giving Desert its Due: Social Justice and Legal Theory* (Dordrecht, 1985), discussed in Campbell, pp. 151–78; George Sher, *Desert* (Princeton, NJ, 1987).

[69] Rawls, pp. 103–4.

(which runs up to 1981) lists seventeen items all of which contain critical comments, and there have been more since.[70] It has become commonplace that it is one thing to say that abilities are themselves deserved and another to say that people may acquire desert on the basis of the use they make of their abilities. The second can be maintained, it has often been pointed out, consistently with the denial of the first.

Against Rawls's suggestion that even efforts have social causes, the critics divide. The hardliners say that so long as effort (that is, voluntary action, in the ordinary sense of the expression) is involved, it does not matter whether or not it has social causes. The soft line approach is to concede the relevance of social causation but then to point out that even Rawls himself claimed only that effort depended 'in large part' on favourable circumstances, and that a complete denial of desert does not follow from such a claim. What both schools of thought share is a dislike of Rawls's treatment of desert.

It is natural to ask where this large literature on desert leaves the discussion of the topic in *Political Argument*. My answer is that I can see no reason for any major revisions. Attempts to build up the range of applications of the concept of desert seem to me to inflate it to the point at which it means, roughly, 'what would be nice'. Thus, George Sher, in his book *Desert*, makes the following claim: 'We do say that someone who has suffered intense or long-standing pain now deserves to be comfortable . . .'.[71] I do not say things like that, and I don't believe that anybody I know would say things like that either. It is true that one might speak of 'undeserved suffering', though only in a context where there was some issue as to the responsibility of the victim for his or her own suffering. But I cannot imagine saying that the person in question deserved to suffer less, since the whole point of saying that the suffering was undeserved would be to deny that desert had anything to do with it.

I am now inclined to think that my own analysis of desert was itself too accommodating, though not as grotesquely as Sher's. The one retraction that I should like to make, therefore, is to

[70] J. H. Wellbank, Denis Snook and David T. Mason, *John Rawls and His Critics: An Annotated Bibliography* (New York, 1982), *sub* 'Desert' (second to sixth subheads) in 'Index of Concepts'.
[71] Sher, p. 19.

withdraw the claim made in the last two paragraphs of VI.4.B to the effect that there is a 'subsidiary sense' of desert in connection with contests so that the person meeting the qualifying conditions for winning is said to 'deserve' the prize simply in virtue of meeting those conditions (p. 112). I am persuaded by David Miller that this is not even a subsidiary sense of desert.[72] It is true that the accolade, and whatever material benefits go along with it, are the due of the person who satisfies the criteria for winning (e.g. being first through the tape without being disqualified). But due and desert are not the same.[73]

This is not to say that it is always out of place to maintain that the person who actually won deserved to win. Thus, suppose it is claimed that somebody other than the winner deserved to win – perhaps that this other person played better but was unlucky with the breaks. Then it might be said in response that on closer examination it would be seen that the luck really evened out. The winner, it might be said in this context, did deserve to win after all. And by extension the objection might be anticipated, and it might simply be said straight off that the winner deserved to win: he or she had trained hard, overcome obstacles, contended with bad luck, and so on.

The essential point remains, however. If it is said that someone other than the person who met the criteria for winning deserved to win, it is no reply simply to reiterate that the person who met the criteria for winning did win. The rebuttal has to be in the same terms as the challenge, dealing in such things as effort, personal qualities and luck. Meeting the criteria for winning in itself established not that one deserves to win but that one has a right to win, in the institutionally-based sense of 'right' distinguished in 4.A. Since a right of this kind cannot provide the foundation for an evaluation, it is always relevant to ask what would be wrong in not giving the prize to the person who has a right to it. But an answer is not far to seek: it would be unfair to award the prize to anyone else in exactly the same way as it would be unfair to

---

[72] Miller, *Social Justice*, p. 84.

[73] 'A just scheme gives each his due: that is, it allots to each what he is entitled to as defined by the scheme itself.' Rawls, p. 313. The assimilation of due and desert is quite widespread: for example, Alasdair MacIntyre treats them as interchangeable when he writes that 'justice, on an Aristotelian view, is defined in terms of giving each person his or her due or desert' (*After Virtue*, p. 188).

offer a reward to a person for doing something and then refuse to pay.

To conclude this part of the discussion, it is worth observing that what has been said applies only to prizes (and the accolade of winning) bestowed in competitions. It is important not to assume that competitions are widespread phenomena outside sporting events deliberately set up to create them. Thus – to jump straight in to the most significant implication – jobs are not in general to be regarded as prizes to which people acquire a right by doing well in a competition. They may be, as when it is announced in advance that places in the civil service will be filled on the basis of a competitive examination. Then someone who scores above the cut-off point has a right to a job founded upon a legitimate expectation, and it is unfair not to honour it. But it is not unfair to refuse to turn a job into a prize in such a way.

Of course, the best candidate should get the job, and this rules out bribery, nepotism, and irrelevant criteria generally. But what makes a candidate the best may not be reducible to prize-winning qualities. It may be that, given the people already employed, what is needed is a woman or a member of a racial minority; or perhaps being able to hit it off with the existing members of a team will be an essential requirement. To put it succinctly: filling a job is appointing someone to perform a function, whereas awarding a prize has no ulterior purpose, except perhaps to encourage the cultivation of the qualities that it takes to win. Prizes are given in respect of past performance; appointments are made in respect of anticipated future performance.[74]

I want to return now to the issue with which I began this discussion of desert. If the repute of desert declined between the 1930s and the 1970s and has since recovered somewhat (though without getting back to the heights of its Victorian heyday), what explanation can be offered? I am aware of two ways of accounting for the decline of desert, but neither seems able to cope with the more recent revival of its fortunes. However, I think that the second can be modified so as to perform that task.

One theory which is quite commonly advanced is that confidence in desert is undermined by the belief in determinism.[75]

[74] See Michael Walzer, *Spheres of Justice: A Defence of Pluralism and Equality* (New York, 1983), pp. 135–9.
[75] See for example Campbell, p. 150.

The idea is supposed to be that desert depends on voluntary actions, and if determinism is true there are no voluntary actions. This is not very plausible, for three reasons. First, as I pointed out earlier, there are 'hard-line' advocates of desert who maintain that non-voluntary virtues and achievements can form the basis of valid desert claims. Suppose, however, that we accept the first premise, that desert depends on voluntary actions. We can still dispute the other premise, that voluntary actions are inconsistent with determinism. 'People are willing to believe both that a man deserves rewards and other benefits for the actions he performs, and that these actions can be explained in causal terms.'[76] A further point is that it would be very hard to contend that the revival in the fortunes of desert has been accompanied by increased resistence to the doctrine of determinism. Most people who accept determinism see it simply as an implication of a uniform order of nature, and as far as I know that is not an idea whose attractiveness has been waning in recent decades. To the extent that the salience of determinism depends on actual scientific discoveries, it should have been enhanced by advances in neurophysiology which have shown more precisely how brain activity relates to thoughts and feelings, since it seems hard to deny that the brain is an electrochemical system subject to causal laws. If the denial of determinism requires the belief in a 'mind' possessed of a 'free will' which enables it to induce human actions contra-causally, it becomes increasingly hard to see how anti-determinism can continue to be sustained except by resorting to a belief in five billion daily miracles.

A second line of explanation for the decline of desert has been put forward by Miller. This is actually an elaboration of the suggestion made in *Political Argument* (pp. 112–13) that '"desert" flourishes in a liberal society where people are regarded as rational independent atoms held together in a society by a "social contract" from which all must benefit. Each person's worth (desert) can be precisely ascertained – it is his net marginal product and under certain postulated conditions (which it is conveniently assumed the existing economy approximates) market prices give each factor of production its net marginal product.' Miller points out that the attribution of a net marginal product

[76] Miller, *Social Justice*, p. 102.

lxi

presupposes a world of independent producers. In a modern 'organized society', however, 'each person is seen as part of a corporate group which collectively supplies goods or services. It is impossible therefore to measure individual deserts by the separate value of each man's products.'[77] Any attempt to apportion contribution is more or less arbitrary.[78]

I believe that considerations of this kind do indeed make it unlikely that desert in a world of large corporate enterprises will ever have the naïve attraction that it has in a society where rewards can be seen to arise more immediately from market relationships. But the size of firms tends over time to increase, and the proportion of self-employed people in the population remains very small. If this is the whole story, then how can we account for a revival in the fortunes of the concept of desert?

One simple answer is that there has been a massive rise in the incidence of sanctimony and smugness among the successful that has nothing to do with any change in the underlying reality. Rather, it has been stimulated by politicians who have realized that it is possible to win power by recruiting the most economically successful forty per cent or so of the population in a crusade to roll back the gains made by their fellow citizens in the previous forty years. And how better to rationalize this than to tell people that they deserve the incomes that the market generates?

I believe this to be a large part of the truth, but I want to suggest that there is also some change in social reality with relevance to the popular status of desert. The 1930s were a period of massive economic dislocation in which millions of sober and industrious citizens found their skills and energies without value. The Second World War then caught up whole populations, giving individuals virtually no control over their fates. The postwar period of reconstruction saw entire industries collapse as production shifted to lower cost countries, and skills became obsolete overnight in the wake of technological change. In these circumstances, there was a basic lack of convincingness in the idea that the unsuccessful had failed because of personal deficiencies while the successful could claim personal credit for their achievements. I do not want to exaggerate the contrast between all this and the present: there is

---

[77] Ibid., p. 308.
[78] Ibid., p. 309.

still unemployment, there is still relocation of industries, and there is still technological change. Nevertheless, people in the advanced industrial societies of the West are perhaps not being unreasonable if they have felt less like playthings of fate in the past decade than at any time in the preceding half century.

What I have been saying presupposes the truth of the claim that the idea of desert fits peculiarly well with a liberal society. This flatly contradicts the assertion put forward in recent years by Alasdair MacIntyre that liberalism is a doctrine lacking the resources to sustain attributions of desert. Let me conclude this discussion of desert by arguing that MacIntyre is plain wrong.

MacIntyre concedes that desert enters in popular contemporary arguments about income distribution, but points out that neither John Rawls nor Robert Nozick (whom he takes to represent the two main strands of liberal philosophizing) has any room for desert.[79] Strictly speaking, Rawls, as we have seen, admits the potential relevance of desert, but maintains that the conditions for its application do not exist, at any rate in relation to income distribution. Nozick has a monolithic theory that makes rights foundational, and thus inevitably has no room for desert.[80]

Nozick's theory is completely misconceived since, as I pointed out in 4.A., there are no particular non-institutional rights such as the right to property appealed to by Nozick. And Nozick has, as a matter of fact, found very few followers in the philosophical community. As far as Rawls is concerned, I have already drawn attention to the universal rejection among philosophers of his views about desert. MacIntyre's notion is that, while ordinary people (confusedly incorporating pre-liberal elements into their thought) continue to talk about desert, philosophers are consistent with the premises of liberalism in eschewing any such talk. That idea is a non-starter, because Rawls and Nozick are both extremely unrepresentative in their rejection of desert.

MacIntyre could still maintain, however, that Rawls and Nozick are right and the rest wrong. According to him, the concept of desert requires as a background to its use a community defined by participation in shared practices which carry with them their own internal standards of achievement.[81] Liberal

---

[79] MacIntyre, *After Virtue*, pp. 232–5.
[80] Robert Nozick, *Anarchy, State, and Utopia* (New York, 1974).
[81] MacIntyre, *After Virtue*, pp. 143, 188.

societies cannot generate the required kind of consensus, so they cannot give rise to claims of desert. The response to this must be that liberal societies all attach a good deal of importance to the generation of wealth, and this provides a basis for the ascription of desert. This does not entail that wealth-production must be treated as a more worthy activity than any other, though the advocates of a so-called 'enterprise culture' would like to see this happen.[82] All that is needed is the notion that 'the labourer is worthy of his hire', and that bigger contributions deserve bigger rewards.

It may still be objected that, where production takes place in large firms, the notion of a definite contribution is too vague and contentious to form the basis for remuneration. (It will be recalled that this was David Miller's explanation for the decline of desert.) But in fact analysis of job-evaluation schemes shows that there is enormous consensus on the factors relevant to the worth of jobs, though there is some variation in weightings.[83] Thus, a sense of just pay differentials based on ideas of desert is quite compatible with the existence of a liberal society.

4.C. *Needs (III.5.A)*. Bearing in mind its extreme brevity (it covers only a little over two pages), the discussion of need in *Political Argument* has attracted a remarkably large amount of attention, almost all of it critical. However, the bulk of this attention has been focused on an issue that seems to me to be rather trivial. Those who make a lot of it do not think it is trivial, but I believe that they are mistaken in this. I should add that the position I take

---

[82] 'An enterprise culture is one in which every individual understands that the world does not owe him or her a living, so we all act together accordingly, all working for the success of UK plc. . . . Successful companies, which regularly make profits and grow, are the flagships of the enterprise culture and their directors are the heroes. . . . In an enterprise culture the whole nation understands that we are locked into competition with other nations. We are soldiers in an economic war. . . . A nation is allowed to put into the economic battlefield any number of its citizens—there are no restrictions. Nor are there any restrictions on the training or the technology given to our economic warriors.' This vision of total mobilization for economic warfare seems to satisfy abundantly MacIntyre's conditions for a consensus on criteria of excellent performance. The passages quoted are from a speech made by the head of the Institute of Directors, reported in the *Sunday Times* 4 March 1990, p. C6.

[83] See Karol Soltan, *The Causal Theory of Justice* (Berkeley and Los Angeles, 1987).

is commonly misrepresented, and is in fact closer to that of my critics than they usually recognize.

I suggested (pp. 47–8) that any statement to the effect that a certain person needs something can be continued with an expression such as 'in order to . . .' or 'in order for . . .'. That is to say, it must be possible to specify a goal of the agent, or an end-state (such as nutrition) that may or may not be a goal of the agent, to which the thing needed is a means. I went on to say, however (p. 49), that there was no linguistic impropriety in suppressing the 'in order to' clause wherever the end-state was of some standard kind such as physical or mental health, and I even went as far as to say that in these contexts it would be pedantic to insert it.

A number of people, including David Miller, David Wiggins, David Braybrooke and Garrett Thomson,[84] have argued against this analysis suggesting that there are two senses of 'need'. One is relative to some end-state, but the other neither requires nor admits the addition of an 'in order to' clause. Of these critics, only Braybrooke acknowledges the second half of my view on the subject, saying that I see 'that the relational formula [i.e. the addition of an 'in order to' clause] gives unilluminating results with basic needs' and that this makes me 'less than a wholehearted champion of the relational formula'.[85] The others fail to recognize how close I am in the end to their own position. The remaining difference seems to me of trivial significance, but for what it is worth all my instincts (inculcated, no doubt, by Ryle and Austin) tell me that it is not very likely that a word such as 'need' would have two different meanings. It is much more plausible to suppose that in any use of 'need' there is always some end-state in the background, but the more obvious and uncontroversial it is the more linguistically odd it would be to spell it out.

The issue is in fact doubly trivial. Not only is there no more than a nuance between the alternatives but nothing turns on the choice of an alternative. This is as far as I am concerned the main issue. My claim was that 'need' has no independent normative status, for the simple reason that the case for meeting a need must

---

[84] Miller, *Social Justice*; David Wiggins, *Needs, Values, Truth: Essays in the Philosophy of Value* (Oxford, 1967); David Braybrooke, *Meeting Needs* (Princeton, NJ, 1987; Garrett Thomson, *Needs* (London and New York, 1987).

[85] Braybrooke, p. 312, note to Chapter 2, section 1.

always be derived from the case for achieving the end-state to which meeting the need is a means. Now the people I have mentioned wish to maintain that, in its alleged non-relative sense (they use different words for this), 'need' stands as a concept with independent normative force. A closer examination of what they say reveals, however, that they do not really mean this. Leaving aside Braybrooke for a moment, we can say that the remaining three theorists take a quite similar line to one another. Miller, Wiggins and Thomson all define a non-relative need in such a way that a person's unmet need will occasion harm to that person.[86] Wiggins also puts forward a formula according to which a person's unmet need will result in (or consist in) the denial of a 'vital interest'.[87]

Suppose, then, that we ask why needs of this kind have some moral weight. Surely, the answer will be that unless these needs are met there will be harm or violation of a vital interest. But then that is the basis for taking the claim of need seriously. My point that need claims are derivative thus stands. Indeed, Thomson says exactly this in the last paragraph of his book. He writes: 'If the point of an evaluation, whether it be moral, political or prudential, is to improve the quality of people's lives in some respect, then the concept of a need will be tailor-made as a basis for that type of evaluation. . . . In other words, needs are a matter or priority in comparison with other evaluative concepts because the point of evaluation is to improve the quality of people's lives or enhance their welfare, and needs cannot be less important than human welfare.'[88] I am quite happy to agree with all that. I merely wish to add that needs cannot be *more* important than human welfare either; and, to press the point harder, needs have whatever priority they do have purely by virtue of whatever priority human welfare has.

It is important to recognize that it is logically possible to recognize the existence of a 'basic need' (i.e. one connected with harm etc.) and yet not thereby be committed to saying that it ought to be the job of a politically-organized society to see to it that it is met. (I should make it clear that 'see to it' does not have to entail direct provision; it can include creating an institutional framework

---

[86] Miller, *Social Justice*, p. 130; Wiggins, p. 10; Thomson, p. 19.
[87] Wiggins, p. 24.
[88] Thomson, p. 128.

within which the need will foreseeably be met, perhaps by family members, perhaps by the workings of a market, or in some other way that is, from the point of view of the state, indirect.) Wiggins recognizes that this is so. He seeks to defend the concept of need from the accusation of 'trying to force our hand or of aiding and abetting some illicit transition from a statement of what must be', and makes an initial move in the defence by pointing out that 'there is no real contradiction at all in saying: 'This patient needs a blood transfusion. But she can't have one. The only suitable blood has been allocated to someone else.'[89]

This is a case where the only reason for not meeting a need is that resources are limited. Can we say, then, that need always constitutes a compelling claim in the absence of resource limitations? No. The temptation to believe that it does stems from the humanitarian presumption that everybody's welfare is valuable. But that presumption is rebuttable. Imagine that Hitler's physician had been recruited to von Stauffenberg's conspiracy against the Führer's life. He might well have said to himself: 'Hitler needs an injection—he'll die without it—so he mustn't have one'.

The target here is not a straw man. It has a flesh and blood embodiment in David Braybrooke. Braybrooke's book is long and complicated, but the gist of it is that the concept of need functions within a 'Selfgovliset' (a 'self-governing linguistic subset' of the speakers of a language) as a way of marking agreed-on priorities for allocation among a 'reference group'—typically the members of the Selfgovliset themselves. Needs are whatever all the members of the Selfgovliset agree should have priority in the distribution of resources—or 'to rule out extreme or bizarre views' perhaps what ninety percent of them agree on.[90]

The most obvious objection to this (and the only one that I shall mention here) is that it has the result of making claims about need occur in the conclusion of an argument about what ought to be done rather than in the premises. Consider the assertion: 'Wheelchair ramps ought to be provided because they're needed by the disabled.' Normally the need would be taken to provide a reason—and a very good one—for the provision. It is not, however, a conclusive reason because it can be countered by the claim that,

[89] Wiggins, p. 5 and n. 7, p. 5.
[90] Braybrooke, p. 64.

although the need is genuine enough, it would cost too much to meet in relation to the benefit in prospect. And at any rate in a poor country where there were many urgent unmet claims on the public purse, such a counterclaim might be very plausible. On Braybrooke's theory, though, anyone conceding that the need existed would thereby be commited, as a matter of linguistic propriety, to accepting that it should be met.

Now as a matter of fact Braybrooke's theory does have instantiations. Thus, British legislation laying a duty on local authorities to make provision for the special needs of the disabled adds that in assessing need the local authority may take into account the costs of provision in relation to the resources available. The only successful litigation under this piece of legislation was a case in which a council official was incautious enough to admit in writing that a need existed while going on to say that the council had no intention of meeting it. What the official should have said, of course, was that since the council could not afford to make the provision the need did not exist. This seems to me a pathological usage of 'need'—a *reductio ad absurdum* of Braybrooke's theory rather than a validation of it.

In *Political Argument*, I drew the conclusion from the derivative value of meeting needs that needs had no distinctive place in the formulation of political principles, and I used this conclusion to explain why needs were never mentioned again in the book. It is now clear to me that this was too hasty, and that needs should be assimilated (making allowance for their derivative status) to pleasure, happiness and welfare. 'Need' is, in fact, especially close to 'welfare', and what I said about welfare can also be said about needs. That is to say, it picks out from all wants (or potential wants) a subset, namely those whose satisfaction prevents harm or serves vital interests, and gives them priority. This makes it *prima facie* an ideal-regarding concept, but, as with welfare, there is a want-regarding as well as an ideal-regarding rationale for it. Thus, David Miller argues that the principle of priority for needs is best seen as simply a strategically-important way station on the road to implementing a principle of equal want-satisfaction.[91] Wiggins, on the other hand, is quite explicit in making the principle of giving priority to meeting needs an ideal-regarding

---

[91] Miller, *Social Justice*, pp. 143–50.

principle.[92] On this view, we may say (following the terminology introduced by Scanlon) that in comparison with preferences needs have 'urgency'.[93]

5. POLITICAL ARGUMENT TODAY

In the earlier part of this Introduction, I laid emphasis on the way in which the intellectual world of *Political Argument* has disappeared. The difference can be simply but entirely accurately characterized by saying that *Political Argument* belongs to the pre-Rawlsian world while the world we live in is post-Rawlsian. No doubt, if *A Theory of Justice* had never come into existence, political philosophy in 1990 would still not be conducted in the same way as it was in 1965. But that does not seem a very fruitful line of speculation. In the actual world, there can be no question that *A Theory of Justice* is the watershed that divides the past from the present.

Although *Political Argument* is more than 'linguistic analysis', the highest it aspires to (at any rate officially) is taxonomy. In practice, it goes beyond that at various points. Thus, as we saw above (4.B), the discussion of desert includes a consideration of the conditions for its popularity—or, to put it more grandly, the metaphysical and sociological presuppositions of the concept. Again, the line taken on the sense to be given to various concepts had a fairly evident bearing on substantive political debates. For example, the argument mounted in Chapters XI–XIII in defence of the concept of the public interest was a response to a movement within political science that reduced claims about the public interest to contentless endorsements of public policies. It seemed to me important to insist that it makes perfect sense to talk about the common interests of citizens, and that the expression 'the public interest' is employed to identify such policies. I am glad to say that this conception of 'the public interest' as embodying a claim of substance has become generally accepted, and I have

[92] Wiggins, p. 43 (and elsewhere). Wiggins speaks of the principle of the priority of need-satisfaction as a distributive principle. It is thus an example (see above 3.D.) of an ideal-regarding (welfare-based) distributive principle.

[93] Thomas M. Scanlon, 'Preference and Urgency', *Journal of Philosophy* 72 (1975), 655–69.

no doubt that it makes for a healthier politics that people can talk about the public interest without having to feel apologetic.

Nevertheless, it remains true that these and others like them are separate and unrelated forays outside a framework of taxonomy. The difference that Rawls made in *A Theory of Justice* was that he raised the stakes in political philosophy to a quite new level. Although the structure of the book works to conceal this, *A Theory of Justice* represents a return to the grand manner of political philosophizing, complete with a theory of the human good, a moral psychology, a theory of the subject-matter (the 'basic structure of society') and the objects (the 'primary goods') of justice, and, of course, an immensely elaborate structure of argument in favour of a specific set of principles of justice. Rawls has made writing general treatments of political philosophy hard in much the same way as Beethoven made writing symphonies hard: much more is involved than before.

Where does this leave *Political Argument*? Obviously, it lacks the theoretical reach of a book like *A Theory of Justice*. But it has some compensating advantages. *Political Argument* aspires to stick close to the linguistic ground, trying to capture as accurately as possible the varieties of usage found in actual arguments about institutions and policies. This seems to me to be a task of enduring utility. Any more systematic political philosophy must, I suggest, come to terms with the data presented in *Political Argument*. We do, for example, actually deploy the complex discriminations between (and within) the concepts of equality, equity, justice and fairness to which I call attention. A systematic political philosophy is not obliged to leave everything as if finds it. But it must convince us that it will not destroy morally significant distinctions.

It is much to Rawls's credit that he accepts the challenge, seeking to show that his principles of justice not only follow from a general conception of the task of a theory of justice but also fit our 'considered judgements' at crucial points. However, as I have shown in Section 3.B, he cannot really manage with three principles related by lexicographic priority except by saying that this might form a basis of agreement under certain special conditions.

Rawls's underlying idea is that we are trying to come up with principles that can serve as a shared, public touchstone for the assessment of institutions in a liberal democracy. If they are to serve this purpose, he suggests, the principles must be few and definite. Moreover, the relations between them must be lexicographic because otherwise it will be open to different people to weight the principles differently and hence arrive at conflicting prescriptions. I cannot imagine that anyone is going to improve on Rawls's effort to achieve the degree of simplicity he believes to be necessary. The conclusion must therefore be drawn that such a degree of simplicity is not to be attained. We shall, I suggest, have to accept the unavoidability of balancing, and we shall also have to accept a greater variety of principles than Rawls made room for.

What, then, is the role left for a systematic approach such as Rawls espoused? For an answer, let me refer back again to Section 3.B, where I pointed to Rawls's fall-back position: that even if lexicographic priorities are not attainable, balancing might still be guided by general theoretical considerations. To repeat the key part of a quotation from there: 'Since in justice as fairness the principles of justice are not thought of as self-evident, but have their justification in the fact that they would be chosen, we may find in the grounds for their acceptance some guidance or limitation as to how they are to be balanced.'[94]

The fundamental idea of Rawlsian 'justice as fairness' is that valid principles must be capable of receiving the free assent of all those affected by them. This is obviously a highly ambitious objective, recalling Rousseau's proclaimed intention, in *The Social Contract*, of finding a form of association that should leave people as free as they were before. Those on the extreme right and the extreme left will alike tend to dismiss it as utopian. Perhaps it is. But if we concede that there is no set of principles capable of gaining the free assent of all, we are committed to saying that societies must inherently be held together by repression—that force is needed no only to maintain compliance with mutually agreeable rules, which (as Rousseau recognized) is unexceptionable, but also to maintain compliance with rules that some people cannot reasonably be expected to accept.

This is not the place to pursue the project further. Much would have to be said about the specification of an appropriate 'original

[94] Rawls, p. 42.

position' (Rawls's is by no means the only one possible) and about the way in which one might try to derive principles from it.[95] My present purpose is simply to explain where the Rawlsian revolution in political philosophy seems to me to leave *Political Argument*. My answer in brief is that it does nothing to undercut the validity of the analysis carried out in *Political Argument*, as far as it goes. (This is not to say, of course, that it cannot be improved upon, and I have offered some suggestions here; but such improvements do not derive from any general theory.) What Rawls, and those who have followed in his footsteps, put before us is the task bequeathed us by the Enlightenment. We have to show that political principles are consistent with reason, not in the absurd sense that they can be deduced from the laws of logic, but in the sense that they are worthy of the assent of reasonable people.

[95] I have offered some preliminary ideas on these points in *Theories of Justice*, Chapter 9.

INTRODUCTION TO THE
1965 EDITION

THIS is a study of the relation between principles and institutions. Its focus is analytical rather than causal. It is concerned mainly with the institutional (practical) implications of certain principles; or, to look at the same thing from the other end, with the principled (theoretical) justification of certain institutions. Only incidentally are those causal, historical questions raised which form part of the domain of the 'sociology of knowledge'—for example, about the origin of certain principles and the extent to which principles are a significant independent motive force in social action. No doubt, though, it can safely be assumed that nobody would spend time studying the implications of principles if he did not believe that they had some causal efficacy in social action. If actions on the stage of politics are controlled exclusively by the glands or the wallet, and principles are merely rationalizations of unconscious drives or material interests, it would surely be foolish to take them seriously.[1]

The scope of the study is also limited in space and time. The principles chosen for treatment are those which have been prominent since 1945 in Britain and the USA. Naturally, most of these principles were also prominent before that but it has seemed to me necessary to have some criterion for selection, however rough. Naturally, too, an analysis which applies to Britain and the USA

---

[1] If the name of Pareto may be associated with the line of thought just presented, that of Charles L. Stevenson summons up one which should be sharply distinguished, although it is superficially similar in appearing also to deprecate the place of reasoned choice in the selection and application of principles. This position does not deny to principles (or, at least, their verbal expression) causal force; on the contrary, it identifies them with this force. At the root of this theory lies a conception of human language which assimilates words to Pavlovian stimuli. Far more so than the first theory, this one depends only on the interpretation of everyday experiences. It is, therefore, amenable to treatment from the arm-chair and I shall criticize it in Chapter II.

will also apply more or less closely to other countries according to their similarity in the relevant respects. Canada, Australia, New Zealand and the three Scandinavian monarchies are examples from the 'similar' end of the spectrum.

What are the 'relevant respects' in which a country must resemble Britain and the USA before my analysis can have a close enough fit to be useful? Accepting the risk of oversimplification, let me state two. Firstly, some working agreement must have been reached on those questions—the extent of national boundaries, the form of the government and the method of changing it, the status of religion and whether there are to be groups with hereditary privileges on grounds of 'race', lineage, language, etc.—which go to the heart of a state's existence. With these fundamental causes of disunity and disintegration somehow reduced to manageable proportions, questions can be raised about the kind of society to which the framework of political order should contribute. Secondly, it is only when the mass of the members of the society have the possibility of living at something above subsistence level that the kinds of rather refined distributive questions which form a large part of my discussion have very much application.

Summarizing these two conditions, I would say that until some minimal amount of order and material welfare has been secured there are technical difficulties but no philosophically interesting problems; the latter arise only where a choice between ends is genuinely feasible. This does not, it should scarcely be necessary to add, mean that philosophically interesting problems are (always or usually) more important than technical difficulties. The extreme undesirability of an all-out nuclear war is so plain as to be philosophically uninteresting; but it is quite likely that philosophically interesting problems, and philosophers to worry about them, will be eliminated from the planet because no generally acceptable means to this obviously desirable end can be found. In relations between states the problem of establishing a peaceful order overshadows all others. No doubt it is possible for substantive general principles to be put forward and widely accepted, e.g. that rich nations have some kind of obligation to help poor nations develop their economies. But any attempt to develop a detailed casuistry of political principles in the absence of a working international order seems a doubtfully rewarding enterprise.

I

EVALUATION

---

1. THE SCOPE OF THE STUDY

1.A. *'Persuasion'*. The good citizen will—or should be—passionately devoted at any moment to a number of general principles, often recently acquired, often part of an ancient intellectual inheritance, often largely contradictory among themselves. In practice, he will unconsciously compromise them, or choose between them in the light of the emphasis being given them in the current flow of rhetoric to which he is being subjected. The effective crusader for good causes will in any campaign of persuasion deliberately or by temperament or in ignorance select for emphasis as supreme above all others at least in the existent circumstances a single general principle, or a small number of presumptively harmonious general principles, and will leave to those hostile to his cause the search for intellectual or practical flaws in his argument. There is a third kind of rhetoric which also has logical and practical claims to merit and to utility, whose task it is to explore the conflicts between principles, to search out the importance of degree, relation, and proportion, to discover for particular values their appropriate place in the process of persuasion. To me this last kind of rhetoric seems a most appropriate one for the academic scholar and providing moral and material support for those who attempt to use it seems the most valuable service a great university can render to the process of reaching worthy decisions on questions of social policy.[1]

This work is a study within the spirit of Viner's 'third kind of rhetoric' and most of its space is taken up with the development and application of a set of concepts which I claim to be useful for such a study. However, in this chapter and the next I shall limit myself to a discussion of some more general questions about

[1] Jacob Viner, 'The Intellectual History of *Laissez Faire*', *The Journal of Law and Economics*, III (October 1960), pp. 62–63.

evaluation and language, trying not to go into more detail than is necessary to provide a basis for later discussions.

To begin with, I want to look more closely at Viner's statement that what is needed is a 'rhetoric' in which one is 'to discover for particular values their appropriate place in the process of persuasion'. I believe that 'persuasion' is too wide. 'The process of persuasion' is presumably any means by which one man gets another to change his mind, and though it is perhaps ironic to include overt threats, appeals to unconscious fears and wishes would certainly be part of the process, as would be outbursts of passion or rage, flattery and similar arts. No doubt this 'process of persuasion' might be studied by a psychologist, but I think philosophers are better adapted to dealing with only that part of the process which consists in providing *reasons* for thinking that some policy is desirable or undesirable. This may well have been what Viner had in mind in the passage quoted, but if so, the choice of 'persuasion' and, to some extent, 'rhetoric' was unfortunate.

1.B. *'Justification' versus 'Evaluation'*. Even if 'persuasion' is rejected as the proper subject of our study, it may still be thought that 'evaluation' rather than 'argument' or 'justification' should be its subject. I shall try to show that there are two significant sources of divergence and that where these occur philosophical analysis must follow argument rather than evaluation.

Let me put first the case for assimilating argument and evaluation. One might say: evaluating a policy is going through a process of reasoning with the object of deciding whether it is a desirable policy or not; but coming to a decision by evaluating is distinguished from (say) flipping a coin by the fact that if you have made an evaluation, you must be able to justify your decision, or argue for it against others. In short, if you *have* reasons you must be able to *give* those reasons. Therefore, to evaluate a policy is simply to take the necessary steps to being able to justify or argue for one's decision about the desirability or otherwise of that policy.

There are two arguments against this. Firstly, someone may review the evidence with the object of arriving at an evaluation on the basis of it, and believe that the conclusion he reaches is justified; yet at the same time he may not be able to formulate verbally the precise principles on which his conclusion is based. (So common is this kind of occurrence that we have words such as 'intuition' and 'hunch' to cover it.)¹ And secondly, even if someone is able to justify the results of his evaluating to some degree by bringing his conclusions under certain concepts or principles, there may be no way in which he can justify (by reference to further concepts or principles) his ranking of one as more important than another. For example, a committee set up to evaluate some (actual or proposed) security arrangements might conclude that they are liable to bring hardship on people for no faults of their own, but that no weaker set of arrangements would safeguard security to an adequate degree; the committee might then conclude that in their view the requirements of national security should be allowed to override the incidental hardship and inequity.²

If I have now succeeded in showing a divergence between evaluating and being in a position to justify (or argue for) a decision, all that is left is to suggest why justification, rather than evaluation, should be the subject of this study. The answer is that the limits of language are also the limits of philosophical analysis. It is no doubt frustrating that nothing can be said in detail about those elements in evaluating which are not susceptible of verbal presentation, but there is no help for it—as Frank Ramsay said, 'what we can't say we can't say and we can't whistle it either'. However, a certain amount can be said about such elements in general, and that is what I shall do in this chapter.

2. RATIONALITY AND INCOMMENSURABLES IN EVALUATING

2.A. *Rationality as Consistency.* In 1.B. I pointed out that someone may be able to say what were the principles guiding his evaluating while at the same time not being able to say why he reached the conclusion he did in the face of a clash between the requirements

---

¹ It is sometimes held that sound *political* judgement is scarcely dependent at all upon general principles. This view is discussed below in IV. 2. C.

² As far as I can see, nothing except complication is added if one supposes instead that the committee is asked to formulate a policy itself, for this can be represented as asking them to evaluate all possible policies and choose the best. In practice, of course, the field would be reduced drastically on the strength of a cursory examination, but it must still be true that if this reduction can be defended (and often it cannot be) it must be possible to claim that no potential winners were among the eliminated candidates or at least that the probability of this happening was so low as to make it irrational to spend more time on the extended list of possibilities.

3

of these different principles. Many would hold that unless all one's principles could somehow be reduced to one 'ultimate' principle, any decision would inevitably be 'blind' or 'irrational'. Mill, for example, wrote:

> There must be some standard by which to determine the goodness or badness, absolute and comparative, of ends or objects of desire. And whatever that standard is, there can be but one: for if there are several ultimate principles of conduct, the same conduct might be approved by one of those principles and condemned by another; and there would be needed some more general principles as umpire between them.[1]

And a more watered-down version of the same idea can be found in W. D. Lamont's *The Value Judgement*, where it is claimed that if a choice is to be made between two possible courses of action it must be possible to bring their anticipated results into relation to some 'common demand' for the choice to be rational.[2]

Against this view I wish to maintain that one can sensibly speak of rational choices on the basis of principles which are not all reducible to a single one provided only that the (actual or hypothetical) choices made show a consistent pattern of preference. We can best begin by looking at our everyday choices as consumers, for it is in this connection that the kind of answer I want to give has been elaborated.

When I decide whether to spend a marginal sixpence on grapes or potatoes (to take the example of a well-known textbook),[3] must I be able to refer them both to some common yardstick before my choice can be regarded as rational? The classical answer would have been that a rational consumer tries to 'maximise his utility' where utility is thought of as a psychological quantity (pleasure or satisfaction). But the answer that would be favoured by most economists now would be to say that a pattern of choices can be regarded as rational provided it is consistent.[4] 'Consistency' means

[1] John Stuart Mill, *A System of Logic* (London, 1898), pp. 620–621. Exactly the same argument for the necessary reducibility of all values to one was used by Professor Hampshire some years ago in a talk in Oxford; on that occasion 'freedom' was the favoured value.

[2] W. D. Lamont, *The Value Judgement* (Edinburgh, 1955), Chapter III.

[3] Alfred W. Stonier and Douglas C. Hague, *A Textbook of Economic Theory* (London, 1953), Chapter 3.

[4] J. R. Hicks, *Value and Capital* (Oxford, 1946), is the basic reference here. See also his *A Revision of Demand Theory* (Oxford, 1956).

not just that one chooses three grapes and four potatoes whenever the choice is open (unless one admits to a change of taste), but also that one prefers five grapes and three potatoes to four grapes and three potatoes.[1]

Whatever may be the case with grapes and potatoes this idea seems to me eminently suitable for application to political principles. Suppose that we imagine there to be only two very general principles which we may call 'equity' and 'efficiency'. (The advantage of considering two only is that they can be represented in plane geometry.) Then for each person who evaluates in terms of these principles we can draw up a set of indifference curves showing along each line different combinations of the two between which he would be indifferent. Thus a person's indifference-map might be supposed to look like this:[2]

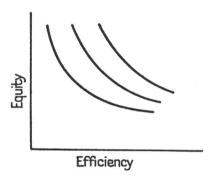

[1] A more elaborate version is to allow the introduction of probability so that people can also be asked whether they would prefer a one in three chance of four potatoes to a two in three chance of two. This of course introduces further possibilities of inconsistency. (See J. von Neumann and O. Morgenstern, *The Theory of Games and Economic Behavior* 2nd ed., (Princeton, 1947); A. A. Alchian, 'The Meaning of Utility Measurement', *American Economic Review*, XLIII (March 1953), 26–50; and R. B. Braithwaite, 'The Theory of Games as a Tool for the Moral Philosopher', Cambridge Inaugural Lecture (Cambridge, 1955). It should perhaps be emphasized that though this method is sometimes said to yield 'cardinal utilities' these still are only ways of talking about patterns of choice and in no way involve a return to the idea of psychological quantities 'underlying' this pattern.

[2] This fundamental idea of a plurality of 'ultimate values' related only by relations of substitutability is more complicated than the assumption of only one 'ultimate value' to which all others are reducible, but that is no reason for

2.B. *Substitution and Importance*. An obvious objection to the idea of indifference curves for such things as efficiency and equity is that unlike grapes and potatoes they cannot be quantified. This is of course true if one is talking about the ability to attach meaningful numbers to them; but it is surely not true if it is taken to imply that one cannot say that one thing is more inequitable than another or that one thing is extremely inefficient whereas another is only slightly inefficient. This is all that is needed for one to be able to maintain that there can be consistent choices of policy even where more than one principle is accepted as 'ultimate'. It would, admittedly, be pedantic to take seriously any actual indifference curves such as those just shown, but it is useful to bear them in mind because ideas suggested by them are relevant to political principles. The fundamental idea that they suggest is that although two principles need not be reducible to a single one, they may normally be expected to be to some extent substitutable for one another. The problem of someone making an evaluation can thus be regarded as the problem of deciding what mixture of principles more or less implemented out of all the mixtures which are available would be, in his own opinion, best.

---

rejecting it if the alternative does not fit the facts; and as far as the evaluations of most people are concerned I believe it does not. However, as soon as the idea that there is only one 'ultimate value' is rejected, it is tempting to introduce a simpler notion than that which I have used, namely, that of maximizing a variable subject to a constraint. I do not wish to deny that particular problems can sometimes be helpfully simplified by regarding them as problems of maximizing subject to a constraint, e.g. a local authority may find it useful as a first approximation to regard its revenue as fixed and see what is the best way of spending it rather than trying to determine by taking into account all relevant values the optimum amount to spend on each item. But this is only tolerable if it *is* kept in mind that it is an artificial simplification of the real problem.

'Casually selected or arbitrary constraints can easily increase system cost or degrade performance many-fold, and lead to solutions that would be unacceptable to the person who set the constraints in the first instance if he understood their implications.

'(Note) We know of studies in which an arbitrary limitation on casualties led to solutions in which at the margin a sum of $100 million was being spent to save a single life. Even if one regards a human life as "worth" this much, the same amount of money could have been spent in ways to save more.' C. J. Hitch and R. McKean, *The Economics of Defense in the Nuclear Age* (Cambridge, Mass., 1960), pp. 186–187.

In the present state of political economy ... we learn that for everything we have we give up something else, and we are taught to set the advantage we gain against other advantages we lose, and to know what we are doing when we elect.[1]

A corollary of the fundamental idea which is familiar in economics but worth bringing out in connection with principles is that where there is no single standard to which all others can be referred, the idea of 'relative importance' becomes very complicated. In fact, it can be given a meaning only in terms of rates of substitution of one value for another at the margin.

Let us go back to the grapes and potatoes. If grapes and potatoes both contributed to the quantity of a homogeneous entity of 'pleasure' or 'utility', the question 'Are the grapes in Jones's diet more important than the potatoes?' could be answered by seeing which provided him with the greater 'flow' of pleasure or utility. (A close analogy would be the question which of two taps was contributing more to the filling of a bath.) But if grapes and potatoes cannot be compared in this way, the question cannot be so interpreted. Instead one must ask: how many grapes would he have to be given to compensate for losing a potato? 'Importance', if it is to mean anything, must be related to the marginal rate of substitution of the commodities.

Exactly the same reasoning can be applied to political principles. If values are incommensurable, then 'He regards efficiency as more important than equity' cannot be understood to mean 'He regards efficiency as contributing a larger amount to the total goodness of a state of affairs than does equity'. For the 'goodness of a state of affairs' is not a quantity to which efficiency and equity contribute but merely a shorthand expression for the total set of the man's indifference curves expressing the trade-offs between equity and efficiency which would leave him equally satisfied. The statement must be understood to mean 'If it's a question of choosing between efficiency and equity, it takes a large potential increase in equity to make him accept a potential reduction in efficiency (and *vice versa*).[2]

[1] Oliver Wendell Holmes, Jr., 'The Path of the Law', *American Thought*, ed. Perry Miller (New York, 1954), p. 202.

[2] 'Importance' can only be predicated of incommensurables in terms of (actual or potential) choices in instances where they are in conflict. If we had two principles whose requirements we could not conceive of as coming into conflict we could never talk about their relative importance.

In putting forward this corollary, I have deliberately over-simplified by talking of *the* marginal rate of substitution between grapes and potatoes or efficiency and equity. In fact, one can only safely talk about the marginal rate of substitution at a certain point. There are really two separate aspects of this, both of which have relevance to political principles: first, indifference curves need not be straight lines; and second, indifference curves need not be parallel to one another. The first implies that if we stick to situations which are all judged equally desirable, it may well be that the more equity and the less efficiency there are in a situation the more important the remaining amount of efficiency becomes; in other words the more equity has to be introduced to compensate for a further diminution of efficiency.

The second aspect deals with the relations of several indifference curves. If one indifference curve plots all combinations of grapes and potatoes which are considered indifferent to three grapes and three potatoes, another may be drawn up for all situations which are considered indifferent to three grapes and four potatoes, and so on. These indifference curves will be parallel only if grapes and potatoes retain the same relative attractiveness at any level of overall satisfaction. But this is unlikely: up to the point where hunger still has to be assuaged, it is reasonable to suppose that to shift someone from an equal number of grapes and potatoes in the direction of more grapes will require a very large offer of grapes per potato; whereas when he reaches a position in which the equal number of grapes and potatoes provides more than enough potatoes for the satisfaction of hunger while additional grapes would still be welcome, he would surely be willing to accept fewer grapes in return for giving up a potato. Suppose we substitute 'food' for 'potatoes' and 'political freedom' for 'grapes', surely we have a recognizable and consistent position (though of course not the only one possible) to the effect that political freedom is more worth having if you can have food as well than if it can only be obtained at the price of starvation.[1]

---

[1] The remarks in the text apply only to the 'demand' side; in order to know what policy should actually be chosen, one must also know the 'supply' side, i.e. how much of one thing has to be given up for how much of the other. For example, even if freedom is worth comparatively little weighed against starvation, it may be that the total eclipse of freedom would gain so little mitigation of the starvation that it is rational to choose freedom.

3. EVALUATING AND POINTS OF VIEW

3.A. *Evaluating and Appraising*. So far I have been taking the notion of 'evaluating' for granted; and on the whole I am more concerned with using it than with adding to the voluminous literature on the subject. However, since most discussions seem to restrict 'evaluation' greatly, compared to its ordinary use, I should perhaps say that I intend it in its ordinary wide sense.

> 'Evaluate' is from the French 'évaluer'; the English word has a use rather like that of the French word. As the structure of the word suggests, 'évaluer' has to do with the notion of drawing or extracting the value from something; thus 'évaluer' connects with 'apprécier', 'fixer la valuer', 'estimer'; thus one can say 'évaluer la valeur d'un terrain'. Similarly, in English 'evaluate' has to do with the notion of drawing or extracting the value from something, but not of course in the sense of deriving value from it: 'evaluate' connects with 'appreciate', but in that sense of 'appreciate' that has to do with sizing up (undoubtedly the primary sense of that interesting word), e.g. 'appreciate the facts', 'an appreciation of the Battle of Jutland'. 'Evaluate' also connects with 'determining the value', 'estimating'.[1]

Ziff, in this quotation, rightly defines 'evaluate' in terms of 'value' so it is necessary to consider that word. 'Value', used as a verb, has two meanings. First, it refers to an activity of determining the worth (generally in money terms) of something. Thus, the Valuation Officer of a local authority, who assesses the rateable value of houses, may say 'I spent the whole afternoon valuing.' ('Appraise' can also be used for this.) And second, 'value' is used to refer to someone's 'state of mind'.[2] To say that one values something in this sense is to say that it is important to one, that it is worth a good deal to one; but it does not usually refer to monetary value. Thus, typical examples of this use would be 'I value his friendship/ services/support/encouragement greatly.' I think it is fair to say (as a mild concession to the 'prescriptive' school) that these can be taken as expressing not only gratitude but a certain willingness to put oneself out to retain what is valued if this should prove necessary.

[1] Paul Ziff, *Semantic Analysis* (Ithaca, New York, 1960), p. 242.
[2] Compare 'I approved that plan ten minutes ago' and 'I approve of the plan's being put into effect'. Also, 'I gave an appreciation of . . .' and 'I appreciate . . .'.

Perhaps just because 'value', used as a verb for the action of determining worth, has pre-empted the field of deciding what price something would fetch (or in some sense 'ought' to fetch), the more cumbersome 'evaluate' does not seem to be used in that sense at all. Indeed, it must be said that it is not used much in *any* sense.[1] The contexts in which, according to my observation, it most often crops up are (*a*) 'evaluating the evidence' (this especially occurs where there is a mass of raw data such as the transmissions from a satellite or the records of a nuclear test) and (*b*) 'evaluating policies' (usually this expression tends to be employed where the policy has already been in force for some time and attempts are then made to see how it has worked—for example, a hospital may evaluate experience gained in applying the policy of abolishing set visiting hours).[2] 'Appraise', which I have already noted may be used as an approximate synonym for 'value', may be used in wider ways as well. Thus, one may 'appraise' a person, which comes to much the same as 'weighing him up', and one may undertake 'logical appraisal'.[3]

If we take 'value' (in the first sense of 'determining the worth of'), 'appraise' and 'evaluate' together, what can be said of them? The most general characterization I can suggest is that they all involve the manipulation of facts in order to answer some question: what would this fetch, what does this prove, etc.? More precisely, they involve 'weighing up', (things, people, evidence), to see what they are 'worth'. I shall call this process 'evaluation' even if some approximate synonym would be more natural.

[1] It is curious that the two key words in the orthodox 'Oxford' moral philosophy are 'evaluate' and 'commend', both of which are very rare words. It is also a damaging reflection, because it suggests that they are not securely anchored in non-philosophical speech. What in fact happens is that 'commend' comes to mean 'call good' and 'evaluate' comes to mean 'decide whether something is good or not'. This is, of course, not much help if the object is to define 'good'.

[2] A typical use occurs in a review of Rachel Carson's *Silent Spring*, by LaMont C. Cole (*Scientific American* (November 1962), pp. 173–180). 'I suspect that the inevitable way to progress for man, as for nature, is to try new things in an almost haphazard manner, discarding the failures and building on the successes. . . . In the long run, unless a new suggestion can be discarded on the basis of prior knowledge, the only way to evaluate it is to try it out.'

[3] See Chapter I of P. F. Strawson, *Introduction to Logical Theory* (London, 1952).

3.B. *Aspects*. Evaluations may be carried out from different *aspects* and using different *reference groups*. These two distinctions can both be included under the heading of *points of view* and that is how they are usually referred to. Thus, in the 'aspect' sense, one may evaluate a new housing estate from the economic, the political or the aesthetic aspects or points of view; a piece of writing might be evaluated from the stylistic, the logical or the factual aspects or points of view; and so on. A roomful of furniture might be evaluated by a carpenter for workmanship, an aesthete for appearance, an ergonomist for comfort and convenience, an auctioneer for cash value and a pyromaniac for combustibility. Which points of view are 'appropriate' in a particular case depends on what one's purposes or attitudes are—and these in turn can of course be appraised by oneself or by others. Nero may be criticized for adopting an aesthetic rather than a fire-fighting point of view in examining the fire in Rome, even if it is granted that he may have been more skilful with the violin than with the fire-bucket. Or someone may be criticized for adopting an exclusively economic point of view when considering the advantages and disadvantages of Britain's joining the Common Market.[1]

3.C. *Reference Groups*. Consider these examples of the 'reference group' sense of 'point of view' from a single short article:

... Problems of international trade from the point of view of a single country. ...

... One situation is actually better than the other from everybody's point of view. ...

... The waste caused by tariffs from the point of view of the universe as a whole doesn't entail that they affect adversely the welfare of a single country. ...[2]

When one speaks of 'the aesthetic point of view' nobody supposes that there has to be an entity 'Aesthetics' with a 'point of view'.

---

[1] Letter in *New Statesman*, 1 December 1961, p. 829, by H. Scott Stokes: 'Mr Douglas Jay does not mention the political importance of the Common Market. It is not easy to see why he avoids this central aspect of the Common Market debate. ... Though it is safe to assume that Mr Jay sticks *deliberately* to economic points, he must be wrong to sum up the Common Market from the economic angle.'

[2] T. Scitovsky, 'A Note on Welfare Propositions in Economics', *Review of Economic Studies* IX, No. 2 (Summer, 1942), pp. 89–110.

The 'point of view' is that of the evaluator, not of the object of his evaluating efforts. When one speaks of 'the point of view of a country' or 'everybody's point of view' it is far easier to suppose that this means *in the opinion of* 'a country' or 'everybody'. And although 'everybody' may be said to have an opinion if there is unanimity, attribution of a view to a group where it is divided raises severe logical difficulties.[1] However, it would be just as much of a mistake to think that 'a country' is what has the view as to think that 'Aesthetics' is what has the view. 'A country' simply points to the range of people the evaluator has taken into account in making his evaluation; I shall call this range of people the evaluator's 'reference group', diverging somewhat in this from the standard sociological use of the term. Thus, someone can say that a certain policy is advantageous 'from the point of view of such-and-such a group' even if the members of it have never heard of the policy; what he cannot do is simply to ignore the interests of some of the members of the group he has put forward as his reference group. If someone objects to his statement that the policy is advantageous from the point of view of the group by saying 'Jones will be worse off and he's a member of the group' he must reply either that this is not so or that in his estimation the loss is outweighed by the gain of the rest of the members of the group. He cannot say 'Jones doesn't count' or 'So what?'

As with aspects, the establishment of a reference-group is preparatory to making an evaluation, though it may itself be the subject of a further evaluation: 'It's selfish of you not to take anyone else's interests into account.' However, except for the use of approbious words such as 'selfish' very little can be explicitly said to convince someone to take one reference group for his evaluations rather than another, though there are perhaps arguments of the form 'Why stop here rather than there?' which would tend to push one towards either egoism or universalism (i.e. taking oneself as reference-group and taking everyone as reference group).[2] Because of the importance of these two extremes I shall refer to them in later chapters by special names: evaluations with oneself or one's family as their object I shall call *privately-oriented*

[1] Cf. I. M. D. Little, 'Social Choice and Individual Values', *Journal of Political Economy*, LX, No. 5 (October 1952), pp. 422–432.

[2] Sidgwick, I think, takes this line in *Methods of Ethics* (London, 1930).

and evaluations with everyone or some large group such as a country as their object I shall call *publicly-oriented*.[1]

Just as disagreements in evaluation may turn not on any difference in principles but rather on one person's giving a number of agreed principles different relative weights from another person, so differences in reference group also account for many disagreements without involving any differences in principles.[2] Indeed, just as problems of a conflict of loyalties give rise to some of the most intractable problems of personal morals, so problems of which reference group to take into account provide many of the most intractable political problems.

I think there would be a general tendency among people to say when asked that when evaluating a policy the proper reference group is comprised of all those who are affected by it. But if so, this verbal response conspicuously fails to correspond to actual evaluations. How many people in this country worried about nuclear weapons while it was only the Russians who were going to be hit by them? How much of our national income would we give away if we were really willing to say that everyone was to count for one and nobody for more than one?

Towards the end of the World Refugee Year a man wrote to *The Guardian* signing himself 'Middle Class Millionaire', saying that compared with the refugees he could be considered a millionaire and he was sending £50 to the fund; and in the following couple of months several hundred more people did the same. I have the greatest respect for these people, who gave far more than I did. But I must point out that if they had asked themselves: 'at what point would a pound cease to do me less good than a refugee?' most of them would have been committed at least to giving ten times £50. So it looks as if hardly anyone counts everyone for one;

---

[1] It would be convenient to be able to use the expressions 'self-regarding' and 'public-regarding' but Mill's confusing use of ('self-' and 'other-') 'regarding' (of actions) for 'affecting' in *On Liberty* has pre-empted it, at least in English philosophical usage. But see Lamont, *Principles of Moral Judgement* (Oxford, 1946), pp. 118–119, for a use of 'self-regarding' and 'other-regarding' applied to ends and referring to the reference group concerned in the judgements.

[2] This is why both are used by Ginsberg in his arguments for uniformities of principle underlying differences in the results of evaluation from one society to another. See M. Ginsberg 'On the Diversity of Morals', *Essays in Sociology and Social Philosophy*, I (Mercury Books, London, 1962).

we are all more or less willing to juggle the addition, whether we make it come out at £50 or at the national average contribution to World Refugee Year of four shillings.[1]

But even if in practice reference groups tend to stop at state boundaries, there has, I think, been a clearly visible move within the last century and probably longer towards treating all the members of one's state as forming a single reference group, rather than picking out particular groups within the state.

> For an aristocracy with special privileges without corresponding special functions to perform, there would seem to be no possible justification. Nevertheless, aristocracies of precisely this character have abounded in history. We are thus forced to ask, Upon what grounds were they justified in the eyes of the people among whom they prevailed? Fundamentally, we must believe that these class distinctions have been recognized because of a more or less vague idea prevalent among the people that there is between noble and base-born a distinction almost as essential as that between mankind and the lower animals. Otherwise, there could hardly have been obtained that popular acquiescence, which for so long a time endured, in the economic and political advantages that were attached to the upper orders.[2]

Racial groups are the most important remaining separate reference groups, and even here, although it would be easy to exaggerate, there is a general tendency for those who wish to justify discrimination to suggest either that Negroes (etc.) are really 'inferior' or that segregation is better for all. One may think these are bad reasons but from the universalist point of view it is surely an improvement over a situation where it is thought that no justification whatever is called for. Would even a Southern white supremacist be willing to echo Maine's Brahmin?

[1] 'There was no complacency about our lecturer, Mr Glover, M.A., and he was even more passionate for social justice than we were. . . . "You'd ask for justice," he'd say, "but do you realise what it entails? And if you do, do you then really want it? Justice for you involves justice for untold millions all over the world; for black men in Africa and Chinamen and the Untouchables of India. Justice won't mean more for you, it will mean less, for compared with black men and Chinamen and Untouchables you already live like princes. And it's all or nothing. If what you want is justice for yourselves and the devil take Chinamen, then you're as selfish as—as Joe Chamberlain." And at that he burst into a splutter of laughter.' W. Allen, *All in a Lifetime* (London, 1959), pp. 135–137.

[2] W. W. Willoughby, *Social Justice* (New York, 1900), pp. 44–45.

14

Sir Henry Maine tells us that he has himself heard a high caste Indian declare that it is the teaching of religion that a Brahmin is entitled to twenty times as much happiness as anyone else, and this not upon the ground of individual merit arising from any conduct or mode of life on his part, but because intrinsically, *qua* Brahmin, he is twenty times the superior of those of a lower caste.[1]

---

[1] Willoughby, p. 36, referring to Sir Henry Maine, *Lectures on the Early History of Institutions* (London, 1914), p. 399. However, my colleague, Mr Ajit Dasgupta, has suggested that the Brahmin might well claim that he was entitled to extra happiness on account of his presumptively extraordinary merit in previous existences. So difficult do human beings find it to avoid trying to give *reasons* (however fanciful) for differences in treatment!

II

LANGUAGE

---

1. INTRODUCTION

1.A. *Argument of the Chapter.* Towards the beginning of the previous chapter (1.B.) I put forward my reasons for believing that the subject matter of the study must be defined as lying in the field of political justification and political argument rather than in that of political evaluation. I suggested that although there may well be aspects of political evaluations which cannot be expressed in language this very feature makes them inaccessible to philosophical analysis too.

My concern in this book is, then, with certain uses of language, namely those which occur in political justification and argument. This being so it seems natural to ask next whether any general characterization of these uses of language can be given. For example, some people might want to say that they are 'evaluative' rather than 'descriptive' uses of language, and that this in turn can be found out by noticing that special 'evaluative' words occur in them. I shall try to show in this chapter why I believe that such a view is, if not strictly mistaken, at any rate not very helpful for my purposes. Although I hope I have succeeded in avoiding technicalities this is in a sense a technical discussion. Let me therefore say here that anyone who is willing to take my word for it that little is to be gained by trying to divide the words with which I shall be dealing into 'descriptive' and 'evaluative' ones or the latter into their 'descriptive' and 'evaluative' components may safely skip the bulk of this chapter and start reading again at the beginning of Section 5 (page 32) without missing anything essential to his understanding of the rest of the book.

1.B. *Method of Proceeding.* The method of proceeding in the next three sections will be as follows. I shall begin by stating two very simple theories of what it is for an utterance to have meaning.

Then, by reflecting on the inadequacies of these two accounts I shall develop what seems a more satisfactory one. After that (Section 4) I shall apply this general theory of meaning to the particular problem in hand—the problem of so-called 'evaluative' meaning. It will be obvious that the subject-matter of these three sections could comfortably fill a large book by itself. I should therefore like to strike two cautionary notes before going further: firstly, that the theory of meaning developed in this chapter is elaborated only in the directions and to the extent necessary for making the points that are directly relevant to my present purposes; and secondly, that where alternative views on the question of meaning are mentioned this is purely as a means to making my own plainer. It would be foolish to pretend to any adequacy in discussing the views of others in such a small compass.

2. TWO THEORIES OF MEANING

2.A. *The Causal Theory.* A convenient stalking horse to start with is the 'causal theory of meaning', according to which

> a sign's disposition to affect a hearer is to be called a 'meaning' . . . only if it has been caused by, and would not have developed without, an elaborate process of conditioning which has attended the sign's use in communication.[1]

Language is thus conceived in Pavlovian terms. An utterance corresponds to the dinner-bell and the effect of the utterance to the dog's salivating.

This theory as it stands is open to a simple, obvious, and decisive objection: if someone does not believe what he is told, it has no effect on him, but the utterance does not lack meaning. As I said, this objection is decisive; but in order to show that no minor alteration (such as talking about 'usual' effects) will do to get around it, it is necessary to say enough to indicate that the failure to deal with false statements is only one symptom of a general weakness.

An unconditioned reflex—a knee jerk, for example—is not mediated by any mental processes (belief, expectation and so on). As I understand it, a conditioned reflex is similar in this respect:

[1] C. L. Stevenson, *Ethics and Language* (New Haven, 1944), p. 57. A more elaborate version of the causal theory may be found in Charles W. Morris, *Signs, Language and Behavior* (New York, 1946).

the dog salivates automatically, not because he 'believes' that food is available. But a better analogy to language than Pavlov's dogs would be a person who hears the gong sound at the hotel where he is staying and comes to the dining-room. He is not *conditioned* into coming: he may only just have arrived. He comes because he has read a notice, been told, or is aware of a general practice of sounding a gong at mealtimes.

Speech and writing do not act directly on people; if they have any effect this is only in virtue of their being understood and believed (or accepted). If someone tells me something and I believe him, or orders me to do something and I do it, it would be misleading to say that the utterances *caused* me to believe the one thing and do the other unless by this is meant simply that I would not have believed it or done it otherwise. It is quite wrong if it is interpreted to mean that the utterance causes the belief or action in the same way as being hit on the head causes one to have a headache. Even in a case where what someone says *causes* one to get angry, it is not the sounds he articulates themselves which have the effect, but the *content* of his utterance. Moreover, (a point I shall return to) the meaning of 'You are a liar' does not include any reference to people getting angry.

2.B. *The 'Intention' Theory.* If the causal theory is rejected, the next simplest theory is the 'speaker's-intention' theory. According to this, the meaning of an utterance is to be identified with the effects which the speaker intends to produce in the hearer.[1] Thus, the gong 'means' a meal is ready because it is beaten in order to produce that belief; the meaning of 'Shut the door' is to be explained by saying that it is uttered by people who want to have doors shut, and so on.

This theory is able to deal, after a fashion, with the objection which I brought against the causal theory: on the assumption that people expect their utterances to be accepted one can say that they intend to bring about the effects which their utterances will have if they *are* accepted. Thus, if a particular utterance is not accepted by the hearer, the ensuing effects (or lack of them) were no part of the speaker's intention. However, this is not an adequate answer, for there is no need to suppose that the assumption made above is

[1] This theory is explicitly stated by Paul Edwards in *The Logic of Moral Discourse* (Glencoe, Ill., 1955), who speaks of the 'Objective' of a speech-act.

valid. Suppose that I know Jones is counter-suggestible; then in order to get him to do *x* (which is what I want him to do) I have to tell him not to do *x*. My intention is that he should do *x* but surely the meaning of 'Do not do *x*' does not change because of this? Indeed, it is precisely because 'Do not do *x*' means what it does that I can use it in order to get Jones to do *x*.

This criticism can be generalized. The meaning of an utterance cannot be equated with the actual intention of the speaker in using it. As well as the case where I tell Jones not to do *x* in order to get him to do the opposite, consider again the case of calling someone a liar. The causal theory had to include 'anger' in the meaning of 'You're a liar' if the actual effect of the utterance was to anger the hearer; but the speaker's-intention theory must include it in the meaning if the speaker intends to produce anger in the hearer. (Whether he succeeds or not is irrelevant for the speaker's-intention theory.)

Criticisms of the speaker's-intention theory can be met partly by introducing a modification due to Grice. According to this, the meaning of an utterance is to be identified with those effects which the speaker intends to produce in the hearer by means of the hearer's recognition of that intention.[1] Thus, even if you recognize my intention of making you angry, it is not now necessary to say that this has any connection with the meaning of 'You're a liar' because I do not intend to make you angry purely by recognition of my intention to do so. In the contrasted case where I say 'Shut the door' my intention is to get you to shut the door purely by recognition of my intention. The counter-suggestion example also falls into place on the present theory. When I say to Jones 'Don't do *x*' I am certainly not trying to get him to do *x* by means of his recognition of my intention. I am pretending that I am trying to get him *not* to do *x*, by means of his recognition of *that* intention, and this is what I must be taken to mean.[2]

[1] H. P. Grice, 'Meaning', *Philosophical Review*, LXVI (1957), p. 383: 'Perhaps we may sum up what is necessary for *A* to mean something by *x* as follows. *A* must intend to induce by *x* a belief in an audience, and he must also intend his utterance to be recognized as so intended.' Grice, in this article, is concerned with finding a criterion for someone's 'meaning something' by an utterance; I am proposing the same criterion for determining *what* he means.

[2] Note that truth and falsity themselves are irrelevant here. It does not make any difference to the issue of meaning whether I am trying to get Jones to

2.C. *The Element of Convention.* Still, the Grice theory is not completely adequate as it stands because it does not enable one to draw a distinction between 'What Jones meant' and 'What these words (used by Jones) mean'. 'What did Jones mean?' can be fairly well construed as 'What effects did Jones wish to bring about by recognition of his intention?' (or, more informally, 'What was he trying to convey?') But 'What did his words mean?' requires a more complicated answer. Roughly, it is equivalent to 'What effects would anyone using those words normally be intending to produce by recognition of that intention?'[1] This still tends to suggest though that 'what people mean' is primary and 'what their words mean' secondary; that the latter is only a statistical summary of the former. But this is quite the wrong way round to conceive the relation. Unless people's words meant something, it would not be possible for people to mean something by using words. Communication by means of language is only possible if there are conventions prescribing the normal intentions that those using the words must have.[2] Of course language can be used unconventionally, in an idiosyncratic way, but it remains true that one can only ascertain what the speaker means in such a case because the words

[1] This distinction is neatly illustrated in the following quotation: 'British lawyers interpret Acts of Parliament and Statutory Instruments in accordance with the commonly accepted meaning, as they see it, of the words in them. Their assumption is that Parliament, or the Minister, meant what they said, and that if they did not they are always free to change the words, in order to make their meaning clearer. . . . But continental lawyers in all the countries of the Six interpret laws by asking themselves what the words in them *were intended to mean.* In order to find these interpretations, they go back to statements in the preambles to laws, or to Parliamentary debates and similar sources.' (Italics in original.) *Not With Europe; The Political Case for Staying Out* by William Pickles (Fabian International Bureau, Tract 336, April 1962), p. 15. Thus, according to Pickles, British lawyers ask of a document 'What does this mean?' whereas continental lawyers ask 'What did the people who framed it mean?' Clearly, there is a distinction here which any adequate theory of language must have room for.

[2] A non-linguistic example would be barbers' red and white striped poles. An individual barber could not use a red and white striped pole to 'mean' that he was a barber (as against drawing attention to his premises) unless there were already a convention connecting such poles and barbers' shops.

believe what is (in my estimation) true by saying to him what is false or *vice versa.* This is indeed generally true of meaning: 'The cat is on the mat' means exactly the same whether the speaker himself believes it or not.

he uses have meanings (where 'having meaning' is to be understood in the way just explained).

I suspect that Grice is able to miss the importance of convention by taking as his central example that of someone conveying information by means of a drawing. But just because the element of convention is minimal, a drawing is a rather bad analogy for an utterance in a language. A simple illustration of this is the ease with which an archeologist can often say what is depicted by graphic representations and the impossibility of his establishing the meaning of inscriptions unless he already knows the language in which they are written (or one like it) or can find the same thing written in the new language and one he does know.[1]

Far closer analogies would be traffic lights or railway signals, which mean what they mean in virtue of a code. These have room for the same divergence between 'what the signal means' and 'what the signalman means' as languages have, whereas drawings do not have room for it. When a signalling device is being operated so as to produce signals which have a meaning in the code there is no point in asking 'What did the signalman mean?' just as there is no point in asking 'What did he mean?' when someone makes an utterance which uses words in normal ways and is not in any way odd in its context. Suppose though that some situation not envisaged in the code arises; the signalman might then try to convey his meaning by an unconventional arrangement of signals and if this happened, the correct response would be not 'What does that mean?' (which would imply that it did have a meaning in the code but one didn't know it) but 'What does *he* mean?'[2] This is analogous to an unconventional use of language.

---

[1] The exception, which proves my point, is a script which is still genuinely pictorial, i.e. one where the symbols are not (as we revealingly say) 'conventionalized' or employed for their phonetic value in transcribing the spoken language.

[2] The exception is again illuminating. If it were an automatic signal then any deviation from the prescribed pattern would necessarily be due to a breakdown. It would then be appropriate to ask of a deviate signal 'What does that mean?' but the sense of 'mean' would be that which it has in 'Clouds mean rain'; in other words, one would be asking not what this was a signal for but what it was a symptom of. (The word 'sign' covers both, which has been responsible for a good deal of confusion).

3. THE 'CONVENTIONAL INTENTION' THEORY

3.A. *Summary.* The theory at which I arrived in the previous section through a criticism of the 'causal' and the 'intention' theories may be labelled the 'conventional intention' theory. In this section I shall begin by stating it, as developed so far, in a more formal way. Then I shall add various complications which are necessary to enable it to cope with the questions raised by so-called 'evaluative words' and 'evaluative sentences'.

Let us call an *utterance* any change in the environment which is intended to produce effects by the recipient's recognition of the utterer's intention; let us further call the recipient the *hearer* and the utterer the *speaker*. An utterance thus takes place at a particular time and place. In contrast to this, let a *form of utterance* be any reproducible kind of use of a medium of communication (defined below). A buzzer sounding on a particular occasion is an utterance, whereas the buzzer's sounding considered as a kind of event is a form of utterance. We can distinguish different *media* of utterance according to the kind of change in the environment produced. Examples of media of utterances are pictures, written marks, coloured lights, buzzers, gestures, spoken sounds, etc. All media of utterance must, to be of any use, allow at least two different forms of utterance to be discriminated (e.g. a light or buzzer must be capable of being either on or off) but beyond this there may be any number of forms of utterance in one medium. Forms of utterance in different media may be correlated (speech, writing, braille and morse code, for example).

Let us call the *content* of an utterance all those effects in the hearer which the speaker intends to produce by means of the hearer's recognition of that intention. And let us call the *normal* content of a form of utterance the content which utterances of that form normally have. The actual content of an utterance may be the same as the normal content of that form of utterance or it may deviate from it; and there need not be any normal content. (The normal content of a form of utterance corresponds to 'what it means'; the actual content of an utterance—in cases where it deviates from the normal content of that form of utterance or where there is no normal content—to 'what the speaker meant'.)

3.B. *Linguistic Forms.* A language is different from a set of signals in that a language has elements some at least of which are not themselves complete forms of utterance and which can be combined in various ways to make an unlimited number of forms of utterance. We can call these 'linguistic forms'.[1] Words are, to the speaker of an analytic language such as English, the obvious candidates; but even in English there are also modifications of words (affixes and inflections) and syntactical elements such as word order, all of which make an independent contribution to the meaning of sentences in which they occur.[2] We can now suggest that the meaning of a word (etc.) is to be found by discovering what is common to the modifications it introduces to the normal content of forms of utterance when it replaces alternative words. The significance of this is that it enables us to see more precisely how it is possible for a speaker to use a sentence which does not have a normal content in order to convey something to his hearer: although the sentence does not have a normal content, the words (etc.) comprising it do have a meaning which is given by their contribution to sentences which do have a normal content.

3.C. *Linguistic Content and Social Content.* What I now wish to suggest is that it is useful for some purposes to draw a distinction between that part of the normal content of an utterance which is due to the meanings of words and that part which is not. I shall call the former the *linguistic content* and the latter the *social content* though these are misleading if their definitions are disregarded. A non-controversial example may help to clarify the distinction which I am putting forward. The meaning of 'large' is (roughly) 'larger than the average member of the class in question' where the class in question depends of course on the noun which 'large' modifies. (See XI.2.B.) Someone who knew that 'large' meant this and also knew the meanings of the other words in a certain uttered sentence would be able to understand its linguistic content, but he might still not know its complete normal content; and it is to cover this contingency that one has to introduce the idea of social content. For example, suppose that someone knows that 'large' means 'larger than average for the class' and also knows the meaning of the rest of the words in 'Fetch a large spoon'. He may still go wrong by having an incorrect notion of the range of spoon

---

[1] Cf. L. Bloomfield, *Language* (New York, 1933), pp. 264 ff.

[2] The clearness of the distinction between words and modifications of words can easily be overestimated. See M. Braithwaite, 'Words', *Proceedings of the Aristotelian Society*, LIV (1953–1954), pp. 209–232.

sizes. If, for some queer reason, he has never seen anything except teaspoons and coffee spoons he may think that a 'large spoon' is a teaspoon and bring that.

It seems to me confusing to say that he has made a linguistic mistake, for this is to assimilate the present case to that of someone who thinks that 'spoon' stands for an eating implement with prongs. Yet it would be even more misleading to classify it as a mistake in guessing the (non-normal) content of the particular utterance in question, for it did not have any. 'Fetch a large spoon' is a perfectly normal sentence and the particular occasion we are imagining (in which it is used to get someone to fetch a large spoon) is a completely standard utterance of it. The mistake is thus quite different from, say, failing to catch on to a strained metaphor or some other obscure concatenation of words, or failing to see the point of someone's using a sentence with a normal content in a context where this normal content is glaringly inapposite.

This mention of the context of an utterance leads me to the final point I wish to make: just as an individual word may have different meanings and one discovers which meaning is relevant by seeing which fits in with the rest of the sentence, so a sentence may have different meanings and one discovers which is relevant by examining the *context* of its utterance, which includes both the linguistic context (what was said before) and the non-linguistic context (when, where and by whom the sentence is spoken, etc.).

3.D. *Kinds of Utterance*. The normal content of utterances can be classified according to the kind of effect which a speaker is taken to be intending to produce in the hearer by the latter's recognition of that intention. For example, a simple tripartite classification would be into utterances intended to produce belief, to produce action, and to elicit a verbal response. This scheme is suggested by the grammatical distinction between declarative, imperative and interrogative kinds of sentence, although there is by no means a complete correlation between kinds of meaning (according to the classification just mentioned) and kinds of sentence. 'Would you mind closing the door?' normally has the intended effect of getting the hearer to close the door rather than eliciting his view on the subject.

My reason for introducing this tripartite division of 'kinds of meaning' is not that I wish to elaborate it; it is more as a prophy-lactic measure. That is to say, I want to bring it forward so as to emphasize that although it may have its uses it should not be taken too seriously. It is, of course, far better to acknowledge three kinds of meaning than one: this at least prevents questions from being reduced to statements that one wants to know so-and-so or inter-rogatives to statements that one wants so-and-so done. But there is no *a priori* reason for supposing that three categories are enough to cover all the phenomena, or that there need be a single definitive answer to the question 'How many categories should one employ?' In any case, surely the right procedure is to develop the categories to fit what one finds rather than force everything willy-nilly into predetermined pigeon-holes. A good loosening-up exercise is to think of some of the ways in which we can characterize utterances: for example, he warned, he praised, he excoriated, he glorified, he condemned, he criticized.[1] Examples of a warning might be 'The pay's low' or 'The roads are icy'. Examples of praise might be 'What a large marrow!' or 'Jones has not been late for work once in ten years'. The significance of these examples—and they could be multiplied indefinitely—is that there is nothing here which could be called an 'evaluative word', unless of course one simply picks out the adjective in each sentence and says that it 'functions' as an 'evaluative word'. But this would merely be a thoroughly confusing way of expressing the fact that it occurs in a sentence which is used to warn, praise, etc. Roughly (and I qualify this later) to warn is to give reasons for not doing something or other, to praise is to say things which reflect credit on someone, and so on. What makes an utterance constitute a piece of warning or praising, etc., is the context combined with what one may call the 'social background'. By this I mean the common knowledge that certain features in a situation do count as reasons for not doing something or other, that certain other features do reflect credit on people, and so on. It is this which enables one to say that the

---

[1] 'He evaluated' and 'he appraised' do not fit in here because they do not refer to speech-performances; evaluations and appraisals may however be *expressed* or *given*, for this is the verbal presentation of the results of the evaluating process. Notice too that 'he valued' does not fit in either. If one said 'he valued' of a speech performance this would not be a general charac-terization but an indirect quotation or paraphrase (equivalent to: 'He said "I value" . . . or words to that effect.')

warning or praising characteristics of utterances can be part of their normal content (given the context) rather than something which the speaker merely hopes the hearer will 'catch on' to, in just the same way as 'large spoon' means (given an ordinary culinary context) 'dessert spoon or larger'. To preface a piece of warning with 'I warn you that . . . ' does not add anything to the normal content except perhaps emphasis and solemnity (compare 'I tell you that . . . ' prefacing an assertion) but one might perhaps say that the normal content becomes linguistic instead of social. In the same way, 'Bring a spoon as large as a dessert spoon or larger' means, in a culinary context, the same as 'Bring a large spoon', but the latter makes explicit linguistically the meaning which in the former was social.

To say, as I did in the previous paragraph, that warning is giving reasons for not doing something (or, sometimes, doing something) is near enough for 'I warned him that . . . ' but it does not cover 'I warned him to . . . ' (plus infinitive) or 'I warned him against . . . ' (plus gerund).[1] The utterance referred to by the sentence 'I warned him not to go' or 'I warned him against going' could simply be 'Don't go!' It could also be 'It would be rash to go' or 'I warn you not to go'. Here one does not give reasons, but one implies that there are reasons which the hearer would accept if he heard them. If the context is such that this is not implied by 'Don't go!' then it may be an order or a plea, but it cannot be a warning.[2]

The significance of the discussion in this section is that it enables us to distinguish between, on the one hand, an expression such as 'I warn . . . ' which is, so to speak, *ex officio* connected with warning and turns any sentence which it begins into a sentence usable only for warning, and on the other hand, sentences in which no such *ex officio* warning signal occurs but which are nonetheless in certain contexts warning utterances as part of their normal (social) content.

---

[1] 'I advise' (to or against) corresponds to 'I warn' (to or against). 'I advise that . . . ', however, simply means 'I inform you that . . . ' in officialese.

[2] Of course, 'I warned him not to go' could equally well refer to the utterance of 'The roads are impassable'; and very often the utterance of 'I warn you not to go' (etc.) is in fact supported with reasons.

4. EVALUATION AND MEANING

4.A. *Language and Evaluating.* Language comes into evaluating at two stages. Firstly, the 'facts' on the basis of which the evaluation is to be made may be formulated verbally, and secondly, the result of the evaluating process may be put in words. To think of the first, take the example of a testimonial or reference. The idea of a testimonial is that it should provide information which is relevant for someone who is wondering whether to give the subject of the testimonial a job.[1]

Everything in the testimonial must, to be relevant, bear on the decision—in other words, characteristics which do not provide reasons either for or against employing a man (and what these are will of course vary according to the job in question) have no place in a testimonial. But to be relevant a characteristic need not be expressed by using an *ex officio* evaluating word. 'Can lift *n* hundredweight' would be a highly relevant piece of information if the job in question required an ability to lift heavy objects, for example.

The second point at which language is involved in evaluating is to express the results of a piece of evaluating activity, and here again there is no special set of words which *have* to be used. Whether or not there is likely to be a handy *ex officio* evaluating word to express the verdict depends mainly on how eccentric was the point of view (aspect) from which the evaluating was carried on. A pyromaniac, for example, might express the conclusions of an evaluation from his own particular point of view by saying with satisfaction that a certain house was 'very combustible'.

It should be noticed, though, that these two ways in which language can come in are not mutually exclusive. A certain utterance may both express the conclusion of an evaluation and at the same time provide part of the material on which a wider evaluation can be based. For example, one might evaluate a politician's tactical

[1] The writer of a testimonial may of course have objects other than this, e.g. he may wish to make sure that the subject of the testimonial gets the job (or that he doesn't get the job) but he will not usually attempt to bring this about by getting the recipient to recognize this intention (e.g. by issuing exhortations, pleas, etc.). He will instead *pretend* to give 'facts' to enable the recipient to decide wisely, but really say whatever he thinks will be likely to achieve his object. The 'normal content' of a testimonial is thus giving information (though information relevant to a judgement) rather than affecting action directly.

skill or oratorical abilities and then put the results of these evaluations together with others so as to form a judgement of his overall effectiveness as a politician. I shall shelve this complication until the next section, however, and turn my attention to the *ex officio* evaluating words.

4.B. Ex officio *Evaluating Words*. Some words are used in sentences uttered in order to state an *ordering* which has been arrived at by evaluating ('best', 'second best' . . .); others state the *grading* which has been arrived at by appraising ('A+, A . . . 100, 99 . . . excellent, good, fair, poor, first class, second class . . . '). Yet others state the attitude or response considered appropriate in view of the qualities of the thing. This may be done in general terms ('commendable, execrable, praiseworthy, admirable'), or it may be spelt out specifically in terms of 'worth' ('worth a pound', 'worth an hour's reading', 'worth going to see if you're in the neighbourhood', etc.).

The above group are completely general as between different aspects—they simply say that the thing of which they are predicated comes up to or fails to come up to the relevant standard for a certain ordering, grading or response to be appropriate. There are some, however, which are a little more specific in aspect. Thus, some are restricted to saying that the thing does some *job* well or badly. These are expressions such as 'efficient', 'effective', 'adequate', 'satisfactory', and 'useful'. Notice that something which is efficient (etc.) is *prima facie* good (etc.) but that something may be good (etc.) without being at all efficient (etc.). Other terms which are specific to a certain aspect are 'true', 'cogent', 'valid', and 'beautiful' which indicate the results of evaluating from the factual, logical and aesthetic points of view respectively.

Finally, there are some words tied to certain rather more specific aspects. Examples are the usual words for personal virtues and vices ('kindness, courage, temperance', etc.) which together provide the criteria for 'a (morally) good man'. Other examples are words for certain 'virtues' and 'vices' of organizations or of actions—'just', 'fair', 'free', etc. There is also a group which expresses the results of evaluating the way in which actions, laws, policies or institutions impinge on someone: that they are 'in his interest', 'conducive to his welfare', 'good for him', 'beneficial to him', 'advantageous to him', 'injurious to him', or 'harmful to him'.

Any enquiry into the 'meaning' of these groups of words takes us into contentious territory, but I think the distinction between linguistic and social meaning throws a good deal of light on the matter. Suppose we consider the stock example of 'good': an adjective, incidentally, with rather little application in moral and political discussion. The standard 'prescriptivist' point is that 'good' cannot have as part of its meaning any reference to 'natural' or 'descriptive' properties because the criteria for a good cabbage and a good king (say) are so different that they surely have nothing in common, yet we do not want to have to say that 'good' has as many meanings as there are nouns for it to go with.

Let us take the first point first. I think there is much to be said for the view, put forward by Paul Ziff in *Semantic Analysis*, to the effect that nearly all attributions of 'goodness' to an object involve the suggestion that the object ministers to some human interest (perhaps 'interest of some sentient creature' would be preferable). I can see nothing implausible in supposing that 'This object ministers to a human interest but is it good?' might be interpreted simply as meaning 'Is there some countervailing human interest to which it is inimical?'

However, the 'prescriptivist' might reply that even if this is so, it is simply a reflection of the fact that to say something is 'good' is to put it in a high (though not the top) grade; and this seems to me acceptable. Indeed, I would apply exactly the same argument to the 'prescriptivist' analysis of 'good' in terms of choosing. Just as one can suggest reasonably that if something is rightly given a high grade there is probably some human (or other) interest which it satisfies, so it is probably sensible—other things being equal—to choose it in preference to something of the same kind graded lower.

The second 'prescriptivist' point that I noted was to the effect that we do not want to say that 'good' has as many meanings as there are nouns for it to go with. Now, this point could equally well be put forward by someone who supported the view that what all uses of 'good' have in common is the assertion that the thing in question satisfies an interest. For the distinctive feature in either case would be the identification of the meaning of the word with the common contribution which it makes to the meaning of all utterances in which it occurs.

But here I should like to recall my discussion of 'large'. It is part of the social content of 'large spoon' (given an English culinary context) that it refers to a spoon of a certain size. And in the same way it is part of the social content of 'good egg' that it refers to a fresh egg—again given an English culinary context.[1] Thus the social content of 'large spoon' depends upon the sizes in which spoons actually come and that of 'good egg' depends upon the features of eggs which in fact make people want them for eating.

If one wishes to restrict 'meaning', when attributed to words, to the common element which the word always contributes, then one must be prepared to say that the normal content of an utterance is sometimes more than is given by the meanings of the words in it and the grammatical structure. In other words, one must be prepared to recognize a social content over and above the linguistic content of utterances. The significance of this is that it is just wrong to suggest that speakers choose their own criteria for goodness and apply them leaving their hearers to 'catch on' to what, beyond the fact that it is graded high, they are saying about the object in question. That good eggs are fresh eggs (or, even more explicitly, that bad eggs are rotten eggs) is part of the normal content of 'good eggs'. A speaker is taken to mean 'fresh eggs' when he says 'good eggs' unless he actually explains that the point of view from which he is evaluating them, or some feature of the situation different from the usual, is such that what makes eggs good in this instance is some other quality.

It might be thought that this point is covered by the idea that words may have 'both descriptive and evaluative meaning'. But this is not so, because (in the case of 'good' at least) all this seems to come to is that if you know the speaker well you may be able to guess what characteristics things of some particular kind must have for him to call them good. This is analogous to seeing a friend cross the road and saying 'That means he's going to the paper shop', i.e. you guess that is where he's going. But of course if it turns out he wasn't going to the paper shop, you can't say he deliberately misled you because he wasn't trying to produce any effect in you at all. The case of someone who says to the grocer, 'Those eggs you sold me were bad' is quite different. Subject to

[1] In a community of English-speaking Chinese who had retained their traditional tastes, 'good egg' might have a social content of 'egg at least n days old'. And in the special context where one was evaluating eggs not for eating but for throwing one might say that a 'good egg for throwing' is a rotten egg.

an explicit disclaimer (which would be almost equivalent to: 'when I say eggs I mean apples') the grocer can properly object if the complaint is *not* that they had gone off. In particular the grocer does not need to know anything about the personal tastes or standards of the speaker in order to understand (not guess) what he means by 'bad eggs'.

Notice that in order to defend himself against deliberate deception it is not enough for the speaker to say that his criteria for badness in eggs are peculiar, for you commit yourself to the normal standards unless you dissociate yourself from them explicitly. Nor will it do for him to say that he didn't know the normal standards, for then he should not have used 'bad' but should have spelt out his complaint. The only defences permissible are (1) that he didn't know what 'bad' meant (in the 'constant contribution' sense) and thought it meant, say, brown; or (2) that he knew what 'bad' meant and *thought* he knew the normal criteria, but was in fact mistaken about them.

4.C. *Final Note.* In this work I shall inevitably be dealing mostly with words which are *ex officio* constituents of evaluative utterances, because the most important and pervasive political evaluations tend to be expressed by using them. But I hope that my analysis will have indicated that the difference between *ex officio* evaluating words and others is not of much importance, since evaluations can be expressed perfectly well without them. Indeed, whether a word is *ex officio* evaluative or not makes only one difference, namely that if it is, then any utterance employing it can be known to be connected with evaluating without one's needing to examine the linguistic context in which the word occurs or the extra-linguistic context in which the utterance occurs. But this suggests (what is, I think, true) that the idea of dividing words into those which are *ex officio* connected with evaluating and those which are not is a great oversimplification once we leave the grading and ordering words. Instead, we should think of some words as requiring *less* contextual information before we can know that they occur in an evaluative utterance, and others as requiring *more*. The words put forward in categories two and three above (efficiency, etc., and justice, etc.) as *ex officio* connected with evaluation would simply be those clustered at the 'less' end of the scale.

5. *PRIMA FACIE* AND CONCLUSIVE ARGUMENTS

5.A. *The Distinction.* In the previous section I pointed out that the same utterance could both give the result of some evaluating and provide part of the material for some further, higher level, evaluating. In this section I want to expand that point, which is of some importance for the understanding of the language used in political, and indeed other, arguments and justifications.

Thus, if I am deciding whether to take a certain job, there might be six headings under which I calculate the pros and cons. For example, I might conclude that I would enjoy the work (pro), but dislike the area (con) and that it would involve a breach of faith with my present employer (con), and so on. Now, clearly, no one of these results could be put forward by itself as *the* answer to the question whether or not I should take the job, if I thought any of the others had force at all. Nevertheless, after getting results for each of the six sub-evaluations I might decide that one was greatly more important than any of the others. For example, I might perhaps think that a breach of faith was far more serious than the other items on the list. If so, then when explaining why I turned the offer down I may simply say, 'It would have involved a breach of faith'. Yet in the case envisaged, this simple statement must be unpacked into three items: (i) on balance the arguments against accepting were stronger than those in favour; (ii) among those against was that it would have involved a breach of faith; and (iii) that argument (ii) was of preponderant importance. Clearly, this complicated use needs to be distinguished from the straightforward one where 'It would have involved a breach of faith' merely gives *one* of the considerations to be borne in mind, without any suggestion that it was preponderant or conclusive. I shall therefore call the latter a '*prima facie*' use and the former a 'conclusive' use.[1]

5.B. *Application to Political Arguments.* The distinction between *prima facie* and conclusive utterances is of considerable importance in the analysis of political arguments for this reason: certain expressions ('in the public interest', 'fair', 'just', 'equitable', 'for

[1] This terminology is not completely satisfactory, since it suggests that a non-conclusive reason is not a real reason at all, but it has the advantage of familiarity. Cf. Sir William David Ross, *The Right and the Good* (Oxford, 1930) and *Foundations of Ethics* (Oxford, 1939).

the common good' and so on) tend to be used as if they were a *conclusive* argument where in fact they are the *main* argument.[1]

To say that some policy is in the public interest, on the present analysis, is to say that it is satisfactory on balance but the thing that is really in its favour is that it is in the public interest. If it were too unsatisfactory on some count (e.g. unfair to a degree which more than counterbalanced its being in the public interest) this new count would be put forward in the guise of a conclusive consideration *against* it (e.g. 'It's not fair').

For example, 'the public' often means 'the consumers'. Now, in this sense of 'public' it would clearly be 'in the public interest' to have working conditions as poor as is compatible with efficiency. Why is this not (openly) recommended as being 'in the public interest'? Surely, because obviously unacceptable proposals are weeded out at a prior stage, thus enabling the ones that are left to be put forward as being 'in the public interest' where this now functions in effect as a conclusive argument. Thus, if a regulatory commission is told to regulate an industry 'in the public interest' this *does* mean that it should regulate it in the interests of the customers;[2] but there is an implied qualification that the industry should get 'fair' profits and pay 'fair' wages.[3] It is not that these are additional criteria of the public interest; it is simply that 'the public interest' can only be used as a *conclusive* argument where it is tacitly understood that other requirements of a good policy are satisfied to a sufficient degree.

Consider in this connection, Rexford G. Tugwell's discussion in *The Economic Basis of Public Interest*.[4] In this he writes that 'the doctrine of the public interest . . . is quite plainly a rule for the definition of economic fair dealing'. (p. 45.) But when he analyses

---

[1] Compare the language of 'cause'. To say that the cause of a road accident was the slippery road is not to deny that it was not a sufficient condition nor that there were plenty of other necessary conditions, e.g. that the car should be travelling at such-and-such a speed, that the camber was such-and-such, etc. It is to assert that this is the particular factor worth focusing attention on (because the other conditions were 'normal' and can be taken for granted).

[2] Bernard Schwartz, *The Professor and the Commissions* (New York, 1959), p. 116: 'There is no doubt that the primary purpose of the regulatory commissions was to protect the consuming public.'

[3] Schwartz, p. 126: 'Regulation in the public interest requires the utility to be limited to only a fair return over and above its costs.'

[4] Wisconsin, 1922.

it further it becomes clear that 'the public interest' is a justification for intervention when the public is damaged because there is a 'harmful price or standard emerging from the market'. (p. 108.) 'Fair dealing' obviously applies in plenty of other cases than those where one party is a 'public'. The significance of fair dealing is not to define 'the public interest'—that is already clear, namely low prices and good quality—but to define the point at which state action should be taken to do more for the public interest than the market is currently doing. To enslave the producers would be 'in the public interest' but just as unfair as to allow them to extort higher prices than are 'reasonable'; it is not therefore put forward as being 'in the public interest' where this would be taken as a conclusive argument for the policy.

III

POLITICAL PRINCIPLES

I. INTRODUCTION

IN the first two chapters we have raised points about evaluation and language which will be used in the rest of the book. This chapter and the two following will likewise be taken up with preliminaries to the analysis of particular principles employed in political arguments; but they will be more specifically relevant to *political* arguments than the first two chapters have been. In this chapter the next section is devoted to clarifying a distinction between two kinds of phenomena which are both commonly described as 'political principles'. Of these two kinds of phenomena, which I call 'personal principles' and 'ultimate considerations', I am concerned in this book only with the second. Then, in the rest of the chapter, I introduce a basic set of categories which can be applied to all 'ultimate considerations', and try to show that they can indeed cope with *prima facie* troublesome concepts.

2. PERSONAL PRINCIPLES AND ULTIMATE CONSIDERATIONS

Suppose one were to ask a candidate for political office what his political principles were. If he replied that he was in favour of peace, plenty, freedom and justice he would quite reasonably be accused of purveying bromides. This is not because these words are 'meaningless'; the difference between peace and war for example is in most situations fairly plain, at least so long as peace is taken as simply the absence of war. No, the trouble is twofold. First, these preferences are too common, and are therefore no use in helping one to choose between rival candidates. And second, so great is the distance between these statements by a candidate and his decisions on particular issues of policy that even if they are completely sincere, they have little predictive value. There may be long and complex means-end chains involved so that a man committed to 'peace' as an end might support any of a number of different policies according to his estimate of their relative chances of producing peace. Again, many words such as 'justice' leave a good deal of room for manoeuvre in interpretation so that different states of affairs might be taken as fulfilling the requirements of justice. And finally, since most decisions in particular cases turn on the relative weights to be given to a number of competing considerations, we can have little confidence in our ability to predict how someone will decide particular questions (even if we know in detail what are the considerations that weigh with him in making up his mind on an issue) unless we also know the relative weights he assigns to these considerations.

At the same time, 'principles' must have a certain generality about them. A list of the candidate's 'stands' on a number of specific issues would be equally defective as a statement of his principles. It too would have limited predictive value for it would not tell us how the candidate would decide any issue which was not on the list. What is required, then, in a statement of principles is something between a string of high abstractions and a list of specific 'planks' in a 'platform'. In particular, it should contain (a) ends of a medium level of abstraction, such as the maintenance of private enterprise or a move towards public ownership, commitment to NATO or to neutrality, and so on; and (b) a statement of the relative weights to be given to medium-range considerations where they seem likely to conflict, e.g. the relative importance of economic growth and inflation, or of the independence of trade unions and the requirements of an incomes policy.

The implications of this are significant. To ask of someone, 'What are his political principles?' is not to ask for the irreducible, ultimate considerations that weigh with him; but to ask for indications of the line he would take on any of a great number of possible issues. A difference in political principles between two people will normally be open to further argument since each will normally be willing to justify his political principles in terms of more general considerations. In particular, a difference in political principles may stem from differing estimates of the *effects* that policies (nationalization, neutrality) or elements in states of affairs (inflation, independence of trade unions) would have.

I shall not in this work be saying much about the sort of

'political principles' which can be ascribed to particular people; but with considerations that lie behind them. It is necessary to be clear about these 'political principles' first, however, because a good deal of philosophical discussion tends to assume that the only principles are 'my principles' or 'your principles'. Thus, T. D. Weldon's view of principles was that they functioned as 'keep-out' notices, which each person could erect wherever he chose in order to avoid having to work out the correct response to each new situation from scratch[1]. But instead of contrasting these *ad hoc* personal principles with the ultimate considerations that underlie them, he assimilated the two and included such notions as 'freedom' among the personal principles.[2]

The term 'considerations' for such things as justice and freedom

[1] This statement is a composite of some to be found in 'Political Principles', *Philosophy, Politics and Society*, ed. P. Laslett (Oxford, 1956) pp. 22–34; and 'The Justification of Political Attitudes,' *Proceedings of the Aristotelian Society, Supplement*, XXIX (1955) pp. 115–130.

[2] 'Political Principles', p. 32. In 'Justification . . . ' he suggests that these various 'principles' (including presumably even ultimate considerations such as freedom) could be 'justified', if at all, by reference to the way of life to which they contributed. This seems to me to be putting things exactly the wrong way round. Ways of life can be justified only by reference to general ultimate considerations. The result was to exaggerate the personal idiosyncratic aspect of political beliefs and to underestimate the significance of widely shared ultimate considerations. The same tendency may perhaps be discerned in some recent moral philosophy. I am thinking here particularly of Mr. Hare's books, where the emphasis on moral *principles*, conceived as 'my principles' and 'your principles' seems to have the same voluntaristic implications as Weldon's emphasis on similarly conceived political principles had. In *The Language of Morals* (Oxford, 1952) Mr Hare gives the impression that the whole of morality is encompassed within the sphere of moral principles. In *Freedom and Reason* (Oxford, 1963) Mr Hare extends the notion of morality so as to include 'moral ideals' which differ from principles in not being universalizable. Clearly, these 'ideals' are even more personal and idiosyncratic than the original 'principles'. However stringently one insists that moral principles must be universalizable this still leaves them very far from covering the same ground as moral rules defining duties and obligations or the concepts which are used to attribute vice or virtue to people. To speak of not lying or murdering as being among one's moral principles is a rather analogous misclassification to that involved in saying that justice and freedom are among one's political principles.

One might say that political principles (in the sense of 'my principles' or 'your principles') are medial and that moral principles (in the same sense) are interstitial. In both cases the picture is distorted if they are put at the centre of it.

has the advantage of vagueness. I shall use it to cover the ultimate determining factors in evaluations, as opposed to the mediate 'political principles' conceived as open to personal adoption and rejection. However, to avoid monotony, I shall speak of these ultimate factors also as 'principles' (e.g. the 'principle of freedom' and the 'principle of justice') but it must be observed that it is not possible to ask whose principles they are or when he adopted them. Thus, if I talk about the 'principle of justice' I shall be referring to the sorts of considerations covered by this word which weigh with people at the present time in Britain and the USA.[1]

3. WANT-REGARDING PRINCIPLES AND IDEAL-REGARDING PRINCIPLES

3.A. *Want-Regarding Principles.* There are doubtless many ways in which political considerations and principles may be classified, and each set of divisions will reflect something about the author's outlook and what he regards as important. To make, as I shall, a fundamental distinction between what I shall call on one side 'want-regarding principles' and on the other 'ideal-regarding principles', involves a decision which can be justified only by the power of the distinction to illuminate political controversies whose foundations are at present obscure. I am willing to make that claim, whether properly or not is for the reader to judge.

Want-regarding principles, then, are principles which take as given the wants which people happen to have and concentrate attention entirely on the extent to which a certain policy will alter the overall amount of want-satisfaction or on the way in which the policy will affect the distribution among people of opportunities for satisfying wants. By calling such principles 'want-regarding principles' the point I am emphasizing is that, in order to evaluate the desirability of a state of affairs according to such principles, all the information we need is the amount and/or distribution among persons of want-satisfaction. In drawing my most fundamental

[1] It is a fundamental presupposition of this work that words such as 'justice' do cover only certain considerations and that they are not extensible to apply to *any* policy, whatever the consideration relevant to it may have been. It seems to me that since, say, 'justice', 'freedom' and 'democracy' are not interchangeable in all contexts they cannot function simply as grading words.

division between principles which involve no reference to any-thing but want-satisfaction and those which take into account other features of a situation in evaluating it, I am suggesting that for some purposes at least it is illuminating to regard utilitarianism and the belief that pleasures and pains should be proportioned to desert without any reference to consequences as closely related ideas within the same liberal tradition.[1]

Thus, although Benthamite utilitarianism is the most obvious example of a want-regarding principle, it would be completely con-trary to my intention in making the classification to restrict it to the utilitarian position. What makes Benthamite utilitarianism an example of the want-regarding theory in operation is its view that 'pushpin is as good as poetry, the quantities of pleasure being the same'. Whether one then goes on to say, with Bentham, that the object is to maximize the total amount of pleasure; whether instead one modifies this to require equal distribution; or whether one believes that the only question is matching want-satisfaction to desert, one has accepted the want-regarding theory. The utili-tarian position is only one variant.[2]

3.B. *Ideal-Regarding Principles.* The ideal-regarding theory can be defined simply as the contradictory of the want-regarding theory, the two thus being jointly exhaustive of the possibilities. The smallest deviation from the want-regarding position would be to allow that the satisfaction of wants is the only criterion by which policies should be judged, but to deny that each person's ranking of the importance to him of having different wants satisfied should necessarily be taken over by the person making the political judge-ment. On this view, a small increment in poetry among a group may from the point of view of an observer more than compensate in value for a large decrease in pushpin even if the people actually

[1] Hare, in *Freedom and Reason,* treats aggregation and distribution as variants of one theory which he calls 'utilitarianism', but he does not apparently include in 'distribution' any principle except that of equality.

[2] For the justification of treating 'pleasure' in Bentham as a synonym for want-satisfaction, see below, 3.C. I emphasize that I am here referring only to *Bentham's* utilitarianism. In particular, if any teleological outlook is treated as being 'utilitarian' (as one sometimes finds today) there is no necessary connec-tion at all between 'utilitarianism' so defined and the want-regarding theory. G. E. Moore's theory of value in *Principia Ethica* is 'utilitarian' in this sense and at the same time the antithesis of a want-regarding theory.

undergoing the change would disagree.[1] More precisely, suppose that whisky is taxed to subsidize the theatre. According to the usual criteria of welfare economics, one finds out whether people are 'better off' as a result of the change in relative prices confronting them, by seeing if there is any combination of whisky and theatres now available to them on a given income which they prefer to the most favoured combination available before. On the alternative criteria now mooted one would find out how their consumption of the two changed and decide whether the rise in theatre-going compensated (in one's own estimation) for the decline in whisky drinking.

A more radical departure from the want-regarding theory would be to say either that the satisfaction of some wants is without any value at all, so that they can be left out of consideration altogether in judging whether one situation is better than another, or (more radically still) that the satisfaction of certain wants is positively bad, so that their suppression is to be counted a virtue in any given state of affairs. Even this does not exhaust the scope of possible variants on the fundamental ideal-regarding theory, for so far we have still kept to views which attribute all value to the satisfaction of wants, though not all wants equally and perhaps some wants not at all. But someone might in addition attribute value to other things besides the satisfaction of good (or at least 'not bad') wants—to such things as people's tastes, characters or beliefs.

If one chose, indeed, one might make the fundamental division here, between theories which hold want-satisfaction of some kind at least to be the only value, and those which include other items; for to say that it is good for certain tastes to be gratified bespeaks a very different outlook from saying that it is good for certain tastes to exist, whether gratified or not. Even if all wants are not given the weighting that the agent would give them; even if the satisfaction of some wants is declared valueless or even intrinsically pernicious; still, it is the satisfaction of *some* wants that has value on the former view, whereas on the latter view, it might be good to cultivate a certain desire even if one had no prospect of ever satisfying it. The former view is still a kind of hedonism,

---

[1] This is one interpretation of John Stuart Mill's doctrine in *Utilitarianism*; but I suspect that Mill would really like to claim that the so-called 'higher pleasures' score higher on some unidimensional scale of 'pleasantness'.

though in its ideal-regarding manifestations it becomes a hedonism of a highly refined nature. The latter view, which breaks with the idea that want-satisfaction in some shape or form is the only good, can perhaps be sustained on a religious basis alone.

3.C. *Want-Satisfaction, Pleasure and Happiness.* The distinction here drawn between a want-regarding theory and an ideal-regarding theory has strong resemblances to Sidgwick's view in *Methods of Ethics* that conceptions of the 'ultimate good' could be divided into those that made it 'happiness' and those that made it 'excellence or perfection'. However, I have several reasons for thinking that it is more useful to define one's fundamental dichotomy in terms of 'want-satisfaction' than in terms of 'happiness'.

First, it should be noticed that 'happiness', in the ordinary acceptation of the word, includes considerable 'ideal' elements. Someone may be satisfying a large number of wants but still not be accounted happy if the pattern arising from satisfying these wants adds up to what is thought of as a radically vicious style of life. Thus the antithesis presented by Sidgwick between 'happiness' on the one side and 'excellence or perfection' on the other fails to be a sharp one.

The second reason, which applies to 'pleasure' as well as 'happiness', is grounded in the development of welfare economics. The experience of welfare economics has a peculiar claim to authority because it can plausibly be argued that there is a direct line of intellectual descent from classical Benthamite utilitarianism to modern welfare economics. Any continuous and long-standing trend of thought among those who have tried most persistently and ingeniously to apply non-ideal-regarding criteria in judging the relative preferability of states of affairs deserves to be taken seriously; so when we find over the period of a century a steady drift away from equating 'utility' with supposedly felt psychological quantities of 'pleasure' or 'happiness' and towards equating it with the bare satisfaction of wants, whatever their objects may be, I think we would do well to follow suit unless there is some powerful countervailing consideration.

The final and most important reason for preferring 'want-satisfaction' to 'happiness' (or, again, 'pleasure') in defining the basic dichotomy is the practical one that political judgements actually tend to turn on want-satisfaction rather than on happiness or pleasure. Freedom, for example, in the 'liberal' or 'negative' sense imputes as I understand it a value to want-satisfaction as such, or at least to the non-existence of human obstacles to want-satisfaction. Mill's statement in *On Liberty* that the promotion of a man's own happiness is not an adequate reason for interfering with his freedom—which is I believe the orthodox 'liberal' view of the matter—seems effectively to rule out the idea that want-satisfaction is merely a means to happiness. It is simply a 'right'.

This can be generalized: consider any contemporary arguments about 'planning', about 'the welfare state', about 'state control' of mass media of communication or about the relative importance of increasing the national income as against maintaining or enhancing other values. Does the dispute take the form of those who take 'pleasure' or 'happiness' as their ultimate value lining up against those who take 'excellence or perfection'? Such a picture is unrecognizable.[1] What we find rather is a division between those who think that wants should be satisfied *qua* wants (characteristically via the 'price mechanism') and those who argue that if a public authority has good reason for thinking that the satisfaction of certain wants will not be conducive to happiness or pleasure ('perfection' is far more rarely introduced) it should see that they are not satisfied and try to arrange things so that different wants are cultivated. Thus, to treat considerations of 'pleasure' and 'happiness' as the mildest kind of 'ideal' consideration rather than the opposite of 'ideal' considerations, brings out the underlying disagreements more clearly.

One is led to the same conclusion—that want-satisfaction as such is something the amount and distribution of which is relevant for political judgements—by looking at distributive judgements in particular. Distributive problems arise out of incompatible wants, and they are not to be allayed by reference to pleasure or happiness. For example, if status or wealth are wanted, this poses

[1] I should make it clear that I mean only that such a picture is unrecognizable in connection with these types of question. There are others—homosexuality, contraception, abortion, euthanasia, suicide, AIH and AID, and to some extent marriage and divorce—where the 'ideal' versus 'happiness' dichotomy has more relevance. Even in these cases however the main 'liberal' point is not 'doing so-and-so will make people happy' but 'why shouldn't people do so-and-so if they want to and they're not doing anyone any harm?' The Wolfenden Report does not argue that homosexuals are happy but that they are harmless.

the question of how they should be distributed. Even if one could show to one's own satisfaction that getting status or income (beyond some minimum) does not conduce to anyone's pleasure or happiness this would not prevent the distributive question from remaining unless one were actually successful in persuading enough of those who had wanted prestige and wealth for the excess demand to disappear. I believe that distributive principles are subtly misrepresented if it is supposed that they must be concerned with the proper distribution of 'happiness' or 'pleasure'. Equality of income as a valued state of affairs is sometimes guyed by taking it to mean 'equality of utility from consumption' (where 'utility' is interpreted as referring to a psychological quantity subject to interpersonal comparisons) and it is then pointed out that this would require paying easily pleased people less than fastidious ones.[1] But why not allow that equality of income may be desired simply because it is thought fair that everyone should have access to an equal value of scarce goods?

4. DISTRIBUTION AND AGGREGATION OF WANT-SATISFACTION

4.A. *The Distinction.* Within the total area of want-regarding principles I draw a distinction between those which direct attention to the distribution of want-satisfaction among people and those which do not. This general distinction is a familiar one and crops up under such titles as 'efficiency versus equity' and 'justice versus expediency' but these expressions tend to be restricted to certain contexts. Efficiency and expediency are both special cases of aggregative considerations as are equity and justice of distributive.

More precisely: an aggregative principle is one which mentions only the total amount of want-satisfaction among the members of a reference group, whereas a distributive principle requires for its statement a mention of the way in which want-satisfaction is to be divided among the members of a reference group.[2] For example it

[1] See Paul A. Samuelson, *Foundations of Economic Analysis* (Cambridge, Mass., 1948), Chapter VIII.

[2] This does not mean that statistics used in connection with aggregative principles cannot be broken down into smaller categories than the whole reference group, but that the categories can be introduced only with an eye to their significance for determining the total amount of want-satisfaction. Thus, road casualties might be divided according to age, on the view that the

might be that the want-satisfaction should be divided equally among the members of the group, or that no member of the group should fall below a certain minimum of want-satisfaction, or that special treatment in terms of want-satisfaction should be related to one set of qualities and achievements and not to any other set. These distributive principles can be further classified as either *comparative* or *absolute* distributive principles. The first kind involve in their application to one person a comparison with the position of some other man or men, i.e. that the person in question should get more, less or exactly the same amount of want-satisfaction as this other man or men. Absolute distributive principles, on the other hand, are of a nature which allows one to specify what one individual should get (given that he falls into a certain category) without requiring one to state this in relation to anyone else's position. Of the examples already given the principle that everyone should fare equally is obviously of the first kind while the principle that nobody in the reference group should fall below a certain fixed minimum level is of the second kind. The principle that special treatment should be given in respect of certain qualities or achievements may be of either kind: it all depends on how the 'special treatment' is specified.

4.B. *Interpersonal Comparisons.* It has been held, especially by economic theorists, that any judgement which involves 'the interpersonal comparison of utility' is either mumbo-jumbo or at any rate cannot involve any process properly describable as 'addition'. Plainly, if either of these assertions is right then the possible contents of the 'aggregative' category are drastically diminished.[1] I shall argue, however, that neither is correct.

The first view, that 'interpersonal comparisons of utility' are mumbo-jumbo, is often put forward as a 'philosophical' or 'scientific' objection, but the philosophical or scientific approach should

[1] See 5.B. for a discussion of the 'optimizing' principle which does not involve any interpersonal comparisons.

---

younger a person is when crippled the more serious this is from a want-satisfying angle, but there would be no room in an aggregative calculation for a distinction between 'culpable' and 'innocent' casualties. Again, it would be a good aggregative move to analyze the distribution as well as the total size of the national income if one held that a pound has more want-satisfying significance for a poor man than for a rich man; but an increase in inequality could not of course be attacked as bad in itself on aggregative grounds.

be, it seems to me, to say with Aristotle that one should ask only for 'as much exactness as the subject matter admits of, for precision is not to be sought alike in all discussions'.[1] Of course, there is no way of reading off on a dial the answer to the question whether a broken leg for *A* is worse than a pinprick for *B*, but that does not mean it is not open to evidence amounting in simple cases to proof. Establishing the relative importance of frustrating or satisfying different people's wants does not seem more (or, no doubt, less) insoluble than, for example, establishing causal dependencies in a complex train of social phenomena.

A more concrete reply to the charge that we can't make interpersonal comparisons is that we do so every day. (A judge who was told that judges can't make law is said to have retorted, 'Yes, they do—I make some myself.') How do we decide at what point slower traffic is balanced by a reduced accident rate? How do we decide on the relative importance of research into cancer, heart disease and the common cold? Or, at a less grandiose level of decision, how does a mother decide that Johnny's shoes have priority over Bill's raincoat?[2] Bentham's position on the whole business of interpersonal comparison seems to me eminently sensible; in this respect at least it is his detractors who show up as naïve and out of touch with reality.

> You might as well pretend to add twenty apples to twenty pears
> ... there would not be forty of any one sort of thing, but twenty
> of each sort, just as there were before. ... This addibility of the
> happiness of different subjects ... is a postulatum without which
> all political reasonings are at a stand.[3]

[1] Lionel Robbins, in *An Essay on the Nature and Significance of Economic Science* 2nd ed. (London, 1948), pp. 139–141, writes: '*There is no means of testing the magnitude of A's satisfaction as compared with B's.* ... If the representative of some other civilisation were to assure us that we were wrong [in thinking that people get equal satisfaction from equal incomes], that members of his caste (or his race) were capable of experiencing ten times as much satisfaction from given incomes as members of an inferior caste (or an "inferior" race), we could not refute him. ... We could not pretend that the justification of our scheme of things was in any way *scientific*.' (Italics in original.)

[2] See the final chapter of Jerome Rothenberg, *The Measurement of Social Welfare*, (Englewood Cliffs, N.J.) for a comment on family decision processes from this point of view.

[3] Mary P. Mack, *Jeremy Bentham: An Odyssey of Ideas* 1748–1792 (London, 1962), p. 244. See also I. M. D. Little, *A Critique of Welfare Economics*, (Oxford, 1957), Chapter IV.

A variant of the argument is to say that although it may not be impossible to get the information to make a sensible aggregative judgement, it nevertheless requires time and trouble. How, then, are we ever to decide at what point to stop collecting information since we don't know how far the further information we might collect would affect our decision? Answers to this question have in fact been produced—answers involving a formidable degree of mathematical sophistication.[1] These answers depend however for their rigour on the assumption that the decision-maker does at least know at the outset the probability-distribution of possible outcomes and then has to ask what it is worth to have more detailed information—e.g. he knows there is a one in three chance of its raining tomorrow and decides whether to acquire a definite forecast. But although this is an idealized picture it is surely true that we generally have *some* idea of the relative likelihood of various outcomes and that this is why deciding how much information to collect is not in fact the completely arbitrary affair that the initial statement of the position made it out to be.[2] We can and do rationally criticize people for collecting too much or too little information, given the knowledge they already had.[3]

The other view that I mentioned above was that although 'interpersonal comparisons of utility' may not be mumbo-jumbo there is still nothing properly describable as 'addition of utilities'. Myrdal, for example, writes:

> We do compare utilities daily. Every political conviction presupposes such a social estimate. But we do it by using our judgement, at best a well-informed judgement based on a correct understanding of the facts, but it remains fundamentally a moral judgement. It expresses what we think should be done in a situation,

[1] See especially Jacob Marschak, 'Towards an Economic Theory of Organization and Information', in R. M. Thrall, C. H. Coombs and R. L. Davis, *Decision Processes* (New York, 1954), pp. 187–220.

[2] Marschak, pp. 196–197.

[3] This is not to say that what later turn out to have been bad mistakes can always be avoided; in the nature of the case even the most rational course of action in a situation of uncertainty may in fact turn out badly. But the problem of defining what, on any given initial information, is the wisest course (given also the comparability of any advantage or gain with any disadvantage or cost) is not theoretically insoluble. (See Hitch and McKean, *The Economics of Defense* . . ., Chapters X and XI, for a discussion of the problems of investment in research on weapons systems.)

46

according to our ideals or according to our desires. The weighting of different people's desires and needs itself involves a new valuation.[1]

As it stands this is very vague, but the general intention seems to be to deny that one can intelligibly say 'This policy would increase the total amount of want-satisfaction but it ought not to be put into effect because it is so unjust', because there is no difference in meaning between the two (whereas between 'This would decrease the mortality rate' and 'This ought to be done' there is).

Against this all one can say is that there *do* seem to be two separate stages and this can be seen from the possibility of applying *either* aggregative *or* distributive criteria to the question of what should be done in a particular case. The mother deciding between shoes for Johnny and a raincoat for Bill may reason along distributive lines: 'Johnny hasn't had anything new for some time whereas Bill had several new things last month' (fair shares). Or she may ask whether shoes would make a bigger contribution to the well-being of Johnny than would a raincoat to the well-being of Bill. Whose 'need' (welfare being the end) is greatest? To suggest that this question is simply a way of covering up the decision that Johnny should get his shoes seems to me to ignore the nature of the considerations which would be relevant here—which child is most likely to catch cold if the item of clothing is not forthcoming, which is most sensitive about his appearance, and so on. The processes of reasoning involved in making a distributive judgement and making an aggregative judgement involving interpersonal comparisons of utility are different to the people who make them and this seems to me the only proof of their difference which is either necessary or possible.

5. TWO DIFFICULT CASES

5.A. *Need.* In this final section I take two principles which are sometimes put forward and which do not at first sight fit into either the aggregative or the distributive category. I shall try to show that inasfar as they do not fit into one or the other this is because they are not independent justificatory principles at all.

Consider first 'need' as a justification for policies. When we see

[1] Gunnar Myrdal, *The Political Element in the Development of Economic Theory* (London, 1953), p. 103.

statements to the effect that human beings need so many calories per day (and that states should make every effort to see that everyone gets this number) or that university teachers need books (which should therefore be allowed by the Inland Revenue as a claim for expenses) we may at first suppose that here is a justification for policies which does not appeal to either distributive or aggregative considerations but to an 'objective' or 'scientific' procedure by which 'needs' are established. But the protean applications of the concept of need are a result not of its being a *sui generis* justificatory principle but to its not being by itself a justificatory principle at all.

Whenever someone says '*x* is needed' it always makes sense (though it may be pedantic in some contexts) to ask what purpose it is needed for. Once an end is given it is indeed an 'objective' or 'scientific' matter to find out what conditions are necessary to bring it about—provided that the end is sufficiently precisely stated, of course. The end in my first example might be mere survival, or good health, or the satisfaction of hunger; and differences in the 'needs' found by different studies might no doubt be largely attributed to differences in the end postulated. Similarly, in my second example, books might be held necessary for a university teacher to function *at all* or only for him to function at his highest potential.

When I say that 'need' is not by itself a justificatory principle, I mean that no statement to the effect that *x* is necessary in order to produce *y* provides a reason for doing *x*. Before it can provide such a reason *y* must be shown to be (or taken to be) a desirable end to pursue. This much is necessary in order to provide *pro tanto* a reason for doing *x*. A *conclusive* reason would require showing that the cost of *x* (i.e. the other desirable things which could be done instead of *x*) does not make it less advantageous than some alternative course of action, and that any disadvantageous side-effects of *x* are outweighed by its advantage in producing *y*.

To speak of needs, then, is to operate on a lower level of generality than that of the ultimate justifications for policies.[1]

---

[1] A category mistake is thus involved in treating 'desert' and 'need' as if they were parallel criteria for income distribution, as is done by S. I. Benn and R. S. Peters in Chapter VI of their *Social Principles and the Democratic State* (London, 1959). To treat need as a *basis* for desert is to commit *two* mistakes: one about 'need' and the other about 'desert'. See, for an alleged example of

'Need' can be used *in conjunction* with justifications of any kind, but not by itself. It can be used, for example, with ideal-regarding as well as want-regarding principles, so that one might equally say 'The town needs a municipal theatre' (in order to *create* a demand) and 'The town needs a municipal car park' (in order to *satisfy* a demand). One can also say 'To destroy life on earth one needs *x* megatons of explosive power'.

So far I have been emphasizing that 'need' is a derivative concept and this seems worth doing because of the danger of treating it as an independent justificatory principle. However, in arguing for this I have left out a certain subtlety in the concept which, when supplied, at least explains why the mistake about it should have been made.

Although, as I have pointed out, one can say in any context that *x* is needed in order to produce *y*, this is not equally true of '*A* needs *x*' where *A* is a person. The concept is no less derivative, but the ends to which it may refer are limited. Any 'objectivity' or justificatory independence of 'need' (e.g. in connection with 'basic human needs') stems from this limitation in ends. At the core is physical health (e.g. the diet example); this extends more weakly to mental well-being (e.g. people need privacy, people need community). Then, spreading further out comes the performance of some function or the achievement of some object (the university lecturer example). Finally, we arrive at the fulfilment of some standard which can be independent of any function or purpose of the person to whom need is ascribed (old age pensioners need more money if their level of prosperity is to keep in step with that of the rest of the community). The nearer to the core the use of 'need' is, the less linguistic propriety demands that the end be supplied in the sentence and, of course, the easier it is to suppose that a need can somehow be established independently of an end. However, this modification does not affect my thesis that no special account has to be taken of 'need', for it is still derivative and the only interesting questions arise in connection with the ends.

5.B. *Pareto-Optimality*. One situation is Pareto-optimal compared to another if at least one person is better off (has more of his wants

---

this, footnote 8 on pages 73–74 of the article by Joel Feinberg, 'Justice and Personal Desert', in *Nomos VI*, edited by John W. Chapman and Carl J. Friedrich (New York, 1963).

satisfied) in the first situation than in the second and nobody is worse off in the first than in the second.[1] Unlike other want-regarding principles such as fairness or equality this one was formulated by a professional economist and is still most often used among professional economists. It is nevertheless a fully-fledged ultimate principle and though restricted under its name of Pareto-optimality it also arises, in a more complex form, as an element in 'the public interest' and 'the common good'. If the principle is taken as saying nothing about the desirability or undesirability of changes which will make at least one person better off and at least one person worse off, it surely falls squarely in the aggregative category. It shares the defining aggregative characteristic that *any* increase of want-satisfaction, to whomever it may accrue, counts equally as an improvement. No question has to be asked about the general distributive effect of the change (does it increase inequality?) or specifically about the title in virtue of which increases occur (do increases go to those who deserve them or are they merely random windfalls, which depend on the possession of some morally irrelevant characteristic?). But it is restricted because it does not operate at all when some who are affected by a policy are affected in a different direction from others. Pareto-optimization and maximization (e.g. Bentham's utilitarianism) then become the two possible sub-divisions within the aggregative branch.[2] Maximization involves a comparison between the gains and losses of different people in order to strike a balance, whereas optimization involves only seeing whether all changes are in the same direction.[3]

The interpretation of the Pareto-optimizing principle which I have discussed corresponds to the terms in which it is usually introduced by those who intend to use it; but rather curiously its actual use is sometimes different. The definition requires that if some gain and some lose in a change from one situation to another nothing can be said about its desirability. But the principle is

[1] Little, *Critique of Welfare Economics*, Chapters 8 and 9.

[2] Etymologically, both expressions are of course superlatives; but the custom of carrying over 'optimal' to a comparison of only two situations is well established. I am extending this usage to 'maximal' as well. ('Melioration' has a somewhat distinct meaning of its own, while no comparative corresponding to 'maximization' seems to exist.)

[3] Compare Pareto's utility *for* and utility *of* a community. Pareto, however, includes *any* non-optimal judgement in the utility *of* a society.

instead sometimes taken to entail that if some people will lose from a change that change should *not* be made. Interpreted in this way, the Pareto-optimality principle becomes difficult to classify, but I suggest that this is due to a basic confusion in it when it is so interpreted. It of course includes in itself the optimizing principle already discussed—that if some gain and none lose there is an improvement, and *vice versa*—but it then goes on to say that if some lose, whether or not others gain, there is *no* improvement. The trouble is, I think, that this rather eccentric principle needs to be brought into relation with some more general principle, before it can be taken as a justificatory move. For why are only losses to be taken into account? Why not turn the principle upside down and say any change in which someone gains (no matter how many lose) is an improvement? No doubt justifications could be found for the principle, e.g. that it is always unjust to make people worse off or that losing is always more unpleasant than gaining, but they would not perhaps be very plausible. Without such a justification the principle demands an inexplicable asymmetry between the treatment of gains and losses. We have a want-regarding principle which claims to provide results while completely ignoring large areas of want-satisfaction, namely gains in a situation where there are also losses. The impossibility of fitting that version of the optimizing principle into the categories I have put forward reflects the incompleteness of the principle rather than the inadequacy of the categories.

The motives leading to the espousal of such a peculiar and unsatisfactory principle seem to be two. The first is that the optimizing principle interpreted as giving answers only where there are gains but no losses (and *vice versa*) has obviously a very limited application, since most changes one can think of involve both gains and losses. The extension of the principle to condemn all changes where anyone loses means that it gives an answer for all possible changes that might be put forward while still not involving 'interpersonal comparisons of utility'. The second motive is ideological: the extended application of the optimizing principle appears by some sleight of hand to achieve the feat of deriving ultra-conservative evaluative criteria from epistemological purity plus the general want-regarding position.

Either way, the argument runs thus: if want-satisfaction is good, and if we cannot compare one man's gain with another man's loss, we can only say that one situation is better than another when at least one person gains and nobody loses. Only such changes should therefore be recommended. The rabbit is smuggled into the hat by the 'therefore'. The most that we can conclude from the premises is that it doesn't make any difference whether we make other changes so long as at least someone gains from them.[1]

[1] In these remarks I have in mind especially L. von Mises in his *Human Action* (London, 1949); and James M. Buchanan, especially in his essay 'Positive Economics, Welfare Economics, and Political Economy', in *Fiscal Theory and Political Economy* (Chapel Hill, 1960).

IV

CONSERVATISM, MAJORITARIANISM AND LIBERALISM

1. INTRODUCTION

IT is one thing to come to the conclusion that some principle would be satisfied if a certain thing were done and another to say that the thing should be done. Since it is in the end judgements of the second kind that matter it is necessary to examine the relation between the two sorts of judgement. This is particularly important in relation to ideal-regarding principles since there is a widely- (and often passionately-) held view that ideal-regarding judgements to the effect that one situation would be better than another should never be translated into judgements of the form: 'In order to bring about the better situation the state should do so-and-so.' The bulk of the present chapter (sections 4, 5 and 6) will be devoted to an examination of this view, which I shall call 'liberalism'. But before this (in sections 2 and 3) I shall quickly pass in review two other theories which would limit attempts to implement principles politically, and which would go further than the 'liberal' view in extending the ban from ideal-regarding principles to *all* principles. I shall call these views 'conservatism' and 'majoritarianism'.

In the nature of the case we shall be treading on slippery ground in these discussions because the arguments involved are of the highest generality. It may indeed be asked whether any argument is possible (let alone fruitful) concerning the most ultimate bases of evaluation. If all arguments were deductive in form, there would indeed be no way of doing it, for in any deductive system there must be some axioms which cannot be proved within the system. But moral and political arguments are not a one-way affair; they may proceed upwards or downwards in generality. Conclusions about particular cases may be used to support higher-level principles as well as (though not, of course, at the same time as) being derived from higher level principles. Moreover, because we are more familiar with thinking about particular cases, we are often more sure about our attitude to them than we are towards general principles. It is, therefore, a legitimate and useful part of argument to attempt to show someone that a principle which he claims to espouse would have implications for certain concrete situations which he is unwilling to accept.[1]

2. CONSERVATISM

2.A. *Definition.* By 'conservatism' I intend here to refer to any view to the effect that all attempts to transform societies in accordance with principles (whether they be want-regarding or ideal-regarding principles) are pernicious: dangerous and self-defeating at once. There are two varieties of this general conservative position which might be called respectively the 'anti-political' and the 'anti-rationalist' variety. The difference is perhaps one of emphasis: the first school emphasizes the dangers of expecting too much from any sort of political action while the second emphasizes especially the dangers of taking principles seriously. I shall offer a brief comment on each.

2.B. *Anti-Political Conservatism.* The first thesis can, I think, be extracted from Hayek's *Road to Serfdom* and de Jouvenel's *Sovereignty.*[2] It may be expressed thus: when the state is generally

[1] Neither a deductive nor an inductive model fits moral or political reasoning accurately. I have already questioned the deductive model which is the most usual one. Prichard stated the inductive one in his 'Does Moral Philosophy Rest on a Mistake?' in *Moral Obligation* (Oxford, 1949). According to this, principles merely summarize our past decisions when faced with particular situations. But if he had ever had to decide something for which his 'intuition' (i.e. training) had not prepared him, he would surely have been forced to proceed by looking for analogies between the difficult situation and situations in which he had no doubts of the right answer. Thus he would be *using* his principles to help decide particular questions.

We are completely sure neither of the lower-level decisions nor the higher-level principles. All we know is that somehow they have to be brought into a consistent relation with one another; but this will often be by a process of mutual accommodation between higher and lower levels.

[2] F. A. von Hayek, *Road to Serfdom* (Chicago, 1944); B. de Jouvenel, *Sovereignty* (Cambridge, 1957).

regarded as no more than an instrument for keeping order at home and repelling foreign invasion, it is of little moment who controls it. The political struggle can thus be kept within bounds. But once people start thinking the state can be made over for the purpose of bringing about social justice or changing human nature, the stakes become too high for the conflict to be manageable and the society is torn apart or brutally unified by a totalitarian government based on terror.

It is difficult to deny that this argument may have an application in some places and at some times; but then it is difficult to deny that almost *any* general statement of this kind may in fact have such an application. What is questionable is whether it has universal application. Consider income redistribution. None of the non-Communist countries where the state is expected to have a policy for personal incomes are in a state of near civil war over the matter and many (especially Britain, Scandinavia, the ex-Dominions and the USA) have a wide degree of internal consensus over it.[1] When applied to ideal-regarding principles (what I called 'changing human nature') the theory becomes more plausible because there is no doubt that at a certain point (e.g. Prohibition in the USA) the cohesiveness of a society is likely to be damaged by attempts to 'legislate morality'. But this is not of course enough to show that *all* attempts to implement ideals lead to similar results as the 18th Amendment did; and I do not see how such a conclusion could be maintained.

A more limited claim, which is perhaps the one which de Jouvenel and Hayek want to make, is that although there may be particular times when competing principles are not so wide apart that attempts to implement them lead to unmanageable strife, nevertheless, it is dangerous for the idea to get around that principles have a legitimate place in politics because you can never be sure when different people's principles won't be disastrously incompatible. But this assumes that there is no way of making a general distinction between permissible and impermissible applications of principles. This is not so. A rough and ready rule for the

---

[1] De Jouvenel oddly enough takes over one of the most questionable parts of Marxism—the idea that material possessions are so important that those with large property incomes will *always* fight against dispossession. From much the same predictions as the Laski of the 1930s, he derives exactly opposite conclusions.

application of want-regarding principles might be that except in an emergency nobody is to be plunged from luxury to poverty if he has once become used to luxury. This underlies suggestions that after a heavy capital levy a substantial part of the income should be paid for one generation. Where ideal-regarding principles are concerned, the specification of a rule is more complicated and will be considered in Section 6.

2.C. *Anti-Rationalist Conservatism*. The second 'appeal to results' has strong claims to being considered *the* conservative argument. Elaborately and eloquently stated by Burke, it has in recent times been endorsed by Oakeshott and Namier.[1] Summarily stated, it is this: principles pick out selected aspects of life and lead their devotees to ignore the cost of pursuing them on other aspects of life no less important. Moreover, human reason is an imperfect instrument and cannot hope to predict more than a tiny proportion of the consequences of any change, if that. So, even if the principles themselves were good the effects of applying them will be bad.

Despite the pedigree of this line of thought, I doubt whether it goes to prove any such sweeping proposition as its advocates suggest. The first half of the argument tells against the incompetent use of principles rather than their use at all. It points out that one may be so obsessed with one thing (say, securing justice) that one ignores others (such as the relation of security to happiness). But nobody as far as I know has shown that it is impossible (or even difficult) to be committed to a number of ideals and principles at once and to realize that the fulfillment of one of them will usually be limited by the claims of the others and that what must be aimed at is the best available balance rather than an outright victory for one at the expense of the others.

The second half of the argument, that human reason is an imperfect instrument, is no doubt well founded. Of course, nobody could predict all the results of making a certain change in

[1] M. Oakeshott, 'Political Education', *Philosophy, Politics and Society*, ed. Laslett (Oxford, 1956); also reprinted in his book, *Rationalism in Politics* (Methuen, 1962). L. B. Namier, 'Human Nature in Politics', *The Varieties of History*, ed. Fritz Stern (Meridian Books, 1956). In the USA Sumner stands as a forceful exponent of the view: 'The Absurd Effort to Make the World Over', *American Thought: Civil War to World War I*, ed. Perry Miller (New York, 1961).

all their ramifications. But what is the significance of this? Before it can be used to show that actions based on principles are likely to lead to bad results, one must add the assumption that the unanticipated consequences are likely to be bad rather than good, and indeed that they will be so bad as to outweigh the good which is nevertheless brought about. At least in some cases, I suggest, it is possible to make a fairly reliable guess that this condition does not hold. Take, for example, the introduction of the National Health Service in Britain in 1948. Undeniably, this must have had many indirect effects not anticipated by those who introduced it; but the question is whether, given their original principles, they should have had good reason for regretting its introduction when they saw how it had worked out; and I think the answer is 'no'. Many other examples could surely be given of major legislative changes which have turned out if not exactly as their sponsors expected at least in a way which they would recognize as an improvement on the *status quo ante*.

What alternatives are offered by those who object to principles? One is to say that instead of relying on discursive reasoning men should put their trust in intuitive judgement. (Often it is added— as by Burke and Oakeshott—that this intuition has to be specially trained and is available therefore only to a privileged minority.) Grant that discursive reasoning is not the only form that intelligence takes.[1] Grant that one can know how to do something without being able to describe it.[2] Even so, principles and ideals have an indispensable role in politics.

Firstly, they are necessary for learning. Observing how the older generation does things can never by itself give one the 'tradition', for without a capacity to generalize one would never be able to apply the experience of the past to fresh situations.[3] To do that, one must know not only *what* was done but *why* it was done; in other words, in what features of the situation brought about by deliberate effort did the value reside? Whether the older generation formulates its criteria for an 'improvement' or whether the younger generation has to work it out from observation, the conclusion is the same: the younger generation must somehow arrive

---

[1] Susanne K. Langer, *Philosophy in a New Key* (Mentor Books, 1948).
[2] Ludwig Wittgenstein, *Philosophical Investigations*, 2nd ed. (Oxford, 1958); Gilbert Ryle, *The Concept of Mind* (London, 1949).
[3] See Hare, *Language of Morals*, Chapter IV.

at judgements of the form, 'It was best to do so-and-so because it would lead to such-and-such', where 'such-and-such' is some *general* description.

Secondly, principles are necessary for securing agreement. Even if one person could make decisions without ever bringing the grounds for them to the surface of his mind, it would not be possible for more than one to do so. Each member of the group charged with the decision could, of course, reach his own recommendation by a subterranean process; but if their recommendations conflicted they would be unable to discuss them. For discussion is only possible if there are general standards to appeal to: 'That would be unfair', 'That would affect the *x*'s adversely', and so on. It has to take the form of trying to show that a certain action will (or will not) bring about a situation to which a certain value (positive or negative) is attached. If there are no general criteria of the form 'value is attached to situations which manifest the following features . . . ' there is no room for arguments purporting to show that such-and-such a situation can be brought under this or that head. 'Intuition' is adequate only when authority is concentrated on one man, a Hitler or a de Gaulle.

3. MAJORITARIANISM

3.A. *The Argument Stated.* The majoritarian argument appeals not to results but to a principle itself; but it asserts that if you accept this one principle you cannot consistently hold any other except in a qualified way to be explained later. The principle in question I shall call the majoritarian principle since it is in that connection that the argument is usually put forward.[1]

It may be put as follows: suppose you agree that all disputes which require political settlement should be settled by majority vote, or by elected persons in accordance with the sentiments of the majority. If so, you can't also adhere to any other political principles. For if you do, they may lead you to say in some instance that *x* should not be done, while the wish of the majority is that *x* should be done. You may thus run into a contradiction. If you really believe that what the majority wants should be done, and the

---

[1] See especially Howard R. Smith, *Democracy and the Public Interest* (Athens, Georgia, 1960), and Jerome Rothenberg, *Measurement of Social Welfare*.

majority wants *x* done, you cannot consistently say that *x* should not be done.[1]

The more generalized form may be expressed thus: if you adhere to any ideal or principle which does not include in it a reference to the opinions of others then it is logically possible that you might be the only person holding it. There could be a situation, therefore, in which you say 'So-and-so should be done' and everyone except you says 'So-and-so should not be done'. You are, in effect, setting yourself up as a dictator.[2] Of course, you probably won't have the power to get what you want done against everyone else's opposition; nevertheless you are saying that if you had the power you would. (You cannot sincerely say 'so-and-so should be done' and then not do it if you have the power.)

3.B. *Primary and Corrected Wishes*. Will a good majoritarian then have only one wish: that a majoritarian procedure be used to settle all disputes? This surely cannot be so, for if everyone took such a view the decision-process would have nothing to work on. There have to be some wants *other* than wants for the procedure itself before it can be brought into play at all. A more precise formulation must make use of more elaborate apparatus. We must distinguish, plainly, between the *primary* wish for a policy, which does not take account of anyone else's views, and the *corrected* wish, which does. Primary wishes, for someone who adheres to the majoritarian principle, may be of any nature; but secondary wishes must be for an outcome which treats one's own primary wish only as one among many. Being a majoritarian, then, involves having a sort of split mind: it requires that one should not always wish one's own (primary) opinions to win. For example, a majoritarian might say 'I am opposed to legalized drinking; and if there is a vote on it I shall vote against it. But if the vote shows that a majority favours it, then I think it should be permitted.'[3] This is

[1] Note A on page 292 contains a comparison between 'majoritarianism' so defined and the superficially similar conception to be found in Rousseau's *Social Contract*. Note B on page 293 provides a brief critical discussion of Richard Wollheim's recent contribution to the problem raised here.

[2] See Arrow's definition of 'dictatorship' in *Social Choice*. . . .

[3] 'In the run-off campaign Black announced his stand on prohibition. Six years had not changed his conviction that liquor was a foremost source of evil, but it had changed his convictions in two other respects. He no longer thought that in the midst of terrible depression prohibition was a paramount issue; and he no longer thought, if he ever had, that it was possible for the

not inconsistent, provided that the first is taken as a qualified assertion. That is, it has to be taken as expressing the way in which the person making it intends to exert his influence on the result (by voting, lobbying or what not) rather than as a wish for that to be the result. An analogy would be someone who tries as hard as he can to win a game, but still only wishes to win if he plays better than his opponent. His behaviour too has an air of inconsistency about it since if the other player plays better than he, he would want him to win while at the same time trying as hard as he can to prevent him. But again, the air of inconsistency can be removed if we recognize that his playing as hard as he can ('trying to win') is a necessary means to the best player's winning, just as it is necessary to vote according to one's own convictions if the will of the majority is to be ascertained.[1]

Once the distinction between the primary and the corrected judgements is grasped, even greater apparent inconsistencies can be shown as justified. For if the actual procedure in operation does not function according to your majoritarian principle, you may have to vote *against* your primary judgement. For example, let us

[1] Another example would be someone who simultaneously hires the best lawyer he can afford to fight his case and wishes the side with the best case to win.

'*That particular goods be properly defended by particular persons matters greatly for the common good itself.* The wife of the murderer, as she fights for the life of the man whom the common good wants put to death, does precisely what the common good wants her to do. It is in a merely material fashion that she disagrees with the requirements of the common good: by doing what the common good wants her to do, she formally desires the common good. The common good formally understood is the concern of every genuine virtue, but it is the proper concern of the public person to procure the common good materially understood, which the private person may virtually oppose.' (Yves R. Simon, *Philosophy of Democratic Government* (Chicago, 1951), pp. 41–42.)

drys to enforce prohibition against a people who did not want it. For himself, he declared, he remained both a personal and a political dry; but the time had come to resubmit the matter to popular vote. As a Senator, he would vote to submit a repeal amendment to the people; as a voter in Alabama, he would vote against it.' (John P. Frank, *Mr. Justice Black: The Man and His Opinions* (New York, 1949), p. 61). The cynical may of course see in this more of Black the shrewd politician getting himself out of a tight spot than Black the dedicated democrat subordinating his own opinions to those of a possible majority; but surely Black must still have thought that the statement was defensible as a position in its own right to have made it at all.

say that your principle takes the form that the majority of those with a definite opinion on any matter should win (rather than a majority of those who vote). Now suppose that in a certain matter your own primary judgement is in favour of X but you know that a disproportionate number of abstentions will be from the ranks of those who favour Y. In this situation, you will be bringing the result of the vote *nearer* to that prescribed by your own corrected judgement if you vote for Y (i.e. *against* your primary judgement) than if you vote for X. (This, however, depends on not too many people following the same rule—the possibility of an infinite regress, in which everyone's action depends on everyone else's, opens here.) Another example would be the position of someone who believed that the result of an election ought to be determined by the popular vote, whereas in fact it was determined by a majority of majorities in constituencies. A Conservative might thus find himself voting Labour if his corrected position was popular-majority majoritarianism and his primary position Conservatism; and a Democrat with the same ideas might find himself voting for a Republican president.[1]

3.C. *The Argument Criticized*. I have tried to show that the majoritarian argument can be defended against a charge of inconsistency. I now have to ask whether one should *accept* it. I believe the main inducement to do so is the dislike of appearing to disregard the wishes and opinions of others. But the majoritarian principle surely jumps to the opposite extreme and commits one (at least in political matters) to the kind of majority-vote relativism of which Broad once accused Hume.[2] To hand over one's judgement as to what measures ought to be taken, without any escape clause, to the majority of a group in which one's own (primary) opinion would count only for one would be rash, to say the least. If Hitler had ever received a clear 'mandate' from the German electorate we would have to condemn on the majoritarian principle not only those who actively opposed him but even those who thought that what he was doing was wrong.

To complete the treatment for attraction to the majoritarian principle, however, its sting must be removed; and the sting lies in

---

[1] The problem of defining 'sincerity' and 'strategy' in voting becomes complicated if we consider the case of an adherent of the majoritarian principle. The point is analysed in Note C on page 294.

[2] C. D. Broad, *Five Types of Ethical Theory* (London, 1930), pp. 114–115.

the accusation that to reject it is to ride roughshod over the opinions and wishes of others. I shall therefore suggest several ways in which one might take account of the wants of others without endorsing it.

The smallest deviation would be to take account of intensity rather than numbers only. The problem of the 'intense minority' is a stock worry of democratic theorists, and clearly if one reserved the right to estimate intensities oneself in deciding what should be done one would sometimes oppose the majority purely in the interests of wishing the side with the greatest 'mass' of intensity to prevail.[1] But the deviation is hardly adequate; surely it is not impossible to imagine a situation where 'the worst are full of passionate intensity'. One might then still wish to oppose the most intense *and* numerous side.

An alternative route away from the majoritarian principle while still keeping the wants of others in sight would be to say that people's wants for *results* should be counted but to refuse to allow that their wants for policies as such should be. In other words, on this view one should respect people's aims but reserve the right to disagree with them as to the policies which are likely to further those aims.[2] This might conceivably leave one as a lone upholder of a certain policy as the right one, and therefore a 'dictator'; yet one would be disagreeing only about the means to the ends desired by the majority. The trouble with this move is, though, that it still leaves one in a position of issuing a blank cheque to the majority, this time not for policies but for results. Perhaps many times when one wishes to hold out against the opinion of the majority it will be because one believes that the policy they support will not lead to the ends they espouse. But it would surely be rash to suppose that a situation could never arise in which it would be the ends themselves which one deprecated, even though they were the ends of the majority.

A more radical departure from the majority principle is to distinguish among the ends themselves, counting only privately-

---

[1] See for example Robert A. Dahl, *A Preface to Democratic Theory* (Chicago, 1956). Whether the problem could be solved institutionally will be considered in Chapters XIV and XV.

[2] Rothenberg apparently allows that one may dissent from the deliverancies of the majority as to where the 'social welfare' lies if it is misinformed. See *Measurement of Social Welfare*.

oriented ones.[1] By 'privately-oriented' I mean having oneself (or at most one's family) as the reference group; or, more precisely, affecting oneself or one's family. When I speak of 'being affected' here I mean having one's life materially impinged upon by some change in opportunities or routine. I do not mean being made to feel, as in the phrase 'an affecting sight'.[2] Thus, in the sense of 'being affected' relevant here a Swiss hotel-keeper, asked if he was affected by the war might reply that it decreased his trade but he could not reply that he was upset by the thought of cities being bombed. Or again, a Northern Negro in the USA is affected by discrimination which prevents him from getting certain jobs or houses, etc.; but he is not affected by what happens in the South.

The justification for counting only privately-oriented wants is that it avoids at one stroke the most objectionable feature of the majoritarian principle, namely the way in which it commits one to handing over questions of right and wrong, justice and injustice, to the majority of a group in which one's own voice counts only as one. Yet at the same time the amendment leaves one free to take account of desires which are put forward simply by people as wants in matters affecting themselves. This may seem high-handed at first sight, but further reflection suggests that what I have called 'publicly-oriented wants' are not actually put forward as wants at all. To treat them as wants is to degrade them and to fall into absurdity.[3]

Suppose that I am making up my mind whether it is fair for the A's to get more of something than the B's; and the A's and B's are the only people directly affected by the division, in the sense of

---

[1] For the introduction of this concept see I.3.C.

[2] 'To be affected' in the relevant sense is not merely *narrower* than 'to feel' (i.e. 'to feel in some matter directly concerning oneself'.) There may be no feeling at all, as in: 'Does the new timetable affect you?' 'Yes, the train leaves five minutes earlier, but I'm perfectly indifferent about it'. Indeed, the relevant sense of 'being affected' can be applied to inanimate things without change of meaning, as in 'The heavy rain in August affected the crop' or 'The storm affected a wide area'. A significant use is that where a type of activity is made the subject: 'Shipping was affected . . . ', 'Farming was affected . . . ', 'Cricket was affected . . . '. Here too, emotional reactions of ships' crews, farmers or cricketers are not in point, though they may occur.

[3] Support for the position taken here is offered, I think, by the fact that it is far easier to swallow the 'democratic principle' when the issue at stake can be presented as a conflict of wants than when it appears as a conflict of opinions as to what is right, fair, etc.

'affected' which I have defined. Should I, in making up my mind, take account of the opinions of the C's in the matter? I may, of course, let them weigh with me as having a certain authority, but surely it would be ridiculous to mix in the wants of the C's for, say, the A's to win, consequential on their belief that the A's have the best case, on an equal footing with the privately-oriented wants of the A's and B's.[1] Suppose, for example, that a vote is being taken on some matter, and some vote on privately-oriented grounds and others only on publicly-oriented grounds: the result of the vote will reflect neither what the majority wants in the interests of its own members nor what the majority thinks (taking a public standpoint) ought to be done, but a fortuitous mixture. Let us say that the question is whether the A's should get more of something than the B's or the same amount. There are more A's than B's, but most of the A's think that (from a public standpoint) equality would be fairer, while the B's are equally divided. If everyone voted according to private wants, the A's would win; if everyone voted according to his attitude based on a public standpoint, the B's would win; but if some vote on one ground and some on another the result is completely indeterminate and depends on how many there are of each and how the numbers are composed.[2]

If, after studying the situation of the A's and B's, I conclude that the B's have the best case, I must also conclude that they ought to get more than the A's—whether or not this will frustrate the publicly-oriented wants of the C's.

Consider a concrete example of a 'cause group': the Howard League. If the Howard League submits a memorandum to the Home Secretary asking for better conditions in prisons, it will no doubt give a number of reasons why this ought to be done; but

[1] An electoral system in which there is no clear understanding as to whether people are supposed to vote on publicly-oriented grounds or on privately-oriented grounds produces precisely the mixture objected to in the text.

[2] Popular opinion in democratic countries seems unwilling to come down on either side. Some people apparently consider that everyone should vote purely according to his own interest, as e.g. a member of a certain class, and rely on the process itself to produce tolerable results; others take the view that one should vote for the party which is 'best for the country as a whole'; most, perhaps, try to avoid noticing the possibility that the two might clash. See, for example, Abrams in *Must Labour Lose?*, ed. Abrams, Rose and Hinden (Penguin Books, 1960).

among them will not be that the members of the Howard League want it done. On the contrary, its members presumably only want it done because it ought to be done.

Unlike a privately-oriented want, which carries a certain automatic claim to satisfaction with it, a publicly-oriented want carries a claim to satisfaction only as being a want for what ought to be done anyway. The want-regarding theory can very well be interpreted subject to a limitation on the meaning of 'want' which makes it equivalent to 'privately-oriented want'. In my opinion at least, the theory becomes far more implausible if publicly-oriented 'wants' are treated as similarly carrying with them an automatic claim to satisfaction, regardless of whether they are frivolous or serious, aimed at justice or injustice.[1]

But what happens when everyone has made his own publicly-oriented judgement based on the privately-oriented wants of a suitable reference group (a 'public')? If, as may be expected, these judgements disagree, there must be some way of deciding between them; are we not then back at majoritarianism? The answer to this is that we may be back at majority voting but we are not back at majoritarianism. The majoritarian principle entailed committing yourself to the (corrected) judgement 'So-and-so should be done' whenever this was the view of a majority. But even if you believe that majority-voting methods are most likely (out of any methods likely to be accepted) to result in the implementation of your principles, your ultimate loyalty is to those principles. Majority voting is only an instrument, liable to be abandoned whenever it appears that your principles would have more chance of being implemented under a different system.[2] It is true that the non-majoritarian, while he *is* supporting majority voting, must support the particular results of majority voting just as the convinced majoritarian does.[3] It would be inconsistent for him to say: 'What the majority wants should be done; but this thing (which the majority wants) should not be done.' Nevertheless, his position and the

[1] The question of the status of publicly-oriented wants is picked up again in a different context in 6.A. below, and is discussed in more general terms in a Note to that subsection, Note E on page 297.

[2] See I. M. D. Little in 'Social Choice . . .' (1952); and Dahl and Lindblom, *Politics, Economics and Welfare* (New York, 1953), pp. 44–45.

[3] Rothenberg makes great play with this and in fact obliterates the distinction between the man who is supporting democracy *pro tem* and the man who is supporting it in principle. ('Conditions . . .'.)

position of a man who accepts the majoritarian *principle* are quite different. To the latter a majority decision which overrules his own primary judgement is superior to his primary judgement; but to the former his primary judgement remains superior, and when he says that the majority should prevail in this case he has his eye on subsequent cases when he hopes to be in the majority and have his judgement implemented. When he says 'So-and-so ought to be done because the majority want it', he is not 'correcting' his opinion; he is merely announcing his continued adherence to the democratic decision-rule. If he could get his judgement implemented in the present instance without adverse long-run effects, he would prefer it; the man who is a majoritarian on principle would not. Therein lies the difference.

4. LIBERALISM

4.A. *Liberalism Defined.* So far I have been discussing two theories with the common conclusion that neither want-regarding nor ideal-regarding principles should be used for prescribing the conduct of political actors. In the rest of the chapter I examine the view that the ban should extend only to ideal-regarding principles in politics. For convenience, I shall refer to this position as 'liberalism'. Classical liberalism had other strands besides this one, no doubt, but one was certainly the idea that the state is an instrument for satisfying the wants that men happen to have rather than a means of making good men (e.g. cultivating desirable wants or dispositions in its citizens).

The scope of the present work extends only to *political* evaluations. Since evaluations may be made from many different aspects, not every judgement that a situation is bad is a political judgement; in order to be a political judgement it must be connected (even if at some remove) to the judgement that some action of a political nature ought to be taken to improve it. An evaluation of, let us say, newspapers, novels or television programmes to the effect that they are not all that they might be, is, so far, not a political evaluation. It becomes one (or, more exactly, it forms the grounds for one) if this state of affairs is attributed to the educational system and it is believed that the state has a responsibility for the condition of the educational system, or if it is thought that the state should do something about the subsidization of the arts, the ownership of newspapers or the control of television programmes. On the other hand, if such activities are thought to be no business of the state, the evaluation remains a full blooded aesthetic one but does not attain any political relevance.

Applying this to the case in hand, it can be seen that it is quite consistent to hold that some desires, beliefs and actions are better than others and yet at the same time to assert that none of this is politically relevant. The proponents of religious toleration in the seventeenth century, for example, usually had little doubt that there was a knowable truth in religious matters (which they were, of course, in possession of); but some at least believed that it was no business of the state to minister to the souls of its citizens.[1] Again, Mill in *On Liberty*, does not doubt that some beliefs are genuinely truer than others, but he rules out in the same essay any intervention by the state with the object of moulding character or beliefs.

4.B. *Illustration: The Wolfenden Report*. Let us now examine the relation between the view that *for political purposes* the want-regarding doctrine alone should apply and the view that in *all* matters the want-regarding doctrine is adequate by taking an actual example. To this end I shall present a simplified and schematized version of the public controversy which attended the publication of the Wolfenden Report on Homosexuality and Prostitution.[2]

Very roughly, then, we can say that there are two questions involved: firstly, is the existence of homosexuality undesirable; and secondly, should the practice of it be prohibited by the state? Four possible conclusions could be reached on the two questions taken together, namely that homosexuality is:

(C1) undesirable and should be prohibited;
(C2) undesirable but should not be prohibited;
(C3) not undesirable but should be prohibited;
(C4) not undesirable and should not be prohibited.

[1] 'In its original use the word implied a certain set of opinions and beliefs and practices approved of by the church or by the State, while certain other opinions or beliefs or practices, though not accepted nor indeed approved of by the powers that be, might yet be "tolerated".' (Ritchie, *Natural Rights* (London, 1924), p. 157.

[2] For simplicity I shall mention only homosexuality.

The third of these positions seems *prima facie* a very implausible one to adopt; if it is left out we have three positions, each of which found many supporters in the discussion.

We can also distinguish four possible sets of premises:

(P1) the want-regarding theory alone should be used to determine both the question about undesirability and the question about prohibition.

(P2) want-regarding theory alone for 'undesirability', but ideal-regarding theory for 'prohibition'.

(P3) opposite of P2, i.e. ideal-regarding theory for 'undesirability', but want-regarding theory alone for 'prohibition'.

(P4) ideal-regarding theory for both 'undesirability' and 'prohibition'.

As before, one can be ruled out: as far as I know, no one has ever espoused (P2), making questions of taste, belief, action or what not, relevant for political but not moral evaluation. We are thus left with three combinations.

Let us take (P1). We know that the same grounds will be held relevant for both the moral and the political judgement. If, therefore, it is held that consenting adult homosexuals do nobody else any harm, there can be no reason for coming to any conclusion other than (C4). If, on the other hand, it is held that they do harm to others, it does not follow immediately that homosexual acts should be prohibited, because prohibition brings many evils in its train—the punishment itself, blackmail, possible corruption of the police and so on. The result here may therefore be either (C1) or (C2) depending on how the person making the evaluation weighs the respective evils of permitting and prohibiting the wrong.

Skipping (P2), which we have ruled out, turn to someone whose position is (P3). This is the man who applies a double standard in his evaluations: he sometimes makes his private judgements on grounds which do not treat all wants as equal, but he is unwilling to impose such judgements by force on others. He may or may not think that homosexuality is wrong in itself, but this does not, in theory, affect his judgement on the desirability of prohibiting it. In deciding the political question, therefore, he simply goes through the same process as the man whose position is (P1). Like him he may finish with C1, C2 or C4. In fact, his only difference is that he has an alternative route to C2, since it is open to him to decide that homosexual practices are undesirable (on ideal grounds) even though they do not affect other people.

Finally consider someone who holds that ideal-regarding considerations are relevant both to the judgement about the desirability of homosexuality and the one about prohibiting it (P4). If he decides that the practice of homosexuality is neither bad for those immediately concerned nor for anyone else, he can reach the conclusion (C4) that it is neither undesirable nor should it be prohibited. But if he decides that it is undesirable, this is for him a *prima facie* reason for prohibiting it. Unlike someone whose premises are of the P3 kind, he does not have to see whether there is a want-regarding case against it before wishing for prohibition. At the same time, he will not necessarily arrive at the C1 conclusion in favour of prohibition, for he might still hold that legal measures would be either ineffective or counterbalanced by other considerations of an ideal-regarding nature such as the risk of blackmail and police corruption. He might thus arrive at the C2 conclusion, that it was undesirable but should not be prohibited.

I have tried to show in this brief and necessarily somewhat artificial analysis that in the hands of different people any of the three conclusions may follow from any of the three premises, depending upon their estimates of the facts of the situation and the precise principles which they invoke.

5. IMPOTENCE OF IDEALS IN POLITICS

In the remainder of this chapter I shall assess two kinds of argument frequently used in support of the 'liberal' position. The first in its simplest form consists of the view that it is futile to employ state power for ideal ends, because character and belief cannot be changed by the use of state power: but this is simply false. Even if the adults are relatively impervious to such efforts, the next generation can certainly be reached. Hitler and the Jesuits both agreed that provided they could get control over children at an early enough age they could guarantee results.[1]

[1] ' "When an opponent declares, 'I will not come over to your side,' " he [Hitler] said in a speech on November 6, 1933, "I calmly say, 'Your child belongs to us already . . . What are you? You will pass on. Your descendants, however, now stand in the new camp. In a short time they will know nothing else but this new community.' " And on May 1, 1937, he declared, "This new

The argument can however be stated more carefully to the effect that no *good* results in terms of character or belief can be produced by political means; so there can be no gains on the 'ideal' side to put forward. If we considered 'political means' as bounded by crude coercion applied to adults, it might perhaps be true. But what about state supported provision of education to children? What about state subsidized or free access to books, music, art, etc.? What about attempts to raise the level of public taste by state control of the design of new buildings?

Suppose though that someone says: 'I refuse to allow that any change in anyone's character can be counted desirable unless it is a result of his own (free, autonomous) decision.' This would, I think, rule out any serious intervention by the state which was actuated purely by ideal considerations; but it is important to realize that someone who makes a statement such as this is in fact *admitting* the relevance of ideal-regarding criteria for political evaluation. For the ground invoked in his statement must itself be an ideal one. This can, I think, be seen if one considers that on the want-regarding theory the only thing that matters is the quantity and distribution (among persons) of want-satisfaction. How these wants originated is irrelevant; the only reason allowed for regarding the satisfaction of one want as more important than the satisfaction of another is that its felt intensity is greater. If this theory is adopted then surely manipulation of wants by the state is in itself neither to be praised nor condemned. It should be praised if it has the result of improving the quantity or distribution of want-satisfaction, and condemned if it results in a deterioration of those factors; but manipulation *per se* is neutral.

On the want-regarding theory, then, the only bad manipulation is unsuccessful manipulation.

> A society is free so far as the behavior it makes appropriate and natural for its citizens—the behavior they feel is good—is also the behavior its controls demand of them.[1]

[1] George C. Homans, *The Human Group* (New York, 1950), pp. 332–333.

Reich will give its youth to no one, but will itself take youth and give to youth its own education and its own upbringing." It was not an idle boast; that was precisely what was happening.' William L. Shirer, *The Rise and Fall of the Third Reich* (Crest Reprint, 1962), p. 343.

Perfect manipulation, which arouses no hostility and makes people want nothing but what they are going to be given anyway, is an excellent practice, on the want-regarding theory; yet on an ideal-regarding theory which makes autonomy its ideal, the more smoothly effective the manipulation is, the worse it is. Aldous Huxley's *Brave New World,* where the process of conditioning has been brought to such a pitch of perfection that nobody is ever dissatisfied with his lot in life, gets its sting exactly from the fact that on the want-regarding theory this *is* utopia.

6. IRRELEVANCE OF IDEALS IN POLITICS

6.A. *Introduction.* What I referred to at the beginning of Section 5 as the second argument against ideals in politics is perhaps better described as a diffuse bundle of misgivings than an argument. At the core of it is an idea which might be crudely put as: 'Why should one lot of people tell another lot of people what to do if the others aren't hurting them?' Or, even more crudely, 'Why don't people just mind their own business?' Nobody has any business on this view to impose his own ideals on others; Jones' opinions on what would make Brown a better man are, politically speaking, impertinent and irrelevant.[1]

What underlies this view is a rejection of any suggestion that an ideal-regarding judgement should be treated as anything other than a peculiar kind of want. If Jones believes that people would get more out of life if they developed a taste for, say, the theatre, this can be translated for purposes of the political calculus into 'Jones wants people to go to the theatre'. Once the translation has been made along these lines the question immediately presents itself:

[1] The view just presented has a strong connection logically and historically with the contractarian tradition of political theory. In this tradition, the only reason for accepting the coercion applied by the state is the advantage of collective self-defence. Any use of the state machinery for purposes beyond these constitutes an infringement of the contract. Locke explicitly moves from the terms of the contract to the conclusion that the state's job should be limited to police functions and specifically that it should not trouble itself with the souls of the citizens. (This is especially clear in the *Letter Concerning Toleration.*) J. S. Mill's famous 'sole right' passage in *On Liberty* does not use the contract framework but rests on exactly the same idea that the state is a justifiable device only while it acts as an agent of 'collective security'. However, Mill's thought is so rich (some might say 'muddled') that he by no means rests his case entirely on this ground in *On Liberty.*

why should people be encouraged to go to the theatre just because Jones wants them to? (Or for that matter because sixty per cent of the population want them to?) Given the question posed in this way it is not too difficult to find a reason for saying that this kind of want should carry no claim to satisfaction.[1] If an ideal-regarding judgement is to be treated as a want, then it must obviously be a publicly-oriented want rather than a privately-oriented want. But, as I have already argued in the latter part of 3.C., publicly-oriented wants do not seem to be candidates for satisfaction merely *qua* wants in the same way as privately-oriented wants do. Jones' want for some future state of Jones might well be thought to be worthy of a quite different sort of consideration from Jones' want for some future state of Brown.[2]

If once the equation of an ideal and a certain kind of publicly-oriented want is admitted, the case for the irrelevance of ideal-regarding judgements becomes a strong one. But need we accept this equation? Why not simply say that there are ideals *and* wants, without trying to reduce the former to a special case of the latter? In the rest of this section I shall try to move away from the picture of implementing ideal-regarding judgements politically as one wherein one person *imposes* his own (publicly-oriented) wants on another and put the emphasis rather on the working out of ideals as a co-operative business in which economic, social and political institutions may well have an important part to play. Although the distinction is not likely to be a sharp one in practice I shall for my own analytical purposes divide the discussion into two parts. In the first part (6.B. and 6.C.) I shall consider cases where someone might reasonably wish to advance his own ideal-regarding judgements. In the second part (6.D.) I shall deal with instances where a man might reasonably be prepared to see others advancing *their* ideal-regarding judgements even when he is personally affected.

6.B. *Supporting One's Own Ideals Politically (i)*. Under what circumstances, then, might someone say 'This society would be a better one if a taste for so-and-so were encouraged' and follow this up by making the *political* judgement 'The state should be used to encourage a taste for so-and-so'? Let me start by taking the case

[1] For an analysis of Mr Hare's treatment of the question in *Freedom and Reason* see Note D on page 295.

[2] This point is further examined in Note E on page 297.

where someone wishes to cultivate the taste in question in himself, and believes that bringing in the state will be the most effective means to this end. Why should anyone ever believe such a thing? Why should anyone wish to tie himself down to making a change in his character which he wants anyway? The answer to this question is that someone may wish to modify his tastes or character but not trust himself to be able to carry out the change unaided. Suppose that there happen to be a large number of such people with respect to a particular matter within a certain political unit. Suppose also that while fearing that they lack the will-power to make in constantly recurring situations the decisions required to produce the change individually (e.g. give up smoking) they think they could summon up enough will-power to vote for a law (or for someone pledged to vote for the law if elected) which will have the effect of changing the structure of incentives with which they are faced every time the choice situation occurs. It would surely be on the face of it rational for this group to press for collective, political action on the matter.[1] As a simple example we might take the one used in III.3.B.: taxing whisky and subsidizing the theatre with the proceeds. It might be rational to vote for this if one were afraid that one would drink too much whisky unless the price were made artificially high, and also afraid that one would not patronise the theatre enough if one had to pay an economic price for the seats. (Modification of prices by tax or subsidy is of course one obvious way of 'changing the structure of incentives'.)

My motive in starting with this kind of case is, I imagine, fairly transparent. Rather than the *prima facie* objectionable situation where one lot of people use the state to impose their ideals on others we have here a situation where people use the state to 'impose' ideals on themselves. It may perhaps be argued that what I have just set out is not an example of a publicly-oriented ideal-regarding judgement at all, but a publicly-oriented want-regarding judgement where the (privately-oriented) wants in question happen to be privately-oriented ideals. I do not object too strongly to this conclusion since the cases I introduce in the rest of the section are unequivocally of publicly-oriented ideal-regarding judgements.

---

[1] Putting the point in a rather grand way reminiscent of Bernard Bosanquet in his *The Philosophical Theory of the State* (London, 1899) one might say that the state could thus embody the best and steadiest judgement of its citizens.

However, I do not in fact think the conclusion is warranted even here, for two reasons.

The proposed alternative classification of the judgement seems to misrepresent what I envisage to be its grounds. I have not been putting forward the case of someone who says: 'So many people want this change made so as to further their privately-oriented ideals that it had better be made so as to satisfy them.' What I have been dealing with is a hypothetical instance of someone saying: 'Since it is a good thing for such-and-such a taste to be encouraged, in myself as well as others, and collective action is the best means of doing so, I should welcome collective action in the matter.'

A man who said this would be, in the technical sense mentioned earlier (3.A.), a 'dictator' in that he would regard voting purely as the means to his end. However, even if we weaken the example and suppose that the man wishes the ideal to be implemented only if there is a majority in favour, the case still does not necessarily collapse into the one I specifically rejected in the previous paragraph. This is because he might hold, as many have, that people make 'better' choices when they make them as citizens than when they make them as private persons, so that the results of n people voting would be 'better' than those of the same n people deciding as private persons.[1] 'Better' here obviously refers to the *content* of the wants expressed in the two kinds of situation, so it is plain that we have here too an ideal-regarding publicly-oriented judgement.

6.C. *Supporting One's Own Ideals Politically (ii)*. If 'ought' implies 'can' then presumably the view that the state *ought* to be neutral between ideals implies that the state *can* be neutral between ideals. The state, on the liberal view, must be capable of fulfilling the same self-effacing function as a policeman on point-duty, who facilitates the motorists' getting to their several destinations without bumping into one another but does not have any power to influence those destinations.[2] If the state, unlike the policeman,

---

[1] For material cited in support of the view that collective decisions elicit different responses from individual ones see Note F on page 299.

[2] Since the idea of the 'night watchman state' is associated with *laissez faire* I should perhaps make it clear that conceptually liberalism as defined here does not entail *laissez faire* or even the 'mixed' economy. The only thing on which it insists is that the state should be conceived as satisfying wants arising independently of its influence.

cannot help but modify the destinations which its citizens desire to reach, then it seems very difficult to argue that it is unjustifiable to raise the question whether the way in which the state modifies wants is the best way; and that, of course, is an ideal-regarding judgement with clear implications for political action.[1]

I shall argue in the present subsection that the state cannot avoid influencing at many points what it is that people want; and my own view is that at these points it is quite right to ask whether the state's influence is for the best and to be prepared to support political changes corresponding to one's ideal-regarding publicly-oriented judgements. My argument against the possibility of the state's total neutrality falls into two parts: firstly, I shall argue that wants depend on the social environment and then secondly I shall argue that the social environment depends on the state.

The dependence of wants on the social environment is a com-monplace of sociology, which could almost be defined as the intellectual consequences of taking it seriously. What Parsons called the 'sociologistic theorem' is precisely the idea that wants (tastes, characters) are neither 'random' with respect to the rest of the social environment nor totally determined biologically.[2] Every culture has its own built-in pressures towards certain approved patterns of wants and away from others which are either disapproved or regarded as insignificant. To define from scratch for oneself a pattern of wants is a strenuous (and, beyond a certain point, impossible) undertaking: indeed it may take so much energy as to leave little over for anything else. It is therefore hardly to be wondered at if every society provides ready-made patterns. If we wish to find out what these are in a particular society we have to ask questions such as: how much money is spent in promoting tastes of various kinds (e.g. cigarette advertis-ing as against subsidies to the arts)? What kinds of people are looked up to, envied or counted as having 'succeeded' (saints, sages or property speculators)? When people talk about 'progress' what do they mean by it (better conduct, better taste, or more cars

[1] Difficult, perhaps, but by no means impossible. If someone insists that it makes good sense to him to say 'We know such-and-such a want arises from a certain feature of the state; but we mustn't ask whether it is a good thing for the state to have that effect' I do not see what further can be said to him.

[2] See Talcott Parsons, *The Structure of Social Action* (Glencoe, Ill., 1949). Leslie Stephen's statement of the view and its political implications still reads freshly. See *The English Utilitarians*, vol. III (London, 1900), pp. 289–297.

per capita)? What is the aim of the schools taken to be ('character', religious or political orthodoxy, learning, or making friends, influencing people and fitting into a well-paid niche in the economy)?

Consider one of the most worked-over, as well as important, examples: the interdependence of character and economic system. Economic development (to take only one aspect) involves far more than supplying goods and services more plentifully; over a few generations it remakes the whole society and the personalities of those in it.[1] Tastes for consumption are altered, by the availability of entirely new goods, by advertising, and by sharp changes in relative prices.[2] The traditional family structure, and very likely traditional religious and political institutions, crumble. Urbanization and industrialism between them change the entire environment in which life is spent.

Again, capitalism requires and nurtures a tendency to personal acquisitiveness and to doing only those things (except for friends and relatives who are 'seen' in an entirely different way) which can be charged for. Life is seen as a matter of 'every man for himself'. Conversely, it is possible to imagine an economic system in which all these were reversed.

> The difficulty of a Soviet couple who fled to the United States in getting used to *meschanstvo* ('living for oneself, without regard for one's brother') and in doing without *yacheiki* ('societies which give one an opportunity to work for collectivity-oriented ends') were described in *The New Yorker* of 16 February 1952. For example, the wife, who worked for Horn & Hardart, was impelled to hold forth to her fellow employees on the great responsibility they all had to keep thousands of residents of the city healthy by supplying them with good food.[3]

Another example is that of the relation between a religion and the other institutions of a society. T. S. Eliot denies, in line with the argument being presented here, that a society can be 'neutral' between Christianity and 'paganism'.

[1] The causal influence of course goes in both directions; I am emphasizing the direction relevant here.

[2] In particular, manufactures become cheaper and services become expensive. See T. Scitovsky, 'What Price Economic Progress?', *Yale Review* (1960).

[3] E. A. Shils and E. C. Banfield, 'Individual Ends and the Structure of Social Choice' (unpublished paper).

The mass of the population, in a Christian society, should not be exposed to a way of life in which there is too sharp and frequent a conflict between what is easy for them or what their circumstances dictate and what is Christian. The compulsion to live in such a way that Christian behaviour is only possible in a restricted number of situations, is a very powerful force against Christianity; for behaviour is as potent to affect belief, as belief to affect behaviour. We must abandon the notion that the Christian should be content with freedom of cultus, and with suffering no worldly disabilities on account of his faith. However bigoted the announcement may sound, the Christian can be satisfied with nothing less than a Christian organisation of society—which is not the same thing as a society consisting exclusively of devout Christians. It would be a society in which the natural end of man—virtue and well-being in community—is acknowledged for all, and the supernatural end—beatitude—for those who have the eyes to see it.[1]

It seems to me that Eliot's assertions here can be equally well accepted by Christians and non-Christians, though they will of course draw opposing practical conclusions.[2]

The second stage of the argument can be presented quickly. It simply involves pointing out that social and economic institutions usually have a legal basis. Thus, to continue the economic example, just as the type of economic system inevitably helps determine the sorts of things people want, so the type of economic system a country has depends in the end on its laws and the actions (or inactions) of its government. Because (as Alfred Marshall put it) 'wants are related to activities', choosing an economic system is not merely choosing a machine for satisfying wants but rather choosing a machine for *producing* certain wants in the future. It is

[1] 'The Idea of a Christian Society' in *Christianity and Culture* (Harvest Book, n.d.), pp. 24 and 27.

[2] For example, I find Eliot's 'Christian society' as described by him repulsive, but I have no difficulty in believing that nothing less would suffice to make Christianity a living reality in most people's lives today. Of course, if God (i.e. Eliot's dismal utopia) were the only alternative to 'Hitler or Stalin' (p. 50) one might reluctantly choose Him in preference to them. But with virtually the entire world moving towards a kind of society markedly different from all three, such a view of the alternatives is extraordinarily implausible. Nor is a modern 'pagan' tradition which boasts works of such noble humanism as Mill's *Utilitarianism* so devoid of content as Eliot suggests.

therefore inevitably a choice to be made partly on ideal grounds.[1] But because any economic system must rest on a legal foundation the choice of an economic system must be in the end a political one. To refuse the opportunity to choose is to opt for the *status quo* without taking responsibility for doing so.

In the special case where political institutions themselves are the subject of discussion the two stages of the argument collapse into one, and it is only necessary to show that political institutions themselves have effects on character; and this is not too difficult to do. Thus, an authoritarian political system will obviously tend to induce a different sort of character from a democratic one, over a long period of time. (One might, for example, correlate the attitude of Americans, Englishmen and Germans to petty regulations such as 'Keep Off the Grass' with their political histories). Even if we confine our attention to political systems which are broadly democratic in form, we can still distinguish very different effects on character among them.[2] One, for example, will make active participation in politics virtually impossible except for the professional politician; another will make participation easy, but only for limited and 'private' objectives; yet another will encourage participation based rather on 'public' grounds.[3]

It should be noticed, finally, that a special twist must be given to the argument to deal with the special questions raised by the upbringing of children. If a society consisted entirely of adults who never died and never had children the liberal presupposition, though as we have seen not completely accurate, might be sufficiently so for many practical purposes. But it is patently obvious that how children turn out depends largely on their upbringing. The complication is that it is indeed possible for the state to take

---

[1] Talcott Parsons in *The Structure of Social Action* shows acutely that Marshall defended *laissez faire* on frankly ideal grounds, as producing a desirably independent and resourceful kind of man, just because he saw that wants are not an exogenous factor. Cf. Paul Streeten in Myrdal, *Political Element* . . . .

[2] For some fascinating survey material on Britain, USA, West Germany, Italy and Mexico relevant to this point see Gabriel Almond and Sidney Verba, *The Civic Culture* (Princeton, 1963).

[3] 'Each citizen is [for Mill] to have a share both in the legislative and administrative functions of the government. Such an education must have a strong influence on the moral characteristics. It may promote or discourage one morality or another, but it cannot be indifferent.' Stephen, *English Utilitarians*, III, p. 291. See also Note F on page 299.

no responsibility for how children turn out; however, whereas with adults it can be claimed with some shòw of plausibility that absence of state intervention leaves people to pursue their own goals, with children it simply means handing them over to parents, private schools, churches, scout troops or any other organization that can get hold of them. Here then the state *can* indeed be neutral; but neutrality simply involves underwriting the moulding activities of others.[1] Now to what extent the state should be involved in the upbringing of children is not at issue here (one obvious answer is that it depends how good the state is and how good the parents and private organizations are) but at least it can be said that the case against the state's being used deliberately to affect character becomes very weak where children are concerned. For the question here is not *whether* deliberate attempts should be made to modify character, but merely *who* should carry out the attempts and in virtue of what title (parent or citizen) he should do it.[2] A child is equally subject to the ideal-regarding judgements of other people whether the *locus* of decision is the political community or some smaller and less inclusive group.

6.D. *Supporting Others' Ideals Politically.* Following the plan set out in 6.A. I shall try now to suggest circumstances in which it might be reasonable for someone to welcome another person's putting into effect that person's own ideal-regarding publicly-oriented judgements. This possibility does not depend on the idea that some men are born to rule; nor does it require that there be different social classes set off from one another by marks of status and deference. What it does depend on is an admission that certain people have, in specific matters, better taste and judgement than others and should be given the chance to exercise them actively.

The best way to see what this admission involves is to examine the consequences of rejecting it. If, for all practical purposes, everyone's taste and everyone's opinion is to be taken as the equal

---

[1] 'Parental choice ranks lower for many than giving children access to the cultural heritage which is theirs. In a given context, truth, beauty and goodness are not necessarily matters of choice.' John Vaizey, *The Economics of Education* (London, 1962), p. 32.

[2] By 'modifying character' I do not mean only indoctrination and 'character training'. The expression as I am using it would equally cover the inculcation of scepticism and autonomy. (Some of the questions raised when one tries to *save* children from indoctrination are discussed in VII.2.C. in the context of the state's relation to church schools.)

of everyone else's, the only criterion of goodness is, as I have pointed out, the satisfaction of wants. Everything is to be looked at from the point of view of a 'consumer' with his 'demand': he who pays the piper, not he who can tell one note from another, calls the tune.

In a society where this assumption is widespread we might expect to find that 'public opinion' will be very important politically, even on matters such as the advisability of running a budget deficit where untrained opinions are worthless. We might expect to find that elected officials are mistrusted if they attempt to act on their own initiative, and that where a matter such as building a new school or a new park requires a majority in a referendum, the electors will often refuse to follow the recommendation of the people they have entrusted with office.[1] It will not be unusual for congregations to sack their preacher if they disagree with the opinions that he has expressed publicly on such issues as segregation. Schoolteachers will be told what textbooks to use by politicians, and what to teach by politicians, parents and children. Universities supported by public funds will be expected to teach only the views and employ only the persons agreeable to those who pay the taxes. The aesthetic judgement (if any) of speculative builders will be more significant for the face of the cities than the judgement of the town planner or the public architect. The content of television programmes will be controlled by the sponsors, themselves anxious not to arouse the susceptibilities of any portion of the audience by the inclusion of controversial matter; any attempt to reduce the amount of inanity and violence will be widely construed (not only by the companies concerned) as 'censorship' or even 'dictatorship'. It would be disingenuous to deny that these examples are all drawn from the USA though many of them could be found elsewhere as well. There are, of course, other phenomena in the USA which point in a different direction; but still, the USA has drunk deeper of the 'liberal' anti-ideals-in-politics philosophy than any other country.

[1] *The New York Times* (Sunday, 26 August 1962, p. 42) contains a story entitled 'Voters Resistant Over Bond Issues' which indicates that about one proposal out of every three made by elected representatives is turned down in a referendum. On one occasion known to me a majority of the electors of a state turned down in a referendum the most important item in the platform of the man it had just elected governor, which was a large bond issue for school improvement.

The alternative to a society of the kind depicted would be one where the institutions and the traditions worked towards giving a great deal of scope to the professional and personal integrity of the qualified, enabling and encouraging them to live up to their own highest standards. Once commissioned (to teach, to write, to produce a television show, to plan a new civic centre) the person entrusted with the job would be left to his responsibility rather than checked at every step by those employing him. The theory of representation would lean on Burke and John Stuart Mill rather than on a rubber-stamp theory of the legislator's job.[1]

As I pointed out at the beginning of this chapter (Section 1), the only way of deciding between the most general principles is to look at their concrete implications. This I have done and I can only leave it to the reader to decide on that basis which set of implications he prefers. In the rest of this section I shall only try to show that if he prefers the sound of the second set, he must abandon liberalism as I have defined it. In other words I shall try to show that the second society can be defended only on ideal-regarding lines. The method used is argument by elimination: I shall argue that no want-regarding principle or combination of want-regarding principles can adequately support the second kind of society.

Take first aggregative principles. On such principles the only time that the competent 'expert' should be given a free hand would be when his desire for it was stronger than the desire of his customers or employers for something other than what he thought best. But the results of following this rule would not be at all the same as that of following the ideal-regarding rule. Suppose for example that there are two architects, one totally incompetent but liable to get very hot under the collar if his designs are not accepted, the other an easy-going genius who can turn out excellent work but

---

[1] For recent moderate statements of the Burkean position see Nigel Nicolson, *People and Parliament* (London, 1958) and Stimson Bullitt, *To Be A Politician* (Anchor, 1961), esp. Chapter IV. Notice that both of them make a distinction between cases where a politician is asked to represent his locality by trying to get concrete local benefits, and matters of principle. Both agree that it is legitimate to follow the wishes of constituents in the first kind of case but that a politician should be prepared to stand out against pressure if necessary in the second kind of case. This supports the view taken here to the effect that privately-oriented wants carry a certain claim to satisfaction *qua* wants, whereas publicly-oriented wants make a claim not as being wanted but as being right.

who doesn't care much whether or not his designs are used; in fact, let us say, he is as happy turning out stuff that he knows to be third rate as he is following his own standards. On the aggregative version of the want-regarding theory the first architect ought often to get his way in a dispute with clients since he will often feel so strongly as to counterbalance their lukewarm opposition. The second architect ought never to get his way in a dispute because he doesn't care what design is adopted. On an ideal-regarding basis the reverse would be true: the good architect should be given a free hand because he is good—whether or not he feels strongly about it has nothing to do with it; the bad architect would be ignored like the unenlightened layman however strongly he felt.

Can any distributive principle do better? The most promising line seems to me to be to say that the competent person should have a free hand as a *reward* for competence and influence. This is less grotesquely irrelevant than the last theory, but it still will not do. A reward is anything which the person wants, given him in virtue of some achievement. Since the only point is to provide some want-satisfaction, it need not take the specific form of giving him a free hand. It would be quite satisfactory, for example, to offer someone a choice between publishing something he has written and a sum of money to suppress it. If he prefers the latter then it is obviously a better reward. Indeed, the publicity consequent upon gaining influence might make it actually painful to some people. Clearly, influence would not be a reward at all to such a man.

The alternative distributive line is simply to assert that everyone has a 'right' to exercise his talents if he wants to, without interference from others. Like the other want-regarding arguments that we have been considering, this one bases itself on the 'want' of the producer for influence or recognition rather than the benefit (conceived in ideal-regarding terms) that the rest of the society may get if it allows him a free hand. It therefore falls into the same trap as the others: it cannot deal adequately with the case of the talented person who has no strong feelings about exercising his talents, or the untalented person who does have strong feelings about it.

Even more seriously, it degrades the exercise of talent from a contribution *to* society into a right claimed *against* society. And when it is put forward as a privilege rather than an opportunity for service it is hard to see why it should be granted. For what has to be claimed is by no means simply the right to be let alone in matters which do not directly affect others; it is the right to affect others profoundly by modifying their tastes and beliefs. Though one might say that the second society is marked by professional freedom, the expression is misleading if it suggests something purely negative. Certainly it involves non-interference by employers and customers; but what they have to refrain from interference in is the use of their money for attempts to alter them, whether they like those attempts or not![1] The difference between what I am talking about and the usual 'civil liberties' can be illustrated by considering 'freedom of speech'. This phrase is usually interpreted to mean that everyone has the right to say and write (subject to limitations such as libel and obscenity) what he likes without legal action being taken against him. The 'ideal' equivalent to this, however, is that facilities be available for those with something important to say to say it with the maximum impact. Thus, it would be concerned with such things as sponsors pressing for changes in a television documentary or newspaper owners telling editors what line to take on an issue; neither of which can be plausibly represented as a personal 'right' of the television producer or newspaper editor. Just as 'there is no constitutional right to be a policeman' so there is no *right* to be a communist schoolteacher or an independently-minded editor. It is only on ideal-regarding lines that these can be defended.[2]

[1] Past treatments of this problem, and especially the fairly modern one which analyses it with the aid of the concept of 'mass society' are discussed in Note G on page 300.

[2] See Chapter VIII for a discussion of 'freedom'. A point relevant to the present topic is the dependence of freedom, even in the minimal 'civil liberties' sense, upon the minority exercising leadership, and especially upon the professions. See Robert E. Lane, 'The Fear of Equality', *American Political Science Review*, LIII (1959) for a theoretical discussion and Samuel Stouffer, *Communism, Conformity and Civil Liberties* (New York, 1955) for some American statistics showing that the average leader, even of organizations such as the Daughters of the American Revolution or the American Legion, is better disposed towards civil liberties than the rest of the population, on average. (The study is summarized by Lipset and Glazier in Bell (ed.) *The New American Right* (New York, 1955): 'The Polls on Communism and Conformity'.

V

TYPES OF SOCIAL DECISION PROCEDURE

1.A. *Why Study Procedures?* The next chapter begins the analysis of particular words and expressions which are used in the course of defending or attacking policies, laws and institutions in Britain and the USA. The only thing remaining to be done before going on to this is to provide a sketch of the various procedures by which conflicts may be settled, and that is the business of this fairly short chapter. A grasp of the variety of possible procedures contributes to the fruitfulness of an analysis of principles in two related ways. First, it is worth bearing in mind that the method of resolving a disagreement on some specific question of 'who gets what, when, how' whereby one side wins over the other by its invocation (or its interpretation) of some principle(s) on which they are both agreed, is by no means the most common. Moreover, it is not even the most common context in which principles are used: principles themselves are more often used in wholesale than retail contexts, in other words not to resolve particular conflicts but to settle the way in which (and, where relevant, the rule according to which) all future conflicts are to be resolved. And second, the exact significance of a word such as 'fair' depends upon whether it is being used in connection with an attempt to resolve a particular conflict or in connection with setting up a procedure to resolve conflicts; and in the former case it depends a great deal what procedure is being applied to the conflict in question.

1.B. *Conflict and Procedure.* Conflict, on my definition, arises wherever two or more actors have incompatible desires (including publicly-oriented wants for this purpose) concerning the future state of the world, and try to do something about it. Thus, if I ask

£2 for the bicycle I am endeavouring to sell and you offer only £1, we are in a state of conflict. I desire a state of the world in which £2 changes hands in return for the bicycle while you desire a state of the world in which £1 changes hands in return for the bicycle; and these are obviously incompatible desires. 'Conflict' is thus opposed to 'spontaneous coincidence of wills', which is what would happen if I had in mind asking 30s. and you had in mind offering the same sum. No harm should come of this extended use of 'conflict' provided irrelevant images of physical violence are not allowed to get in the way of what is being talked about.

Where two actors (they may be individuals, organizations or states) arrive at incompatible desires by taking different reference-groups (see I.3.C. for this concept) it may be possible to resolve the conflict if they both take a wider reference-group, which includes them both. For example, if I have set my price by deciding what would suit me best and you have set your offer by deciding what would suit you best we may both decide spontaneously that a 'fair' price (taking both of us as a reference group) would be something between my privately-oriented price and your privately-oriented offer. This would then become our first preference and we would have arrived at a 'spontaneous coincidence of wills'.

However, the actors may not spontaneously reach the same decision even if they are using the same reference group; and of course they may well *not* use the same reference group. It is in these cases that procedures come in. The actors may argue about the rights and wrongs of the matter; they may make threats, fight, toss up or vote; they may have a contest of some kind (agreeing in advance to let the result determine the outcome in some way); or they may agree to hand the decision over to somebody else. Finally, one actor may settle the question unilaterally, invoking his authority to do so. It is to a review of these possibilities that I now turn.

2. AN OUTLINE OF SOCIAL DECISION PROCEDURES

(1) *Combat.* The first way in which disputes may be settled is by one side forcing the other into submission by fighting it, starving it and so on, in short by making it preferable to the other side to give in rather than to resist. This procedure is rarely ever used by itself. At the least, one or both sides will usually attempt to achieve

its ends by threatening to impose sanctions rather than by imposing them first; and very often in addition there is discussion on merits as well. For example, the relations between states (where there is a conspicuous lack of settled means for deciding disputes) are a tissue of moral and legal arguments, threats and manoeuvres designed to make the threats plausible, and actual attempts at coercion.

(2) *Bargaining*. The second possible procedure is bargaining, by which I mean to refer to any discussion into which the merits of the question are not introduced. Within this area of bargaining there is a distinction to be made upon which an entire metaphysic of liberalism has been based, namely between bargaining where the only sanction is not coming to a deal and bargaining which involves threats.[1] In the first case, the two sides are simply left where they were before if no agreement is reached, but in the second case one side at least says that it will make the other worse off than it was at the start unless it accepts certain terms. So far the definition of 'bargaining' given includes talking as a necessary part of it, and this is I think the normal use of the word. Analytically, however, the presence or absence of discussion is of no significance. If the shopkeeper puts up a placard with a price written on it and the buyer offers him that amount, the situation is analytically identical with that which would have obtained if they haggled about it.[2] I shall therefore extend 'bargaining' to cover any situation where one party offers another either some advantage or the removal of the threat of some disadvantage in return for the other party's performing some specific action.[3]

At first sight 'contract' might appear more suitable than 'bargaining', but it is both too wide and too narrow. It is too wide because contracts may be reached on any grounds—including discussion of the merits. It is too narrow because the results of

[1] Cf. von Mises, *Human Action*; and Hayek, *The Constitution of Liberty* (London, 1960). The distinction also plays an important part in the law of contract according to which duress invalidates a contract.

[2] Does 'bargaining' in this case collapse into 'spontaneous coincidence of wills?' Not necessarily, for the buyer might like to charge more and the consumer to pay less and each be deterred by the 'sanction' of not making an exchange.

[3] 'Threatening', like 'bargaining', as normally conceived has a linguistic element in it; but we certainly use it for non-verbal threats as in 'threatening someone with a gun'. It is the wider sense which is relevant here.

'bargaining' in neither the originally introduced sense nor the extended sense need be legally binding. Moreover, contracts are invalid in at least the most flagrant cases of agreement due to threats.[1]

(3) *Discussion on Merits.* As an 'ideal type' this involves the complete absence of threats and inducements; the parties to the dispute set out (from initially incompatible positions—otherwise we have 'spontaneous coincidence of wills') to reach an agreement on what is the morally right division, what policy is in the interests of all of them or will promote the most want-satisfaction, and so on. Also included are arguments about the correct interpretation of some rule or set of rules which the parties accept as providing the answer to their dispute. 'Negotiation' will be used to cover both bargaining and discussion on merits.

However difficult the line may be to draw in particular cases between discussion on merits and bargaining, it is easy to state in principle. If agreement is reached by means of discussion on merits, the parties to the dispute have changed their minds about what they want; even if one party had the power to get its way completely it would not want to change the solution. Agreement reached by means of bargaining, on the other hand, merely involves a recognition on the part of each side that it cannot hope to get more of what it wants than is represented by the settlement. But each side retains its wish for the solution it originally entertained and if it had the power to achieve that solution it would use it to that end. Of course, many (perhaps nearly all) negotiations involve both bargaining *and* discussion on merits, but this does not dissolve the difference because (*a*) there are still clear-cut cases and (*b*) even in the combined cases one can often distinguish the respective contributions to the agreement of bargaining and discussion on merits.

For example, in analysing a wage negotiation one might be able to say that the initial gap between the union's demand and the employer's offer was halved when each became genuinely convinced that its claim was excessive and its offer too low respectively; but that the other half of the gap was only mediated by the fact that each stood to lose by a strike. Or again, let us consider a jury deliberating. Part of their initial disagreement may be

[1] For a rejection of the view that 'the price mechanism' is a procedure see Note H on page 301.

resolved by one convincing another (as in 'Twelve Angry Men') but the remainder may be resolved by horse-trading: you say it's murder, I say he's innocent so we'll call it manslaughter. I choose this example deliberately to emphasize that bargaining is quite consistent with publicly-oriented attitudes. This is, I believe, completely consistent with ordinary usage: to say that a man is a tough bargainer is not necessarily to say that he uses his bargaining skills for selfish purposes (either his own or anyone else's). Indeed, he may be easy-going where privately-oriented matters are at stake but inflexible and unscrupulous in advancing ends which he conceives to be good.[1]

(4) *Voting*. Where there are more than two parties to a dispute one way of settling it is to take a vote on it. The vote may be a snap one, or it may be the culmination of a long process of negotiation.[2] Also (and a different distinction) it may be publicly- or privately-oriented. Voting may be open or secret. Any proportion over half may be required for a decision.[3] These various possibilities are mentioned here (without being dwelt on) because the pro's and con's of voting as a procedure in any given instance must depend on the precise form it takes, exactly as the precise set-up in a bargaining situation must be known before one can decide whether one approves of it or not.

(5) *Chance*. A quite different way of settling disputes is to employ some chance mechanism—tossing a coin, throwing dice, picking straws, etc. Perhaps the most important modern use of chance to decide how something should be allocated is the American use of an element of chance in the procedure by which men are chosen for military service. Generally, its use is somewhat peripheral (e.g. breaking a tie in elections) but it gives rise to an

---

[1] For a discussion of the status of 'compromise' see Note I on page 302.

[2] The difference between bargaining and discussion on merits is neatly illustrated here. Discussion on merits is as effective when the vote is secret as when it is open, because if someone is convinced that x is the right policy to vote for he will presumably vote for it whether or not anyone is looking over his shoulder. But bargaining is only of use where voting is open, for by definition someone swayed by bargaining is only convinced that it is better to do x than go without y or suffer z. Secret voting makes it impossible for anyone to associate y or z with x—unless of course he is willing to take the person's word.

[3] At unity we pass from 'voting' to multipartite negotiations. A body such as the UN Security Council has characteristics of both, because the veto introduces an element of negotiation as part of the constitution.

idea of fairness as arbitrariness which as we shall see below has ramifications beyond strictly chance procedures.

(6) *Contest.* Discussion on merits will sometimes take the form of a dispute as to which of the various parties is 'better at' something, and this may be inconclusive because each can bring forward certain evidence of past achievements to support his case. One way of settling the question is to set up a contest. This does not actually settle the original question, but it replaces it by another which is at least easier to settle; you may however claim that though you lost the contest this was because you were unlucky or had an off-day—you are still, in general, better. Subject to this qualification, though, it may be said that the easiest way to find out who can run a hundred yards fastest is to have a race; the easiest way to find out who is the best angler is to see who catches the most fish in an afternoon. Those faced with a question, 'Who is best at *x*', may thus settle for the rough but objective justice of a contest rather than, say, take all past performance as their criterion.

By a contest then I mean such things as a race, a boxing match, a competitive examination or a fishing contest. In general, a contest is a way of allocating something which makes the allocation depend on comparative achievement, those who are eligible for the allocation knowing in advance what the criterion of achievement is (number of fish, weight of largest fish, weight of total catch) and during what periods of time their efforts will count towards the result. (If the chairman of the fishing club announces at the *end* of the day's fishing that he will give £5 to the angler with the heaviest catch, that does not turn the afternoon's fishing retroactively into a contest.) A restriction on 'contest' in ordinary usage is that the amount to be allocated should remain somewhat invariant with respect to the quality of the field of contestants.[1] But in my use of the word, I wish to ignore this limitation, because everything I shall have to say about fixed-allocation contests will also apply to fixed-standard trials.

---

[1] I say *somewhat* invariant because we do ordinarily say that there is a contest even when the number of prizes (say) is reduced because of low quality. But if the number were also increased to whatever number was necessary to ensure that everyone who reached a certain standard got a prize of fixed amount, this would normally take it out of the realm of 'contest' and into that of, say, 'qualifying trial'.

(7) *Authoritative determination.* This, my final category, contrasts with the previous six in that in them the dispute was settled, if it was settled at all, by all the parties together.[1] 'Authoritative determination', however, I define as any resolution of a conflict by a party recognized by all of those concerned as legitimate. Both 'authority' and 'legitimacy' are words to conjure with and rather than plunge into a morass of definitional problems I shall try to elucidate the category of authoritative determination by contrasting it with those already introduced.

If two parties discuss their dispute on its merits and do not reach an agreement they may set up an arbitrator to decide between them and then present their respective cases to him. The situation then becomes an example of authoritative determination, the authority of the arbitrator arising unproblematically from the consent of the two parties involved. It will be noticed that I defined authoritative determination in such a way as to leave it open whether the party with authority is also one of the parties to the dispute or not. In this case he is not.

Now take instead a case where one party takes the initiative and acts unilaterally in a situation where another party is involved— e.g. a civil servant assesses someone's income tax or an Executive Council turns down someone's claim for replacement false teeth— the analogy here is not with discussion on merits but with bargaining, and very one-sided bargaining at that. This is the view at which one arrives by looking purely at the power relations involved. It was the view of the legal positivist John Austin and has been recently stated by N. W. Chamberlain.[2]

There is nothing *wrong* in classifying legislation as a species of bargaining; but at the same time if one is asking for a classification which will be useful in connection with an analysis of evaluations there are good reasons for not doing so. The difficulty of making precise the notions of authority and legitimacy does not mean that

[1] Voting (with a simple majority rule) and contest guarantee a decision one way or another, when once the step of setting them up has been taken; the other procedures do not.

[2] *A General Theory of Economic Process* (New York, 1955), p. 262: 'Sovereignty thus stands revealed as simply a bargaining power relationship, distinguished only by the special kinds of coercive powers available to the government to increase the other's cost of disagreement on its terms. ... To label the legislative process a form of bargaining is not intended as a figure of speech but as a precise classification.'

the difference between being stopped by a policeman and being stopped by an armed robber can be ignored. The usual reason why people obey laws is not because they are coerced but because they think the law is right, or because they think they should obey the law (except in extreme cases) whatever its content. If legislation backed by sanctions is 'bargaining', then legislation not backed by sanctions must go in a different category; yet from many points of view this difference hardly seems essential.

Finally let us compare authoritative determination with contest. It might be suggested that if two contestants set up an umpire this is not significantly different from two people who set up an arbitrator. But the sense in which the third party on the one hand and the parties directly concerned on the other may be said to 'determine' the result is different in the two cases. In the first case the skill and effort of the contestants (and some luck) is expected to determine the result; to say that the umpire determined the result would generally be thought a criticism either of the umpire or of the rules (for excessive vagueness). But in the second case it is quite all right to say that the arbitrator determined the result, and it would be a criticism of the arbitrator or the procedure to say that the relative skill of the parties in arguing their cases determined the result. In the second case what stands in the same relation to the decision as 'the skill and effort of the players' is 'the intrinsic goodness of their cases'.[1]

3. MIXED PROCESSES AND COMBINED PROCESSES

A single decision may involve more than one of the seven procedures just outlined. I shall say that in this case the process by which the decision is reached is a mixed one; it mixes two or more procedures. Thus, to take an example already mooted, a certain negotiation might be made up partly of merit-discussing moves and partly of bargaining moves. This process of reaching a decision would amount to a mixture of the two procedures. It is possible to imagine cases of decisions which would simultaneously satisfy almost any pair out of the seven possible categories though

[1] L. Fuller, 'The Forms and Limits of Adjudication', (unpublished paper), p. 16: 'The distinguishing characteristic of adjudication lies in the fact that it confers on the affected party a peculiar form of participation in the decision, that of presenting proofs and reasoned arguments for a decision in his favor.'

in practice the only other one of importance is probably a mixture of contest and authoritative determination. An example would be a local authority filling grammar school places partly on the results of a written test and partly on teachers' estimates of aptitude.

Mixed processes, though important in practice, are of little theoretical interest, and I have introduced them mainly in order to get clear the distinction between them and combinations of processes. One process (procedure or mixture of procedures) is combined with another if the two are distinct decisions yet one is a necessary condition of the other's occurrence. For example, the membership of some body will be chosen in a certain way and the body will then reach its decisions in a certain way. The choosing of the members is different from the members taking a certain decision, but unless the members had been chosen they could not have taken the decision.

Once we recognize that processes may be used 'end-on' we need a vocabulary to deal with the different *types of decisions*. So far I have concentrated attention on ground-floor decisions that a certain thing shall be done in a certain situation: unique determinations for specific disputes. But a decision may instead be not that a certain action be done but that future actions should satisfy certain general requirements. For example, there may be a decision that in future a certain rule will be followed, a certain principle be applied or a certain end be pursued. Another type of decision is a decision to appoint someone to a decision-making position. And lastly, there may be a decision to the effect that a certain process be used under some specified circumstances.[1]

Before giving examples, it would be as well to introduce a notation to refer to the various procedures and types of decision. The procedures will therefore be referred to by the numbers given them in Section 2 as follows:

1. Combat.
2. Bargaining.
3. Discussion on Merits.
4. Voting.
5. Chance.
6. Contest.
7. Authoritative Determination.

[1] Cf. Kenneth J. Arrow, *Social Choice and Individual Values* (New York, 1951), p. 90.

The types of decision will be given letters of the alphabet as follows:

S. Specific decisions resolving individual disputes.
R. Decisions that certain rules, principles or ends be adopted.
A. Appointments to decision-making jobs.
P. Decisions to employ a certain procedure.

Example (i)

A decision by a civil servant (S7) rests on an instruction from his superior covering such cases (R7) made on the strength of some delegated legislation (P7) authorized by an Act of Parliament which lays down the ends of the Act (R4) and the procedure for delegated legislation under it (P4). Both bargaining and discussion on merits may have underlain the vote (R2 and R3). The civil servants concerned are appointed after a competitive examination (A6) conducted by the Civil Service Commissioners, themselves appointed (let us say) by the Cabinet on a majority vote (A4). The Cabinet is responsible to the House of Commons (simplifying, say, A4) which is in turn elected (A4). The constitution can be changed, to all intents and purposes, by a simple majority of the House of Commons (P4).

Example (ii)

As a result of bargaining two people enter into a contract. A contract simultaneously sets out a rule for future action and a means of determining disputes (i.e. appeal to a court). It is therefore in this case (R2) and (P2). If there is a dispute about the requirements of the contract it is settled by a court (S7) of which the judge is appointed by a superior official (A7) or elected (as in some parts of the USA)—(A4). A contract is, in short, a means by which private citizens may place themselves under obligations having the force of law.[1] It is not itself a procedure, but a means of invoking one.

---

[1] The court may of course refuse to enforce the contract or read into it fictitious 'understandings' in order to arrive at an equitable result. If you bring in public procedures you also bring in, almost inevitably, public values.

VI

JUSTICE AND FAIRNESS

I. INTRODUCTION

IN the rest of this book, the main concern will be with want-regarding principles; this chapter and the following three will be mainly about distributive want-regarding principles, while the last six will be mainly about aggregative want-regarding principles. However, where a want-regarding principle runs parallel (or appears to run parallel) with an ideal-regarding principle I examine the relation between them. For example, in Chapter VII, I analyse the differences between the want-regarding principle of equality and the ideal-regarding principles of integration and non-discrimination; and in Chapter VIII, I discuss the various reasons—both want-regarding and ideal-regarding—that one might have for holding that certain kinds of personal freedom are desirable.

I have tried in the second half of Chapter IV to substantiate my view that although many people might assent to the 'liberal' view when it is stated in the abstract, far fewer would be prepared to agree with its implications in every single case.[1] If this view is correct, then it is a fair question (and not a hypothetical one—the point has been put to me) whether there is any point in making a detailed analysis of want-regarding principles. If conclusions drawn from want-regarding principles are always liable to modification on ideal grounds should one not write them off?

My answer to this is that the relation between want-regarding principles and ideal-regarding principles where the latter modify the former is not analogous to the relation between one explanatory theory and a superior one where the latter modifies the former. If it were, one could happily espouse the second and write the first

---

[1] See IV.4., 5. and 6. 'Liberalism' is defined in IV.4.A. as the belief that one should try to implement politically only want-regarding judgements—never ideal-regarding judgements.

off. A more apt analogy would be two forces acting in different directions on a single body. The second force certainly modifies the effect of the first force but this obviously does not mean that the second eliminates the first so that in predicting the path of the body one could ignore the first force. Unwinding the analogy: want-regarding principles do not cease to have any efficacy because they are not the only kind. If you insist you can call the conclusion indicated by want-regarding principles a first approximation, but only if you make it clear that the second approximation cannot be reached without passing through the first. People use want-regarding principles *and* ideal-regarding principles; there is no reason why these two kinds of principle should not be subject to the same trade-off relationships as any other values.[1]

This still leaves open the question whether it is justifiable to concentrate on want-regarding principles rather than ideal-regarding principles. Justifiable or not, my reason for doing so is that there seems to be more scope for saying something about want-regarding principles than about ideal-regarding principles. Many concepts of the former kind are in almost universal use and even when it is difficult to express their uses it is usually easy to tell whether one has done so correctly or not. Ideal-regarding concepts are far more idiosyncratic, fluctuating and vague so that it is only by a kind of courtesy that one can speak of 'ideal-regarding principles' at all.

This is not a mere accident; it lies in the nature of the difference between them. The need to reconcile conflicting wants is urgent and universal; and the range of principles that one can hit on to regulate the outcome seems to be fairly fixed. The implementation of ideal-regarding considerations has a less immediate bearing (in the short run at least) on societal survival; and the ideals themselves are liable to wide variation from one person to the next. Moreover, ideal-regarding principles tend to have very little structure compared with want-regarding principles. Once you have decided that a good kind of human being would have the qualities x, y and z and that this is a *political* judgement then everything else connected with it is either a question of means to that end or a question of trade-offs between this particular principle and others which you also hold and which, given the state of the world, compete

---

[1] The notion of trade-off relationships among values is explained and illustrated in I.2.

with it for scarce resources. Neither of these problems—real as they may well be—allows much scope for a general discussion.

At the beginning of the present section I said that the next few chapters would be concerned mainly with distributive want-regarding principles. This chapter will deal with Justice and Fairness, Chapter VII with Equality, Chapter VIII with Freedom and Chapter IX with Equity. However, before turning to some detailed remarks on Justice and Fairness let me interpolate here a rather tiresome but I am afraid unavoidable disquisition on the wider and narrower senses of 'justice', 'fairness' and 'equity'.

A rough analogy for the ways in which these three words have both wide and narrow senses would be provided by the way in which the word 'cat' is used indifferently for the domestic puss and the cat family (including lions, tigers, etc.). But this analogy greatly understates the complexity of the matter, for the three terms differ in both their narrow and their wide senses although the latter overlap. Very roughly, the position seems to be as follows: 'justice' in its wide sense includes all distributive considerations, whether comparative or absolute.[1] (This is the sense in which, for example, 'justice' is contrasted with 'expediency'.) 'Fairness' and 'equity' in their widest sense are usually used to indicate that some *comparative* distributive consideration is relevant (without saying which).

Equity (Chapter IX) has two narrow applications: firstly, it has a semi-technical use referring to modifications of general rules to meet special situations; and secondly, it is used in contexts where precise comparisons are made within a general distributive pattern which is not itself questioned. These are connected by the notion of 'interstitial' criticism. The subject of this chapter is 'justice' and 'fairness' in their narrow senses. In the next two sections I take up uses which tie them very closely to the correct carrying out of certain social decision procedures. In the remaining two sections I shall consider first 'justice' as the requital of desert and then two uses of 'fair': 'fair shares' and 'fair exchange'.

[1] For the distinction between comparative and absolute distributive judgements see III.4.A.

2. PROCEDURAL FAIRNESS, BACKGROUND FAIRNESS AND LEGAL JUSTICE

2.A. *Procedural Fairness.* To say that a procedure is being fairly operated is to say that the formalities which define the procedure have been correctly adhered to. A fair race, for example, is one in which the competitors start together (nobody 'jumps the gun'), do not elbow one another or take short cuts, and in which the first person past the line and not disqualified is recognized as the winner; a fair fight is one in which the contestants are not allowed to get away with fouls; and so on. Fairness in the operation of the authoritative determination procedure has more or less content according to the detail with which the procedure is specified in any given case. A 'fair trial', for example, must satisfy elaborate procedural safeguards, whereas a 'fair administrative decision' need mean only that the official taking it was impartial or 'fair minded'.[1] In terms of formalities an administrative tribunal or an official inquiry occupy an intermediate position.[2] The fair application of a chance procedure requires the procedure to be genuinely random (a true die, for example) so as to give everyone a 'fair chance'. A 'fair election' rules out ballot stuffing, double voting, miscounts, etc.

This leaves the first three procedures. 'Fair war' has no use (though 'just war' has): 'All's fair in love and war.' The explanation is that war does not specify rules to be followed before what is happening can be called 'war'; indeed, it is the negation of orderly procedures.[3] War in its fullest sense is an attempt to impose one's will on another by violence; as soon as conventions come in (if you capture place *A* or man *B* you win) an element of contest enters in. Winning becomes not merely *being in a position* to impose your will

[1] 'Impartiality as an obligation of justice may be said to mean being exclusively influenced by considerations which it is supposed ought to influence the particular case in hand, and resisting the solicitation of any motives which prompt to conduct different from what these considerations would dictate.' J. S. Mill, *Utilitarianism*, Chapter V.

[2] See the Franks Report (Cmnd 218, 1957), *passim*.

[3] It is quite correct for the old saw to include 'love' in the same category, at least if it is taken to mean 'attaining the object of sexual desire'. There are no rules, no formal requirements, to satisfy before you can get your girl (or your man); you may have all the virtues but if you don't happen to have appeal you don't win.

but *being allowed* to impose your will in virtue of having satisfied a certain standard.[1] A duel is a contest just as a boxing match is, because if it settles, say, who gets the lady, it does so by convention: 'Let the best man win.'[2]

The notion of 'fair discussion on merits' also has no obvious use, again because there are no prescribed formalities to be observed; nor has 'fair bargaining' in general any use, since if threats are included it is simply the verbal counterpart to combat. Under more restricted conditions, however, considerations of procedural fairness can be invoked. Thus, in a context where threats are supposed to be ruled out it is 'unfair' to make threats. More subtly, in a context which is supposed to be one of 'perfect competition' it is unfair for a rich company to sell below cost in order to drive out its competitors. 'Fair trade', the traditional name for all restrictive practices aimed at protecting the inefficient producer and retailer, in theory usually means this, while in practice it normally degenerates into an attempt to guarantee 'cost plus' all round.[3] It is also used in connection with the closely similar proposal of tariffs against foreign 'dumping', which again generally comes to mean 'effective foreign competition'.

2.B. *Background Fairness.* While still concentrating on the way the procedure works, some evaluations in terms of 'fairness' dig a little deeper and ask whether the background conditions are satisfactory. Some examples should make the notion of 'background conditions' clear. Procedural fairness rules out one boxer having a

---

[1] I am not saying that war, still less combat in general, cannot be limited in its means (or in its ends) but that there cannot, by my definitions, be a conventional connection between achieving a certain feat and winning; the only connection can be that the other side in fact gives up. A strike or a lock-out, for example, can be limited in means (no shooting, no sabotage) and ends (a rise of 5 per cent or a reduction of 5 per cent). But it is still combat and not contest because each is aiming directly at changing the attitude of the other, not at some separate standard of achievement which is then taken as settling the dispute. A contest would occur if the Trade Union and the employer agreed in advance that whichever side was the first to cost the other a million pounds should get its demand fulfilled.

[2] A duel *à l'outrance* of course removes the loser not conventionally but necessarily; but the removal is still in the course of an activity with formal rules. If we have a duel fixed for tomorrow it would still be 'unfair' for me to shoot you in the back today as you walk along the street.

[3] E.g. the 'Codes of Fair Practice' produced under the NRA, in the New Deal.

piece of lead inside his gloves, but background fairness would also rule out any undue disparity in the weight of the boxers; similarly background fairness would rule out sailing boats or cars of different sizes being raced against one another unless suitably handicapped. In a court case the fact that one side's counsel showed far greater forensic skill than the other's would be grounds for complaint under the rubric of background fairness but not procedural fairness. Background fairness in voting might be thought to require that the opportunities available to those supporting the different sides should be equal, or roughly proportional to their strength among the voters. On these grounds one might well object to the two-to-one superiority in resources of Republicans and Conservatives or to de Gaulle's use of the government monopoly in radio and television to further his referenda. Chance has no room for background fairness alongside procedural fairness, nor, except in a loose sense, has bargaining. Exactly why this is will be examined in Section 3 when I consider the justification of evaluations in terms of procedural and background fairness.

2.C. *Legal Justice.* Procedural fairness and background fairness are concerned respectively with whether the prescribed formalities have been observed and whether the initial position of the parties was right. There is a third type of evaluation which is based on the working of procedures: legal or (more generally) rule-based justice.

Henry Sidgwick noted that one of the clearest and most frequent uses of 'justice' is in a legal context: a verdict is just when it is a correct application of the relevant rule of law. He also noted that it is not the *only* use of 'justice' because we can for example say (*pace* Hobbes) that a law is itself unjust.[1] The restriction to legal rules does not correspond to any difference in terms or evaluations; if the rules of the club allow expulsion for cheating and I am expelled without having cheated this is unjust in exactly the same way as a punishment inflicted by a court can be unjust. I shall therefore use the same term 'legal justice' whether the rule in question is a rule of law or not.[2]

The criterion of legal justice can be employed only where a decision is reached in the light of some rule(s), held by those taking

[1] H. Sidgwick, *The Methods of Ethics*, Book III, Chapter V.
[2] Sidgwick indeed extended the term 'legal justice' to cover promises and similar social obligations.

the decision to give the answer in cases of that kind. It can therefore be used only in conjunction with the authoritative determination procedure. There may also perhaps be a marginal application to contest: a bad interpretation of the rules could at a pinch be called unjust; but it is more natural to say that it was unfair. This is closely bound up with a point made in the previous chapter: a referee does not determine the result of a football match in the same way as a judge determines the result of a trial. A bad decision by the referee only gives an 'unfair advantage' to one side; the other side may still win. When I try to think of a referee's decision for which I should feel 'unjust' to be the appropriate epithet I immediately light on something like sending a man off the field or recommending his suspension, which are of course examples of a direct effect on the player rather than (or at least in addition to) an indirect effect on the result of the game.[1]

3. JUSTIFICATIONS

3.A. *Legal Justice.* So far I have simply presented procedural and background fairness and legal justice. It must now be asked why the honorific names of 'fair' and 'just' should be applied to the correct carrying out of procedures and the correct application of rules. Unless one is a 'rule worshipper' one must presumably ask for a justification of these procedural considerations in terms of conduciveness to some more general consideration, either aggregative or distributive.[2]

I shall begin by advancing three reasons of this more general kind for taking legal justice seriously. One argument is that any consistent application of a rule creates a primitive variety of equity—like cases being treated alike—though this is a rather weak sort of distributive principle because the basis of 'likeness' is

[1] The *result* of a match may be unjust in that it does not reflect the relative merits of the teams, but this is a different use of 'unjust' bound up with desert. An unjust result in this sense may be due equally to a bad decision or an unlucky gust of wind.

[2] See J. J. C. Smart, *An Outline of a System of Utilitarian Ethics* (Melbourne, 1961). Smart's 'utilitarianism' appears to be *entirely* made up of a rejection of 'rule worship'. Not only is the position he defends not (necessarily) hedonistic; it is not even aggregative. This—formerly, I should have thought, the sole distinguishing mark of non-hedonistic utilitarianism—is abandoned when Smart admits that different utilitarians may disagree on distributive questions.

stipulated by the rule and it may be outrageous. Another argument is that if known rules are applied, everyone can if he chooses avoid the consequences of infringing them; this applies to any rule, good or bad, unless it prescribes penalties for something nobody can do anything about (such as being a Jew or a Negro) or for past voluntary actions done before the rule was promulgated (such as having joined the Communist Party in the nineteen thirties). Both distributive and aggregative justifications underlie this second argument. Reasoning on aggregative premises one may say that following rules of the required kind prevents insecurity (the knock on the door in the early morning) and allows punishment to be deterrent rather than a dead loss of total want-satisfaction. On distributive premises one may say that if the required kinds of rule are followed then at least nobody will suffer for something he could not have helped doing, and this is at least a *part* of the criteria for 'desert'.

Finally, legal justice tends to reduce the incidence of unfulfilled expectations. The principle that unfulfilled expectations should be avoided if possible can itself be justified on both aggregative and distributive grounds, and then applies to legal justice as a special case.[1] The aggregative argument, for what it is worth, was elaborately worked out by Bentham in his analysis of the competing (utilitarian) claims of security and equality.

... ' the *advantage of gaining* cannot be compared with the *evil of losing*.' This proposition is itself deduced from two others. On the one hand every man naturally expects to preserve what he has; the feeling of expectation is natural to man and is founded on the ordinary course of events, since, taking the whole sum of men, acquired wealth is not only preserved but even increased. All loss is therefore unexpected, and gives rise to deception, which is a pain —the pain of frustrated expectation. On the other hand the deduction (or addition) of a portion of wealth will produce in the sum of happiness of each individual a deduction (or an addition) more or

---

[1] Sidgwick, in *The Methods of Ethics* suggests that the avoiding of unfulfilled expectations constitutes most of the Common Sense idea of 'justice' but (at least nowadays) 'justice' does not seem to be used so widely. There still seems to be agreement that there *is* a value in not frustrating expectations, however. Consider the contrasting attitudes of many people to death duties on one hand and a capital levy on the other. (I am referring to the opinions of those who are naïve enough to believe that death duties, as currently operated in the UK, are effective in reducing fortunes.)

less great according to the portion deducted and the remaining or original proportion.[1]

The distributive argument is of more limited import and refers specifically to cases where people have invested money, changed jobs, moved house, etc., in the belief that the state of affairs which induced them to do so would continue indefinitely. If they have, then it is wrong for this state of affairs to be suddenly changed.[2]

When a legislature passes a law, not for any temporary purposes, nor limited as to the time of its operation, and which therefore may be reasonably expected to be permanent,—and persons, confiding in its permanency, embark their capital, bestow their labour, or shape the course of their life, so that their only hope of success is founded on the existence of the law,—the rights which they have acquired in the reliance upon its continuance are termed 'vested rights;' and persons in this situation are considered as having a moral claim on the legislature for the maintenance of the law, or at least for the allowance of a sufficient time to withdraw their investments, and to take the measures necessary for guarding against the loss consequent on so large a change.[3]

3.B. *Procedural and Background Fairness.* Now take procedural and background fairness. What, first of all, is the relation between a fair trial and a just verdict? The answer seems to me to be the empirical one that fair trials tend to produce just verdicts more often than unfair trials and that the more respects in which a trial is fair the more likely it is to eventuate in a just verdict.[4] The value

---

[1] In Halévy, *The Growth of Philosophical Radicalism* (Beacon, 1955), p. 40. Note that the second argument would sometimes *favour* redistribution. Take £10 from a man with £1,000 and give it to one with £100. You decrease the happiness of the former by 1 per cent, but increase the happiness of the latter by 10 per cent. The argument in any case rests on a peculiar assumption about the marginal utility of money—far more questionable than the simple diminishing marginal utility idea.

[2] Sidgwick's claim that 'just' is used to refer to fulfilling expectations would be more plausible if restricted to cases which fall under this argument.

[3] Sir George Cornewall Lewis, *Remarks on the Use and Abuse of Some Political Terms* (London, 1832), p. 25.

[4] When I say that this is a matter of fact I do not mean that the dovetailing of fair procedures and just results is an accident, for the criteria of a fair trial are selected with an eye on this dovetailing. What I am denying is any analytic connection between the two such that a just verdict entails a fair trial or a fair trial entails a just verdict: there can be fair trials which still produce unjust verdicts.

of fairness is thus a subordinate to that of justice: fair procedures and background conditions are to be valued for their tendency to produce (rule-based) justice. Procedural fairness provides the minimum conditions while background fairness constitutes a refinement.[1]

Now consider contest. Again the criteria of fairness are empirically related to a tendency for fair contests to produce the 'right' results; and it is even clearer than before that the criteria for fairness are drawn with this requirement in mind. In Section 2 and again above I have used the expression 'the right result', and this bears the same relation to the contest procedure as 'rule-based justice' does to 'rule-based authoritative determination'. But whereas one can define 'justice' as 'conformity with the rule', one cannot give a general characterization of 'the right result' except as 'a result which is an accurate index of the quality which the contest was supposed to be testing'.

Procedural fairness (conformity with the procedural rules) is always more likely than not to produce the 'right results'—whatever they may be—because it merely specifies that everyone does the same thing. Whatever it is that the race is supposed to be testing, it is hard to see how its reliability would be improved if some competitors got away with jumping the gun, except in the perverse case where the race is a blind and the real test is in gun-jumping ability.

The criteria of background fairness, on the other hand, vary according to the 'right result'. If all that is being tested is ability to knock out an opponent, there is no need for any limits on disparity of size between boxers; but if the boxing match is supposed to be a test of skill, 'background fairness' must be brought in to specify the maximum disparity beyond which skill is secondary in determining the result to brute force. Again, if an examination is supposed to be testing *effort*, a different method of marking will be required from that necessary to test *ability*.

As with rule-based authoritative determination, the main justification for procedural and background fairness lies in its tendency

---

[1] Indeed, it is quite plausible to suggest that background fairness is only relevant to trials inasfar as they partake of contest, by their use of the adversary system which thus places a premium on equally matched counsel. Courts do not *have* to be so organized. See Sybille Bedford, *The Faces of Justice* (London, 1961).

to produce certain results. If these results are good then fairness, as a means to them, is also good; if not, not. The results of contest are to match rewards and deprivations (perhaps only immaterial ones such as prestige and chagrin) to performance, and for this to be desirable the scale of rewards and deprivations must be such that when it is adhered to they are appropriate to the perform- ances. 'Equality of opportunity' (the honorific name for back- ground and procedural fairness) is not very important if the achievements which are rewarded are base or trifling.[1] However, as before, we can suggest that there are certain virtues in pro- cedural and background fairness in a contest regardless of the result to which the contest is directed. These are, as before, the minimal equity of like cases being treated alike (even though 'likeness' may be defined in any way) and the fact that contestants at least know what they are supposed to be trying to do. It must be allowed that these general considerations seem to be a good deal weaker than those raised in connection with rule-based authorita- tive determination.

The link between justifying procedural and background fairness and justifying the use of the procedure itself comes out even more clearly if we look at voting. If we suppose that the object of the voting procedure is to ascertain the opinions of the voters then plainly the formal requirements are a necessary condition of this. If in addition we say that the object is to secure their informed opinions we have to introduce the background conditions as well. If these objects are good then the means to them are good.

I have now covered the three procedures of whose operation both procedural and background fairness can be predicated. Of the rest, chance, I remarked, is liable to procedural fairness (or unfairness) only. This follows from the rather peculiar fact that there is no end in view when a chance procedure is employed

[1] Compare 'equality before the law', the honorific name for procedural fair- ness in connection with rule-based authoritative determination: 'equality before the law' does not guarantee that outrageous actions are not rewarded and good ones punished. It should hardly need saying that neither form of procedural 'equality' has anything to do with substantial equality though the possibility of confusion is convenient for those who prefer the rhetoric to the reality of equality. (See, e.g., C. A. R. Crosland, *The Future of Socialism* (London, 1956)). Plato in *The Republic* and Michael Young in *The Rise of the Meritocracy* (Penguin Books, 1961) have both given us pictures of extremely hierarchical societies based on 'equality of opportunity'.

beyond settling something on a random basis.[1] Since the end is identified with the actual mechanical procedure there is no room for background fairness. Indeed, procedural and substantive fairness are merged since the distributive value *is* the randomness.

I also suggested that bargaining is in the reverse position. It cannot be procedurally fair (or unfair) but at least in a loose sense background fairness (or unfairness) can sometimes be attributed to it. Indeed, I may add that the same can sometimes be said of combat. This odd state of affairs arises whenever something which those taking part in it define to themselves as combat is at the same time being evaluated by a third party as if it were a contest. This observer, but not the combatants, may then speak of fairness—but only loosely and perhaps one might even say improperly.[2]

So far I have dealt with justifications for fairness taking one procedure at a time; but are there general reasons for following a prescribed form which applies to *any* form? I can suggest two. One is the argument (offered by Rawls) from 'fair play'.[3] This is essentially a distributive argument, which runs as follows: if you have accepted benefits arising from a certain practice then (unless you have given notice to the contrary) it is only fair that you should continue to adhere to it even when in some specific case it would suit you better not to. The other is an aggregative argument to the effect that the more a society is divided on substantive values the more precious as a means of preserving social peace is any agreement that can be reached on procedure. The connection between liberalism and an emphasis on 'due process' is not fortuitous. Procedures cannot be justified by the results they produce because a result which one approves of another disapproves; the adherence to procedures is justified instead by saying that everyone agrees on them and this is the only thing on which everyone does agree. Whether these considerations are sufficiently

[1] An apparent exception would be the use of a random device in the belief that God will arrange for a substantively good result; but then the arrangement is not (in the eyes of the people operating it) to be regarded as invoking a *chance* mechanism.

[2] This point is pursued in the context of J. K. Galbraith's 'concept of countervailing power' in Note J on page 303.

[3] John Rawls, 'Justice as Fairness', *Philosophical Review*, LXVII (1958). Reprinted in F. A. Olafson (ed.) *Justice and Social Policy* (Spectrum 1961). (Page references are to this reprint.) Also reprinted in Laslett and Runciman, Second Series.

universal or compelling to account for the importance which is often attached to a meticulous adherence to prescribed forms I shall not guess. Perhaps there is an element of 'rule worship' which can be supported by neither aggregative nor distributive principles; but the rationality of general adherence to prescribed forms is high on almost any principles.

Apart from the 'legal sense' of 'justice' the only other narrow one seems to be that which is analytically tied to the requital of 'desert', so it is to 'desert' that we must now turn.

4. DESERT

4.A. *Criteria of Desert.* To ascribe desert to a person is to say that it would be a good thing if he were to receive something (advantageous or disadvantageous) in virtue of some action or effort of his or some result brought about by him.[1] Notice that it is not necessary that one should go on to say that some specific person or body should actually provide the advantage or disadvantage specified. To say that a venture deserves success does not necessarily commit one to saying that steps ought to be taken to see that it gets it. Notice also that the 'something' which the person deserves to get need not be specified at all precisely, though it may be specified with complete precision. At its vaguest it can simply be 'He deserves a break' or 'He deserves something pleasant'. At its most precise it may specify 'an eye for an eye and a tooth for a tooth'. But one may endorse a certain specific allocation as 'deserved' without saying that this exact amount is derivable from the concept of 'desert'. I can say that Jones deserved the prize of £100 that he won without having to claim that £90 would have been less than he deserved and £110 more; or I can say that Smith deserves his sentence of six months imprisonment without having

---

[1] Compare Feinberg, *Justice and Personal Desert.* 'In general, the facts which constitute the basis of a subject's desert must be facts about that subject. If a student deserves a high grade in a course, for example, his desert must be in virtue of some fact about *him*—his earlier performances, say, or his present abilities. Perhaps his teacher *ought* to give him a high grade because it will break his neurotic mother's heart if he does not; but this fact, though it can be a reason for the teacher's action, cannot be the basis of the student's desert.' As Feinberg notices, this limitation of possible bases for ascribing desert to a person to 'some facts about him' gives a necessary but not a sufficient condition.

to claim that contemplation of the idea of desert tells me that six months (rather than five or seven) is exactly right.

What general features of a person's conduct are the right ones in virtue of which to attribute desert to him? This question has much exercised modern writers on desert.[1] I think there is no doubt that desert *is* attributed on the basis of actions, efforts and results produced, and any attempt to say that we are always (confusedly) rewarding and punishing (say) efforts seems to me quite misguided. Sometimes it is an actual contribution to human welfare or human knowledge (as when one says that so-and-so 'deserves' a Nobel prize); sometimes it is an act itself ('murderers deserve hanging'); sometimes it is purely the intention behind the action ('his good intentions deserved more success'). Sometimes it is the skill shown ('he was the better player and deserved to win'); and sometimes the pure effort ('he deserves praise for trying so hard').[2]

When, however, we consult 'common sense' or 'the moral consciousness (or whatever oracle we favour) about what the basis *should* be, its counsels are apparently divided. On one hand, there is the principle that since the amount and direction of effort is the only thing under a person's control, it is the only factor which can decently be praised and blamed, rewarded and punished; and this seems attractive. On the other hand, there seems to be a certain absurdity in paying one man more than another for doing a certain job because, though the first is slower and produces a worse result, he finds it more of an effort than does the second.

I am not rash enough to suggest a solution, or even (more fashionably) a dissolution of this conundrum. But I believe that it can be shown to be less acute than briefly stated it appears, and I shall advance three arguments in support of this view. Firstly, any idea of a clear-cut division between 'effort' and 'results' is a mistake.

[1] See Sidgwick, *Methods of Ethics*, Book III, Chapter V, and L. T. Hobhouse, *Elements of Social Justice* (London, 1922) Chapter VII, for two acute discussions.

[2] Where there is a contest the person or side that deserves to win is the one which has to a highest degree the qualities which the contest is to test. This is rather analogous to the legal use of 'just' in that it takes the criteria (for 'winning', as compared to 'crime') for granted. But though it is analytic that those with the qualities to be tested deserve to win, there is no necessary connection between winning and getting a prize; this is the contrast with the rule-based sense of 'justice'.

To say, in connection with a contest for example, that someone deserved to do better (or worse) than he actually did is to say that some factor which was irrelevant to what was being tested helped to determine the result. Thus skill and effort might be contrasted with luck ('They deserved to win the Test but lost the toss in each match') or with some initial advantage ('He deserved to win but his opponent, though an inferior boxer, was so much bigger'). The side that had done most training might be said to deserve to win or the side which tried hardest on the particular occasion of the contest. In each case 'effort' is being contrasted with 'results' but in each case a different contrast is being made.

Secondly, if we take the most extreme example of concentration on effort, the last, it is hard to see why this one in particular should be singled out as the only relevant criterion. If, in the interests of finding something that a person 'could have done otherwise' at a certain moment we eliminate all consideration of the way his capacities and opportunities came about, we are surely leaving out highly relevant material.

Thirdly, the essential point of the principle that desert should be tied to effort can be retained even if the principle, with its vagueness and unacceptable implications, is dropped. This essential point is, I suggest, that a person's having been able to have done otherwise is a *necessary condition* of ascribing desert; but it does not have to be the *sole basis*. This proposal is supported by English usage in an interesting way. I have noted that 'desert' may be used where advantages and disadvantages are not geared directly to the amount and direction of effort, but it is true that we can only speak of 'rewards' and 'punishments' where there is voluntary effort involved at some point. Isolating someone with a contagious disease or interning an alien during a war is not 'punishment' and it would not be justified by saying that they deserved it. Conversely, though not everyone has the initial physical equipment to win an Olympic gold medal, nobody can win without making an effort; though a strong swimmer risks less by jumping in to save someone than does a weak swimmer, each could equally well have turned away; and though there may be a lot of luck in being the one to make a scientific breakthrough, it is quite an effort even to be in the running. Such actions are therefore suitable for rewards and for talk of desert.

4.B. *A World without Desert.* If we want to know how important the considerations represented by 'desert' are, the best way of finding out is to imagine a world which did not employ the concept and to see how it would differ from that with which we are familiar.

Let us take first the necessary condition for ascribing desert which has just been canvassed. Leaving out the distributive terminology we can paraphrase this principle as follows: specially strong countervailing reasons must be forthcoming before it is ever justifiable to connect advantages and disadvantages with anything except a person's voluntary actions and their consequences. Without appealing to the value of distributive justice, could one justify the principle? Let us consider first a rule that where x is normally punishable and a person 'does' x, he is not punished if the action was not voluntary—if he was asleep, in an epileptic fit, insane, etc.[1] The simple aggregative case for this rule is that since these 'actions' are non-voluntary, attaching sanctions to them will not affect behaviour. There is, however, an aggregative reply which takes this form: if it becomes known that people who commit crimes are 'let off' under certain conditions, there will be some who could have avoided committing a crime (and would have avoided it had the punishment been certain) who will now commit a crime hoping to convince a court that they could not help doing what they did. In short: if you let off genuine hard cases you may encourage would-be (and perhaps even successful) fakers. If a man is found not guilty of murder on the ground that he killed in his sleep, may not others kill deliberately hoping to get away with the same defence? P. J. Fitzgerald has added a second argument which goes even further:

> It might prevent conduct that is not involuntary if potential criminals said to themselves, 'See, this Draconian code even punishes those who cannot help stealing—the kleptomaniacs, too. We, therefore, who can help stealing would be shown no mercy, so we had better refrain from committing crimes altogether'.[2]

[1] See P. J. Fitzgerald, 'Voluntary and Involuntary Acts', and H. L. A. Hart, 'Negligence, *Mens Rea* and Criminal Responsibility', in A. G. Guest (ed.), *Oxford Essays in Jurisprudence* (Oxford, 1961).

[2] 'Voluntary and Involuntary Acts' in Guest (ed.), *Oxford Essays in Jurisprudence*, p. 19.

There is, however, an aggregative reply to these arguments which is precisely the same as that advanced against legal injustice above, namely that the possible advantages would be bought at too high a price in personal insecurity. If even involuntary actions may bring about the severest penalties, who could ever feel safe?

Secondly, let us consider a rule that instead of, or in addition to, a criminal's being punished, certain specified people, or people in a certain specified relation to the criminal—kin, neighbours, class-mates—shall be punished. This rule has certain *prima facie* advantages in aggregative terms, though the details vary according to the precise application. I offer these general observations: (i) where the group or person to be punished is defined without reference to the criminal, some deterrence can be assured even without looking for the criminal, provided of course that the potential criminal is affected by the threat to these people; (ii) a potential criminal may actually be more deterred by threats to certain others than to himself—this, however, is most likely to be true of people in a speci-fied relation to the criminal, which entails that the criminal be identified, even if not caught; (iii) as well as the advantages in ease of execution and effectiveness on the criminal, the method may also be an effective means of controlling criminals via the group to be punished in their place. If a man's kinfolk or neighbours will suffer for his misdeeds they are likely to try and restrain him.[1]

The aggregative argument *against* all this is the same as before: personal insecurity. This would not be a sufficient argument if there were no other way of controlling crime, but would our imaginary society be very different from existing ones in that respect? Although, in the society we know, a value is attached to 'not punishing the innocent' we are still willing to override it, e.g. in time of war when we intern aliens. And if Britain does not experience collective fines and suchlike at home does not this merely prove that they haven't been needed? Wherever order is threatened these methods come into play. They have for example been of great importance in British colonial policy (e.g. collective fines for villages in Cyprus). And if an analogy from Britain itself is wanted one may instance the crushing social and economic dis-advantages inflicted on illegitimate children, which have only been reduced in this century. Children themselves obviously cannot help being illegitimate; but these arrangements were justified as

[1] See E. A. Ross, *Social Control* (New York, 1922), p. 119.

being necessary to prevent people from having illegitimate children. And they have been attacked less on abstract grounds of justice than on the grounds that they caused more misery than their (very modest) deterrent value warranted.[1]

The principle that in general specially good reasons have to be given for 'rewarding' or 'punishing' non-voluntary actions would, then, retain its force even if it were not backed by the explicit distributive value of 'desert'. But of course 'desert' in many instances goes beyond this and specifies that such-and-such an action (contribution, effort, etc.) *deserves* a certain increase or decrease in want-satisfaction. How similar would a society without *this* sort of 'desert' be to one with it? The difficulty in giving a general answer to this question lies in the fact that it depends *what* matters are regarded as deserving *what* rewards and punishments.

However, I think it can be suggested that the main outlines of 'desert' would be duplicated by aggregative considerations of incentive and deterrence. That is to say, given that desirable behaviour deserves good treatment and undesirable behaviour bad treatment, giving people what they deserve will often come in practice to the same thing as giving people what is necessary to encourage desirable behaviour and discourage undesirable behaviour. But there is certainly no guarantee that they would come to exactly the same thing. Desert looks to the past—or at most to the present—whereas incentive and deterrence are forward-looking notions (i.e. someone ought to be given something in virtue of a past action *because* this will encourage similar actions by him and others in the future).[2] It would be a remarkable coincidence if following the former criterion *always* led to the same results as following the latter. For example, if pay were fixed solely

[1] It has often been argued that aggregative principles unrelieved by any others would justify 'punishing the innocent' (or, to avoid verbal quibbles, let us say 'treating innocent people in a way physically indistinguishable from punishment'). This is of course true. What is less often noticed is that any mixture of aggregative and distributive principles is liable to have the same result in some circumstances. But this does not seem to me to show that nobody is an aggregationist—quite the reverse. I think most people would accept (reluctantly, no doubt—but still accept) that in some imaginable situations the 'innocent' could justifiably be treated in a way physically indistinguishable from punishment.

[2] 'It follows from our analysis of desert statements that to say that "S deserves X because giving it to him would be in the public interest" is simply to misuse the words "deserve".' (Feinberg, 'Justice as Desert', p. 91.)

by incentive considerations, jobs for which people felt they had a vocation would be paid lower than jobs similar in every respect except this; and if an industry was declining it would cut its rates of pay for skilled workers who were too old to change to another occupation (even though the work itself would of course be just the same as before) counting on not having to recruit fresh employees.[1]

This example is deliberately chosen as one where 'desert' might be taken to prescribe specific amounts or differentials. But, especially in connection with the contest procedure, there is a use of 'deserve' which only claims that *given* the prize is so much, so-and-so 'deserves' it more than anyone else in that he fulfils the conditions laid down better than anyone else. The prize may have been set up not to reward desert but to stimulate productions of suitable kinds; nevertheless, it *generates* a use of 'desert' in the subsidiary sense just noted. In these cases, 'procedural fairness' will carry the entire load, for 'desert' does not say that there should be a prize or how big the prize should be.[2]

Where the contest procedure is in use, then, the abolition of the concept of 'desert' will make no difference except in cases where 'desert' is defined *independently* of the contest as a criterion for setting up the contest. Compare, for example, 'Anyone who can climb that rock deserves £50 and I hereby offer it' with 'Since £50 has been offered for climbing the rock and I have climbed it, I deserve it'.

4.C. *The Revolt Against Desert.* In contrasting the 'world without desert' with the familiar one, I have ignored the fact that the 'familiar world' is changing in this respect. In examining the concept of desert we are examining a concept which is already in decline and may eventually disappear. 'Desert' flourishes in a liberal society where people are regarded as rational independent atoms held together in a society by a 'social contract' from which all must benefit. Each person's worth (desert) can be precisely

[1] Justice as expectation-fulfilment would come in here, however, and as I pointed out in the last chapter this has a certain aggregative justification.

[2] But can procedural fairness be justified if one is not allowed to say that it ensures the prize's going to the man who deserves it? I think it can, for as I argued in 3.B., whatever may have been someone's object in setting up a contest that object will normally be most effectively achieved by procedural fairness.

ascertained—it is his net marginal product and under certain postulated conditions (which it is conveniently assumed the existing economy approximates) market prices give each factor of production its net marginal product. Life is an obstacle race with no special provision for the lame but if one competitor trips up another, the state takes cognizance of this fact; thus compensation is given only when there is negligence on one side but not on the other.

Compared to this paradigm—approximated most closely by Britain and the USA in the second and third quarters respectively of the nineteenth century—there has already been a widespread movement away from 'desert' as a prime consideration in determining income distribution. Roscoe Pound has commented on this in his discussion of changing 'jural postulates':

> Another emerging jural postulate appears to be that in the industrial society of today enterprises in which numbers of men are employed will bear the burden of what might be called the human wear and tear involved in their operation. Some such postulate is behind workmen's compensation laws. But in the administration of those laws there is much to suggest a wider proposition. There are also other indications of a third proposition, which may come to include the second, namely, that the risk of misfortune to individuals is to be borne by society as a whole. Some such postulate seems to be behind what has been called the insurance theory of liability and is behind much social security legislation. Perhaps a reaching out for something of the sort has been behind a tendency for juries to hold that, whenever anyone has been hurt, someone able to respond in damages ought to pay.[1]

Workmen's compensation, mentioned by Pound, is a clear example, and so is a welfare state which (in theory if not in practice) pays special attention to the old category of the '*un*deserving poor'. If we turn to the criminal law we can say that at least in official discussions pure retributivism is not respectable, so that opinions on, say, the death penalty, however they may in fact be formed, are argued in terms of deterrence. Even in the operation of the law, more attention is being paid to rehabilitation and deterrence, and less to seeing that the criminal gets his 'just deserts'; while the Streatfeild Committee has proposed that this

[1] Roscoe Pound, *Social Control Through Law* (New Haven, 1942), pp. 116–117.

should go a lot further, sentencing being regarded as a pragmatic administrative task.[1]

I have already suggested that a world in which 'desert' had completely disappeared would not necessarily be radically different from one with it. But this leaves two questions. First, would the changes be improvements? And second, might it not be possible for the changes to be very great if the requirements of incentive and deterrence could be disposed of? Marx, for example, in the *Critique of the Gotha Programme* (1875) gave an affirmative reply on each count.

> The right of the producers is *proportional* to the amount of labour they contribute; the equality consists in the fact that everything is measured by an *equal standard*, labour. . . . This *equal* right is an unequal right for unequal labour. . . . In a higher phase of communist society, after the enslaving subordination of the individual to the division of labour, and therewith also the antithesis between mental and physical labour, has vanished; after labour has become not only a means of life but life's prime want; after the productive forces have also increased, with the all-round development of the individual, and all the springs of co-operative wealth flow more abundantly—only then can the narrow horizon of bourgeois right be crossed in its entirety and society inscribe on its banner: 'From each according to his ability, to each according to his needs!'[2]

The first answer is that the 'bourgeois' conception is 'narrow'. As Bernard Shaw suggested in *The Intelligent Woman's Guide to Capitalism and Socialism* there is something ridiculous in trying to compare the 'worth' of different jobs; and surely there is something degrading about a court having to decide whether some victim of a ghastly accident was 'negligent' or not and whether or not he therefore 'deserves' compensation. The second answer which Marx gives is that once society has been thoroughly reconstructed it would not be necessary to offer differential pay in order to attract people into certain jobs.[3] Clearly, inasfar as this is so, the

---

[1] Streatfeild Committee on the Business of the Criminal Courts, Cmnd. 1289, H.M.S.O., 1961.

[2] Karl Marx and Friedrich Engels, *Selected Works*, II (Moscow, 1962), pp. 23–24.

[3] Compare Mill, *Autobiography* in *Essential Works of John Stuart Mill*, ed. Max Lerner (New York, 1961), p. 137: 'Education, habit, and the cultivation of the sentiments, will make a common man dig or weave for his country, as readily as fight for his country. True enough, it is only by slow degrees, and a

pattern of distribution can differ from that required by 'desert' far more so than in a society where incentives must still be offered. Criminal law offers an analogy: if it were not necessary to keep an eye on the deterrent effects of the way in which convicted people are treated, a more radical break with 'just deserts' would be possible.

5. FAIR SHARES AND FAIR EXCHANGE

5.A. *Fair Shares*. In this final section I want to examine two uses of the elusive word 'fair': 'fair shares' and 'fair exchange'. What are fair shares? One way of characterizing them is to say that they are shares which are equal except insofar as there is some good reason for diverging from equality. 'Fair' and 'reasonable' often go together and we now have to ask what are reasonable grounds for divergence from equality. John Rawls has suggested that the only permissible ground is that everyone should gain from the deviation, but at least as a description of usage this seems too limited; desert is also a ground for deviation which is compatible with fairness. But simple maximizing considerations will not do, so we cannot say that a demand for fair shares among a group is no more than a demand for the whole group to be treated as a single reference group.

To take fair shares as *prima facie* equal shares is not however to get to the bottom of the notion. A deeper analysis would, I think, make equality a special case; the general case would be proportionality. This is especially so where the distributive question arises in the context of sharing a burden rather than a benefit: what is the fairest way of sharing the costs of UNRRA, the United Nations, NATO? The answer to such questions is likely to be that contributions should be assessed as proportions of national income, or some other index of 'ability to pay'.[1] It is important to note that desert plays no part in this conception of fairness: there is no suggestion that the rich countries should pay more per head to expiate for some past wrongdoing. Nor is it an egalitarian

[1] Thomas C. Schelling, *The Strategy of Conflict* (Cambridge, Mass., 1960), p. 67, esp. fnt. 6.

system of culture prolonged through successive generations, that men in general can be brought up to this point. But the hindrance is not in the essential constitution of human nature.'

conception: if the intention were to equalize per capita income the USA and (perhaps) a few other countries would pay the whole cost.[1]

So far I have been considering 'fair shares' where it occurs as a principle used to determine a pattern of distribution, but it may also be used within an already established pattern (which need not itself be based on fairness). There is an exact analogy with 'desert' which may be used either as a basis for setting up a pattern of distribution or as a basis for claims arising under such a pattern. 'Desert' is used in the second way when the pattern relates distribution to efforts or actions requiring deliberate efforts; 'fairness' is used in the second way when the pattern relates distribution to some other factor. Whatever the basis underlying the ground rules for administering a fund, any party which believes it is receiving less than it is entitled to under these rules can complain that it isn't getting its 'fair share' of the funds.[2]

5.B. *Fair Exchange.* 'Fair exchange' is a fairly sophisticated economic notion. A fair exchange is one which would occur under conditions of perfect competition. The notion of generalized 'values' which are equal in a fair exchange cannot be conceived except by reflecting on the processes of the market. 'Fair exchange' in fact bears exactly the same relation to 'fair competition' as does 'just verdict' to 'fair trial': the first is the ideal consequence of the second. But whereas 'just verdict' can be defined independently of 'fair trial' a 'fair exchange' simply *is* the exchange which would take place in a perfect market. Whereas 'fair trials lead to just ver-

---

[1] The difficulty of applying a principle of proportionality where *benefits* are to be distributed may be illustrated by asking what would have been a (proportionally) fair way of dividing Marshall Aid up among OEEC countries. If some ratio were to be applied it would presumably have to be between poorness and amount received. But this relation could not be expressed in any simple formula akin to that in the case of burdens and wealth. Moreover, since the benefits were given for a specific purpose, i.e. putting the economies of Western European countries on a sound basis, wouldn't fairness have been out of place as a primary principle? Surely more relevant criteria for distributing the money would be: an aggregative one of using the money where it will do most good, a quasi-distributive one of getting countries back to their prewar position and perhaps in the background an egalitarian one of bringing up the poorer countries.

[2] It does not follow that it can claim it *deserves* more unless, of course, the criteria themselves relate to efforts made. If the criterion is, e.g. that damage done by the war should be made up, this does not generate a use of 'desert' in even the weakest sense.

dicts' is a well-founded empirical observation (though the criteria of a fair trial have of course been chosen with the end of making the generalization true), 'perfect competition leads to fair exchange' is a *tautology* offering a definition of the technical term 'fair exchange'. The notion of a fair exchange as the exchange of equal abstract 'values' could only arise after people had observed markets in operation and invented a model in which the imperfections of actual markets were left out. To look for value as something 'behind' goods and services, leading to their exchange at certain ratios is to put the cart before the horse. Their 'value' just *is* their (idealized) rate of exchange.

Although not itself a 'procedural' value, 'fair exchange' is defined in terms of procedure (i.e. the procedure of perfect competition). The notion of 'fair exchange' is an instrument of commerce and as such has an important function: it is not always convenient or possible to have anything approaching perfect competition in all exchanges. In such cases the parties may have resort to bargaining based purely on relative strength of will and economic force; but this is wasteful and the delay and inconvenience may well make both parties worse off than a quick settlement. The most obvious solution is for them to agree on the rate of exchange that *would* have obtained *if* there had been more buyers and sellers. (Cf. in this context 'fair market price' in connection with compulsory purchase orders and the definition of 'fair wages' in government contracts as 'wages paid by reputable employers', i.e. the going market price of labour.) 'Fair exchange' is thus transferred from its analytic home in the bargaining procedure to a grander prescriptive home in the procedure of substantive decision.[1]

[1] 'More important for present purposes was the medieval doctrine of the "just price" and, though to a lesser degree, of the "just wage". The scholastics maintained that it was a violation of commutative justice to sell at a higher price or to buy at a lower price than the "just price", which they explained as the price according to "common estimation". Until recently, this has been commonly interpreted as meaning the fixing of prices by civil authorities or by wise men, in the interest of justice and as a restraint on the avarice of merchants, and as demonstrating that the medieval Church was hostile to the free market. Modern scholarship, however, has conclusively demonstrated that, except for a few nominalists, the standard late-medieval meaning of "common estimation" was market price under free competition, and that some of the scholastics even used the term equivalent to "common estimation in or by the market". That they meant by the "market" a competitive market,

But it is not (*pace* Aristotle) by itself an ultimate distributive value, because it pays no attention to the *titles* of those who exchange. It ensures that everyone who buys or sells gets a 'fair deal' but this is, after all, no more than to preserve the *status quo*: value exchanges for like value. The fair rate of exchange between a bicycle and a pair of shoes does not depend on whether the bicycle was found, stolen or inherited and the shoes made by the seller. Though fair between *goods* it is not necessarily fair between *people*.[1]

In order to suggest that a fair rate of exchange guarantees a more fundamental fairness, theorists have found it necessary to restrict the conditions under which this can be claimed. In particular, it is sometimes claimed that fair exchange is distributively *just* provided the initial stock of value of each party was come by due to his own personal efforts. Naturally this poses difficulties if the context is one of capitalist apologetics, since inheritance seems ruled out; but even if we consider fortunes made in a lifetime we must surely wonder whether the *size* of the fortunes made by the successful capitalists really bear any relations to their deserts when compared with the foremost statesmen, writers, artists, thinkers, etc., including undeniable benefactors to mankind such as the Curies or Sir Alexander Fleming. If the capitalist makes so much more than they by free exchange, can free exchange be reconciled with any notion of desert which has not lost all connection with personal worth? Perhaps it just might, if one accepts unquestionably the axiom that 'giving people what they want' is the only worthy activity. This will get rid of some counter-examples: if the artist starves in his garret this is because nobody wants his paintings enough. But it still doesn't get rid of the problem that some talents are so much more effectively exploited than others by a 'fair exchange' system: a scientist cannot sell his ideas at their market value anywhere near as easily as a businessman can.

[1] See F. H. Knight's essay 'Freedom and Reform' in his book of collected essays bearing that name.

---

operating under normal circumstances, they made sufficiently clear by their uniform condemnation of all monopolies, and by the exceptions they made for appeal to official or non-market determination of prices when abnormal conditions, such as famine or siege, or unusual absence of business skills or lack of bargaining power, made particular individuals unable to cope adequately with market processes.' Jacob Viner, 'The Intellectual History of Laissez Faire', *The Journal of Law and Economics*, III (October 1960), 53.

VII

EQUALITY, INTEGRATION AND NON-DISCRIMINATION

1.A. *Introduction*. This chapter provides a good chance to test the usefulness of the distinction between want-regarding principles and ideal-regarding principles, for it is maintained in it that a large proportion of the arguments which are put forward in terms of the want-regarding principle of 'equality' can actually be made to work only if they are taken to depend on one of two ideal-regarding principles, which I call integration and non-discrimination. In order to show this, I shall take first the copiously documented example of the US Supreme Court's handling of racial cases, and then two issues in whose discussion principles often play a somewhat less prominent part: schooling and medical care.

But before this, it is necessary to say a little about the meaning of 'equality', 'integration' and 'non-discrimination' so I shall give the present section to this.

1.B. *Equality*. By 'equality' I am referring to a distributive notion, not to the wider notion of a reference group (I.3.C.). Statements that human beings (or some group of them) are 'fundamentally' or 'spiritually' equal, if they are not intended as purely theological propositions, usually seem to amount to claiming that human beings (or a certain group of them) should form a single reference group; in other words that *some* principle or other must be invoked if people are to be treated differently.[1] If you like, you can say that 'fundamental' equality underlies equality in other senses

[1] For a use of 'spiritual equality' in this way see W. W. Willoughby, *Social Justice*. Quite frequently (as in the examples cited in the next footnote) this kind of 'fundamental' equality is simply referred to as 'equality'.

(meaning that you have to establish a reference-group before you can say that relations among its members are, or should be, equal) but of course it is then equally true to say that 'fundamental' equality underlies justice or the greatest happiness of the greatest number. There is no *special* connection between 'fundamental equality' (i.e. the establishment of a reference-group) and equality as a distinctive want-regarding concept.

Those who wish to disparage the distributive principle of equality often seek to do so by suggesting that its adherents are committed to holding either that men *are* 'equal' in their personal characteristics or that they *ought* to be 'equal'. Then, since 'equality of personal characteristics' does not seem to make much sense it is suggested that equalitarians presumably mean 'identical' when they say 'equal'. As this idea is absurd, too, distributive equality can be conveniently dismissed as an unintelligible concept. The cosy conclusion can then be drawn that when people demand 'equality' they are either confused or they are demanding 'fundamental' equality; that is, for some group (perhaps the human race) to be treated as a reference group. What equality 'really means' it is claimed is that some reason or other must be adduced to justify treating people differently.[1] The incoherence, however, lies not in the concept of equality, but in the hostile formulation itself. To say that people should be equal is to say that their opportunities for satisfying whatever wants they may happen to have should be equal. Whether or not one agrees with the claim in any particular case it surely cannot be denied that it is a reasonably intelligible one, and one not involving any implausible prescriptions or descriptions involving uniformity or identity.

Thus—to take what I shall call the 'weak' sense of distributive equality—asking for racial equality between black and white does not entail asking that everyone should be an identical intermediate colour, nor does asking for equality between the sexes entail asking for universal hermaphroditism. What one is demanding is that a person's chances of satisfying his wants should not be

[1] See, for examples of this emasculation of the concept of equality, Benn and Peters, *Social Principles* . . . and W. von Leyden, 'On Justifying Inequality', *Political Studies*, XI, No. 1 (February 1963). Giovanni Sartori, in *Democratic Theory* (Wayne University, 1962), carries the process to a further stage of refinement by distinguishing (at inordinate length) between 'equality' and 'uniformity' and then using 'uniformity' for equality (which he dislikes) and 'equality' for inequality (which he favours).

affected by his or her skin colour or sex.[1] Red-headed people are equal to others in Britain not because they dye their hair or because nobody notices the colour of their hair, but because one's chances of getting deference, a council house, a job, or admission to Oxford do not vary according to the colour of one's hair.

One use of 'equality' in a distributive context is, then, to deny that a certain characteristic (generally one which people can't do anything about) should be taken as a basis for treating people differently. 'Equality of x's' (where x is the characteristic in question) is, as I have pointed out, a common form in which 'equality' occurs here. 'Equality of opportunity' refers to a sub-class of cases, where the irrelevant characteristics are whatever characteristics give rise to background unfairness by improperly influencing the results of contests or authoritative determination.

But equality in respect of one quality (say, colour or sex) is perfectly compatible with great inequalities in respect of other qualities.[2] And 'equality of opportunity' is sometimes expressly defined as 'equal opportunities to become unequal'. Let us therefore distinguish this 'weak' sense of 'equality' from a 'strong' sense which comes into play to describe or demand a state of

---

[1] This is distinctly more stringent than demanding 'fundamental equality'. Someone could accept that (some or all) members of the two races or the two sexes formed a single reference-group and then go on to say that there *was* some 'relevant difference' between them which justified treating them differently. But just this move is ruled out by the demand for *distributive* equality between the races or sexes.

[2] Thus, writing of what he calls the 'status' ends of Chicago Negroes, James Q. Wilson says: ' "Status" ends are those which seek the integration of the Negro into all phases of community on the principle of equality— all Negroes will be granted the opportunity to obtain the services, positions, or material benefits of the community on the basis of principles other than race. Such principles include the ability to pay and personal achievement or qualification. Status ends which have been sought in the Chicago Negro community include the integration of all public schools, the opening of all-white public housing units to Negroes of comparable income, the desegregation of private hospitals, the equal treatment of Negroes in the allocation of public offices and honours, and the establishment of the principle of open occupancy in the real estate market'. *Negro Politics* (Glencoe, Ill., 1960) p. 185. Not altogether surprisingly, Wilson reports that this kind of 'equality' has proved more popular with middle class Negroes than the rest, who tend to be more interested in direct material improvements such as better housing and better schooling.

affairs in which all the members of a group get an equal share in some (tangible or intangible) good, regardless of *any* personal characteristic. In this use, when the phrase 'equality of *x*' is employed, the *x* refers not to a personal characteristic which is to be irrelevant (race, sex) but to a good which is to be equally shared ('equality of income', 'parity of esteem'). In the adjectival form of the phrase, instead of 'racial equality' or 'sexual equality' we have 'economic equality' or 'social equality'. The full implementation of the principle of equality in this 'strong' sense would of course often conflict with the full implementation of other principles— not only aggregative principles but also other distributive principles. For example, inequalities based on considerations of incentive or desert would be ruled out. This fact is sometimes used as an argument against taking the concept of 'strong' equality seriously, but the argument would only be valid if it were irrational to adhere to a principle which cannot be implemented fully without its coming into conflict with other principles. As I have suggested in I.2.A. there need be nothing irrational in so doing; and if it *were* irrational so to do then it would be very hard to hold any principles at all.[1]

1.C. *Integration and Non-Discrimination.* So far I have presented what I call 'strong' and 'weak' equality as distributive considerations concerned with the proper distribution of tangible or intangible goods—money, building sites, prestige, etc. But there are also ideal-regarding principles which in many instances run along the same lines as these distributive want-regarding principles, but at crucial points diverge from them or go beyond them. The two ideals in question I shall call 'integration' and 'non-discrimination'. By 'integration' I refer to the belief that it is a desirable state of affairs for people who differ in certain given respects to mix socially and to share the same clubs, churches, political parties, housing areas, shops, schools, theatres, swimming pools, etc. By 'non-discrimination' I refer to the belief that there is something degrading in treating differently people who differ in certain ways (e.g. in the colour of their skins).

In the rest of this chapter I shall be exploring the relation

[1] Sir Isaiah Berlin in his article 'Equality', *Aristotelian Society*, Supplementary Volume LVI (1955–1956), reprinted in Olafson (ed.) *Justice and Social Policy*, is the only recent writer I know to have taken seriously the strong sense of equality as an independent value.

between these principles and the two principles of equality previously introduced. First, however, it may be useful to illustrate the differences between them. Integration differs from strong equality because it is possible to imagine conditions under which there would be equal distribution of goods (even intangible ones such as prestige) but still no mixing. Conversely, there can be mixing without equality. An example of the former would be two men receiving the same pay for the same job in different (segregated) parts of the same factory. An example of the latter would be two men working side by side at the same job but receiving different pay on account of race.[1] Non-discrimination differs from weak equality because the former entails objecting to treating people *differently* (according to their possession or non-possession of a certain characteristic), whereas the latter entails only objecting to treating them *worse*.[2] 'Separate but equal' facilities in a context of equality of power and prestige would satisfy the latter but not the former.

It can be seen moreover that integration differs from non-discrimination because it is possible for the requirements of the one ideal to conflict with those of the other. For example, the only way of achieving racial integration in an area may be to have a quota system. Without such a guarantee 'tipping' is almost certain to take place.[3] But a quota system involves treating people differently according to their race (e.g. applicants for housing will have to state their race).[4] Again, the demand for predominantly Negro wards or Trade Union locals to be represented by Negroes (thus guaranteeing integrated governing bodies) conflicts with the demand that the best man should get the job regardless of race. Again, a university seeking a 'balance' between public school and maintained school products would adopt a different approach from

[1] A single movement may well advance one principle and set back the other: Jim Crow gained ground rapidly in the 1880s as the South's response to Reconstruction.

[2] This use of 'non-discrimination' thus takes the word 'discrimination' quite literally and diverges from the ordinary use inasfar as this is taken to mean '*unfair* difference in the *quality* of treatment'.

[3] 'Tipping' is the often-observed phenomenon of an area changing rapidly from overwhelmingly white to overwhelmingly Negro due to panic selling by white house-owners when the proportion of Negro occupancy rises to a certain figure (which need not be half).

[4] J. Q. Wilson, *Negro Politics* (Glencoe, Ill., 1960), pp. 184–185.

one which intended to admit applicants without any reference to the type of school from which they came.

Because in practice segregation and inequality almost always go together it is not easy to tell in a given case whether segregation is being attacked as an evil in its own right (on the basis of the ideal of integration or the ideal of non-discrimination) or whether desegregation is merely regarded as a means to achieving greater equality of material goods, status, opportunity, etc. On the second view, if equality could be achieved without desegregation there would be nothing left to object to.

2. EXAMPLES

2.A. *Segregation and the Supreme Court.* The Fourteenth Amendment guarantees citizens of the USA the 'equal protection of the laws'. This is clearly the language of distributive judgements. How then does it apply to segregation? The two most interesting cases here are Plessy *v.* Ferguson (163 US 537) and Brown *v.* Topeka Board of Education (347 US 483). The first held that segregated schools are 'equal' provided they have equal facilities and the second rejected this. The court's opinion in the second case did not however say that segregation is always and under all circumstances unequal, but that it always is in public education—and the famous 'sociological' evidence was then brought it. Although the opinion is apparently limited in this way, the decision in Brown *v.* Board of Education has subsequently been cited as the authority for *per curiam* decisions in fields other than education: declaring, for example, legally segregated transport facilities unconstitutional.

This is an awkward situation and it arises, I suspect, from the court's trying to fit its own ideal-regarding principles into the constitutional mould of distributive want-regarding principles. Thus, in the Brown case, it could be claimed (whether correctly or not) that 'segregation with the sanction of law . . . has a tendency to retard the educational and mental development of Negro children and to deprive them of some of the benefits they would receive in a racially integrated school system'. Segregation can thus be called 'unequal' because it causes an actual loss (of educational advancement) to the Negro children. But what effects analogous to this do segregated buses have? Here, surely, one could only say that the segregation itself was 'unequal', given the context of white political supremacy.

Wechsler has questioned this line of thought: he asks whether making racial segregation a denial in principle of equality to the group that is not dominant politically does not involve

> an inquiry into the motive of the legislature, which is generally foreclosed to the courts? Is it alternatively defensible to make the measure of validity of legislation the way it is interpreted by those who are affected by it? In the context of a charge that segregation *with equal facilities* is a denial of equality, is there not a point in *Plessy* in the statement that if 'enforced separation stamps the colored race with a badge of inferiority' it is solely because its members choose 'to put that construction upon it'? Does enforced separation of the sexes discriminate against females merely because it may be the females who resent it and it is imposed by judgements predominantly male? Is a prohibition of miscegenation a discrimination against the colored member of the couple who would like to marry?[1]

We can point the question further by asking whether segregation would still be unequal in a context of political equality if, in addition, the bulk of each race approved of the segregation? Or, again, what if the state law provided only that there must be facilities open only to Negroes but that there must not be facilities open only to whites?[2] Wechsler himself wishes to make the rejection of segregation turn on the denial by states of 'freedom to associate',

> a denial that impinges in the same way on any groups or races that may be involved. I think, and I hope not without foundation, that the Southern white also pays heavily for segregation, not only in the sense of guilt that he must carry but also in the benefits he is denied.

Does not the problem of miscegenation show most clearly that

[1] Wechsler, 'Toward Neutral Principles of Constitutional Law', 73 *Harvard Law Review* 1, 26–35 (1959).

[2] This example is not as fanciful as it may sound. Although there are some bus stations in the South where the writ of the ICC does not run and restaurants are still fully segregated, there are others (especially in larger towns) where the two restaurants are still kept going but the ex-white one is de-segregated while the ex-Negro one remains wholly confined to Negroes. Since the Negro has, in these circumstances, a choice of non-segregated and segregated facilities, where is the 'inequality' here?

it is the freedom of association that at the bottom is involved, the only case, I may add, where it is implicit in the situation that association is desired by the only individuals involved.

The difficulty of this is, as he recognizes, that

if the freedom of association is denied by segregation, integration forces an association upon those for whom it is unpleasant or repugnant.

From the constitutional angle, the problem is then:

Given a situation where the state must practically choose between denying the association to those individuals who wish it or imposing it on those who would avoid it, is there a basis in neutral principles for holding that the Constitution demands that the claims for association should prevail? I should like to think there is, but I confess I have not yet written the opinion. To write it is for me the challenge of the school-segregation cases.

Let us widen this: is there *any* principle (not just a constitutional principle) which condemns segregation where facilities are genuinely equal? 'Freedom of association', as Wechsler in effect admits, is a broken reed because if we are simply balancing want-satisfactions we have to take into account wants for non-association.[1] Wherever we are not willing to accept the conclusions of a want-regarding appraisal we must turn to ideal-regarding considerations. The reason for preferring the 'freedom' of those who wish to associate with members of other races can then be simply that they are a more desirable type of human being, and their number should be swelled as much as possible.

2.B. *Schools and Medical Care*(*i*). The advantage of racial segregation as an example is that a good deal has been written about it and that the US Constitution forces attention on to the fundamental principles involved. Its disadvantages are also great. First, it is difficult to conceive of racial segregation in an atmosphere of racial equality because in fact segregation has always been an instrument of inequality and probably will remain so until both are destroyed together. And secondly, most men of good-will outside the southern USA (and a good many inside it) are convinced that

---

[1] It does not appear that we can dodge this problem by ruling out the wants for non-association as publicly-oriented wants. (See Note E on page 297). The desire not to live, work, eat or travel with a person of another race must surely be counted as a privately-oriented want.

segregation is an evil, so that discussion tends to turn on finding principles to support a conclusion one is already quite sure of rather than an anxious weighing of pros and cons; yet it is in the latter kind of situation that the most valuable reflections on principles arise.

Let us therefore turn to a field in which opposite views can easily be found and look for the principles that underlie them. The essential question which arises in connection with both schools and medical care is the same: can an attempt to create a common system of schooling or medical care for the bulk of the community be justified on want-regarding grounds alone (such as equality) or must the ideal-regarding principle of integration be introduced?

A school system which satisfies integrationist criteria will be one attended by the bulk of schoolchildren in a given community; exceptions will be distributed across racial, class, occupational and religious lines so that the bulk of the children in any subdivision will be attending the common schools while the schools catering for children outside the system will not draw support from any particular group. This is, of course, an 'ideal type' though all the conditions except the last can be found in some places.[1]

I have deliberately said 'school system' because I want to concentrate on an issue other than the question whether children of different ability should be educated in the same school (or even in the same class) or whether separation based on intelligence and aptitude is justifiable. It is fairly obvious that integrationists will tend to favour comprehensive schools and ungraded classes within each age-group, though they might admit aggregative and distributive considerations to form a counter-argument. Similarly, integrationists will favour co-educational schools rather than single-sex schools. But where a school system contained schools segregated by race, religion, social class, etc., this would indeed be anti-integrationist in the way I am concerned with in this section, and the same question would arise, 'Well, why shouldn't they be?'[2]

[1] That is to say, there are places where most of the children in any category one considers attend the common system; but the schools outside the system cater for particular categories. A partial illustration would be the fact that most Church of England children attend local authority schools but there are special Church of England schools.

[2] It is of course well known that segregation can come about de facto by quite informal means when each school has a fixed catchment area, since the

A medical care system will be integrated if it is used by the bulk of the population and the same conditions about exceptions hold. The easiest way of bringing about an integrated school or medical system is of course to make it illegal for anyone to avail himself of schooling or medical care outside the public system. A less extreme method is to make it a good deal cheaper to use the public system by making the public system free or available at a heavily subsidized price while making everyone contribute through taxes, national insurance, etc., to the cost of doing this whether or not he actually uses the system. Private provision would not of course be subsidized publicly and might even be taxed.

The value of integration is raised once proposals are made to divorce public responsibility from (integrated) public provision. In other words, it may be suggested that the education or health of citizens is a legitimate public concern and that nobody should go without some minimum of schooling or medical treatment because of inability to pay; but unified state provision of the education or the treatment, rather than a sum of money to cover some standard quality, should be rejected. Thus, in the field of schooling it has been suggested in the USA that the appropriate public authority should give parents vouchers for so much per child of school age and allow the parents to choose at what school they will spend it. Standards of attendance for children and efficiency for schools may be imposed by the public authority, but the publicly provided schools will not have a preferred position in any way, charging whatever they cost to run.[1] In Britain too there are

[1] Milton Friedman in R. Solo (ed.), *Economics and the Public Interest* (New Brunswick, N.J., 1955). John Vaizey in *The Economics of Education* (London, 1962), Chapter II criticizes Friedman's proposal, but his objections are of many different kinds and not systematically arranged. One is that there are aggregative and distributive objections to making parents pay fees (or more than nominal fees) for the education of their children. Another is that the state may need to step in between the parents and the child to make sure that the child gets a sufficient quantity and quality of education, whether or not the

boundaries can be drawn to cut along racial or class lines. Cf. Wilson, *op. cit.* p. 186: 'Although there is no legally defined segregation in Chicago schools, school district lines tend to follow the lines of racial communities, and as a result, the great majority of all children attend schools which are racially homogeneous.'

frequent suggestions to the effect that parents who send their children to private schools should be subsidized either by direct payments or by tax relief; and in fact there are many ways in which a private education can be secured below cost, such as covenants taken out by grandparents and scholarships for the children of the managerial staff of some firms.

Alternatively, direct subventions may be made from public funds to privately-controlled schools. Grants to denominational schools in Britain are on a very generous scale, whereas in the USA the constitutionality of anything beyond free transport to denominational schools is still (1964) in question. Contributions to churches are, however, tax deductible and this is a concealed subsidy of formidable proportions.

There are analogous proposals in the sphere of medical care. Analogous to the first educational proposals would be one for universal insurance providing standard amounts of money for given treatments, while leaving doctors and hospitals to organize privately and charge what they will. Analogous to the second would be direct public support to the costs of running private hospitals.

2.C. *Schools and Medical Care (ii)*. I think the importance of these possibilities is that almost the only thing against them is their anti-integrationist effects. They therefore force one to decide whether or not one values integration for itself and, if so, how much. If (contrary to the integrationist view) one assumes that the only object of the public authority is to make sure that everyone reaches some certain level of education or medical treatment, both distributive and aggregative arguments can be advanced in favour of divorcing public responsibility from public provision. On distributive grounds one may say that it is unfair for someone who chooses to obtain the service privately to be penalized compared to someone who chooses to obtain it publicly. An irrelevant factor (i.e. whether the service is obtained from a public or private

parents want it to. But Friedman allows for subsidies and for minimum educational standards: provided these were high Vaizey's criticism on *these* points would presumably be met. However, inasfar as Friedman appears to allow that only the 'neighbourhood' (external) effects of education can be the subject of the minimum or the subsidy, it would be subject to Vaizey's strictures. I have omitted this qualification from the proposal considered in the text.

source) is allowed to determine its cost.[1] On aggregative grounds it can be pointed out that it leads to an irrational allocation of resources to subsidize only the publicly-provided service. The artificial difference in cost will cause many who would have been willing to pay the cost of the privately provided service if it were put on all fours with the public one, to use the public one instead, since they are paying for it in taxes, etc., and do not get a rebate if they don't use it when entitled to. There is thus a waste here in that people are allowed to get the public subsidy only if they use the public service, whereas some would prefer to take the subsidy and put it towards the cost of private service. This is sometimes varied by saying that even if only *part* of the subsidy were returned to those who use a private service there would be a clear gain in efficiency because there would be some who would then switch from public to private service (*ex hypothesi* these would welcome the new arrangement) and since they would only receive part of the subsidy, those sticking to the public service would also gain (the rest of the subsidy of each person who switches can be divided among those who remain).

All this case against confining the subsidy to those who use the public service (and it applies even more strongly against special taxes or a ban on private services) depends on the initial assumption that there is no advantage in public provision as such. It also ignores any possible want-regarding arguments on the other side. I shall consider the latter first. It may be said that private schools of high prestige and social exclusiveness militate inevitably against equality by giving some children an unfair start in life. No parent should be able to buy such special advantages for his children. Now this argument works against the top English 'public' schools, but it does not serve as any basis for an objection to full subsidies for parochial schools wherever their standards and prestige are *lower* than those of state-run schools. If therefore one objects to such subsidies it cannot be on these grounds. Moreover this argument does not have any application to medical care: private doctors and hospitals do not seem to produce the same objectionable 'old boy' advantages over and above the specific advantages (if any) of the private services.

[1] If the private service is more expensive intrinsically, so being educated or treated privately costs more, this is a 'relevant' circumstance. It is differences in cost over and above this which are condemned on the present basis.

An alternative distributive objection to the proposal is that education and/or medical services are too important to be rationed by the price mechanism rather than being distributed equally. There are two ways of avoiding this objection. One would be for public and private provision to have exactly the same ceiling in expenditure per head. The objection would thus be met; therefore, if one still dislikes the result it cannot be on these grounds. Instead of meeting the objection by adding a restrictive condition to the proposal one might instead ask if the objection is well founded. Food, for example, is important. Should it therefore be rationed? Surely there is no point in prescribing a maximum which anyone can spend on any particular item unless the total amount for distribution is fixed and cannot be increased merely by an increase in the price. (This is a necessary, not a sufficient condition.) During and after the war, for example, the total amount of food was more or less fixed for the country as a whole, so that if one person had more food another had to have less. Normally, however, this is not so. I can have more food without decreasing anyone else's by my foregoing something else. The extra food is (very crudely) produced instead of the 'something else'. To limit the amount I can spend on food has no advantage under these circumstances, at least on want-regarding grounds; it is not a distributive but a sumptuary measure.[1] Schooling and medical care are only to a very limited extent analogous to food during the war; the proportion of the national income spent on them is largely open to (public or private) choice. This is particularly clear with regard to bricks and mortar, books, equipment, etc., but even staff could quite easily be increased over a quite small number of years if the demand were there. The number of schoolteachers, particularly, is limited mainly by pay and training facilities. If the National Health Service and the national school system are second rate this has little to do (directly at least) with the existence of private institutions.[2]

We are left, therefore, with the conclusion that if one is against the proposal under discussion even where it would not incur

[1] It would on standard economic analysis reduce the price of food, if food-producing is an increasing-cost industry. But this would be an extraordinarily inefficient way of producing distributive effects. The distributive object could be achieved by providing a free or subsidized amount of food for each person or simply by redistributing incomes.

[2] For a discussion of contrary views expressed by A. D. C. Peterson and John Vaizey see Note K on page 305.

criticism on either of the distributive grounds just canvassed this can only be because one places value on integration as such. Once integration is accepted as a principle, one's view of the whole subject changes. Instead of every departure from equal treatment of public and private provision being looked at askance, every departure from a complete ban on private provision must be regarded as a concession. People should be grateful for being allowed to get out of the public system rather than complaining because they are not paid for it as well. The common position whereby people are neither helped nor hindered from opting out can then be seen as a compromise between integration and other competing values. It will sometimes be too severe and sometimes too lenient, according to the numbers who wish to opt out when the position is in force and their distribution within the population as a whole. But it has the advantage of being a simple and unique solution, which at least usually is enough to keep the bulk of a population within the public system.

3. DOUBTS AND QUALIFICATIONS

Integration is, as I have pointed out, little recognized explicitly as something valuable in its own right. I have offered reasons for thinking that integrationism must, however inchoately conceived, underlie certain commonly held political views; but it still seems to me uncertain whether my account so far has got to the bottom of the problem or whether it is something slightly different from integration which is valued. Perhaps only integration in *certain* situations is regarded as valuable, which means that what is valued cannot be described *simply* as integration. In the present section I shall see what can be said for the idea that wherever a measure appears desirable some reason other than an integrationist one can always be found, while integration without any supporting reasons ceases to appear desirable.

Consider once again the school example. Even if we agree that in some circumstances a disinclination to see the public system merely one of many and catering to a minority can only be justified on ideal-regarding grounds, must the ideal be an integrationist one? What if the only school in an area was that run by a certain religious denomination? This would be integration but would it be desirable? Or again suppose the public system were less 'enlightened' than almost any of the private schools; would one not welcome a move which enabled more children to get into the latter?[1]

I am inclined to say that what these examples show is that for me at least integration is a very *weak* value (i.e. that it is easily over-ridden by other considerations) but not that it is non-existent. If the private schools were only a little more 'enlightened' than the public ones I should favour pressure toward use of the public system, but not if the disparity were great. The first example raises in addition the question how far the value of integration is reducible to that of democracy. As far as each parent determining the education of his child is concerned private schools offer as much scope as public in principle since private schools may be run by the parents of the children attending them. But if what one values is that the members of the community should determine as one group how the next generation is to be educated, there is no substitute for public schools.[2] If democracy is interpreted as a means to *communal* determination of the content of education (rather than as a means to individual want-satisfaction) isn't this in fact the integrationist principle in an extended form rather than a quite different principle?

A second line of attack would be to say that integration as a general principle can itself be justified on more ultimate grounds. On this line of argument it is not denied that integration is always a value (if a weak one); all that is being denied is the belief that it cannot be reduced to some other value. (This would make integration a 'focal aim' analogous to 'negative freedom'—See VIII.3.A.,

[1] The word 'enlightened' is used here not in order to beg questions but to avoid saying 'better' since that would involve the distributive objection considered in the previous section. The public schools must be regarded as being *as good* in the relevant sense for distributive arguments (i.e. their products get just as good jobs, as many university places, as much social prestige, etc.) but objectionable in the sorts of opinion they instil and the kinds of character they tend to produce.

[2] At any given time only those adults with children of school age would be determining the education of children under a regime of private schools; with publicly-controlled schools all adults could influence policy. Another point, first raised in IV.6.B., is that people may make different ideal-regarding choices (e.g. for their children) when participating in a collective decision than when making an individual decision, and the former might be preferred on ideal grounds. Notice that this argument would work even if the decision-making group were identical in the two cases.

p. 145.) Three possible justifications for integration would be: (i) that it is conducive to economic efficiency; (ii) that it is conducive to social and political stability and (iii) that it is conducive to the protection of the poorer and less powerful sections of the community. All these justifications seem to me cogent ones. Thus, on the first count, one can suggest that a community in which different groups have an entirely different way of life, with different institutions to take care of every contingency from birth to death is liable to serious splits to heal which there will be no shared experiences and standards.[1] On the second count, it can be urged that a stratified society will allow positions of power to be occupied by those who are comfortably situated already and have everything to lose from change, while keeping out those with more intelligence and drive.[2] On the third count it can be pointed out that so long as those with money can buy exemption from the common lot the rulers and the generally dominant groups in a society will have little motive for making sure that the public facilities are of good quality.[3] If every cabinet minister knew that he had an average chance of entering a state institution for the aged or that his children were going to a state school would this not make a difference?[4]

[1] Michael Young's *Rise of the Meritocracy* illustrates the possibility of combining this state of affairs with 'equality of opportunity'.

[2] See Vaizey, reported in *The Guardian* (22 November, 1962), p. 6 and C. A. R. Crosland, *The Conservative Enemy* (London, 1962).

[3] This is equally true when the poorer groups have their own representatives, since the representatives themselves may be richer than those who voted for them. Many Labour MPs send their children to non-state schools, for example. My point is not that these MPs are inconsistent even if they advocate the abolition of such schools (any more than it is inconsistent to advocate a change in the rule of the road in Britain while continuing to drive on the left) but that the existence of private provision allows for a divorce between the experience and outlook of the representative and his supporters.

[4] 'If the wife of a wealthy Rhode Islander fell ill he would send her to some place like Butler or the Hartford Retreat or Chestnut Lodge. This is cheaper, for a large taxpayer, than paying a proportionate share of the upkeep of an adequate hospital system.

'The public-school system in any city, whether Providence or New York, has to combat the same form of negative larceny. The man of property sends his kid to a private school when young, to a preparatory school and an endowed but expensive college later. His only interest in the public schools is to see that as little money as possible is spent on them. Schools never fare worse than during a "reform" administration.

The difficulty posed by these arguments is that they are almost too good. By this I mean that if they *always* justify integration, how are we to tell whether integration is a value on its own or not? However, though there is a danger in resorting to thought-experiments in such cases we can at least try to settle the question by taking parochial schools and imagining a situation where all religions have a fair cross-section of the population as far as power is concerned and where religion does not appear to be divisive. We might then ask whether the case against integration would fall to the ground. I find it very difficult to answer this question, but for my own part I believe that these conditions would enormously weaken the case for non-segregation, without destroying it.

'When people barely in the economic middle class become ill their families send them to voluntary hospitals, just like the wealthy. This is not cheaper for them than it would be to pay a pro-rata share of a higher tax rate, which would provide decently maintained public hospitals. They have no alternative. The rigorous economy grafters, and the newspapers that are their mouthpieces, have shoved the level of public education and public hospitals so low that the poor little white-collar gulls have to shun them too. Then, since the public schools and hospitals are no good to them, these invertebrates dissociate themselves from the fate of public institutions. And the economy hogs let things run down some more.

'I often wonder what would have happened if all men of military age hadn't been compelled to go into the same public armed services during the most recent war, and if there had been a nice private auxiliary army available for the sons of large taxpayers. I believe that rations, clothing, medical attention, and pay would have been lousy in the ranks of the public army. To compensate for these drawbacks, discipline would have been much more severe, and the newspapers would have been full of editorials against coddling public soldiers.

'There was no attempt to run war on that system, and I sometimes doubt that we should run peace that way.' A. J. Liebling, *The Press* (Ballantine Books, New York, 1961), pp. 76–78.

VIII

FREEDOM AND NATURAL RIGHTS

I. FREEDOM AS AN AGGREGATIVE PRINCIPLE

1.A. *Introduction*. Any discussion of words used in political judgements must obviously deal with 'freedom', for some would say that this is the most important single justification for any policy. But definitions of 'freedom' differ a great deal (far more so than actual uses of the word) and the value of freedom is explained in different ways: these two points are connected, as I shall try to show. In the present section I shall briefly examine two definitions of 'freedom' that would make it an aggregative want-regarding principle. Then in the following two sections I shall take up one definition that would make it an ideal-regarding principle (Section 2) and one that would make it justifiable on various grounds but mainly on distributive want-regarding ones (Section 3). In the final section of the chapter I shall discuss briefly the related concepts of 'natural rights' and the 'national minimum'.

1.B. *Freedom as Want-Satisfaction*. The simplest way of defining 'freedom' is to identify freedom with want-satisfaction itself. The freedom of one person (considered alone) is increased when his opportunities to satisfy his wants are increased. The freedom of several people (taking them together as a reference-group) is increased on balance when there is an overall increase in want-satisfaction in the group—that is to say, whenever the aggregate gain in opportunities is greater than the aggregate loss of opportunities. An assertion that freedom should be increased as much as possible then becomes equivalent to the aggregative want-regarding assertion that want-satisfaction should be maximized.[1]

[1] See for exponents of this definition of freedom Bertrand Russell in R. N. Anshen (ed.), *Freedom, Its Meaning* (New York, 1940), p. 251; and Dahl and Lindblom, *Politics, Economics and Welfare*, pp. 28–29.

There are two snags with this definition. The first is that it does not correspond with usage: to enslave someone is not normally said to increase the slave-owner's freedom though it certainly decreases the slave's. This is trivial by itself, but the serious objection underlying the point is that the definition does not then allow one to make the distinctions within wants for which 'freedom' is normally used. A useful concept for making distinctions which are relevant to political judgements is destroyed by extending it.[1]

1.C. *Freedom as Non-Grievance.* It is possible, however, to recognize the disadvantage of this definition of 'freedom' as want-satisfaction while claiming that it can be altered in such a way as to leave 'freedom' with a special aggregative significance. Graham Wallas, in *Our Social Heritage*, takes as a stalking horse a typical statement of the definition just considered to the effect that personal liberty is 'the practical opportunity that we have of exercising our faculties and fulfilling our desires'.[2]

He then goes on to say that when our desires are frustrated

the reaction depends more on the nature of the obstructing cause or agent, than on the nature of the obstruction.

Common usage refuses to say that the liberty of a Syrian peasant is equally violated if half his crops are destroyed by hail or locusts, half his income is taken by a Turkish tax-gatherer, or half his working hours are taken for road-construction by a German or French commander. . . . The reactions to human obstruction take the form, first of anger and an impulse to resist, and then, if resistence is found to be, or felt to be, useless, of an exquisitely painful feeling of unfreedom; and similar reactions do not follow non-human obstruction. Wounded self-respect, helpless hatred, and thwarted affection, are, that is to say, different psychological states from hunger and fatigue, though all are the results of obstructions to the carrying out of our impulses. When Shakespeare wishes to describe the ills which drive men to suicide he gives,

> The oppressor's wrong, the proud man's contumely,
> The pangs of despised love, the law's delay,
> The insolence of office, and the spurns
> The patient merit of the unworthy takes,

[1] One may compare the disadvantage of extending the concept of 'power' so that it, too, becomes equivalent to 'getting what you want' rather than to exercising control over the actions of other people.

[2] Graham Wallas, *Our Social Heritage* (London, 1929), p. 158. Quotation from Sidney Webb, *Towards Social Democracy* (Westminster, 1916).

and does not mention the want of food and clothing from which he must himself have suffered during his first wanderings from Stratford.[1]

Wallas goes on to say that not all human hindrances produce a feeling of unfreedom, but only those inconsistent with 'normal' relations in a primitive society; this is in line with his general belief that men are not well adapted except by accident to the 'great society'. He thus suggests that a man who is denied access to a woman who loves him or from whom a faithful wife is taken feels differently from one who is denied access to a woman who does not love him; that though Ahab and Nathan both had 'wants' in connection with the vineyard only Nathan can feel 'the oppressor's wrong'; that the Germans invading Belgium were no doubt fulfilling their desires, but were hardly become more free; and that whether the property-less feel unfree or not depends on whether they picture the social environment as 'human' or 'natural', and on whether they regard their lack of property as due to the working of the 'normal environment' or as due to 'abnormal action of . . . fellow human beings'.

This idea is not peculiar to Wallas. Frank Knight has written that

> Scrutiny of any typical case of unfree behaviour reveals that the coercive quality rests on an ethical condemnation, rather than the ethical condemnation on a factually established freedom. . . .
>
> All taxes and legislative or administrative regulations take away property values, but they do not 'confiscate' if sound social-moral reasons clearly underlie them. We do not feel constrained in having to take the right side of the street or sidewalk. We simply do not have the feeling of coercion except in connection with one of ethical disapprobation.[2]

[1] Compare A. M. Schlesinger, Jr., *The Coming of the New Deal* (Cambridge, Mass., 1959), p. 476: 'The political consequences of the New Deal aroused perhaps the gravest concern—in particular, the conviction that affirmative government was destroying American freedom. Government was coming to seem, first of all, arbitrary and personal; in a phrase much revived in these years, it appeared a government of men and not of laws. In a thoughtful article in 1935, *Fortune* suggested that, although no businessman ever liked regulation, what really infuriated him about New Deal regulation was "the sense of personal action, personal will; the feel of the human interferer".'

[2] F. H. Knight, *Freedom and Reform: Essays in Economics and Social Philosophy* (New York, 1947), pp. 10 and 11.

The advantage of the kind of definition of freedom given by Wallas and Knight is that it enables one simultaneously to allow for the fact that not all satisfaction of even privately-oriented desires counts as 'freedom' and to say that this limited sense of 'freedom' is of special aggregative significance because the denial of it adds to ordinary lack of want-satisfaction 'an exquisitely painful feeling of unfreedom' or 'the feeling of coercion'. To be unfree is thus both to have certain desires frustrated and to have unpleasant feelings of 'unfreedom' or 'coercion', so it should be counted twice in any aggregative calculation.

The trouble with this analysis is that although it gives a meaning to 'feeling free' it does not give an independent one to 'being free'.[1] Freedom becomes a matter where 'thinking makes it so'. If I feel (however unreasonably) that I am being coerced by having to walk on one side of the street I am thereby 'unfree'. Conversely, a slave who has never imagined that he might be anything other than a slave and therefore does not feel resentment about his lot must be regarded as 'free'. Ordinary usage, appealed to by Wallas, will surely not support this. A purely subjective definition of 'freedom' rules out of court any attempt to give criteria for it independent of the feelings of the people of whom freedom is predicated. More subtly, it tends to misrepresent the usual reasons for taking freedom seriously. If a man believes, however unreasonably, that he is being treated unjustly there is perhaps a *prima facie* case for removing the source of his belief, if this can be done without much trouble. But if he *is* being treated unjustly, surely the *main* reason for doing something about it is that injustice is bad; whether or not the man concerned is fretting about it does not alter the moral case for putting things right. The same goes for 'feeling unfree'.

2. FREEDOM AS AN IDEAL-REGARDING PRINCIPLE

If we suppose that 'freedom' means something other than either getting what you want or not feeling aggrieved, what does it mean? The next possibility I shall consider would make it an ideal-regarding concept. To say that someone is free is not, on this view,

[1] 'Feeling slighted' can be understood as 'believing (with appropriate emotional overtones) that one *has* been slighted'; but 'feeling unfree' must be understood as 'feeling (with appropriate emotional overtones) that one has been unjustly treated, wronged, etc.'

merely to talk about his opportunities or frustrations. It is to say something about either the content or the origin of his wants.

Ideal-regarding conceptions of freedom, then, can be divided into those which look at the content of a person's wants and those which look at the origin of his wants. The first equates freedom with virtue, the second with self-determination. In spite of the perennial fascination which the first kind of definition has exercised over philosophers I doubt whether it has ever (at least in the countries I am dealing with) been accepted widely by non-philosophers—or even by philosophers outside their studies. The idea that nobody can freely do bad—whether the criterion of badness be motive or intention—is surely too paradoxical to commend itself to Common Sense, as Sidgwick would have said.[1]

The alternative kind of definition of 'freedom' which makes a man's freedom depend on the origin of his wants seems to sit better with ordinary sentiments. For example, someone acting under post-hypnotic suggestion may feel free and he may be able to do what he wants to do yet one would be uncomfortable about saying that he was acting freely; similarly with someone who bought ice cream as a result of subliminal advertising during a film. Once these are admitted one can be presented with cases of people who act compulsively (compulsive liars or compulsive truth tellers, compulsive slackers and compulsive workers, for example), people exposed to massive and one-sided advertising or propaganda campaigns, and people who are 'slaves' to custom, fashion or the opinion of those with whom they associate. Galbraith's attack on 'synthetic' wants and Riesman's obvious preference for the 'autonomous' man rather than the 'inner-directed', 'other-directed' or custom-bound type are recent illustrations of writers who have been driven to adopt self-determination as a criterion in order to make their criticisms.[2] Earlier, de Tocqueville had sug-

[1] See the Appendix to *The Methods of Ethics*, and the *Lectures on the Ethics of T. H. Green Mr Herbert Spencer and J. Martineau* (London, 1902), Lecture III on Green's Ethics, for acute criticisms on this score of Kant and Green, respectively.

[2] J. K. Galbraith, *The Affluent Society* (London, 1958) and David Riesman, *The Lonely Crowd* (Anchor Book, 1950). An interesting complication is that Galbraith tries to force his case into a want-regarding framework and thus has to say that the satisfaction of 'synthetic' wants should be ignored in the calculations of welfare economists. Since however 'synthetic' wants certainly *are* wants this is surely confusing.

gested that 'democracy' might bring about a new kind of 'despotism', and since he claimed that one of the most significant features about it would be that people would accept it cheerfully, he was clearly not referring to lack of freedom in a want-regarding sense.[1]

3. 'NEGATIVE FREEDOM'

3.A. *Justifications of 'Negative Freedom'*. The most usual way of defining 'freedom' is none of those dealt with so far. It is not extended to the satisfaction of all wants but neither is it restricted to virtuous or self-directed wants. And, though it tends in practice to cover the same things as the 'non-grievance' definition, it is not defined in a subjective way. This usual definition is that people are free when they can satisfy wants which fall within particular categories. In this sense 'freedom' is contrasted with interference, censorship, control, regulation, restriction, constraint, etc. Examples are freedom of speech, freedom of worship, freedom of travel, freedom to paint one's house any colour one chooses. 'Freedom' used in this way is generally interchangeable with 'liberty', whereas this is far less true of the other uses considered. Following Berlin, I shall call it 'negative freedom'.[2] To show that negative freedom so defined is valuable one has to bring it into relation with some ultimate justification. Want-regarding justifications of both aggregative and distributive values may be adduced, as may ideal-regarding justifications.[3]

The distributive argument is the simplest, since it takes the form of an assertion that (subject perhaps to overriding aggregative considerations) people have an absolute right to do whatever they

[1] The difficulty for any theory of freedom as self-determination is of course whether any cases of a self-determining person could ever occur, for if they cannot this makes the distinction pointless. What has to be shown is that criteria can be produced according to which some actions are at least 'more self-determined' than others or according to which some people are 'more autonomous' than others. My own view is that this can be done and that it need not involve any assumption that actions can be 'uncaused' or 'undetermined'; but it is enough for my present purpose to indicate the sort of distinction to which I am referring.

[2] *Two Concepts of Liberty* (Oxford, 1958). To lump together the want-satisfaction definition and the two ideal definitions as 'positive' seems to me, however, to obscure the matter.

[3] All three are used, for example, by John Stuart Mill in *On Liberty*.

want in certain matters. What these matters are may be specified in general terms, as with Mill's 'very simple principle' or they may be spelt out individually as in the US Constitution and the various statements of 'natural', 'basic' or 'human rights'.[1] But however the matters are specified the claim is always the same: that in these matters a man has a *right* to do what he likes even if this impinges on other people in ways that they dislike.[2] And this claim is presumably to be classified as a want-regarding distributive one.

Any defence of negative freedom in aggregative terms must seek to show that adherence to the principle will always bring about a maximum of want-satisfaction, or at least that it will only in very extreme cases be justifiable on aggregative grounds to override the principle of negative freedom. Such a defence may take one of two forms. One of them is to say that the wish to carry out the acts in the area claimed for inviolable freedom is always as a matter of fact stronger than the desire to suppress such acts.[3] Plainly, this assertion will be far more plausible if publicly-oriented wants are ruled out when making the aggregative reckoning, since many of the wants to be counted against negative freedom would be of this nature.

It might at first sight seem that *all* the opposing wants would be publicly-oriented, and if this were so the result of the calculation would be unproblematical indeed. But things are not so simple. 'Freedom of speech' for example does not mean freedom to speak when nobody is listening—it means freedom to attempt to com-

[1] ' . . . the sole end for which mankind are warranted, individually or collectively, in interfering with the liberty of action of any of their number, is self-protection. . . . '
'The only part of the conduct of any one, for which he is amenable to society, is that which concerns others. In the part which merely concerns himself, his independence is, of right, absolute. Over himself, over his own body and mind, the individual is sovereign.' John Stuart Mill, *On Liberty*, Chapter I, 'Introductory'.

[2] Mill's criterion might seem to rule out the possibility of others being adversely affected; but he recognizes that one can only strictly speak of *predominantly* 'self-regarding' actions.

[3] This line of argument obviously involves the same psychological assumptions as the definition of freedom as the absence of feelings of grievance. But whereas on that view all oppression, when felt as such, constituted 'unfreedom' (by definition), the view at present being considered merely maintains an empirical connection between the absence of certain restraints (defined independently of anyone's feelings) and acute frustration.

municate what one has to say either to as many people as possible or to as many members of some selected group as possible. Inasfar as someone taking advantage of this freedom is successful then he will impinge on the lives of his intended audience. If they don't want to hear what he has to say this would be a privately-oriented want. Moreover, even a desire to stop *other* people hearing something—on the face of it a publicly-oriented want—would be derived from privately-oriented wants if the motivation behind the desire were a fear that people hearing the message might be liable to behave differently in a way that would affect one personally.[1]

An ideal-regarding justification for negative freedom can be constructed on the same lines. It can then be said that, whether or not the desire for negative freedom is more intense than the desire to suppress it, it is a more worthy desire and should therefore be preferred on ideal-regarding grounds.[2] What all these three

---

[1] Presumably those who were in the forefront of the campaign to prevent Communist propaganda from functioning in the USA were not (at any rate consciously) doubtful of their own steadfast devotion to 'the American way of life'. But neither (except in the more fanatical cases) was the motive behind it a purely disinterested desire to prevent the weaker brethren from being led into temptation. It was, rather, the belief that Communist converts in sufficient numbers would alter American society at large—which would of course affect the non-Communists too. This is the rationale of Justice Holmes' famous 'clear and present danger' test for the constitutionality of a limit on freedom of speech. 'The question in every case is whether the words used are used in such circumstances and are of such a nature as to create a clear and present danger that they will bring about the substantive evils that Congress has a right to prevent.' (*Schenck* v. *U.S.* 249 U.S. 47 (1919), reprinted in *The Mind and Faith of Justice Holmes*, ed. Max Lerner (New York, 1943), pp. 294–297). Schenck was held responsible for distributing leaflets to conscripted men in wartime urging them to 'assert their rights', and Holmes, speaking for the Court, argued that the intended effect of the document and its actual tendency was to impede conscription. Thus Schenck's free speech affected the privately-oriented wants (dependent on winning the war) of others.

[2] The ideal-regarding principle most relevant is that of self-determination. Thus, the ideal-regarding justification of negative freedom would come close to the definition of 'freedom' in terms of autonomy which was canvassed in Section 2. But there is of course still a big difference between *defining* 'freedom' as autonomy and asserting that (negative) freedom (defined independently) is a *means* to autonomy. The relationship is analogous to that mentioned in a previous footnote between the *definition* of 'freedom' as non-grievance and the assertion that (negative) freedom is a *means* to non-grievance.

justifications of negative freedom have in common is their picture of the person who is enjoying the freedom benefiting at the expense of the rest of the community. The exercise of freedom is an indulgence, making the person exercising it more satisfied and perhaps even better; but the rest of the community must simply put up with it. Communicating an idea, for example, is if anything an imposition on its recipients—it is not regarded as satisfying them or making them better.[1]

Alternative (or, if they are slightly reinterpreted, supplementary) to these justifications for negative freedom are justifications which concentrate attention on the benefits which an exercise of negative freedom provides for those *other* than the person exercising it. Again, the argument can take either a want-regarding or an ideal-regarding form.[2] In its want-regarding manifestation it requires the assertion that in the long run it will be in the interests of everyone to allow or even encourage innovation in behaviour and ideas.[3] The ideal-regarding version of the argument requires one to maintain that whether or not it satisfies people's wants to have innovation in behaviour and ideas this is still something desirable. One reason for saying so would be a belief that people are made 'better' by being forced to choose between alternative patterns of life and thus act willy-nilly on the dictum that 'the unexamined life is not worth living'. An alternative reason would be the quasi-aesthetic one that a world with a great variety of human types in it is preferable to one with fewer—virtually irrespective of *what* the types are.[4]

[1] See Mary McCarthy, 'The Contagion of Ideas', *On The Contrary* (New York, 1961) and Robert Paul Wolff, 'Reflections on Game Theory and the Nature of Value', *Ethics*, LXXII (April 1962), pp. 171–179. Also compare IV.6.D. above.

[2] The want-regarding line of justification can take only an aggregative form because, *ex hypothesi*, there is no conflict of interests.

[3] The *locus classicus* for this argument is John Stuart Mill's *On Liberty*, where it is maintained that non-innovating societies will not merely remain stationary but go backwards.

[4] One strand of German Romanticism consisted in an assertion of this value judgement and, in an attenuated form, it makes up one of the many strands of Mill's argument in *On Liberty*. For a treatment of German Romanticism from this angle see Chapter X, 'Romanticism and the Principle of Plenitude' in A. O. Lovejoy's *The Great Chain of Being* (Cambridge, Mass., 1948). On page 107 he summarizes the view in question as follows: 'If the world is better the more variety it contains, the more adequately it manifests the possibilities of

An interesting point that arises here is whether these two justifications for negative freedom are not 'too strong' in the sense that they justify *more* than negative freedom. If innovation is so desirable why stop short at tolerating it? Why not actively encourage it? If, for example, the case against deliberately suppressing the dissemination of new and challenging ideas is the advantage to society of such dissemination, will not the same consideration require that the state take an active hand in *ensuring* the dissemination of these ideas? And if so should not negative freedom be swallowed up in some more comprehensive principle?

I think one might accept that these two arguments for negative freedom have further implications but still deny that 'negative freedom' could usefully be superannuated. This denial would be based on the fact that the principle of negative freedom lies at the confluence of a *number* of ultimate considerations. As a sort of lowest common denominator it offers a basis of agreement for people whose ultimate principles are widely divergent.[1] If we adopt this approach we can surmise that some categories of negative freedom will be more strongly supported on some grounds than on others. Mill's mistake, I would suggest, lay not in advancing alternative reasons but in not distinguishing where they applied. Toleration of homosexuality and various other practices may, for example, be supported on the grounds that it doesn't do other people any or much harm (the distributive or first aggregative argument). Freedom of speech, publication, etc., on the other hand, may be supported more effectively on the second ideal-regarding argument; and so on right through the list of things covered by the umbrella of 'negative freedom'.

[1] Cf. C. L. Stevenson on 'focal aims', *Ethics and Language*, pp. 179, 189–190.

---

differentness in human nature, the duty of the individual, it would seem, was to cherish and intensify his own differentness from other men.' The implication, which was unhesitatingly drawn, was that a diversity of good and bad is better than a uniformity of good. 'What would the uniform repetition of even the highest ideal be? Mankind—time and external circumstances excepted—would be everywhere identical. . . . What would this be in comparison with the endless variety which humanity *does* manifest?' (quoted p. 308). Similarly with the arts: diversity not quality is the test. 'Every offspring of the brain, everything that wit can fashion, has an unchallengeable right of citizenship in this larger understanding of the creation.'

3.B. *Application to Groups.* The same justifications which were given for securing negative freedom to people considered individually may also be applied to people in groups (families, clubs, states, etc.). On distributive grounds one may describe freedom of association, freedom of assembly and national self-determination as 'natural', 'basic' or 'human' rights. On aggregative grounds one may point to the frustration of having the affairs of a group of which one is a member interfered in, and to the indirect contributions made by people in groups to the long-run satisfaction of others' wants. And finally one may appeal to group freedom as an essential means of cultivating a spirit of independence, initiative, etc.[1]

The grounds for interference, on the other hand, can be more numerous where a group is concerned. I shall deal first with those grounds for interference with the freedom of a group which take the group itself as reference-group and then with those which take a wider group as reference-group.

(1) Interference with a group, where the group itself is the reference-group, may be proposed on either ideal-regarding or want-regarding grounds. Ideal-regarding grounds would be that what the group was doing was immoral or otherwise undesirable even if those in the group wanted to do it. The prohibition of homosexual relationships among consenting adults or the prohibition to be found on the statute books of some American states of certain kinds of sexual intercourse even by married couples might be justified (or might once have been justified) in this kind of way.

Want-regarding grounds for interfering in the affairs of a group can be either aggregative or distributive. Aggregative grounds would be that on balance the group frustrated more wants among its members than it satisfied; while distributive grounds would be that the group distributed want-satisfaction wrongly. Where the operation of such grounds seems possible, it may be thought desirable for the courts to review the actions of a club or a trade union for conformity with its rules; or for the rules themselves to be amended on the grounds that they are unfair between the members or that they are undemocratic. An illustration of the second is the tutelage exercised over local authorities by the central authority in (for example) Britain and the USA, where this is employed not in order to counter spillover effects from the local

[1] See for the last R. A. Nisbet, *The Quest for Community* (New York, 1953) and W. Kornhauser, *The Politics of Mass Society* (London, 1960).

area but in order to prevent substantial injustice. Another would be A. A. Berle's suggestion that the state (perhaps through the judiciary) should take a hand in supervising the labour policies (especially with respect to dismissals) of firms.[1] An illustration of the third would be provided by proposals for the state's insisting that trade union constitutions be democratic and for compulsory workers' participation in the management of firms.[2] In addition, group (negative) freedom may conflict with individual (negative) freedom, i.e. if the group is left alone it may use its freedom to suppress the freedom of some of its members.[3]

Plainly, nobody in his right mind would continue to belong to a group in which he was being badly or unjustly treated if it were almost costless in terms of want-satisfaction for him to leave the group and either join another group satisfying the same wants or switch to satisfying different wants. Intervention on want-regarding grounds therefore becomes more important the more costly it is for a member to leave the group. For example, trade union membership (where there is a closed shop) or membership of a professional association (where this is necessary to practice the profession) obviously involve one's livelihood, and to move from the area where one lives so as to escape a local or national jurisdiction is awkward if possible at all. At the other end of the scale there are groups where the penalty for resigning is so small that it can be quite reasonably claimed that anyone who belongs to the group has chosen freely to do so. Intervention could not therefore increase want-satisfaction since (*ex hypothesi*) belonging to the group is of negligible importance or there are other groups just as good.[4]

[1] *The Twentieth Century Capitalist Revolution* (Harvest Books, 1954), Chapter III, 'The Conscience of the King and of the Corporation'.
[2] See Austin Albu in *New Fabian Essays* (London, 1952), ed. R. H. S. Crossman.
[3] See especially Henry S. Kariel, *The Decline of American Pluralism* (Stanford, 1961) for a full account of such clashes in the contemporary USA. The infamous AMA with its power to ruin a man for speaking out against the official line or engaging in 'socialistic' practices is of course the stock example. Kariel suggests that one of the prime tasks of the state is to *rescue* people from more intimate groups—a welcome note of qualification to the rising tide of pluralism.
[4] See Kenneth Boulding, *The Organizational Revolution* (New York, 1953), p. 51. 'No system of political checks and balances can make a dean so amenable to a professor's point of view as an agreeable letter in the professor's pocket from some other dean.'

(2) Now let us consider justification for curtailing the freedom of a group where a wider reference-group than the group in question is invoked. This covers cases where the actions of the individual or group impinge on others either unfairly or in such a way that the satisfaction of the individual or group amounts to less than the dissatisfaction of the others affected. Many restrictions on these grounds apply in much the same way to both individuals and groups, although of course inasfar as a number of people acting collectively are more likely to be effective than the same people acting separately the case for restricting the freedom of groups is greater. (A mass rally may be a threat to public order where a speech would not be, for example.) But, in addition, special grounds for restriction may arise in the case of groups from their prohibiting people who wish to from becoming members: examples would be golf clubs or trade unions with racial restrictions.[1]

Just as intervening in the affairs of a group for the sake of the members became more clearly justified the greater the loss incurred by leaving the group, so in the same way the greater the loss from not joining the group the stronger the case on distributive want-regarding grounds for preventing it from keeping out would-be members. Discrimination in the single golf club in an area is more serious from this point of view than discrimination in one of a dozen tennis clubs all within easy reach. Some groups do not provide any service at all; their sole *raison d'être* is that their members like one another's company. In such cases although one may say on ideal-regarding grounds that it would be better if they were the sort of people who could be congenial with other races (etc.) there is no tangible commodity to be distributed and the only intangible one, congenial company, would be destroyed if unwanted members were forced on the group. Ideal-regarding grounds alone might still lead one to wish to prevent such groups from functioning, but it would surely be tyrannical (i.e. unreasonable limitation of 'freedom of association') even if it were possible, to insist that people choose their marriage partners or friends impartially.[2]

[1] As Wechsler in effect admitted in the article referred to in VII.2.A., the term 'freedom of association' is far more naturally applied to letting people who wish to associate do so (so that laws prohibiting miscegenation would fall under its ban, for example) than to forcing people to associate with others because those others wish to associate with them.

[2] 'I do know . . . that in thousands of ways there exist restrictions which always have existed, and always will continue to exist, by which people are

4. NATURAL RIGHTS AND THE NATIONAL MINIMUM

One of the commonest justifications of negative freedom is the claim that it is a 'natural', 'human' right. But there are also rights of this kind which require positive state action, and it is worth looking at these as well. Examples from the *Universal Declaration of Human Rights* (1948) are:

> Article 22 (the right to social security); Article 23 (the right to work); Article 24 (the right to rest and leisure); Article 25 (the right to an adequate standard of living; the right of mothers to special care and assistance); Article 26 (the right to education); Article 27 (the right to participate in cultural life; the right of protection of scientific, literary and artistic productions).[1]

The inclusion of these 'positive' rights has been objected to on the grounds that they aren't the sort of thing that can be *demanded* of a government unconditionally. The government can only provide them if the economic basis of the country is sufficiently advanced. But to this it has been replied that the Declaration offers a *standard of achievement* against which the achievements of governments may be measured and judged. The question then becomes whether these are adequate as a standard of achievement. It seems to me that to express these positive demands in the language of absolute distributive principles is to use the wrong conceptual apparatus.[2]

Why, for example, an *adequate* standard of living? Surely, other things being equal, the object should be the highest possible average income, properly distributed. Setting up arbitrary minimum standards to which each person must come up is an attempt to avoid having to deal in both distributive and aggregative values,

[1] Quoted by N. S. Marsh in Guest (ed.), *Essays*, p. 242 n.

[2] 'Absolute' because there is no reference to relative positions of different people or groups which are to be maintained. See Chapter III.4.A.

---

enabled to exercise choice with respect to their friends and neighbours. (quoted by Dennis Lloyd, *Public Policy* (London, 1953), p. 144). The case in which this was said by one of the judges was a Canadian 'racial covenant' case, the question being the validity of such a covenant. Since such possibilities are always open it is surely not necessary to lend them reinforcement in the teeth of both distributive and ideal considerations. ('Distributive' because there is a tangible good at stake: 'certain property situated at a summer resort'.)

but I do not see that it can work unless these 'rights' are claimed only as rules of thumb derived from ultimate principles. The traditional civil liberties on the other hand can be aptly put into an absolute distributive form, since they do not require any reference to *amounts*. An analogy to 'an adequate standard of living' would be 'a moderate amount of free speech' but the latter is not what is called for in a declaration of rights.[1]

The same comments apply to the idea of a 'national minimum' if this is taken as resting on an absolute distributive principle. To say that everyone should be guaranteed 'subsistence' or kept out of 'hardship' leaves the principle on which the relevant amount is to be fixed up in the air. It could of course be taken to mean that the only obligation of the state is to keep its citizens barely alive and this would at least provide some sort of fixed point. Normally, however, comparisons of various kinds will be brought in, but

---

[1] Mr Maurice Cranston has argued in *Human Rights Today* (Ampersand Books, 1962) against the inclusion of these 'positive' rights in declarations of human rights on the grounds that they lack the two essential qualities of *paramount importance* and (universal) *practicability*. But it is not at all clear that the 'negative' rights are of paramount importance compared with the 'positive' ones, if this is taken to mean that wherever one of the former kind conflicts with one of the latter kind the first should always prevail. (If there were never any conflict between 'negative' rights and other values one could not speak of their relative importance at all, as was argued in I.2.B.)

In a paper prepared for the International Political Science Association in 1964, Cranston suggests that there is a duty to relieve suffering but not to promote actual pleasure, and then attempts to assimilate 'negative' rights to relieving suffering and 'positive' rights to the promotion of pleasure. But even if the assumption of a moral asymmetry between pains and pleasures is accepted (and my own view is that it is merely a reflection of the fact that pains tend to be more intense than pleasures—as Epicurus for example held—so that an unweighted felicific calculus will inevitably give pains more significance) the attempt to assimilate 'negative' rights to prevention of pain and 'positive' rights to promotion of pleasure doesn't work. The alleviation of hunger and disease is not included in the traditional 'negative' rights but it obviously falls under the 'relief of suffering' category rather than the 'promotion of pleasure' category.

As for practicability, it does not seem certain that the statement of the 'positive' claims might not successfully be whittled down until they were at any rate as generally practicable as many of the 'negative' ones. Surely the important point is that even when this had been done the particular level of well-being put forward as a right would still have no unique significance: it would be an arbitrary stopping place in a matter where it was true to say, 'The more the better.'

vaguely, so that it is impossible to tell upon exactly what the level of the 'minimum' is supposed to depend at any given time.[1] For example, it is said that pensions and public assistance should keep up with rising prosperity; but this leaves the initial relation between them and the level of prosperity completely arbitrary.[2]

Alternatively, these vague comparisons can be replaced by precise ones, e.g. between a man's lifetime earnings and his retirement pension or between his average earnings and his sick pay. But these raise complex problems of equity, and it is to that notion that I now turn.

[1] Benn and Peters, *Social Principles and the Democratic State*, pp. 144–146 suggest that the notion of 'basic needs' is inflated *pari passu* with the rise in the national income per capita. Inasfar as this is so (and I doubt whether it is, except to a very minor extent) it is an interesting psychological fact but it does not turn an absolute distributive principle into a comparative one.

[2] 'In 1959 the Government promised those receiving assistance "a share in increasing prosperity". It has not had the courage or the honesty or the clarity of mind to go on to explain what this means. Does it mean that assistance payments will rise to reflect the average increase in personal income during a year, half the average, or what?

'Why is the new increase in the rate for the single person to be 6s.? Because, the Minister of Pensions told us last Monday, there was a 4s. increase last September and this puts the total increase on a par with the increase in national insurance. Why should the full rate for a single person now be 63s. 6d. rather than, say, 70s. or 80s.? This is no doubt the exact amount that the Government thinks it can afford and get away with, but can a political democracy do no better than that? Is there nowhere a rational explanation, nowhere a principle?' Peter Townsend, *Observer*, 24 February 1963, p. 10.

IX

EQUITY

1. EQUITY AS AN INTERSTITIAL PRINCIPLE

THE principle of equity is that equals should be treated equally, and unequals unequally. If the principle is taken to include within itself criteria for determining what makes people 'equal' and what makes them 'unequal', then it swallows all other comparative distributive principles. But it may instead take the general outlines of the distributive pattern as given and concentrate attention on 'anomalies', 'inconsistencies' and 'incoherences'. The last Oakeshottean term serves to bring out the conservative implications of 'equity' when used in this second, interstitial way.[1] It may also remind us of the familiar objections to any attempt to maintain that such a limited form of criticism is the only proper one. If criticism is to be confined to pointing out incoherences, one cannot reject an entire tradition or system, however repulsive.[2] And no room is allowed for the injection of new conceptions. Oakeshott says that the only possible argument for giving women the vote was that their position had already changed in other ways. But the main reason for this was the series of Acts of Parliament in the latter half of the nineteenth century, such as the Married Women's Property Act, which were passed under the influence of an 'abstract' idea of equality.

The advantage of appealing to 'equity' is that in cases suited to it one can derive results from it without having to bring in any independent criteria at all; they may instead be found within the system to which the principle of equity is being applied. One may simply say: in this system, x is admitted as relevant yet *here* it is not allowed to make a difference between the treatment of A's, who have x, and B's, who haven't x; or, conversely, x is not

[1] Cf. 'Political Education' in Laslett, First Series.
[2] See R. H. S. Crossman, *The Charm of Politics* (London, 1958), pp. 134–138.

admitted to be relevant yet *here* it *does* make a difference. All that is
needed is a sharp eye for inconsistency. Thus, one may criticize a
series of decisions or a set of rules as inconsistent with one another
without having to look any further and see whether there is anything wrong with the general principles or laws underlying the
decisions.

Here are two simple examples: firstly, an analysis of the decisions of conscientious objectors' tribunals in the Second World
War suggests that one's chances of being enrolled as a conscientious objector depended to a large extent on the part of the
country one came from. The proportion of applicants whose
claims were accepted varied widely, as did the proportions within
this number accepted on different grounds (e.g. religious or non-
religious). Secondly, whether someone is prosecuted for homosexual activities in private or for mild speeding depends largely
on the composition of the Watch Committee the opinions of the
Chief Constable or on even more fortuitous factors—such as being
caught in the first place.

Now the point about the concept of 'equity' is that we can
criticize such situations as inequitable without committing ourselves to such questions as: 'Should the law prohibit homosexuality in private?' 'What criteria should conscientious objectors' tribunals apply?' We merely have to take our stand on the
principle that whatever is to be done should be done equally to all
who are alike in what the rule itself declares to be the relevant
respects.

Thus, equity (as Aristotle pointed out in Book V of the
Nicomachean Ethics) can operate as a refinement on legal justice.
Legal justice is satisfied when the rule covering a case is properly
applied, but equity can make finer distinctions. To revert to the
conscientious objectors' tribunals: it would be very hard to show
that any of the tribunals actually contravened the relevant laws;
there was therefore no legal injustice. Yet at the same time people
alike in their arguments and apparent sincerity (which all tribunals
agreed to be relevant factors) were treated differently from one
tribunal to another. All the tribunals were legally just and any one
would have been equitable by itself, i.e. consistent in its own
decisions; but taken together they were inequitable. Again, no
legal rule is infringed when only some practising homosexuals or
speed-limit offenders are prosecuted. If you are prosecuted the

fact that other offenders haven't been prosecuted is not an admissible defence; but you have a certain cause for complaint on grounds of equity.

Cases where equity is a refinement of legal justice in the way Aristotle commented on are important but by no means exhaust the applications of the notion of equity. Any policy or rule may be criticized as inequitable on internal grounds (i.e. taking the assumptions of what's relevant from within the system) wherever there are anomalies affecting distribution.

Wayne A. R. Leys, in his book, *Ethics for Policy Decisions*,[1] gives an extract from the record of an American wartime arbitration tribunal in which we see the labour representative, German, put a mining company to rout (soon after this exchange, Leys records, the company asked for an adjournment and conceded the point):

> *German:* 'I've never been down in a mine, so you'll have to explain this to me. You say that you buy the carbide, but the miners buy the lamps?'
>
> *Company:* 'That is correct.'
>
> *German:* 'I see. I suppose you have an office up above the mine where the miners work.'
>
> *Company:* 'Of course.'
>
> *German:* 'And in the office, you supply the carbide, but the clerks have to buy their own lamps?'
>
> *Company:* 'Certainly not. In the offices we use electric lights.'
>
> *German:* 'Oh, I see. You supply the electricity, but the clerks have to buy their own bulbs and fixtures.'

Another example would be provided by a state of affairs in which very similar goods (e.g. desks with inkwell holes and desks without them) are subject to purchase tax at widely differing rates. This might be described as an *anomaly* and further as *inequitable* as between buyers or as between manufacturers of the two kinds of goods. All that is required for calling such a situation inequitable is a judgement of 'similarity' between classes of goods, and though this allows room for dispute the dispute is not over ethical principles but based on common sense or fiscal policy. The objector tries to show that two differently taxed objects are closely similar; the defender tries to show that the two objects are different in some respect relevant to fiscal policy, e.g. that one is mainly for industrial or educational use, the other for domestic use. Of course, the

[1] (New York 1952), p. 283.

objector may not accept the fiscal policy underlying the distinctions drawn by the defender, but provided that the treatment of the goods in question has been shown to be consistent with such a policy, the first attack, of simple inconsistency or anomaly, has been successfully repulsed. If the attack is to be continued this can only be done by an appeal to principles brought in from the outside. And these the defender may refuse to accept in a way in which he could hardly refuse to accept the implications of his own principles as extracted from the system he defends.

In the next section of this chapter I shall subject the notion of equity to critical scrutiny in three brief examples: taxation, wages and land. Then, in Section 3, I shall offer an extended analysis of a single example, that of child allowances. Here, as well as commenting on the application of 'equity' to the question I shall try to show more generally how any acceptable proposal is likely to be a compromise between the various policies which would completely satisfy one principle at the cost of failing to come near to satisfying any others.

2. THREE EXAMPLES

2.A. *Taxation.* If one had to pick out the sphere of discourse in which 'equity' plays the largest part it would surely be that of taxation, especially when 'impartial' academic economists and Royal Commissions are doing the talking. Does it perhaps function as a term of art, with a special significance in connection with taxation? It does not appear so. It is still used as an 'interstitial' concept, as may be gathered from the approximate synonyms which are employed for it: 'anomaly', 'discrimination', 'difference of treatment', 'harsh treatment' and so on.[1]

If one asks how it can come about that arguments about the proper way to raise the vast sums of money required by modern governments are conducted in terms of an interstitial notion, the only answer is an historical one. In the nineteenth century, when the pattern for this kind of talk was set, the amounts to be raised were small and in the general climate of opinion of the time it seemed reasonable to take it as an axiom that they should be raised as far as possible without changing the pre-tax distribution of

[1] These examples are drawn from the Minority Report of the Royal Commission on Taxation of Profits and Income, 1955.

income. 'Equity among taxpayers' was understood in this way and the adherents of the 'equal sacrifice' and the 'proportional sacrifice' theories fought their battles in these terms.[1]

The more fuzzy idea that taxation should be based on 'ability to pay' is plainly from the same stable as these, though it leaves more room for a complete exemption from taxation of those with the lowest incomes. The essential point of all these views is that they shun any open evaluation of the post-tax position by the application of general distributive criteria, assuming that pre-tax differentials are to be kept more or less intact. But one is bound to ask why, if the pre-tax distribution could be improved, the tax system should not be consciously designed with an eye to this. To J. S. Mill's justification of the 'equal sacrifice' theory on the ground that 'equality ought to be the rule in all affairs of government' Pigou could reply:

> There is at least as good a case for taxation that makes net satisfaction equal as for taxation that makes sacrifices equal. Indeed, there is a better case. For people's economic well-being depends on the whole system of law, including the laws of property, contract and bequest and not merely on the laws about taxes. To hold that the law about taxes ought to affect different people's satisfactions differently, while allowing that the rest of the system may properly affect them very unequally, seems not a little arbitrary.[2]

A particular disadvantage of the 'equity' approach is that it inevitably leads to a confounding of two entirely independent questions, namely (1) what is a desirable post-tax income-structure? and (2) how much should be spent on state-provided services? If it is supposed that there is some 'equitable' way of sharing out any given tax burden, the main determinant of post-tax income distribution will be the *amount* of money raised in taxes, so that if (for example) the tax system is progressive those who seek greater equality of post-tax incomes will have to favour greater state expenditures and vice versa. Once the 'equity' approach is aban-

---

[1] 'Equal sacrifice' of 'utility' was generally taken to entail taxation proportional to income, while 'proportional sacrifice' of 'utility' (i.e. each person to lose the same proportion of his total annual flow of 'utility') was generally taken to entail a modestly progressive income tax structure. These deductions rested on the postulate of the decreasing marginal utility of money.

[2] Quoted by Fagan in *Readings in the Economics of Taxation*, American Economic Association (London, 1959), p. 42.

doned the two questions can be considered independently and the tax system organized to satisfy the answers to both.[1] It goes without saying that the two questions of resource allocation and income distribution are rarely in public discussion dealt with separately as I have suggested. What is more disappointing is to find even the 'left wing' minority of the Royal Commission on Taxation of Profits and Income (1955) still arguing within the 'equity' frame of reference. Perhaps the explanation can be found partly in the terms of reference of the Commission but there is no internal evidence that the members regarded the task set them as peripheral or pointless. The Minority indeed recognized the danger of piecemeal applications of the concept of 'equity':

> When a base on which a tax is levied lacks precise definition the system is particularly exposed to the danger that successive concessions, designed to take care of special situations, will cause a progressive erosion of the tax base until its efficacy as an instrument of taxation is seriously weakened. For once a new principle is admitted into a tax system on the basis of which additional concessions are given, the pressure for further concessions based on arguments of close analogy becomes well-nigh irresistible. Every time some particular interest can make out a case of inequitable treatment under the existing provisions of the law and a fresh concession is granted, it invariably follows that some other interest finds itself disadvantageously treated as a result and can make out an even stronger case for a further concession that can be shown to follow logically from the original concession made.

But their suggested solution lies merely in a better application of 'equity'. The difference between the Majority and the Minority about the propriety of taxing capital gains—a difference actually based (quite properly) on their opposed political outlooks—was

[1] See R. Musgrave, *The Theory of Public Finance* (New York, 1959), pp. 5–6. It should be noted that if the total amount of public expenditure required is small but the degree of redistribution wanted is great it may be necessary to have straight transfers of income between different sections of the community, by giving those with low incomes 'negative income tax', that is a supplement to their earned income under P.A.Y.E. rather than the usual deduction. Incidentally, the 'benefit theory' of taxation is a special case of the present proposal for separate enquiries into the allocation of resources into public goods and the post-tax income distribution; it is what one gets with the element of redistribution set at zero. See K. Wicksell, 'A New Principle of Just Taxation' in Musgrave and Peacock (eds.), *Classics in the Theory of Public Finance* (London, 1958), pp. 72–118.

represented as a disagreement over the correct definition of 'income' for taxation purposes. Whether or not capital gains should be taxed (and if so, how heavily) is one question; and various considerations of both an aggregative and a distributive kind are relevant to it.[1] Whether or not capital gains are 'income' is another question and not a very profitable one, the answer being that they are like ordinary examples of 'income' in some respects and not in others.

A second example will illustrate the limits of 'equity' further. The Majority points out that earned income relief had been first introduced in 1907 on the grounds that this would compensate for the greater precariousness of earned incomes. But since the introduction of superannuation relief, there was a danger of the same thing's being allowed for twice over. The Minority however said:

> We believe . . . that whatever the historical reason for the introduction of the differentiation may have been, 'precariousness' should not be regarded as the sole, or even the most important, reason for maintaining a difference in treatment as between incomes from work and incomes from property. In our view there is a strong case for making some allowance—even though the cost cannot be precise—for the real cost involved in working as opposed to owning property: for recognising the fact that in performing work, a man, in the words of Adam Smith, 'must always lay down the same portion of his ease, his liberty, and his happiness'.

The argument is that equal incomes should be treated unequally if their 'cost' is different; but the 'cost' of unearned income is nil, so if the Minority's principle is followed it would seem to entail that unearned incomes should be taxed away entirely. This is a perfectly reasonable view but it is not the minor 'difference in treatment' which the Minority was using the argument to justify. Surely the only way of dealing with the question—once one is willing to raise the possibility that the *source* of a given amount of income may be relevant to the rate at which it should be taxed— is to examine the justification for private property and its existing distribution, and then if changes are desired, to work out the best means of bringing them about.

[1] For example: does speculation serve a useful purpose? Is the present distribution of private property radically unjust? How far is it fair for any group in the population to be insulated against inflation?

2.B. *Wages.* Wages may be determined by bargaining, backed (except where strikes are illegal) by the threat of combat; they may be determined by discussion on merits between employer and employee; or they may be authoritatively determined. In the countries with which I am dealing compulsory arbitration under the auspices of the state with the results binding on employers and employees is not acceptable to either of the parties which would be involved directly, because it is thought that such a proposal would restrict the autonomy of economic groups (especially trade unions) too much. Nor do governments seem keen to impose solutions on the entire economy, perhaps thinking that it would be impossible to find a universally agreeable wages policy and dangerous to its authority to try to impose one which was not universally agreeable. This leaves bargaining, discussion on merits and authoritative determination on the initiative of the parties immediately concerned in a dispute. At the same time there is a general expectation that wages should be 'fair', in other words, justifiable by reference to some distributive criteria. Bargaining has no automatic tendency to produce 'fair' results (at least where perfect competition does not prevail) so there is an inevitable tendency for independent tribunals to be called in wherever discussion on merits fails to produce agreement.[1]

In practice, such tribunals cannot forget that their authority depends on the sufferance of the two parties.

> In these conditions it would be logical, if slightly cynical, to ascribe to the arbitrator the role, not of dispensing justice, but of preventing strikes.[2]

But this is not the whole story.

> . . . in practice decisions are constantly being reached by one means or another; and these decisions, whatever the processes by which they are actually determined, are always presented as the outcome of argument and counter-argument in socially responsible terms . . . Even arbitrators, on the rare occasions when they show their hands and confess to the grounds of their own decisions, never admit that

---

[1] See however Note J on page 303, for a discussion of the possibility of governmental manipulation of the relative bargaining power of the parties.

[2] Barbara Wootton, *Social Foundations of Wage Policy* (London, 1958), p. 95.

they have split the difference between the parties because they could not think of anything else to do; they, too, defend their judgements as being 'fair' and 'reasonable'.[1]

But what is 'fairness'? Without generally acknowledged distributive principles trade unions, employers and tribunals fall back on 'equity'. The general outlines of distribution are taken as given and then within these comparisons are made by each side in such a way as to advance its own case.

> Nobody knows in this context what justice is, and no Socrates walks the streets pestering us to find out. That is where conservatism comes to the rescue. Change—always, everywhere, in everything—requires justification: the strength of conservatism is that it is held to justify itself. It is not therefore, surprising that the maintenance of standards, absolute or comparative, should be woven as warp and woof into the texture of wage discussions; or, to change the metaphor, that history should be summoned to fill the void when moral actions must be performed without moral principles to guide them.[2]

Comparison may be made with the previous purchasing power of the same wages, with the rise in average pay (or national income) since some date, with some more specific category (e.g. professional earnings, skilled workers' earnings) or with some other specific job.[3] Common to all these comparisons is a lack of any justification for taking one comparison rather than another and a failure to enquire whether the earnings of the job compared, or at the date taken as a base, were right.[4]

Since Lady Wootton wrote her book, the situation has (1964) changed to some extent. Cabinet ministers no longer pride themselves on not issuing 'instructions or guidance of any sort' to arbitration tribunals.[5] The 'guiding light' has been institutionalized in the shape of a 'National Incomes Commission'. But the object still seems to be no more than trying to hold down average

---

[1] Wootton, p. 121. See also 98–99.

[2] *Ibid.*, p. 162.

[3] *Ibid.*, pp. 133–34.

[4] 'The outstanding feature of these comparisons is the measure in which they amount to purely circular arguments.' Wootton, p. 132. See also 'Wage Policies in the Public Sector', *Planning*, XXVIII, No. 476 (19 November 1962).

[5] Sir Walter Monckton, quoted by Wootton, p. 170.

wages to a level which will avoid inflation. The Commission's first report, on the Scottish building industry, appears to be based on the assumption that its job is to determine (or rather postulate) an average level of annual wage increases which will be non-inflationary and then apply this figure to all cases that come before it.[1] This is a shift from 'comparability' but its effect is exactly the same: to freeze the existing differences between the pay of different occupations. No attempt has been made by the National Incomes Commission to settle the proper position of Scottish builders' wages in the overall income pattern of the UK; nor would the opinions on this matter of an 'impartial' (i.e. politically irresponsible) body be of much value. As Baroness Wootton has said, this kind of question is the stuff out of which party platforms are (or should be) made.

Meanwhile, her conclusion still stands.

> Custom (the rule that whatever is is right), scarcity of labour supply in relation to planned requirements or to market demand, the title of superior skill or heavier responsibility to higher pay in its own right, or, conversely, the intrinsic virtues of equalitarianism—all these are *possible* principles in terms of which the merits of a total wage and salary structure could be judged, or a rational decision reached in a particular case. But without any such principles to refer to, either explicitly or by implication, judgements can be neither intelligent nor defensible.[2]

2.C. *Land.* Before discussing land compensation and control I would like to emphasize that I am not aiming at a systematic treatment—a complete book would be too short for that. As an illustration, however, problems arising out of the private owner-ship of land have the great advantage of allowing 'equity' to reach its fullest flowering with a minimum of support from other principles. Of course, land prices are determined, in a private-ownership system, by 'the market'; but whereas in the case of other goods their price can be represented as covering the cost of producing them and therefore 'just' (i.e. deserved by the seller), land (considered purely as location, as for development purposes) has no cost of production. Its value arises purely out of its scarcity. In fixing compensation which shall be 'equitable', comparison is all; there is nothing independent of what the land might in certain

---

[1] *The Guardian*, 23 April, 1963, p. 3.　　[2] Wootton, p. 120.

circumstances fetch, or what was paid for it, to which appeal can be made. This arbitrary quality was clearly realized by Cannan in his evidence to the Royal Commission on Local Taxation, 1899, when he said:

> ... the present land tax would be a most inequitable tax to impose, since it would not treat holders of equal amounts of property equally; and would disappoint legitimate expectations; but after it has been imposed for one or two centuries, and both the properties subject to it and the properties not subject to it have been bought and sold over and over again, always on the assumption that it would continue, it would be inequitable to abolish it, since the abolition would not treat holders of equal amounts of property equally.[1]

In modern town and country planning we find 'equity' playing a similar part, and on similarly arbitrary foundations.[2] The 1947 Town and Country Planning Act was designed to peg at 1947 prices the price at which land should change hands—a completely equitable business between landowners. Compensation was to be paid by the state for compulsorily acquired land at those prices. Existing owners should be compensated for losing their right to collect the profit from selling their land for development; after this, their profit should go straight to the state as a 100 per cent 'development charge'. Unfortunately, however, this scheme ran into various difficulties, including the important one that since it eliminated the profit from development it became impossible to provide a carrot to encourage people to sell land for development.

The Conservatives, in Acts of 1952 and 1954, abolished the development charge and kept the principle of tying compensation to 1947 prices (plus one seventh). Here is where 'equity' begins to exercise the squeeze. Justice as fulfilment of expectation is perfectly satisfied, as Self points out:

> The permanent limitation of compensation claims to 1947 values is not in principle unjust, since owners have been consistently warned since that date to expect nothing more.[3]

But any solution which puts public compensation on a radically different basis from market values has unfortunate effects on the

---

[1] In *Readings in the Economics of Taxation.*
[2] P. Self, *Cities in Flood* (London, 1961), pp. 147–164.
[3] Self, p. 156.

behaviour both of private owners and of local authorities. First, it creates an appearance of injustice in the fortunes of different owners. Justice in this context is wholly relative. As has been said, there is nothing inherently unjust about the 1954 Act's principle of compensation. But if some owners are allowed to make profits out of land and others are not, the latter feel aggrieved—especially of course if they bought their land on the opposite assumption.[1]

It is interesting to note here that, exactly as in wage negotiations each party selects other groups for equitable comparison to suit itself, so here a landowner who is prevented by planning controls from developing his land compares himself with landowners whose land has appreciated, not with those whose land has retained much the same value purely because nobody happens to want to develop their land.

This sort of compromise having run into objections on grounds of 'equity', what about the final solution: compensation at market values? This is perfectly equitable between landowners (if we take for comparison landowners whose land would be equally profitable to develop—not lucky and unlucky land-owners); but highly inequitable between landowners and the public.

> The more effectively the State plans, the bigger becomes the compensation bill, and, by the same process, the larger becomes the betterment which fortunate owners collect. In such a situation, the relative injustice to one group of owners tends to blind the public to the greater injustice which is being inflicted upon the taxpayer. But when the taxpayer eventually protests (or rather the Treasury does so on his behalf) the likely result is an abandonment of planning.[2]

The discussion in this section has of course been very general and entirely negative. But that has really been the whole point: to show the limitations of 'equity'. According to 'equity' one must treat like landowners alike, but this is consistent with any number of actual policies, each of which will have its own effects on land values. The choice must rest on aggregative considerations (what arrangements will produce the best planning?) and on more deeply considered distributive principles than equity, e.g. the principle that nobody should make windfall gains out of communal efforts (in effect an appeal to desert). Once the choice has

[1] Self, pp. 158–159.   [2] Ibid., p. 160.

been made, 'equity' has a limited place in saying how the policy should be carried out to avoid 'anomalies', 'hardship' and so on.

3. CHILD ALLOWANCES

3.A. *Introduction*. In this section I discuss the principles on the basis of which the size of child allowances might be determined; and in particular, the role of equity in this. The method employed —a catalogue of possible principles and their implications for child allowances—may perhaps be criticized as 'academic' in the most pejorative sense: remote from life and devoid of any personal involvement. But the object of this study is not to provide answers to problems; it is rather to make it easier to understand how answers may be reached. And for this purpose family allowances are useful as an example for at least two reasons. The first is that there are many different principles which can be applied to the question and they lead to widely divergent policy recommendations if taken one by one in isolation from one another. The second is that there is no 'conventional wisdom' on the subject, which eliminates preconceptions. Too often a discussion of principles turns into a game of 'hunt the rationalisation' where 'we all know the right answer' and the only problem is to deduce it.[1] Here men of good will can reach diametrically opposite recommendations by stressing different principles (especially relief of hardship as against incentive effects) and the systems of different countries are very different.[2] Indeed, Britain luxuriates in two entirely unrelated systems (family allowances and income tax relief), not to mention a third—now being run down—for university teachers (a £50 allowance for each child including the first).

With such a wealth of clashing principles having application to family allowances, any scheme is bound to represent the *locus* of several principles. The exact position adopted will depend on the principles whose validity is accepted and the relative importance assigned to them. Even if one set of circumstances were to be

[1] This complaint has especial relevance to discussions of utilitarianism. Even so large-minded a man as Sidgwick managed to derive the details of Victorian sexual morality from the general principle of utility.

[2] Compare A. Carter, *Too Many People*, Fabian Society (1963) and John Vaizey, *The Economics of Education* with Peter Townsend in *Conviction*, for recent examples.

dealt with and there were no disagreements on the probable effects of various policies, an immense variety of schemes could still be justified by appealing to different combinations of principles and assigning different relative importances to them. But little could be gained by starting with the full complexities of the position, and the present analysis is nothing if not exploratory. I shall therefore deal most of the time with the implications of each principle considered in isolation from the rest, and leave the reader to put them together according to the relative weight which they have in his own mind.

3.B. *Incentive and Desert.* To begin with, let us take the straightforward argument from incentive for making concessions to parents. This argument will obviously apply only to situations where a higher birthrate is desired by the public authority than that forthcoming without such concessions. If the birthrate were too high without family allowances the same argument would justify penalizing parenthood with a tax.[1] It is, I think, generally agreed that the main motive behind the establishment of family allowances in Britain was the highly publicized fear of a declining population, and that this dictated the form of the family allowance: it being assumed that couples would have one child anyhow if they were going to, no allowance was given for the first child. It seems highly questionable whether the family allowance should be continued on this ground and whether relief through the income tax allowance should not be stopped.[2]

[1] Two possible ways of penalizing parenthood would be to increase national insurance contributions of those with children, and charging something for attendance at state schools. 'The size of family, it seems, is tending to rise quite fast. A more realistic notion of the cost of having children might not be a bad thing for many parents, therefore, over the next ten years. This would substantially ease the problem of providing teachers for a rising number of children of primary age. (There is also an interesting ethical problem. Roman Catholics are forbidden to use customary means of restricting the size of their families. Is it fair that Anglicans, Jews and atheists should be taxed to support the consequences of religious beliefs which they reject?) Before the war, when the fear was that the race might die, the problem was exactly the opposite: how to encourage people to have children. It can be seen, then, that circumstances alter cases; fees might be wrong then but right now.' John Vaizey, *The Economics of Education*, pp. 34–35.

[2] A more sophisticated variant of the incentive argument would support the abolition of the family allowance but not the tax relief. Since a time before anyone worried about the declining overall birthrate, enthusiasts for

An alternative, distributive, way of deriving similar recommendations would be to say that if the birth-rate is below the 'optimum', those who have more children than would suit them personally are doing a service to the community and deserve to be rewarded; but if it is above the optimum those who have the number of children that suits them are behaving to some extent anti-socially and may even deserve to be made to pay the rest of the community for the cost they are imposing on it. This line of argument would lead one to espouse different practical proposals from the argument based on incentive only inasfar as people were not in fact open to manipulation by material incentives and disincentives. Those who (for religious or some other reasons) were committed to accepting whatever size of family their normal sexual habits produced, would presumably be impervious to encouragement or discouragement. If they could be effectively identified the stick or the carrot could be withdrawn from them, since it would not modify their behaviour. But if the object of making extra payments to parents or imposing extra costs on them was distributive, i.e. rewarding desert or punishing anti-social conduct for its own sake, there would not be the same case for withdrawing these payments or costs from those whose behaviour would not be altered by them.[1]

[1] The expression in the text 'there would not be the same case' is deliberately vague, for on a Kantian view one would have to say that people whose breeding happened to be socially advantageous but who did not particularly *aim* to have a large family whether it were socially beneficial or not, are not manifesting a virtuous will and are therefore not fit recipients for reward. But if one thinks that people should be rewarded for doing the right things, whatever their motives may be, one would reward all parents if one were going to reward any.

It is interesting to notice a certain similarity between the 'Kantian' line on

---

'eugenics' have been worried about the fact that the higher income groups were being outbred by lower income groups. Since intelligence does seem to have an hereditary factor and since there does seem to be some correlation between income (at least earned income) and intelligence, there might therefore be reasonable grounds for mild alarm about the long run consequences. (See for example Ginsberg's appraisal, 'The Claims of Eugenics', in *Essays in Sociology and Social Philosophy*, I, and Eysenck, *Uses and Abuses of Psychology*.) Income tax relief strongly discriminates in favour of the affluent—to those who do not get enough to pay income tax anyway it is worth nothing whereas to those paying super-tax it can be worth over £100 per child, including the first—so it presumably has rough-and-ready 'eugenic' properties.

3.C. *Hardship and Equality.* Even if we leave out the argument from incentive, which depends for its force on there being a 'sub-optimum' birth rate, there is still an aggregative argument for family allowances. This takes the form of saying that people with large families will suffer hardship without special financial help and that in particular their children will. The overall level of well-being will therefore be increased if money is transferred to those with children from those without.[1] This argument is really no more than a variant of the utilitarian justification of an equal income distribution derived from the postulate of diminishing marginal utility and the assumption that everyone's utility function with respect to money is about the same.[2] What this utilitarian argument justifies, it is not always appreciated, is not equal pay for each wage earner but an equal payment to each human being. A believer in economic equality for its own sake should surely attach himself to the same principle rather than to that of equal pay for each worker.

But by whatever route one arrived at the principle of an equal income for each person, it would be necessary to modify it to provide for incentives unless labour were to be directed; even variations for the sake of incentive though could be brought under the principle of equality if one took one's principle to be that incomes should be equal *net of work*.[3] Higher pay for unpleasant jobs in unpleasant places on this principle is actually necessary for equality to be achieved.[4] Sickness and retirement pay under such

[1] Cf. Wootton, *Social Foundations . . .* , pp. 185–186.

[2] See Halévy, *Growth of Philosophical Radicalism* (Boston, 1955) for Bentham, and F. Y. Edgeworth, 'The Pure Theory of Taxation', *Classics in the Theory of Public Finance*, ed. Musgrave and Peacock, pp. 119–138.

[3] By 'net of work' I mean that the difference between pleasant work and unpleasant work should be compensated; not that the difference between working and idleness should be (if indeed many people really prefer idleness to work). Willingness to work, if this were accepted, would have to be the condition of receiving the standard income during unemployment.

[4] Higher payment for living in unpleasant areas would be in principle due to everyone and not just those working; but it would be difficult to establish the relevant differentials except by seeing what incentives were necessary to attract workers to the area.

desert and the ultimate refinement in the application of 'incentive' such that only those whose conduct was actually affected by the bait would receive it. The difficulty in either case is to put the principle into operation unless one is God to whom the hearts of all men are open.

a modified egalitarian system could be either the standard (pre-incentive) income or related to total (standard plus incentive) income. Both would come to the same thing from the point of view of equality, since on the second scheme any given degree of incentive could be achieved with less extra payment during health and before retirement than on the first scheme.[1]

3.D. *Equity and Child Allowances*. So far in this section I have considered as alternative justifications for family allowances an aggregative argument from incentive and its corresponding distributive principle of desert, and an aggregative argument from the diminishing marginal utility of money and its corresponding distributive principle of equality. Against this background the limited role of 'equity' can be better appreciated. The principle that equals should be treated equally can be paraphrased as the principle that 'irrelevant' factors should not be allowed to make a difference in people's positions. One application of this to family allowances would be to claim that two couples with an equal income should not have an unequal standard of living because one couple has children and the other does not (or because one has many and the other few).[2] If 'standard of living' is interpreted in terms of material possessions, travel and entertainments, holidays, etc., the allowance would certainly be large on this basis, and quite plausibly might be directly proportional to income.

This proposal would in effect assimilate having children with being the victim of illness, accident or natural disaster, and there are two immediate objections to this. The first is that parenthood is, since the advent of reasonably reliable contraceptive methods, something which can be freely chosen or rejected.[3] The second is that the relevant 'equality' should be not 'standard of living' but

[1] The point would however have different implications from the point of view of *equity*, as I shall show in the next sub-section of this chapter.

[2] The French scheme of family allowances, which adds about a third to one's income for each child might be thought to satisfy this requirement, though the motive behind its introduction seems to have been increasing the population.

[3] This of course applies only to places where contraception is not illegal. It may be asked whether one should not also include as exceptions those whose religious (or other) convictions prevent them from availing themselves of contraception; but I do not think so. The analogy would still be not with someone who gets hit by a car but with someone who jumps under a car from religious conviction.

'standard of want-satisfaction' and most people at least appear to regard children as something they would rather have than not.[1] This partly coincides with the first argument, since the most conclusive evidence for saying that someone prefers x to y is that he chooses it, and many people choose parenthood even at the cost of a drop in living standards as defined originally. But it also includes the case of people who have 'unwanted' children and do not afterwards regret it, in spite of a drop. It will not include people who do regret it, however; in this case equity, as envisaged here, might in theory require some compensation unless it were possible for parents to have their children adopted.

A wider objection to the proposal is also possible, namely that alternative criteria of a 'relevant difference' might be put forward. For example, one could suggest that it is inequitable for a *child's* standard of living to depend on the ('irrelevant') accident of its parents' income and wealth. So far from making family allowances rise with parental income one would on this principle rather arrange for them to increase with the parents' poverty. But the underlying principle here is equality in what I called the strong sense of the term, for what is being maintained is that *nothing* is 'relevant' where differences between children are concerned. If it is asked whether there is any reason for favouring equality among children even if not among adults, two replies—aggregative and distributive—can be given. Present financial incentives are not necessary with children as they are with adults (inasfar as there is any need for incentives these can consist in the knowledge that what one does in childhood will affect one's prosperity as an adult) and if people deserve different incomes for different contributions to the general welfare this does not apply to children. It is, however difficult to see how equality for children can be combined with inequality for parents except in a universal boarding-school system with negligible holidays at home. There are also objections of principle, though I think they can be greatly exaggerated. On incentive grounds it can be argued that incentives will not be effective if people cannot use extra money to give extra advantages to their children, and on desert grounds it can be argued that if people deserve extra money they deserve to be able to spend it

[1] See Vaizey, *The Economics of Education*, p. 33: 'It is by no means self-evident that a family which chooses to have children is thereby lowering its standard of living unless children are regarded as an unmitigated curse.'

how they like. One answer to this is that already there are a number of things one cannot buy, such as slaves, votes and peerages; and restrictions on the way money may be spent can be made up by increasing all rewards proportionally.[1]

Of two possible applications of equity as an original principle one is implausible and the other reduces to the strong sense of 'equality'. But equity could have interstitial uses in conjunction with the principles whose application to family allowances was discussed previously. For example, equity might be added to inconvenience as an argument against offering incentives or disincentives only to those liable to be influenced by them, even though the rationale of the system as a whole were admitted to be incentive in nature. Thus, even if it were held that the only reason for making a difference in treatment between those with children and those without was a desire to increase or decrease the birth rate compared to what it would be without such a difference being made, it might still be held inequitable to withdraw the bonus or penalty from, say, Roman Catholics on the grounds that their conduct would not be affected by it.[2] The reason for asserting this to be inequitable would be that the only basis for treating people differently under the scheme should be the number of children they have, and that their imperviousness to incentives or deterrence should not be relevant. This assertion would I think be compatible with allowing that the only justification for having a system of family allowances in the first place was to influence behaviour.[3] In short, equity may be used to insist that *if* differences are to be made, they must cut along certain lines, even if these lines are not completely suitable to the purpose of making the differences; but it cannot be used to say whether or not (subject to this limitation) differences *should* be made. An analogy would be

[1] The truth of the first is questionable anyway. Are childless people noticeably less ambitious and hard-working?

[2] For analytical convenience I am assuming this to be true of Roman Catholics though in fact it is not.

[3] This divergence from the requirements of incentive or deterrence cannot I think be explained by reference to the need to specify a 'practice'. A 'practice' of leaving out Roman Catholics could be specified and its unattractiveness does not seem to lie in utilitarian side-effects, but squarely on inequity. If there is an independent (albeit secondary) principle operating here may it not also be operative in objections to 'telishment'? (See John Rawls, 'Two Concepts of Rules', *Philosophical Review*, LXIV (1955), pp. 3–32.)

grammar, which does not force one to say anything at all, or prevent one from having a great choice of things to say, but does impose a limit on the combinations of words which are acceptable out of all possible combinations.[1]

A special application of equity is the 'What if everyone did that?' principle. (Note that it is the *act* and not the *maxim* which is submitted to test of generalization.)[2] Thus in the present example, suppose that a birth-rate of more than an average of 2·5 children per fertile married couple would be disadvantageous to the community, and that this number is being exceeded. Since each child beyond *n* thousand per year adds equally to the burden—whether it is the couple's second or twentieth child—it would be consistent with incentive (modified by practical problems and the application of equity considered above) and also with desert to reduce the bonus or increase the penalty equally for all children, whether they be the second or the twentieth.[3] Yet this might well be thought inequitable, and the reason would be (as far as I can see) that if nobody had more than three children and some had two the excess would not arise. One can say simultaneously that every child adds an equal share to the burden and that those parents who have more than three children are especially responsible for the burden. An analogy would be to say that someone who brings ten suitcases on to the bus is more responsible for overloading it than those who bring one, although of course the relief of the overloading would be equally noticeable whichever suitcase were

[1] 'Arbitrariness' is a word often used to make this kind of criticism of an arrangement. See Note L on page 306 for a brief discussion of the concept.

[2] If the criterion of 'universalizability' is applied to 'maxims' or 'principles' it is compatible with any of the principles dealt with in this study. Sidgwick, for example, accepted the criterion but went on to say that the only principle he was willing to hold in this way was that the flow of pleasure in sentient creatures should be maximized. The 'Kantian' criterion does not in itself impose *any* limits on aggregationist principles. Benn and Peters' attempt to modify the latter by adding the former as a limiting condition is misconceived; but if they were to put forward a stronger version of the 'Kantian' criterion as a defining feature of morality (or even equity) it would become plain that most appraisals were ruled out as immoral and inequitable.

[3] I think this is plain in connection with incentive, but it may need arguing in connection with desert. The point is that if payments are to be made only for contributions to the community, then since a given couple's second child is as much of a burden or benefit as its twentieth it does not 'deserve' any more bonus or any less penalty.

removed. The 'relevant difference' for policy would here be defined in terms of the results of nobody's having more than some given number of children. The disincentive effort would be applied above that number per fertile couple which would be satisfactory if nobody exceeded it.[1]

[1] Obviously because of the indivisibility of children this formula could not be precisely adhered to (where an average of 2·5 was wanted). A third child would presumably attract some proportion of the penal rate.

X

THE CONCEPT OF INTEREST

ALTHOUGH the main thread of the previous four chapters has been provided by the various distributive principles which have been examined in turn, I have already, by way of comparison and contrast, made frequent reference to aggregative considerations. The fact that this could be done without any need to talk about specific 'aggregative principles' is itself highly significant. All distributive considerations which may be advanced in particular cases are applications of *specific* distributive principles; but aggregative considerations need not be applications of anything more specific than the general aggregative principle itself. Or, to put it another way, there is no such thing as '*the* distributive principle'; but there is '*the* aggregative principle', at least, if we are willing to allow that it may take either an optimizing or a maximizing form (III.5.B.). Because of this there is little need to indicate explicitly that one's argument is aggregative in nature. Someone who presents a distributive argument usually (though by no means always) pushes it home by saying that the thing he condemns falls under a specific distributive principle: that it is unfair, inequitable, unjust, etc.; but someone who makes an aggregative objection is unlikely to do the same thing by finishing up 'it will not conduce to the greatest total happiness' or 'it isn't Pareto-optimal'. Far more often, a proximate result will be adduced and the connection with any ultimate principle left to be filled in by the hearer: 'It will increase the road-accident rate', 'It won't help economic growth', or 'It will cause hardship'.

There are, indeed, specific principles of an aggregative kind but these take the form of drawing attention to certain types of consequences which are always relevant to aggregative judgements. Two of these principles have already been noticed in earlier chapters. In Chapter VI, I noted that rule-based justice and justice as the fulfilment of expectations have an aggregative justification (VI.3.A.) and in Chapter VIII I looked at aggregative justifications for freedom defined as the absence of certain kinds of grievance (VIII.1.C.) and the absence of certain kinds of restraint VIII.3.A.). These are clearly only partial aggregative arguments because they make a selection from all wants.[1] Thus, as part of an attempt to decide whether something was justified on aggregative grounds one might, in examining all the wants involved, have to weigh up on one side its fulfilling an expectation and on the other side its diminishing negative freedom. But these two considerations are not distinct 'aggregative principles' (in the sense that justice as desert is a distinct 'distributive principle') because they can be brought together within the general aggregative principle of maximizing want-satisfaction.[2] They are more like mnemonic devices to ensure that no significant classes of want are overlooked than they are like independent principles.

This chapter and the next are devoted to an examination of several basic concepts which often occur in aggregative judgements. The first of these is the concept of interest, as it is used in expressions such as 'in so-and-so's interest', 'in the public interest' or 'in the common interest'. Because of the remarkable complexity of the concept I spend the whole of the present chapter on its elucidation. In the next chapter I discuss more briefly 'good' and 'welfare' and then such compound expressions as 'the public interest' and 'the common good'.

2. THE DEFINITION OF 'INTEREST'

2.A. *Three Definitions Rejected.* Most of the words I have been dealing with are equivocal, and, far more seriously, nearly all are vague. But while the word 'interest' no doubt has different

---

[1] In VIII.1.B. I also considered a definition of 'freedom' as want-satisfaction that would make the principle of maximizing freedom equivalent to the maximizing form of the general aggregative principle. So this too is not a *kind* of aggregative principle.

[2] Of course I would wish to maintain that two distributive principles—say desert and equality—might be 'brought together' in the sense that trade-off relationships between them could be established (see I.2.B.). But this is in no way equivalent to treating them as aspects or subordinate parts of some further principle.

meanings, the expression 'in so-and-so's interests' is neither equi-vocal nor vague. The explications of the phrase which have been offered are correspondingly clear, although, I think, incorrect. There seem to be three available. The first makes 'x is in A's interests' equivalent to 'A wants x'.[1] This rules out one's being able to ask 'A wants x but is it in his interests?' Another makes 'x is in A's interests' equivalent to 'x would be a justifiable claim on the part of A'.[2] This rules out asking 'x is in A's interests but would it be justifiable for him to claim it?' Since these two ques-tions are perfectly sensible and one can easily think of situations where the answer would be 'No', these two suggestions as to the meaning of 'in so-and-so's interests' are obviously wrong.[3] The third explication of its meaning equates 'x is in A's interests' with 'x will give A more pleasure than any alternative open to him.'[4] There are two objections to this. One is that a person can be said without self-contradiction to find pleasure in advancing the in-terests of others—where this means something quite different from 'in pursuing his own interest he unavoidably has to advance those of others.' The other is that a solicitor can be retained to 'look after A's interests while he is away' and can make a good job of it without knowing what gives A pleasure. Conversely, an arrangement calculated to provide one with enjoyable conversa-tion may well be described as giving pleasure but would hardly be

[1] C. B. Hagan, 'The Group in Political Science', in R. Young (ed.), *Approaches to the Study of Politics* (London, 1958).

[2] S. I. Benn, 'Interests in Politics', *Aristotelian Society* (1960); John Plame-natz, 'Interests', *Political Studies*, II (1954). Benn supposes that one asks a farmer 'What are your interests?' (This strikes me as a peculiarly phrased question to start with. 'Would it be in your interests for [say] Britain to enter the Common Market?' is surely a more natural kind of question.) He then says that the farmer would not give a vast sum of money as the answer to the question; but this is not because getting a large sum of money would not be in his interests but because it so obviously is. Indeed, I shall suggest that it is a paradigm of something that is in a person's interests.

[3] I add the point about the answer's sometimes being 'No' to cover the objection that one can also perfectly sensibly ask, 'Is a bachelor an unmarried man?' It is not the only way of disposing of the objection, but it seems to me the simplest.

[4] This is a common sense identification, though seldom offered as an explicit definition. Bishop Butler and Hume seem to treat 'interest' and 'pleasure' as interchangeable, as when Butler says, 'interest, one's own hap-piness, is a manifest obligation'. (Preface to *Sermons on Human Nature*, ed. W. R. Matthews (London, 1914).)

described as being 'in one's interests'. However, these objections are slight compared to those I had to make of the other two explications, and the connection between 'interest' and 'pleasure' is indirect rather than non-existent.

2.B. *'Interest' Defined*. We can approach a precise characterization of what it is about an action or policy that makes it in someone's interests, in two stages. As a first approximation let us say that an action or policy is in a man's interests if it increases his opportunities to get what he wants.

> Wealth and power . . . are potential means to any ultimate ends. . . .
> It is primarily these generalized means to any ultimate ends, or generalized immediate ends of rational action, to which Pareto gives the name 'interests'.[1]
> Civil interests I call life, liberty, health and indolence of body; and the possession of outward things such as money, lands, houses, furniture and the like.[2]

The necessary qualifications to this first approximation can best be introduced by thinking of wealth and power as assets. They can be saved (i.e. held ready for future committal) or committed. If committed, they can be either invested (i.e. tied up in a way not desired intrinsically in hopes of having *more* to commit in the future), or transferred to the use of another to do with as he thinks fit, or consumed. If consumed, they may be used to satisfy one's own wants or those of someone else. Under what circumstances would it be rational in a man to wish his possession of these assets to be less than it might be? If he takes as his point of departure a reference-group including others beside himself he will almost certainly conclude that it would be better (from the point of view of the group) for the disposal of some assets to be in the hands of other members of the group.[3] He would thus be led to favour a

---

[1] T. Parsons, *The Structure of Social Action* (Glencoe, Ill., 1949), p. 262.

[2] John Locke, *The Second Treatise of Civil Government and A Letter Concerning Toleration*, ed. J. W. Gough (Oxford, 1948), p. 126.

[3] It is not *necessary* to arrive at this conclusion by taking other people into consideration. You might, for example, wish for the happiness of others, but believe that this was more likely to be achieved if you obtained power or money and used it on their behalf. (Cf. Philip Wicksteed, *The Common Sense of Political Economy* (London, 1910) on 'non-tuism'). There are, however, many reasons for wanting others to have resources to use as they think fit; reasons of an ideal-regarding kind (independence develops character), of a distributive

diminution of his own assets if this were necessary to provide the amount for others which he thinks they ought to have. But although one could say that under such circumstances the man *wants* his assets to be reduced, this does not in the least entail that he thinks *it is in his interests* for them to be reduced. Rather, it is to be described as a case where he allows his principles to override his interests. To take care of this we must say that, in the phrase 'if it increases his opportunities to get what he wants', wants for *others* to have their share of assets are not included.

However, even if a man takes as his reference group himself alone, he may still, if he is rational, want to reduce either his assets or at least his opportunities for committing them. He will do this not (*ex hypothesi*) out of any regard for the interests of others but because he knows he is likely to be irrational in the future and it will therefore pay him to take precautions in advance. A man who knows he is carried away by the gambling spirit will avoid going to the races with more money in his pocket than he can afford to lose; a homicidal maniac in his lucid moments, a somnambulist in his waking hours, and an alcoholic or drug-addict when able to think clearly may all welcome restraint.[1] And if someone isn't himself able to make the rational calculation others can try to think their way into the man's value system, or impute what seem reasonable values to him (based largely on the value systems of more rational people) and prevent him from doing things he will regret later or make him do things he will be pleased later to have done.[2]

[1] *McCall's*, November 1961: '. . . a time-lock cigarette case for problem smokers . . . can be set to open only at fixed intervals during the day!'

[2] An example is provided by a conversation (published in *The Observer*, 10 March 1963) between Kenneth Harris and a barrister. Defending the division between solicitors and barristers the latter said:

(Barrister): 'As things are, the barrister can concentrate on winning his case; he doesn't have to consider conducting the case in a manner which will satisfy "the gallery", or his client.'

(Harris): 'But might a client want his case conducted in a way which would increase his chances of losing it?'

(Barrister): 'Indeed he might. He might, for instance, be so splenetic that he would much rather bring out in public his view that the other party is a

kind (each person has a right to a certain amount or proportion of the assets available) and of an aggregative kind (people want the chance to exercise initiative and are likely to know what is best for them).

This applies to any committal of opportunities, whether investment, transfer or consumption—not only to consumption.[1] Here we have a genuine qualification to the assertion which I put forward as a first approximation, that an increase in one's assets is always something which is in one's interests; but its status as something exceptional is often indicated by the use of a special expression 'best interests', 'real interests', 'true interests', etc.

3. IS INTEREST A WANT-REGARDING CONCEPT?

3.A. *Introduction*: '*x is in A's Interests*' *and* '*A wants x*'. If my analysis of 'interest' is sound the question arises whether it is a one hundred per cent want-regarding concept or not. By pursuing this question in the present section I shall at once be saying more about the concept of interest and more about the 'want-regarding' category itself. Until now I have managed to avoid committing myself to a particular view of exactly what is to count as a 'want' for the purpose of the 'want-regarding' category, beyond suggesting that publicly-oriented wants should not be counted. I shall try to be a little more specific here but I should like to put forward now two propositions that I believe to be true: (*a*) that a great deal more could be said on the subject and (*b*) that the conclusions which one might reach by saying a great deal more would probably not alter very much the validity of anything else in the book. In other words, it seems possible to operate effectively with the category of 'want-regarding judgements' even if the criteria for counting something as a 'want' are left a little vague.[2]

[1] Cf. Lamont, *Principles of Moral Judgement*, pp. 106–107.

[2] It follows from this last point that although the enquiry carried out in the rest of this chapter is fairly important for the argument of the book as a whole it is not essential. Unfortunately the converse of the Duke of Wellington's celebrated dictum that 'easy writing's curst hard reading' does not necessarily hold so that though the rest of this section has cost as much pains as almost any other piece of equivalent length I cannot pretend that it makes easy reading. Anyone who finds the next few pages unduly hard going might therefore be well advised to skip them—either temporarily or permanently.

blackguard and a cad and lose the case than stay quiet and win it. As it is, a barrister's whole training from his earliest years, both in advising and in fighting cases, is to think of nothing whatever but the client's real interest.'

In this passage the barrister assumes that a litigant's 'real interest' lies in winning the case rather than in giving vent to his feelings: by preventing him from being able to influence the barrister, it is suggested, the system increases rationality.

My method of proceeding will be to look in turn at five ways in which 'x is in A's interests' can differ from 'A wants x' and consider the implications of these differences. I have just dealt (2.B.) with one difference, namely that even if something satisfies all the other criteria for being 'in a person's interests' it may still be denied that it is 'in his best interests' if it is claimed that he would grossly misuse the assets unless restrained. Consideration of the implications of this point will be left to the last since it raises special issues.

3.B. *First Difference.* There is one fairly clear way in which 'x is in A's interests' is narrower than 'A wants x' and it is this: in 'A wants x' the x can refer to some way in which A wants himself or others to be affected, whereas in 'x is in A's interests' the x normally refers to a policy or action (of A or of somebody else).[1] This point emphasizes the tight connection between talking about what is or what is not in people's interests and evaluating policies and actions. Compare 'x is in my interests' with 'I was (or will be) adversely affected by x'. One can ask: 'Were you adversely affected by the cold weather?' (or some other natural phenomenon) but hardly 'Was the cold weather in your interests?' or 'Was it in your interests for us to have cold weather?' As things are, these would only make sense if it were thought that one could reasonably engage in celestial lobbying about the weather. If the weather could be controlled by government scientists the question would be perfectly appropriate.

An important corollary of the limitation of the x in 'x is in A's interests' to actions or policies is, however, that it enables one to see how people can 'mistake their interests' while knowing very well 'what's good for them'. For what is generally meant by saying that a person has mistaken his interests is not that he is unaware that, e.g. an action or policy giving him more money would be in his interests, but that he does not know what results the action or policy in question will have—whether it will provide more money

[1] For the notion of 'being affected' see IV.3.C., p. 63. To say 'Getting more money would be in A's interests' is admittedly possible, but it would surely occur in a context of teaching someone how to use the expression 'in so-and-so's interests' rather than one of giving information about A's circumstances. The only other use would be to deny that A's was a case where the limitation of opportunities to satisfy his wants would be 'in his best interests'.

or not.[1] And surely nothing is more common than to be doubtful or mistaken about the results of actions or policies. Nor is this only a matter of the difficulty of prediction. Even when the policy has been put into operation there can still very well be much doubt and dispute about the degree to which some subsequent changes (and the absence of other subsequent changes) are attributable to it.

What are the implications for the 'want-regarding' status of 'interest' of the limitation of the x in 'x is in A's interests' to actions or policies? As I have been using the 'want-regarding' category so far, one could say that a man ranked one *situation* higher than another on want-regarding grounds; but if we employed instead an 'interest-regarding' category we could not talk about the relative rankings of situations. We could only say that one *action* or *policy* was ranked higher. Now of course it can reasonably be said that there is no point in ranking situations unless this has implications for the ranking of alternative conceivable actions or policies. Nevertheless it is sometimes useful to be able to talk in terms of situations directly and it therefore seems to me preferable to follow unrestricted 'wants' here rather than 'interests' in drawing up the criteria for the 'want-regarding' category.[2]

3.C. *Second Difference.* When someone says 'x (an action or a policy) is in A's interests' we still have not established that this is in any way different from saying that A wants the action or policy x to be done or enacted. But it so happens that so far from being equivalent the two never mean the same thing (though there may of course be an empirical connection between them—that is to say it may usually be the case that when one is true the other is true). That a policy's being in one's interest cannot be logically equivalent to one's wanting that policy may be easily seen if one con-

[1] See Note M on page 307 for a discussion of the consequences of W. D. Lamont's not distinguishing actions and policies on one hand from ways of being affected on the other when analysing the criteria for saying that something is 'good for' someone.

[2] Notice that nothing has been said in this subsection to deny that *where* actions or policies fill the x place, 'x is in A's interests' is equivalent to 'A wants x'. And nothing so far precludes 'x is in A's interests' from being equivalent to 'A wants x *in the sense relevant to the want-regarding category*', provided x is an action or policy. All that has been denied is that 'A wants x' (full stop or in the 'want-regarding' sense of 'want') can always be translated into 'x is in A's interest'—for the x in 'A wants x' could be a situation.

siders these facts. (*a*) Whether or not a given policy would be in someone's interests can be established quite well without benefit of the information that the person in question does or does not approve of the policy; indeed he may never have heard of it. And (*b*) one of the main reasons why people wish to find out if a policy is in their interests is precisely so as to know whether to support it or not. But trying to find out if a policy was in one's interests so as to know whether to support it or not would be an absurdity if supporting the policy *was* its being in one's interests.

What, then, is someone saying about the action or policy *x* when he says *x* is in *A*'s interests? I have already suggested the answer to this question in 2.B.: he is saying that it will increase *A*'s opportunities to get what he wants, where 'what he wants' does not include wants for others to have such opportunities. But to give this answer at the moment would introduce all the restrictions on 'interest' compared with 'want' at once, whereas I want to bring them in one at a time. Therefore, to introduce the minimum restriction which is necessitated by the point made in this subsection, let me say that when someone says the action or policy *x* is in *A*'s interest he is saying that it will have results that *A* wants.

Thus, wants for policies have now been ruled out from the concept of interest. When you say that *x* is in *A*'s interest you are talking *about* an action or policy but what you are saying about it is something about its results. However, what you are saying is that the results are wanted by *A*. So although '*x* is in *A*'s interests' is never equivalent to '*A* wants *x*' it is always equivalent (on the present simplified definition) to '*A* wants the results of *x*'. Now comes the same question that I asked in the previous subsection: do we wish to follow 'interest' here in constructing the 'want-regarding' category and restrict the range of 'wants' to results as against policies? This time I am inclined to answer: yes.[1] It seems difficult to maintain that there can be value in a person's getting the action or policy (on his own part or on others' part) that he wants, when this is considered in complete isolation from the results of that action or policy. The action or policy is surely the means to an end: there is an element of double-counting if we

---

[1] This answer is anticipated in IV.3.C., page 62, where it is argued that in disagreeing with a majority on an issue of policy one might 'say that people's wants for *results* should be counted but . . . refuse to allow that their wants for policies as such should be'.

count both as 'wants' for the purposes of the 'want-regarding' category. There are great difficulties involved in any attempt to distinguish 'an action' from 'its results' and it is I think generally recognized that the same gross physical changes may be either 'part of an action' or 'one of the results of the action' depending on the situation, and especially that part of the situation which consists in what the agent was intending to do. Moreover, given a very extended application of 'results' the principle that one should attribute value only to the results people want can be tremendously illiberal. For example, one might argue that the main result anyone wants is to go to heaven rather than hell. If the Inquisition is a means to this then it is giving its victims what they want. I mention these difficulties but I do not intend to tackle them because they represent too big a job to be undertaken here. I shall just say that pretty clearly if the interpretation of the 'want-regarding' category in terms of wants for results is to be tolerable the 'results' must be of a short-run kind and, where the person making the evaluation differs on the means to these results from the person who enters into his evaluation, he must be sure that the means he is assuming to be the appropriate ones would be agreed to be such by any competent person. (This is, of course, not the solution but a sort of rough sketch of what the solution might be like.)

3.D. *Third Difference*. The terms of the comparison have now been amended so that we are comparing 'x is in A's interests' with 'A wants the results of x (where x is an action or policy)'. Are there in addition limits on what 'the results of x' can be? There are indeed; and the remaining three subsections, dealing with a 'difference' apiece, are devoted to them.

The first of these three limits on 'the results of x' is that results concerning people other than A are not directly relevant. This point was made in 2.B. where it was argued that the satisfaction of a desire for *other* people to have assets was not 'in one's interest'. If we compare this position with that of the 'wants' in the 'want-regarding' category it is obvious that it is equivalent to the rejection of publicly-oriented wants as suitable material for the want-regarding calculus.[1] In this respect, then, 'want' (in the 'want-regarding' formula) and 'interest' again run parallel.

[1] The case for including only privately-oriented wants in want-regarding judgements is argued out fully in Note E on page 297, so I shall not give any arguments here.

3.E. *Fourth Difference.* The second limitation of 'the results of x' in 'A wants the results of x' is a serious one and gives rise to a clear distinction between 'interest' and the class of wants taken account of in want-regarding judgements. To quote Parsons again, from 2.B.: interests are 'generalized means to any ultimate ends, or generalized immediate ends of rational action'. As we have seen, Parsons is too sweeping in saying that something which is in one's interests will *always* help one towards one's ends, or that it is *always* rational to pursue one's interests; for one's ends may include some advancement of the interests of others. But Parsons is still right in emphasizing that interests are *generalized means* to, at any rate, a wide range of ends.

To say, therefore, that an action or policy is in somebody's interests is not actually to say that it satisfies his immediate wants at all; it is rather to say that it puts him in a better position to satisfy his wants. Policies or actions that will bring me more pay are 'in my interests' but once I start spending the money 'interest' no longer applies. Suppose I spend a bit of it by going to the cinema, and enjoy myself there. The money has been spent wisely and profitably then, but was it 'in my interests' to go to the cinema? We can imagine a situation in which this could be truly said, but it would be a situation where some ulterior purpose would be served by going, e.g. impressing my employer with my highbrow tastes and thus disposing him to give me a rise.

Since some of a person's wants at least are for some state of himself (other than the state of possessing the 'generalized means' to further ends) it is clear that some want-satisfaction does not consist of interest-enhancement. More informally, if enjoying yourself is not in your interest (and I have argued that it is not) then it is obvious that people want to do things other than those which are in their interest.[1]

Thus, summing up so far, 'interest' and 'want' (for the purposes of want-regarding judgements) are similar in two respects out of the four considered: they both concentrate on results rather than actions or policies in determining whether something is 'in some-one's interests' or 'wanted' by him; and they both rule out

---

[1] This is not the same as saying that they want to do things which are not in their interest. They do, but only where they mistake their interests or act on principle. Going to the cinema in an ordinary situation is neither *in* one's interests nor *contrary* to one's interests.

publicly-oriented wants. In the other two respects 'interest' is more restrictive: actions and policies can be 'in somebody's interest'—not situations; and it is only its resulting in one's possessing means to satisfying wants rather than in its resulting directly in satisfying wants that an action or policy comes to be 'in one's interest'

The significance of 'interests', from a want-regarding angle, is that they form a very useful guide to the amount and distribution of want-satisfaction. Evaluations in terms of 'interest' (especially when this is reduced to money) are far more practicable than evaluations in terms of want-satisfaction. If one were simply given a list of the wants which someone had satisfied in 1964 and a list of the wants he had satisfied in 1965, it would be impossible (quite apart from the conceptual and practical difficulties involved in the drawing up of the lists) to say whether he was 'better off' on a want-regarding basis in 1964 or 1965. One would also have to know how important each want was to him. If the problem were then extended to dealing with a large number of people's levels of want-satisfaction, the absurdity would become even more manifest. To operate instead with *opportunities* for want-satisfaction, expressed in a common medium such as money, is a workable alternative although open to theoretical objections on the grounds that it does not measure exactly the same thing.

3.F. *Fifth Difference.* Finally, I come to a case where someone is checked 'in his best interests': that is, because if he did use his assets he would use them so as to damage himself. Here we are explicitly concerned with the way in which a man is likely to use his assets; if he is to be justifiably prevented from doing what he wants with them, must this not be on ideal grounds alone? So far, the divergencies of 'interest' from 'want' (in the sense defined for the 'want-regarding' category) have made interests into a sub-class of wants—an evaluation in terms of interests would thus be a partial want-regarding one. Does this fifth difference alter the position and make interest an ideal-regarding concept? I do not think it need do so, at least in ordinary cases. The kind of example we are thinking of when we speak of limiting a man's opportunities to get what he wants 'in his own (best) interests' is surely one where by doing what he wants now he will produce results that he doesn't want in the future (including very commonly, a lack of

opportunity to satisfy *whatever* wants he may have in the future).
The contrast is thus not between want-satisfaction and something
other than want-satisfaction, but rather between want-satisfaction
now and want-satisfaction later.[1]

Attempts to show that this is an inadequate account tend to
inflate 'interest' to an inordinate degree. Thus, Benn claims that
one might frustrate a child's wants simply in order to change the
wants he will have in the future (i.e. on ideal grounds) and that
this could be defended as being 'in the child's interests'; but this
seems to me not so, except inasfar as one is inculcating habits such
as prudence and industry which could be plausibly regarded as
useful for the satisfaction of any particular wants the child may
conceive when he is older.

> I think, however, that there may be a sense in which one might
> judge something to be in a person's interest without necessarily
> implying that he wants it, or would want it if he rightly understood
> the position, or even that want it or not, he would be pleased with
> it if he got it. When we act in the interests of a child, we may not be
> much concerned with what he wants but rather with educating him to
> be a person of a certain sort. . . . It might be in the child's interests to
> deny him satisfaction of some of his desires to save him from
> becoming the sort of person who habitually desires the wrong sort
> of thing.[2]

Benn's mistake stems, I suspect, from not noticing that 'acting
in the interests of a child' involves very special contexts. Parents,
for example, do not in general 'act in their children's interests';
they 'bring them up' or 'raise them'. Schools, again, 'educate'
children—also a different notion from 'acting in their interests'.
The main contexts in which one might expect to come across the
phrase would be such as these: a local authority checking on
foster parents to see that they were not exploiting the children in
their care, and a court deciding whether the executor of a will
leaving property in trust to a child had managed the estate 'in the

[1] It should be noticed that there is a genuine 'conflict of interest' here
between present and future in that the wants at both times can be of the self-
affecting kind relevant for 'interest'. This kind of situation is not analogous
to that where someone mistakenly wants a policy thinking it to be in his
interests; for here, though there is indeed a conflict of wants, there is no
conflict of interests. This is because the want for a policy does not count as a
component of 'interest'.

[2] S.I. Benn, 'Interests in Politics', pp. 130–131.

child's interests' or had enriched himself at the child's expense. But of these the second is a straightforward application of the idea that increases in future opportunities (via money) are in a person's interests, while the first concentrates attention on the degree to which the child is left free time to do what he wants, rather than acting as an unpaid servant. Neither involves any reference to altering or moulding the child's character on ideal-regarding grounds.

The 'fifth difference' then, in spite of its superficially greater divergence from 'want' is in fact quite compatible with it. Want-satisfaction must be considered as a flow over time and at a certain point one is entitled to decide that someone who satisfies his present want is going to reduce his chances of satisfying future wants to an unreasonable degree.

XI

OTHER AGGREGATIVE
CONCEPTS

1. 'GOOD' AND 'WELFARE'

1.A. *'Welfare'*. Before turning to the compound expressions 'public interest', 'common good' and so on, it will be of some use to complete our introductory survey of single words by asking the same questions about 'welfare' and 'good' (in the sense of 'for so-and-so's good') that were asked in the previous chapter about 'interest'.

Turning first to 'welfare' we may first notice that the word is sometimes qualified with the adjective 'material', the contrast apparently being 'spiritual' or 'moral'.[1] The point of 'welfare' is much the same in the three contexts, namely, health and the conditions making for health.[2] Confining ourselves to 'material welfare'

[1] Charles A. Beard suggests in *The Idea of National Interest* (New York, 1934) that 'material interest' (what I have simply been calling 'interest') represents a species of a more widely conceived genus 'interest' and that the narrowing down of 'interest' to 'material interest' paralleled a whole movement of thought. 'For a long time the term [interest] was employed indifferently in its wider psychological sweep; in fact, until the secular revolution which opened in the latter part of the 15th century spread out to the borders of thought. When political economy took the place of theology as a central concern of the intellectual elite, interest shrank to an economic conception in writings and negotiations involving policy, statecraft and social affairs generally. The word was taken over into German in the later Middle Ages and meant in law "the share which arises from the property of any person through the activities of another, a utility lost or a damage suffered." Materially conceived, it now means a gain in wealth as measured by the prevailing economic standards—a gain in land, houses, material capital, money, credits and exchangeable commodities.' (p. 155).

[2] A neat example of a refusal to assimilate health to the status of an 'interest' is provided by the following: 'For the Ministry of Health the Solicitor General, Sir Peter Rawlinson, Q.C., said that the Minister was concerned with the health of the community and also with the interests of the taxpayers. . . .' (*The Guardian*, 15 December 1962, p. 3.)

we can suggest that a local authority concerned with the welfare of certain old people or children would have a finite list of things to look at which would not include an investigation of the actual wants of the old people or children. It would see whether they had the food, shelter, clothing and medical attention necessary to maintain a state of health. It makes perfectly good sense to say that a person's welfare has gone up though his overall ability to satisfy wants (e.g. his income) has gone down or that his welfare has increased but his happiness (pleasure in life) decreased. It also makes sense to say that a person or a whole community place a comparatively low value on welfare as against, say, the maintenance of religious practices.

Since most people in fact want health and the material conditions conducive to it, we can think of 'welfare' as a constituent in partial want-regarding judgements—'partial' in that it concentrates attention on a selection out of all possible wants. If we ask why this range of wants should be singled out for special attention three reasons can be adduced. Firstly, the very fact that welfare is so generally desired makes it reasonable to demand that governments should guarantee it, and if necessary provide the material basis themselves. Secondly, welfare is the sort of thing which *can* be provided by governments in the sense that it is fairly directly subject to governmental efforts. A 'welfare state' is easier to provide than an across-the-board want-satisfying state, quite apart from the fact (implied in the first point) that the conditions of welfare are far more uniform among different people than the conditions of want-satisfaction. Finally, welfare lends itself to fairly clear statistical treatment in a way that want-satisfaction in general does not. Infant mortality rates, hospital beds per thousand, the number of people whose diet falls below some minimum standard of nutrition: these can be discovered and expressed in figures which mean something.

However, I do not think this is the whole story: 'welfare' can also be used with an ideal-regarding tinge, so that one criticizes someone for sacrificing his health or his life in the pursuit of other wants (e.g. the desire for nicotine in smoking or the desire for a kick in Russian roulette). Of course, one could seek to bring this criticism within the want-regarding category by saying that it was not in his (long-run) interests to satisfy these wants: satisfying them now is liable to decrease drastically his chances of satisfying wants in the future. But I think some people at least might be willing to brush this aside and say that one *ought* not to endanger one's life and health 'unnecessarily'. Suicide, for example, has been condemned not just as imprudent or hard on those left behind but as intrinsically wrong—this is presumably an ideal-regarding judgement.[1]

1.B. *'Good'*. 'Good' in phrases such as 'for the good of *A*' or 'for *A*'s good' can cover a wide range of things but at least two things can be said: that a very characteristic use of 'good' is in contexts where someone is prevented from doing something or appealed to not to do something 'for his own good'; and (perhaps associated with this) that it is rather infrequently used as a synonym of 'interest', though it is sometimes used synonymously with 'best interests'.

Beyond this it is difficult to go. A hard core of meaning seems to lie in the healthy functioning of an organism. This includes non-human organisms as in 'Raw meat is good for dogs' or 'Manure is good for cabbages'; and, even more significantly, it also includes those analogues of organisms, human organizations, as in 'What's good for the USA is good for General Motors' (the correct version of Charles E. Wilson's famous statement at the hearing before his appointment as Secretary of Defense) and in references to 'the good of the school' or 'the good of the regiment'. It is the survival, growth and improvement of the organization that is referred to here; statements about the good of an organization are not equivalent to statements about the good of their members. Even to suppose that they must be connected more indirectly would be to make the proposition that organizations exist for the good of their members into an analytic truth rather than an exhortation.

Though, as I have said, the use of 'good' to refer to the healthy functioning of an organism gives us an important part of its meaning, there are many other uses not covered by this. For

---

[1] The view that an observer may regard a person's welfare as being more important than the person himself does when that person assigns to welfare a certain position among his settled purposes, is strengthened if we turn from 'material' or 'spiritual' welfare. These are presumably to be defined according to moral and religious criteria and are therefore straightforward ideal concepts specifying what it is proper to want.

example, the Obscene Publications Act provides that no conviction or order for seizure can be made

> if it is proved that publication of the article in question is justified
> as being for the public good on the ground that it is in the interests
> of science, literature, art, or learning, or of other objects of general
> concern.[1]

The 'public good' here seems to be an ideal-regarding concept in that science, literature, art, etc., would presumably be said to be 'for the public good' even if a majority of 'the public' didn't want them to be advanced. However, though 'the public good' is distinguished here from 'what the public wants', what is 'for the public good' is not that people should have or satisfy certain wants but merely that if they do have such wants they will not be prevented from satisfying them.

But 'good' is also used in contexts where an ideal of character is being mooted. For example, the sometimes stated view that suffering is 'good' for people seems to rest on a belief in the ennobling effects of suffering. In this wide sense, 'a man's good' may be said to reside in the possession of certain qualities irrespective even of their contribution to his happiness: T. H. Green for example appears to have believed that it lies in 'perfection' which is not equivalent to 'happiness'.

2. PUBLIC AND COMMON INTERESTS

2.A. *'Public'*. The definition of the meaning of 'the public interest' which I propose makes it equivalent to 'those interests which people have in common *qua* members of the public'. I shall treat 'public' in this section and 'common interests' in the next.

A hundred and thirty years ago, Sir George Cornewall Lewis offered a general definition of 'public' which it is impossible to improve upon:

> *Public*, as opposed to *private*, is that which has no immediate relation to any specified person or persons, but may directly concern any member or members of the community, without distinction. Thus the acts of a magistrate, or a member of a legislative assembly, done by them in those capacities, are called public; the acts done by

[1] *The Trial of Lady Chatterley*, Introduction by C. H. Rolph (Penguin Books, 1961), p. 4.

the same persons towards their family or friends, or in their deal-
ings with strangers for their own peculiar purposes, are called
private. So a theatre, or a place of amusement, is said to be public,
not because it is actually visited by every member of the community, but because it is open to all indifferently; and any person
may, if he desire, enter it. The same remark applies to public
houses, public inns, public meetings, &c. The publication of a book
is the exposing of it to sale in such a manner that it may be pro-
cured by any person who desires to purchase it: it would be equally
published, if not a single copy was sold. In the language of our law,
public appear to be distinguished from private acts of parliament,
on the ground that the one class directly affects the whole community, the other some definite person or persons.[1]

Bentham's discussion in 'Principles of the Penal Code' has some
extra points highly relevant for my purposes, while resting on the
same general distinction as Lewis.[2]

1st. *Private Offences.* Those which are injurious to such or such
assignable individuals. An *assignable* individual is such or such an
individual in particular, to the exclusion of every other; as Peter,
Paul, or William other than the delinquent himself.
2nd. *Reflective Offences, or Offences Against One's Self.*
3rd. *Semi-public Offences.* Those which affect a portion of the community, a district, a particular corporation, a religious sect, a commercial company, or any association of individuals united by some
common interest, but forming a circle inferior in extent to that of
the community.

It is never a present evil nor a past evil that constitutes a semi-
public offence. If the evil were present or past, the individuals who
suffer, or who have suffered, would be assignable. It would then be
an offence of the first class, a private offence. In semi-public offences
the point is a future evil,—a danger which threatens, but which as
yet attacks no particular individual.
4th. *Public Offences.* Those which produce some common danger to

---

[1] *Remarks on the Use and Abuse of Some Political Terms* (London, 1832), pp.
233–234. Here is an additional example, from the many which might be given.
'Pious and charitable' bequests tend to be distinguished by their 'public
purpose' and we find, not surprisingly, the same criterion. 'A charity, in
the legal sense, may be ... defined as a gift—for the benefit of an indefinite
number of persons. ...' (Supreme Court of Massachusetts, in Jackson *v.*
Phillips, 14 All 539 Supreme Court of Massachusetts, 1867.)
[2] *The Theory of Legislation* (London, 1931), p. 240.

all the members of the state, or to an indefinite number of non-assignable individuals, although it does not appear that any one in particular is more likely to suffer than any other.

So much for 'public' as an adjective; but how about 'the public'? Here again the emphasis is on 'an indefinite number of non-assignable individuals'. The main (though not the only) kind of situation which gives rise to 'publics' is that where people are affected as consumers, using the term broadly. A rail strike would inconvenience 'the public' (i.e. it will inconvenience travellers and those sending goods by rail). 'The public' (i.e. those using the park as opposed to, say, the municipal gardeners) are requested to keep off the grass in the park. For doctors 'the public' is patients; for theatre managers it is theatregoers or potential theatregoers, for civil servants it is citizens (i.e. roughly, consumers of government services) and so on. Clearly, the qualifications for being 'a member of the public' vary from one situation to another, and we cannot therefore speak of what 'the public interest' requires until we know the particular context in which the question is being raised.[1]

2.B. *Common Interests: Introduction*. To say that two or more people have common (or divergent) interests is to make an incomplete statement. Nor is it complete to say that they have a common interest in a certain policy's being put into effect or a certain action's being taken. This is due to a feature which 'interest' shares with 'good', 'welfare' and 'favourably affected', namely that they are necessarily comparative. You can ask 'would this policy be fair?' without introducing a comparison with some other policy. In other words, 'This policy is fair' does not for the sake of completeness require expansion into 'This policy is fairer than that policy'. But if you ask whether a certain policy would be in someone's interest (etc.) this *does* require expansion into 'Is this policy more in his interests than that policy?' 'Being in someone's interests' is at least a triadic relation between a person and at least two policies.

This phenomenon of a concept not on its face comparative

---

[1] 'The membership of the public is not fixed. It changes with the issue: the actors in one affair are the spectators of another, and men are continually passing back and forth between the field where they are executives and the field where they are members of a public.' Walter Lippmann, *The Phantom Public* (New York, 1927), p. 110.

being in fact comparative is quite common. Hume remarked on it in the following terms:

> That there is a natural difference between merit and demerit, virtue and vice, wisdom and folly, no reasonable man will deny: yet it is evident that, in affixing the term, which denotes either our approbation or blame, we are commonly more influenced by comparison than by any fixed unalterable standard in the nature of things. In a like manner, quantity, and extention, and bulk, are by everyone acknowledged to be real things: but when we call any animal *great* or *little*, we always form a secret comparison between that animal and others of the same species; and it is that comparison which regulates our judgement concerning its greatness. A dog and a horse may be of the very same size, while the one is admired for the greatness of its bulk, and the other for its smallness. When I am present, therefore, at any dispute, I always consider with myself whether it be a question of comparison or not that is the subject of controversy; and if it be, whether the disputants compare the same objects together, or talk of things that are widely different.[1]

It is of considerable importance to make a distinction between *standards* and *criteria* so as to avoid drawing from this wider conclusions than are warranted.[2] The criterion remains the same from one context to another; the comparison affects only the standard. The criterion for 'being larger than' is the same whether one is talking about dogs or horses; it is only the standard defining the minimum size which an animal has to be before it can be called 'large' which varies from one kind of animal to another. A good golfer by local standards may be a mediocre one by national standards, and a good one by national standards mediocre by world standards; but the criterion of a 'good golfer' is always the ability to turn in scores lower than the average of the relevant class. Similarly, if the standards of university entrance go up, all this means is that students have to be better to gain a place; but the criteria of 'being a better student' need not alter. (They may of course alter but this would be an independent change.)

[1] 'Of the Dignity or Meanness of Human Nature', *David Hume's Political Essays*, ed. Charles Hendel (New York, 1953).

[2] Hume, in the passage quoted, is plainly resisting the temptation to suppose that the point about comparisons proves more than it in fact does when he says that 'quantity, and extention, and bulk, are by everyone acknowledged to be real things' although the comparison 'regulates our judgement'.

The application of this distinction to 'interest' (etc.) may now be traced. A certain policy can be 'in so-and-so's interest' when it is compared with one alternative and 'contrary to so-and-so's interest' when compared with another alternative. The standard which the policy has to meet alters between one comparison and the other. But at the same time the criteria for 'one policy's being more in somebody's interest than another' do not alter; and I would of course claim that they are as set out in the last chapter.

Neglect of the way in which all statements about 'interest' carry a 'secret comparison' between one policy and another is responsible for a good deal of shadow boxing in arguments as to whether or not a policy (e.g. a certain specific reduction in particular tariffs) is in my, your or everybody's interests. Two people may agree on what kinds of results any policy must have for it to count as being more in a person's interests than an alternative. They may also agree on what the actual results of policy x will be if it is adopted. Yet they may still disagree on whether it would be in their (or everyone's) interest for it to be adopted because each is forming a different 'secret comparison' between x and possible rival policies. One disputant may be asserting that x isn't in his interests because he can think of a policy that would be even better for him. Another may say that it *is* in his interests because it would make him better off than the *status quo*. And another may take an intervening position, comparing x not with all logically possible alternatives, however absurd and unlikely (e.g. prohibitive duties on toothpaste, everything else admitted free—probably the policy most in the interests of a toothpaste manufacturer) but with the half dozen or so which stand some chance of being enacted; and compared to these he may assert that x is (let us say) in the interests of most people but not all.

The same neglect is responsible for statements that there are no interests common to all the members of a society. The grounds advanced for the view are that any proposal which becomes practical politics is opposed by some group.[1] This is superficial

---

[1] For example: Arthur F. Bentley, *The Process of Government* (Indiana, 1949), p. 122: 'We shall never find a group interest of the society as a whole.' David B. Truman, *The Governmental Process: Political Interest and Public Opinion* (New York, 1951), p. 51: 'We do not need to account for a totally inclusive interest, because one does not exist.'

because it ignores the question: why are some logically possible proposals never advocated by anyone at all? Why, for example, is nobody in the USA in favour of having the Strategic Air Command take off and drop all its bombs on the USA? Obviously, because nobody at all believes this would be in his interests. To point out as if it were a great discovery that all proposals *which are actually put forward* meet opposition is as naïve as expressing surprise at the fact that in all cases which reach the Supreme Court there is something to be said on each side. (If there isn't, someone has been wasting an awful lot of money.)

Once we remember that 'being in A's interest' is at least a triadic relationship (between A and at least two policies) we can easily see how empty it is to talk in general about common and divergent interests. For any given proposal there is nearly always at least one that compared to it is in someone's interests and at least one that compared to it is contrary to someone's interests. To say that two or more people have a common interest is to say that there are two policies x and y such that each of them prefers x to y from the point of view of his own interest. On this definition it is safe to say that *any* two people have a common interest as between *some* two policies and *any* two people have a divergent interest as between *some* two policies; and the same is (by the same reasoning) true of groups.

Common interests are ubiquitous even among enemies[1] and so are divergent interests among allies.[2] Instead of speaking in

[1] See Thomas C. Schelling, *The Strategy of Conflict* (Cambridge, Mass., 1960), pp. 4–5, 11; and also Schelling, 'Reciprocal Measures for Arms Stabilization,' *Arms Control, Disarmament and National Security*, ed. Donald G. Brennan (New York, 1961), p. 169: 'It is not true that in the modern world a gain for the Russians is necessarily a loss for us, and vice versa. We can both suffer losses, and this fact provides scope for cooperation. We both have— unless the Russians have already determined to launch an attack and are preparing for it—a common interest in reducing the advantage of striking first, simply because that very advantage, even if common to both sides, increases the likelihood of war. If at the expense of some capability for launching surprise attack one can deny that capability to the other, it may be a good bargain.'

[2] E. E. Schattschneider, *Politics, Pressures and the Tariff* (New York, 1935), p. 224: 'The very nature of tariff legislation, since it involves a vast number of independent conflicts of interest, is such as to bring out the fissures in almost any group, however homogeneous it may seem in other relations. Indeed, in tariff legislation it is often the interests which lie nearest to each

blanket terms about people or groups with common or opposed interests, we should speak of people or groups whose interests coincide or conflict with respect to the adoption of *x* rather than *y*. If once we do this, it becomes plain that there are considerable possibilities for 'common interests' so interpreted, among all the citizens of a country as well as among wider groups.

A final point in this introductory section is that a person may be affected in a number of different ways by a certain policy as he is impinged upon by it in different roles or capacities. As a motorist, tighter enforcement of the speed limit is not in his interest, as a pedestrian it is; as an importer of some raw materials it is not in his interests to have higher tariffs all round, as a seller who has to compete with foreign rivals it is; and so on. I shall therefore distinguish between a man's interests *as a φ* (that is, in some particular capacity) and his *net interest* in a policy (that is, how he is affected overall, striking a balance between the pluses and minuses incurred in his various capacities). So far, I have been thinking only of net interests, but the interests which people share with one another in virtue of similar roles or capacities, even if these interests are overlaid with others which diverge, are analytically and practically important too.

2.C. *Common Interests in Policies.* Though common net interests in particular actions even extending to a community are not impossible in principle it must be agreed that between pairs of particular actions actually proposed it is unlikely that one of them would be better for everyone than the other. This is particularly true where the benefit redounds to assignable persons, that is, where each person can say precisely what he has gained. More promising are cases where some hazard is averted which might indifferently have struck any member of the community but would probably not have struck all. For example, suppose high seas will cause flooding costing £100 per head to half the population unless the dykes are strengthened at a cost of £10 per head to the whole population. The action of strengthening the dykes would be in everyone's interest *provided* nobody knew in advance whether or not he would

---

other in the families of industries which have contradictory needs. Add to this the fact that trade associations may be formed on many bases, most of which bear no reference to the tariff, and it may be seen that interests within single groups are often complex.'

be among the half who would be flooded. If some know they will be safe anyway, the levy will represent to them a £10 loss rather than a bargain-rate insurance with an expected value of (0·5 × £100 =) £50.

But it is policies rather than particular actions which provide the most scope for common interests among the members of communities and this is again because the incidence of benefits and losses arising under it cannot be accurately predicted in advance. An insurance policy is an example of what I mean here by 'a policy': it says that if at any time you suffer a certain loss you will be compensated. Retrospectively, each person can work out whether he has gained or lost from having his house insured against fire; but prospectively, he is simply forced to work out whether, given the premium and the risk of fire, it is worth having insurance. He knows that at the end of the year he will either be glad or sorry that he insured his house. But that is no help to him in making up his mind because he has no way of telling now whether he will be glad or sorry.

Many government programmes—medical care, unemployment relief, etc.—are of this kind. Though the benefits and costs are always specific, nobody can know whether over the course of his life he will gain from them or not so it may be in everyone's interest to support such programmes and save worry. This is the sort of thing I refer to as a *policy*; it consists not simply of a decision to give *A* ten pounds a week but to give everyone in such-and-such conditions ten pounds a week. Most laws are 'policies' in this sense; indeed, laws which specify individuals to be punished are distinguished as 'acts of attainder' (and prohibited under the US Constitution).

Very often where there is not common interest in a specific act *x* there will be a common interest in a policy under which acts of type *x* will be carried out. For example, there may be no single road in a country to whose building cost it would be in everyone's interest to contribute; but it may still be in everyone's interest to contribute to the costs of a policy under which roads will be built all over the country wherever some criterion of 'need' is satisfied.

Rousseau's use of the distinction between what he calls 'laws' and 'decrees' is precisely the same as that which I have been making between 'policies' and 'particular acts'. Since in supporting a policy you are in effect writing a blank cheque which events may in future write your name on, it behoves you to be careful. Before voting to make the penalty for murder severe, remember you may some day be in the dock. Before voting to make it lenient remember you may some day be the victim.[1] In voting on particular actions, however, the people are not making a 'general' judgement, because the gainers and losers are assignable. This is a job of deciding between interests and should, Rousseau says, be left to executive or judicial agencies.

The mental block against accepting this point of view which some people appear to have may arise from confusing it with a crude 'harmony of interests' theory of the kind Pareto dissected as follows:

> Some writers, such as Pufendorf, Hobbes, Spinoza, and Locke, think that there is a sanction for natural laws in the fact that the individual who violates them does harm to Society and hence to himself as a member of society. The fallacy lies (1): In disregarding the amounts of gain or loss, on the assumption that *all* individuals are to act in one way or *all* in another, and in not considering the case where some individuals are to act in one way and some in another. (2) In going to extremes along the line of the above and considering gains only, or losses only. In fact, let us adopt the premise that if *all* individuals refrained from doing *A* every individual as a member of the community would derive a certain advantage. But now if all individuals *less one* continue refraining from doing *A*, the community loss is very slight, whereas the one individual doing *A* makes a personal gain far greater than the loss he incurs as a member of the community.[2]

Pareto's strictures do not, however, apply to Rousseau (or, I suspect, to the authors mentioned by him). Rousseau does not deny that it may be in your interest to *break* a law which benefits you *qua* member of the community; all he says is that it is certainly in your interests to *vote* for it, and that if you have voted in favour of a certain punishment for a certain crime you have no business to complain if your wish for a certain general policy is applied to you in a particular case. Exactly the same point may be made about

[1] Cf. John Rawls, 'Justice as Fairness', *The Philosophical Review*, LXVII, No. 2 (April 1958), pp. 164–194, reprinted in Olafson (ed.), *Justice and Social Policy*.

[2] Vilfredo Pareto, *The Mind and Society* (*Trattato di sociologia generale*) ed. Arthur Livingston (New York, 1935), pp. 945–946.

contracts: it is in your interests to enter into some contracts even though it would be even better for you if you could avoid performing your part of the agreement.

The complexity of modern society makes it hard to see this principle at work, so I offer this example:

The Eskimos living in the Coronation Gulf live mainly on seals. Small seals are taken home by the hunter and cooked; the wife

> either invites the neighbors to join in a meal at her house or sends portions of cooked food to families that are known to be without fresh meat.
>
> When a hunter secures a bearded [large] seal he does not take it home but stands on a small ice hummock with hands outstretched long enough to turn around three times slowly. All hunters who see him doing this gather, and the most influential of them cuts the seal into as many pieces as there are hunters present.[1]

The hunter gets the last piece, the divider next to last—an interesting solution to the 'problem of fair division'.

The policy described probably could not be changed so as to make everyone better off so long as everyone played the game. If some slacked or stopped sharing, this would be in the short run good for them but the rest would soon call a meeting to decide what was to be done, and no doubt everyone would find that the only policy which could command unanimous agreement would be one of *enforcing* the old rules. It would be in everyone's interest to agree to this rather than be excluded, since an individual hunter is quite likely to starve sooner or later between catching one seal and another; but it would of course be even better to agree and then break the rules. Everyone is better off in the first position than the second except undetected rule-breakers; so far the 'harmony' theorists are right. Everyone is better in the second position than the broken-down form of the first position; this is what Hobbes and Rousseau point out. But if you can escape detection in the second position you may be even better than keeping the rules in the first position; and if you can break the rules in the first position without this having a perceptible effect on others (either in the direction of joining the racket or beating it) this is best of all: thus Pareto.

[1] Vilhjalmur Stefansson, 'Was Liberty Invented?', *Freedom—Its Meaning*, ed. Ruth Nanda Anshen (New York, 1940), p. 400.

But if the popular error is to underestimate the areas of common interest in policies, this is no reason for going to the other extreme and supposing that the uncertainty of the future is the password to the rehabilitation of common interests in all areas of social life. This is an error which can be generated by confining one's attention too exclusively to the simpler parts of the criminal law (e.g. the law prohibiting murder) and 'much of our Road Traffic law'.[1] There are many other matters where a person's qualities affect his prospects under different policies.

Consider qualities such as being highly educated or not, skilled or unskilled, intelligent or unintelligent, white or coloured. These are unlikely to alter very much over one's life-span, at least without considerable effort, and they will inevitably place their owners differently under different general arrangements. A white man could hardly be counted on to oppose Negro slavery on the grounds that he might later turn into a Negro, for example. Thus, many of the basic issues on which there is a *prima facie* conflict of interest are not alleviated much by the fact that the future is unpredictable. People voting on political and economic arrangements are not simply choosing a set of roles on the understanding that they will have an equal chance of getting assigned any role; they have a fairly distinct idea of the general position they will occupy. And in practice I believe that it is impossible to explain actual voting behaviour unless we do assume that people are willing to count on getting one role rather than another. For example, suppose that the Southern representatives at Philadelphia had been asked to choose between, on the one hand, a $\frac{1}{4}$ chance of owning three slaves and a $\frac{3}{4}$ chance of being one (or generally a $1/n$ chance of owning n-1 slaves and an $n—1/n$ of being one); and on the other hand the certainty of neither being nor owning a slave. I suspect that most would have chosen the latter alternative; yet the Southern representatives certainly did not take the opportunity to press for slavery to be ruled out by the new constitution—on the contrary.[2]

[1] John D. Mabbott, *The State and the Citizen*, p. 67.

[2] See William Vickrey, 'Utility, Strategy, and Social Decision Rules', *The Quarterly Journal of Economics*, LXXIV (1960), pp. 507–536. Another point made by Vickrey is that even if the impossibility of predicting future roles were complete, people might still vote for different role-sets unless they had identical feelings about risk and identical ideas about the marginal utility of money at different incomes. (I think these are intuitively distinct concepts

2.D. *Common Interests in Rules for Choosing Actions and Policies.*
Must the idea of 'common interest' stop at policies? Not necessarily. Under favourable conditions it may be that everyone can
reasonably expect to gain if a higher-order policy is adopted which
specifies some criteria and says that *any* action or policy which
satisfies these criteria is to be put into effect. An example would be
a general rule to the effect that aggregatively justified changes
should always be made. The classical economists, from Bentham
to Edgeworth, often adopted this line of justification for utilitarian
recommendations;[1] and in spite of Lord Keynes's dictum that 'in
the long run we're all dead', J. R. Hicks revived the idea in the
1940s.

> If the economic activities of a community were organized on the
> principle of making no alterations in the organization of produc-
> tion which were not improvements in this sense [that is, changes
> where the gainer *could* compensate the losers and still be better off]
> and making all alterations which were improvements that it could
> possibly find, then, although we could not say that all the inhabi-
> tants of that community would be necessarily better off than they
> would have been if the community had been organized on some
> different principle, nevertheless there would be a strong proba-
> bility that almost all of them would be better off after the lapse of a
> sufficient length of time.[2]

The limitations on this approach are fairly easy to see: some
decisions would have such large effects on distribution that it
would be idle to expect them to be more than cancelled out by
small changes. Nevertheless, where decisions have fairly small
effects on distribution and do appear to be justified on general

[1] See Gunnar Myrdal, *The Political Element in the Development of Economic
Theory*, tr. by Paul Streeten (London, 1953), pp. 211–212.
[2] 'The Rehabilitation of Consumers' Surplus', *Review of Economic Studies*,
VIII, No. 2 (February 1941), p. 111.

even if there is no way of distinguishing them operationally.) Otherwise, one
man might prefer a role-set which gave him a big chance of a low income
and a small chance of a high income, while another might prefer the reverse
and a third a certainty of some intermediate income. A corollary of this is
that even if *laissez faire* produced the highest real income measured in, say,
expected-value terms, a rational agent might still prefer a lower expected
value if he preferred a certain income to a gamble with a higher expected
value but carrying the possibility of destitution.

utilitarian grounds public authorities often carry them out with general approval, and it is plausible to think that underlying this is a general assumption that in the long run everyone will gain if public authorities always act on this basis.

Instead of rules such as that just canvassed, which would still have to be applied, a group might find a common interest (compared at least with the prospect of not settling them at all) in settling things according to some automatic procedure, such as chance or voting. With chance each person might hope to be favoured by the winning policy as much on the average as anyone else, while with voting he might hope to be in the majority more often than not. (How majority voting may be expected to work is discussed in Chapters XIV and XV.)

It should be observed that where such a higher-level policy is in operation, it is that which is 'in the public interest' and not the particular policies and actions which are carried out because they satisfy it; i.e. that it is the 'majority-principle' or the 'principle of utility' which is 'in the public interest', rather than this or that application. In just the same way, where some particular policy is in everyone's interest in its own right (2.C.), it is incorrect to say that the specific actions carried out under it are in everyone's interest. For example, even if it is in everyone's interest to hang murderers, it is obviously not in any given murderer's interest to be hanged.

3. PUBLIC GOOD AND COMMON GOOD

Before proceeding to the business of the next chapter, which is to look at 'the public interest' in more detail, I wish to turn aside briefly to extend the analysis of 'public interest' and 'common interest' already given to 'public good' and 'common good'.

'Public good' presents few problems; it appears to work in exactly the same way as 'public interest' except inasfar as the meaning of 'good' diverges from that of 'interest'. That is to say that whereas 'the public interest' tends to be restricted to contexts where the means of general want-satisfaction are at stake, 'the public good' can be used more widely as in the Obscene Publications Act already quoted, which allows 'science, literature, art or learning' as elements of the 'public good'. Between the most typical uses of 'common good' and 'common interest', however, there seems to be a wider difference than can be accounted for by the different shades of meaning represented by 'good' and 'interest'. This can be seen in two differences between typical uses of 'common good' and 'common interest' which, though related to the difference between 'good' and 'interest' themselves, are not wholly reducible to those differences.

The first difference is that the common interest of the members of a group is often held to lie in something which would benefit them at the expense of someone else.[1] The common interest of employers is formulated with reference to employees, and *vice versa*. 'Common good', on the other hand, seems to be used almost exclusively for talking about the relations *within* some group rather than the relations between the members of a group and those outside the group.

The second difference is that 'the common good' is invoked in order to justify a particular allocation of scarce resources but not to justify an arrangement whereby incentives and deterrents are fixed with the object of modifying behaviour. A system of rewards to encourage work or of punishments to discourage law-breaking might well be supported by saying that it was 'in the public interest' but hardly that it was 'for the common good'. There is another way of putting what is, I think, the same point. 'The public interest' is used where an institution or a political action is to be defended; *par excellence* it is an administrator's concept. 'The common good' is typically used in a very different way, namely in the context of an *appeal* to individual people to do something or other which is contrary to their net interests. Thus, where a greater use of incentives might be supported as being

[1] The tendency is even stronger with 'the national interest', which extremely often refers to the interests of the inhabitants of a certain country in that country's relations with others. Even where this is not superficially so, as when wage claims or speculation in foreign exchanges are said to be 'contrary to the national interest' it is still usually the external relations of the state which are being thought of, e.g. its balance of payments or its exchange rate.

'The national interest' may either mean the interests of the members of the state which they have in common *qua* members of the state, or it may sometimes mean the interests of the members of the state considered as a group for aggregative purposes. In Chapter XIII, I notice a way in which 'public interest' degenerates into an undifferentiated aggregative concept; but it is far easier to treat 'the nation' as a (fictitious) entity having a single 'interest' than it is to treat 'the public' in the same way.

'in the public interest', the alternative of an appeal to those concerned to work harder without extra pay would be couched in terms of 'the common good'. Of course, for there to be a net sacrifice involved in doing something 'for the common good' the result to be brought about plainly cannot be in the net interests of everyone concerned; it must rather be in their interest (or 'for their good') in the 'as a ϕ' sense. In other words someone who is asked to make a net sacrifice for the common good is being asked to place those elements in his own good which he shares with others above those elements the pursuit of which benefits only him.

I have taken the case where the pursuit of the common good entails a net sacrifice as being more typical. But it is possible to conceive situations where a 'natural identity of interests' obtained, especially in a small group, such that a man's net interest lay in pursuing those interests which he shared with the rest of the group. For example, if there are six people in a lifeboat and all of them must either row or pump if any is to survive then the common good and each individual's good coincide in requiring the same actions. But such cases are surely unusual. Where the group is larger and the conditions are less extreme (so that results are 'more or less' rather than 'all or nothing') it is more likely that the amount of damage a person does himself *qua* group member by pursuing his private interests exclusively will not on balance make it worthwhile (from a purely self-interested point of view) for him to further the interests he shares with the group at the expense of those he does not. A man who makes a fortune selling substandard goods to the army in a war, for example, makes defeat more likely, let us say; but the increased probability of defeat is so fractional that it is not likely to be more significant *to him* than the certain fortune he can make. T. H. Green appears to have laboured under the belief that before someone could be expected to pursue the common good he must somehow be convinced that he was thereby pursuing his own greatest (net) good.[1] It is surely more consistent with common sense to say that people may put the common good before their own individual good for purely altruistic reasons or from a belief that it is only fair to make

[1] It was in order to make this work that he declared a man's greatest good to lie in a desire to pursue the common good; unfortunately, 'the common good' can then only mean a community where everyone has such desires.

a contribution to those sources of one's own good which are provided by the efforts of others. For example, if others shovel snow off the pavement in front of their houses 'for the common good' so that one benefits from cleared pavements, it is surely fair to shovel the snow outside one's own house too. Similarly, if others burn smokeless fuel 'for the common good', thus giving one the benefits of a less smoky atmosphere, it is fair to do the same oneself.[1]

Notice that these are (or, at least, may well be) true cases of a divergence between the common good and an individual's own good in that the amount of benefit *he* would get from clearing *his own* pavement will quite likely be not worth the effort. Of course, the benefit from *everyone's* clearing his own pavement may still be greater for each person than the cost in effort to each person of clearing his own pavement; indeed, if this were not so for at least most people it would be better (on aggregative grounds) for nobody to bother about clearing the snow at all. But unless he thinks his own decision will affect others by example this calculation has no relevance for a purely self-interested individual deciding whether or not to clear his own pavement.

If appeals to 'the common good' were ineffective it would be possible to introduce a rule with sanctions requiring everyone to clear the pavement outside his house (cf. Smokeless Zones). This would be supported on the grounds that it was 'in the public interest' and it might well be in the *net* interest of everyone to vote for it. If it were once passed, there would no longer be any need to appeal to 'the common good' in order to get people to clear their pavements; provided the sanctions were great enough and were

[1] These examples can be brought under the principle put forward by John Rawls in 'Justice as Fairness' to the effect that if one enjoys the benefits of a practice there is a *prima facie* obligation to undertake the burdens prescribed by the practice also; but in order to do this one would I think have to widen Rawls' notion of a practice. The benefits of smoke control and snow clearing do not depend upon there being a rule saying everyone (or everyone in a certain category) should do it. Even if only one man burns smokeless fuel or clears the snow outside his house this helps; and the essential point is that additional people following suit help strictly in proportion to their numbers. (This is always on the assumption that uncleared pavements are merely inconvenient. If there were only a path and if one uncleared stretch made it impassable there would be no point in anyone clearing his section unless everyone did. Under *these* circumstances one would have the makings of a Rawlsian 'practice'.)

enforced against a high enough proportion of offenders it would be possible to rely on self-interest (i.e. the fear of a penalty).[1]

[1] It is the existence of this phenomenon which explains how there can be both a 'natural identity of interests' in some matter and an 'artificial identity of interests' in the same matter. There can be a natural (i.e. independent of any law) identity of interest in *having* a law with penalties to make everyone do so-and-so or refrain from doing so-and-so (i.e. a law that will produce an artificial identity of interests). Lindsay, for example, decries the Benthamites' espousal simultaneously of natural and artificial identity of interests: *Modern Democratic State*, p. 142. His own confusion is sharply brought out in his virtual equation of anarchy and *laissez faire*: *laissez faire* is the theory that everyone will gain relatively to any other economic policy if everyone pursues his own interests within a certain framework of laws (e.g. enforcing contracts). It is thus a good example of natural *and* artificial identity. The same failure to appreciate that there may be an identity of interest in maintaining a coercive structure incidentally vitiates Lindsay's strictures on Hobbes in the same volume.

XII

APPLICATIONS OF
'THE PUBLIC INTEREST'

1. INTRODUCTION

IT has become fashionable in some quarters to dismiss the concept of 'the public interest' as devoid of content. Its use as a counter of public debate is said to be fraudulent, since there is no such thing as a 'public interest', and it is claimed that if it has any social function it is merely that of casting an aura of legitimacy around decisions which are in fact the outcome of group pressures.[1] In the previous chapter I have criticized this position from a theoretical angle in trying to show that given workable definitions of 'interest' and 'common interest' it makes good sense to suppose that there are interests common to all the members of a community. I shall now follow this up by examining some examples of contexts in which 'the public interest' is often used and trying to show that in these contexts to say '*x* is in the public interest' has a fairly clear meaning and is by no means equivalent to nothing more precise than 'I favour *x*'.

[1] I have already quoted A. F. Bentley and D. B. Truman in this connection (XI.2.C.). In addition see Frank J. Sorauf, 'The Public Interest Reconsidered', *Journal of Politics*, XIX (November 1957), pp. 616 ff.; Howard R. Smith, *Democracy and the Public Interest* (University of Georgia, 1960); and Glendon A. Schubert, *The Public Interest: A Critique of a Concept* (Illinois, 1961). Summaries of Schubert's book may be found in 'The Public Interest in Administrative Decision-Making', *American Political Science Review*, LI (June 1957), pp. 346 ff. and 'The Theory of the Public Interest in Judicial Decision-Making', *Midwest Journal of Political Science* II (February 1958) pp. 1 ff.; or in C. J. Friedrich (ed.), *Nomos V: The Public Interest* (New York, 1962), pp. 162–176. For a similar if less extreme Anglo-Australian view to set beside these American ones see J. D. B. Miller, *The Nature of Politics* (London, 1962), Chapter IV; and for an explicit critique of Miller see my paper on 'The Public Interest', *Proceedings of the Aristotelian Society*, Supplementary Volume XXXVIII (1964), pp. 1–18.

The kinds of instance in which 'the public interest' gets used can be put into two groups, and although the demarcation line is not sharp at the edges it is useful enough for the purpose of dividing up my discussion. The first class of cases I shall call *negative* applications of 'the public interest'. In these cases what is said to be 'in the public interest' is preventing someone from doing something which will have adverse effects on an indefinite group of people. 'Negative' planning, which has as its aim the prevention of eyesores such as corrugated iron sheds in front gardens and flashing neon lights in the Cotswolds, is a perfect example of action of a negative kind based on 'the public interest'. So is the operation of the criminal law, at any rate considered in prospect when 'future victims' are still an indefinite group. 'Positive' applications, on the other hand, occur when a facility is actually provided for an indefinite group of people. A local authority, for example, acts 'positively' in the public interest when it provides such things as parks and roads.[1] The exact point at which a public authority imposes so many restrictions on, say, the development of a site that it moves from a 'negative' to a 'positive' application of 'the public interest' can be argued over, but the central cases are clear enough.[2]

In Section 2 I shall investigate negative applications of 'the public interest' mainly by looking at one example, namely the concept of 'public policy' which is invoked by judges when they

[1] When I analysed the notion of something's being in an individual person's interest (Chapter X) I suggested that something is in a person's interests if it puts him in a position to satisfy wants. This meant that if something directly satisfied a want the concept of 'interest' was not relevant to it. But given that 'the public interest' covers the kinds of thing mentioned in the text, does this involve a redefinition of 'interest'? I think not; for providing a facility such as a public park, or enforcing minimum standards of goods for sale, enables members of 'the public' to satisfy wants more effectively whenever they may happen to wish to do so. A particular person may never benefit from a particular facility but it is there if he wants it.

[2] It is interesting to notice that the distinction between 'negative' and 'positive' action by a public authority has legal relevance in the USA. States have power to prevent harm to the public without giving compensation; but if they are held to be making a private person secure a benefit to the public they have to give compensation. For example, a person can be prevented from building above a certain height but he cannot be prevented from building at all so as to leave the land as a park or a parking lot. See Alison Dunham, 'City Planning: An Analysis of the Content of the Master Plan', *Journal of Law and Economics*, I (October 1958), pp. 170–186, esp. 180–182.

refuse to enforce the terms of otherwise valid contracts thereby (it is hoped) discouraging the kind of activity to which the contract is incidental. Not all 'public policy' grounds involve 'the public interest' but I shall try to show that the categories I have developed are helpful in analysing the grounds that are invoked.

2. NEGATIVE APPLICATIONS: PUBLIC POLICY

2.A. *The Public Interest in Public Policy.* No doubt the phrase 'public policy' is used in many different contexts but in this section I shall take account of only one, namely, the legal context in which otherwise valid contracts are declared void on the ground that it would be 'contrary to public policy' for a court to enforce them.[1] Here, the state does not provide anything, but it tries to discourage certain forms of conduct by refusing to enforce contracts made in connection with them. The decisions of courts that certain types of action are to be discouraged thus provide a useful quarry of relevant examples. The kinds of reasons given by judges (or attributed to them by scholars) for invoking 'public policy' can be divided into 'public interest', 'public good' and 'public conscience'.

The first, 'public interest', covers cases where a contract has economic or political repercussions, thus affecting others as citizens or consumers.

> Rules have been established based on the interest of the state or politically organised society in its security *vis-à-vis* other states, as when contracts with enemies even when they stipulate for suspension during war, or contracts having in view hostile activity against a friendly state, or possibly even violations of the law of friendly states, are held void. The social interest in the integrity and efficiency of political institutions has based rules forbidding traffic in public offices and honours, contracts to influence governmental policy for private purposes, or to use public authority or office agreeably to private directions, or to assign salaries and pensions attached to the exercise of public office. In particular, the great social interest in the integrity of legal and especially judicial

---

[1] 'Within narrow limits the judges are thus given room to manoeuvre and to refuse to countenance a transaction which, without coming within the four corners of a legal prohibition, nevertheless strikes at the roots of the social order.' Dennis Lloyd, *Public Policy* (London, 1953), p. 128.

institutions has led to the striking down of contracts to stifle prosecutions for felony, of contracts of indemnity against the forfeiture of bail, or contracts of maintenance and champerty.[1]

The common law doctrine against contracts providing for 're-straint of trade' has been partly directed to fairness between the parties and partly to the protection of consumers; it is in the latter respect that it involves 'public interest'.[2] The Restrictive Practices Act of 1956 is also relevant in that it gives the criteria for invalid agreements in terms of 'the public interest'. Section 21 Part i begins:

> For the purposes of any proceedings before the Court . . . a restric-tion accepted in pursuance of any agreement shall be deemed to be contrary to the public interest unless the Court is satisfied of any or more of the following circumstances. . . .

The first two 'circumstances' (a) and (b) are that the restriction is necessary to protect the public against injury and that its removal would

> deny to the public as purchasers, consumers, or users of any good other specific and substantial benefits and advantages enjoyed or likely to be enjoyed by them as such.

Two others (e) and (f) refer to unemployment and the balance of payments while two more (c) and (d) exempt agreements whose effect is to counteract the restrictive practices of others and to enable those operating the restriction to deal on equal terms with others. (a) and (b) clearly fit well into the concept of the public interest which I have been building up, and so, by and large, do (e) and (f), since unemployment and the balance of payments have general economic effects. But it seems to me that (c) and (d) are directed at the prevention of unfairness between producers rather than the protection of non-assignable persons, and that to lump *all* the relevant considerations under the heading of 'the public interest' is therefore a mistake. It might however be said that although (e) and (f) do not constitute factors to be included in 'the public interest', the point is that the public interest should not be allowed to *override* other factors (such as fairness between producers). 'The public interest' would then be working as a

---

[1] Julius Stone, *The Province and Function of Law* (Sydney, 1946), pp. 501–502.
[2] Cf. Lloyd, *Public Policy*, pp. 34–54; and Stone, Chapter 23.

conclusive argument even though it does not in fact cover all the relevant considerations. (See Chapter II.4.B.). On this analysis, restrictive agreements are to be stopped on the grounds that they are contrary to the public interest unless some other ground outweighs it in importance.

2.B. *Public Good in Public Policy.* If we take the 'public interest' element in 'public policy' to cover the interests (in a wide choice of goods at low prices and in the working of the political and legal system) of those not party to a contract, this leaves 'public good' to cover other respects in which contracting parties may affect other non-assignable persons adversely. For example, it may be thought that a certain pattern of marriage and family life is 'good for' people and that the 'public good' therefore requires discouragement of any contracts which are liable if generally indulged in to alter the institution to some other form.

> The social interest in the preservation of the family as a stable social institution has led under the cloak of public policy to the creation of comprehensive rules, avoiding contracts which forbid an unmarried person to marry; mercenary contracts of marriage brokage; contracts by a spouse to marry a third party after the existing marriage terminates by death, or divorce, if at any rate, the contract is made while the spouses are living together normally; contracts contemplating future as distinct from immediate separation, and contracts by parents tending to nullify their parental responsibilities other than by the regular procedures of adoption permitted by law.[1]

If 'the protection of the family as a stable institution' is indeed the rationale in these cases, then we have a genuine example of contracts which are held to damage unassignable third parties, namely all those who benefit from the institution which is supposedly being undermined by the contract.[2]

---

[1] Stone, p. 502.

[2] Judicial intervention on behalf of the 'public good' raises in particularly acute form the question whether judges, who (especially in this country) tend to be drawn from a narrow social class and to have received a narrowly technical training are well fitted to decide (*a*) whether a certain institution is 'good for' people as it stands or whether it would not benefit (or at least not be harmed) if modifications were allowed to occur and (*b*) *what* effects striking down contracts of a certain kind would in fact have on an institution.

2.C. *Public Conscience in Public Policy.* At the beginning of 2.A. I said that the grounds on which contracts were voided as a matter of 'public policy' could be divided into three. The first is that the kind of action which it is hoped thereby to discourage is contrary to the public interest. The second is that the action is against the public good. And finally, the third is that the action constitutes an affront to the public conscience.

Let me explain how I am planning to use the expression 'public conscience'. I shall say that an action 'affronts the public conscience' when it does not directly affect 'the public' (that is, a non-assignable group) but where nevertheless 'the public' (which for this purpose is equivalent to 'a substantial body of opinion with a common political authority') thinks the action ought to be discouraged or prohibited. For example, how a person treats a domestic animal which he owns need not affect others, especially if the person lives in a deserted area. Yet this may still be a matter of public conscience in the sense that many people will consider cruelty to animals to be something which ought to be prevented. Similarly (if we abstract from the ways in which others may be affected) with the hunting or trapping of wild animals and birds. 'The public conscience' is a convenient phrase in that it clearly separates these cases from 'public interest'. Indeed, the 'public conscience' is quite often active in situations where it conflicts with 'the public interest' as when bad working conditions or low pay in some occupation are improved with a resultant rise in the cost of the product.[1] The emancipation of the slaves in the West Indies with compensation provided by British taxpayers might also be given as an example of public conscience triumphing over public interest. We admit readily enough that a particular person will want to bring about some states of affairs because he conceives them to be in his own interest or for his own good, while other states of affairs he will wish to bring about although they do not affect him at all: exactly the same remains true of men as members of collectivities.

[1] Another frequent configuration is that of public interest modified by public conscience, as when in 1948 the Statement on Personal Incomes exempted those with the lowest incomes from the proposed wage freeze. The later National Incomes Commission did not appear to conceive of itself as charged with any responsibility for altering differentials between different incomes but merely with keeping the general level of increases down. (See IX.2.B.)

The kinds of action taken by or on behalf of a 'public' when the 'public' is not itself affected can be divided into those actions which are motivated by want-regarding considerations and those motivated by ideal-regarding considerations.[1] Want-regarding intervention is aimed at securing equitable relationships among specific people or preventing people or groups from acting 'contrary to their interests'. It is also involved whenever a politically organized group taxes itself in order to provide more want-satisfaction for others outside the group.[2] Ideal-regarding considerations are involved wherever actions of individuals and groups with assignable members are declared illegal not because they affect others adversely but simply as being wrong. The prohibition of homosexuality and abortion in this country appear to be examples of this.[3]

When we come on to 'public policy' specifically, we find that contracts are declared void as affronting public conscience in both its want-regarding and ideal-regarding manifestations. Thus, taking want-regarding grounds first, we find that contracts are declared void if they are unfair as between the parties even if 'the public' is not directly affected in an adverse way.[4] And if we turn

[1] Compare VIII.3.B.

[2] For states to do this is just as much contrary to the principles of Locke and Mill as is a state's interference in the affairs of its own citizens except for 'self defence'. See E. C. Banfield in *Public Policy*, ed. C. J. Friedrich (Cambridge, Mass., 1962). For a rejection of the view that states in their external affairs should be concerned with anything more high-minded than their own national interest, see George F. Kennan, *American Diplomacy, 1900–1950* (Mentor Book, 1952).

[3] Even the degree of discouragement for homosexuality and prostitution recommended by the Wolfenden Committee seems to require an ideal-regarding judgement of this nature to underpin it, as Lord Devlin has argued. See Note N on page 307 for a discussion of the point.

Lord Devlin has also argued the wider thesis that many cases which are *prima facie* questions of public conscience are on further analysis to be regarded as questions of public interest. His view is considered in Note O on page 308.

[4] Even when 'the public' is affected, as in 'restraint of trade' cases, Lloyd claims that unfairness between the parties is still the most important factor in the minds of judges. 'The test is whether the agreement is unreasonable as between the parties and as regards the public. Yet notwithstanding the declared relevance of public policy in such matters, the modern decisions show a strong tendency to ignore or pass over the public interest in the transaction and to concentrate on the manner in which the agreement affects the parties thereto as individuals'. (Lloyd, p. 50.)

to ideal-regarding grounds for intervention, of a 'public conscience' type, we discover contracts furthering so-called 'immorality'—especially as one might expect sexual 'immorality'—being struck down.[1]

3. POSITIVE APPLICATIONS

3.A. *The Public Interest.* Negative applications of 'the public interest' and 'the public good' typically involve action by a public authority to prevent some harm to unassignable persons, where the meaning of 'harm' depends on whether it is 'interest' or 'good' which is invoked. Positive applications involve action by a public authority to provide a benefit for unassignable persons, the meaning of 'benefit' similarly varying.

If we start with 'interest' we may give as examples of things which are in the 'public interest' the provision of defence against foreign enemies and the maintenance of full employment and conditions favourable to economic growth. Contrasted with positive action in the public interest is positive action which benefits determinate persons. Subsidies and tariffs are often, for example, advantageous to particular industries or particular firms, but so far from being in the interests of 'the public' they may well actually operate at its expense.[2] Appleby gives these examples:

[1] 'Agreements in consideration of illicit cohabitation provide the typical transaction which both English and French systems of law will annul on grounds of immorality.' (Lloyd, p. 55.) 'Even a promise of marriage conditioned upon pregnancy arising from such future intercourse, has been held to be void by a New Zealand court.' (Stone, p. 502.)

[2] For tariffs see E. E. Schattschneider, *Politics, Pressures and the Tariff*, p. 21: 'It is probable that a very large portion of the separate items in the schedule represent a subdivision of the policy carried to the point where the duties constitute substantially private tariffs levied for the benefit of very small numbers of producers and often for the benefit of single producers. Indeed, in those cases in which separate provision is made for industries which are not only controlled by one or two producers but are, in addition, very small, it may be said that the tariff is more than private, being approximately personal.'
C. A. Beard in *The Idea of National Interest* suggests that at least until the administration of F. D. Roosevelt (when the book was written) 'the national interest' was equated with the separate interests of exporters and foreign investors without any questions being asked about whether anybody benefited except the exporters and investors themselves. Cf. Thurman Arnold, *The Folklore of Capitalism* (New Haven, 1937).

Industrial employees are surely to be classified as members of their organizations; even before the industrial revolution had got well under way they turned to government to act in behalf of their special concerns as members. The principal source of demands for tariffs has been the producers seeking protection of their private interests. The Dairy Bureau of the United States Department of Agriculture owes its existence to the influence of dairy farmers seeking private benefits.[1]

And here are two small examples from Herring: the US government at one time carried out statistical researches for the National Canners' Association, and on one occasion prepared a report on filberts for the Pacific Nut Growers Co-operative Association.[2]

Finally in this brief list of examples consider the silver policy passed by Congress and reluctantly accepted by Roosevelt in the early New Deal.

> The silver policy represented the most remarkable—as well as the least remarked—special-interest triumph of the period. A minor industry, employing in 1939 less than five thousand persons, the silver industry, in effect, held the government to ransom, extorting nearly a billion and a half dollars in the fifteen years after 1934— a sum considerably larger than that paid by the government to support farm prices over the same period. The silver acquired under the legislation played little part in the American monetary system, and the American silver policy only complicated the monetary problems of countries, like China and Mexico, where silver constituted part of the circulating medium. No legislation passed in New Deal years had less excuse.[3]

Herring, in his book just quoted, provides copious examples of government activities which have the effect of benefiting assignable groups, and his constant refrain is to ask whether they are 'in the public interest' or sometimes whether they contribute to the 'general welfare'. But the answer to this question is easy: they don't or at any rate they don't inasfar as they benefit only

[1] P. H. Appleby, *Morality and Administration in Democratic Government* (Baton Rouge, 1952), p. 20.
[2] E. Pendleton Herring, *Public Administration and the Public Interest* (New York, 1936), p. 40.
[3] A. M. Schlesinger, Jr., *The Coming of the New Deal* (Cambridge, Mass., 1959), p. 252.

assignable groups.[1] The interesting questions are: whether the government should nevertheless undertake these activities; if it does whether it should not at least charge the cost of them to the beneficiaries; and so on. Only confusion is generated by lumping the two kinds of question together, and it is not surprising that those who (like Herring) adopt this vicious approach come to doubt whether 'the public interest' has any distinct meaning. For if one insists on treating 'the public interest' as an all-inclusive criterion for good actions and policies, scepticism about its usefulness amounts to no more than the conclusion that there is no such single criterion; and from that conclusion I at least would not wish to dissent.

I shall hold over until the next chapter a discussion of the question whether there are indeed good reasons for saying that governments should be particularly (or exclusively) concerned with the promotion of interests shared by non-assignable persons rather than the interests of members of determinate groups. In the rest of this chapter I wish only to illustrate some positive applications of 'the public interest', 'the public good' and 'the general welfare'. Before doing so I should perhaps once again enter the *caveat* that I regard the distinction between positive and negative applications as an analytical convenience but by no means as a hard and fast distinction.

A person's interests are (roughly) advanced when his opportunities to get what he wants are increased. A state can advance the interests of 'the public' in three ways which involve arranging for positive provision. Firstly, it can provide internal law and order and attempt to defend the country from attack by other countries. The reason for calling these 'interests' is that they underlie the satisfaction of nearly all more specific wants.[2] Secondly, it can provide goods or services for 'the public'—either without their having to pay for them or at full cost price or at some lower price.

[1] Herring's question would be defensible if it meant: do these government activities *also* have the effect of benefiting non-assignable persons? But Herring in fact seems to want to ask whether they are in the public interest purely in virtue of benefiting an assignable group.

[2] Of course, being alive is even more basic compared to the satisfaction of particular wants and if so-called 'defence' seems likely to lead to the death of a great number (perhaps nearly all) of the inhabitants of the country in question it must be doubtful whether on these terms it must not give way to the *more* basic interest of bare survival.

Usually the 'public interest' is invoked only where it is a question of making the good or service available for people to take advantage of if they so wish. Services such as street lighting or refuse collection which actually benefit nearly everyone rather than merely being available to everyone tend to be described as being for the general benefit, etc.—where, indeed, they are referred to any more abstract justification at all.[1]

Finally, the state can lay upon private persons or corporations duties of a positive rather than a negative kind. An example would be the 'common carrier' obligations with which Parliament has traditionally burdened the railways; these did not merely say that *if* a train was to run it must meet certain conditions but specified that certain trains *must* be run whether the railway company wanted to run them or not. Another example, at least potentially, is the American Federal Communications Commission. Here again the state has granted valuable privileges of a semi-monopolistic kind to private producers and in return has placed on them an obligation to serve 'the public interest' and at least in the view of the first Chairman appointed by President Kennedy this requires the programmes to satisfy all tastes.[2] British commercial television,

---

[1] As I pointed out in X.1. many things whose justification is of an aggregative kind are not normally defended in terms of any general principle at all. That it satisfies wants and is therefore desirable for people to see their way in the streets or have their dustbins emptied may well be regarded as too obvious to be worth mentioning.

[2] Newton N. Minow, 'Television and the Public Interest', a speech given on 9 May 1961, before the 39th Annual Convention of National Association of Broadcasters. Reprinted in *Etc.* XVIII, No. 2:

'What about adult programming and ratings? You know that newspaper publishers take popularity ratings too. The answers are pretty clear: the most popular parts of a newspaper are always the comics, followed by the advice-to-the-lovelorn column. But, ladies and gentlemen, the news is still on the front page of all the newspapers; the editorials are not replaced by more comics; the newspapers have not become one long collection of advice to the lovelorn. . . .

'Let me make clear that what I am talking about is balance. I believe that the public interest is made up of many interests. There are many people in this great country and you must serve all of us. . . . You are not only in show business; you are free to communicate ideas as well as relaxation. You must provide a wider range of choice, more diversity, more alternatives. It is not enough to cater to the nation's whims—you must also serve the nation's needs.' (p. 139.)

with an even stronger element of private monopoly, is similarly supposed to provide 'balanced' programmes.

3.B. *The Public Good.* It is most convenient for the present purpose to take 'the public good' in its wide sense as the form of expression used where the provision of a good or service is justified on ideal-regarding grounds. The clearest instance of this would be the provision of something in order to create or develop a certain taste. But one must also include the very important type of case where the provision is intended to satisfy a pre-existent demand although it would not be justifiable on want-regarding grounds to make the provision. For example, suppose (to take a very simplified case) that a thousand people in a town and its environs are willing to spend five shillings regularly to go to a symphony concert but none are willing to spend more. The most the concert can make is £250, and if this is not enough to cover its costs the concerts should not take place on aggregative want-regarding principles. For it would in general be 'inefficient', from the want-regarding point of view, to subsidize the concerts if they could not pay for themselves, since this would be to apply money where the beneficiaries themselves did not most appreciate it. Suppose a subsidy of £250 per concert were necessary: since none of the patrons is in fact willing to spend more than five shillings on the concert it follows that all would prefer a cash bonus of five shillings and no concert to a five shilling concert subsidized at the rate of another five shillings per head.[1]

It may perhaps be thought that the example given was simplified too far by the introduction of an assumption that a thousand (which we will suppose to be a capacity attendance) will pay five shillings and none will pay more. It is quite true that if we relax this assumption and imagine (more realistically) that some number less than a thousand would pay six shillings, a smaller number

[1] However, suppose that the concert-going public more or less coincided with or was more or less contained in some independently-defined class of persons who required additional income on want-regarding principles (either distributive or aggregative). If there happened to be some practical or political difficulty in providing the supplementation in the form of a cash bonus, the concert subsidy might be justified as a clumsy way of redistributing real income. This is a pretty far-fetched supposition in the case of concert-goers but the idea does have genuine applications in other cases—e.g. food subsidies. Governments have been concerned with keeping down the price of bread in particular (in places where bread is the staple) for millennia.

seven shillings, and so on, it may turn out that although there is no price at which the concerts can be made to pay, the total amount that the thousand would be willing to pay *would* be enough. If the money each would be willing to pay rather than forego the concert could actually be collected there would be no need for a subsidy; it is only because it cannot that a subsidy is necessary.[1]

But before assenting to the view that a subsidy would be justified in this case on aggregative want-regarding grounds one must, in principle, compare the intensity of want-satisfaction which the subsidy provides and that which is stopped by the marginal increase in taxation which it necessitates. For example, those who would be willing to pay the most for the concert may be not the most enthusiastic but the richest; so unless the tax is also levied on the rich the effect of the tax and subsidy is to redistribute income from the rest of the community to the music-loving rich. Moreover, even if this aggregative argument did not hold there would still be the distributive objection: why should the rest of the community subsidize this particular group? The fact that the group *would* be willing to pay its own way is surely not enough if it is not actually made to.

I have seen a distributive argument in favour of subsidization in a case such as the amended example which takes the form of saying that those who are willing to pay their share of the economic cost of a concert (etc.) should not be penalized merely because not enough others are willing to join with them. For example, if eight hundred will pay ten shillings for a seat they should not be denied the concert because the other two hundred necessary are not forthcoming. But this is surely not plausible unless one has already decided, on ideal grounds, to give concerts special treatment. If I would like to travel from Stoke-on-Trent to Ascot by chartered coach I surely cannot complain if the company refuses to put on a 32-seater coach (in return for my offer to pay one thirty-second of

[1] Charging different amounts for different seats complicates the statement of the problem without necessarily contributing anything to the solution. We simply have to say what each person would be willing to pay for each kind of seat. The problem of the text could only be solved if seats of identical attractiveness were priced differentially according to the amount each customer was willing to pay rather than go without—which of course requires information not accessible to the people running the concerts, and would in any case be regarded as inequitable.

the cost) because not enough other people want to come too. And in general there must be vast numbers of goods which never appear on the market because at any price sales would be too low to cover costs; yet nobody as far as I know has ever suggested that any good which some would like should be supplied to them at a price which would be enough to cover its cost *if* it had a market of some arbitrary size.

I do not want to deny that there is a quite widespread feeling that railway and electricity authorities (for example) have a duty to provide a 'public service' which is not necessarily defined in terms of each operation covering its costs. But I think that this idea can be broken down into three elements: (*a*) the 'consumer surplus' idea already mentioned. The inhabitants of an area may be benefited by public transport to an extent not measured by fares: (*b*) an indirect effect—the mere existence of public transport is a comfort even if one never uses it; (*c*) a deliberate distributive effect, e.g. the extention of electrification below cost to isolated places to counter rural depopulation. Here the effect could be achieved alternatively by cash payments for staying combined with charging the full cost of electrification. This last does not seem relevant to the 'cultural' examples I am considering at the moment, for the object is not to make electricity cheap but to make living in isolated areas attractive, and there does not seem to be anything analogous in the case of concerts, museums, etc. The second, however, does have some application: could we not regard 'culture' as a sort of public service which it is comforting to have available even if one does not actually wish to avail oneself of it at the moment? This would establish subsidies on a secure want-regarding basis provided the desire to have the concerts, etc. *available* were strong enough.

But although this line of thought may be sufficient to justify some subsidized public provision on want-regarding principles, there is no reason to suppose that it is always so. Tyrone Guthrie's outburst (*The Observer*, 12 March 1961) at the news that the National Theatre would not be proceeded with due to lack of 'public demand' has a ring of plausibility too:

> I am sure that if a plebiscite were taken there would be no wide-spread public demand for public money to be spent on a National Theatre, repertory theatres or theatres of any kind. Would anyone,

however, maintain that, unless the National Gallery had been founded over a century ago through the exertions of a small group of influential persons, it would stand the slightest chance of coming into being now, in response to 'widespread public demand'? If a plebiscite were to be taken as to whether several million pounds were to be expended upon paintings—few of them of a popular character, many of them distinctly 'unpleasant'—would such expenditure be endorsed? 'Ten thousand times, No,' cry the Puritans. 'No,' shouts Philistia. Suburbia echoes, 'No.'

I have been at some pains to enquire into the rationale of subsidies to performances of the arts because this is quite often defended as a 'liberal' idea, in that it widens the possibility of choice.[1] I have tried to show that since 'widening choices' by subsidy 'narrows choices' (or at any rate chances to satisfy wants) by taxation it is more difficult to justify subsidies to the arts on want-regarding grounds than might at first sight appear. On ideal-regarding grounds, of course, one is free to suggest that the availability of *particular* options (whose content is actually specified) is so important that it is worth preserving even at a certain cost to the community in terms of aggregate want-satisfaction. To decide that the local theatre and recreation ground are worth keeping open at a loss, whereas the local cinema, pub, fish-and-chip shop and football club should be allowed to close if they can't cover their costs necessarily involves an ideal-regarding judgement. To put the point another way, the apparently quantitative notion of keeping a wide range of choices open already covertly includes certain preferred options.

This point is, I think, worth making because those who support the conception of keeping open cultural options tend to speak as if anyone who thinks the state should have any concern with the cultural level of the community is a prig and at heart a 'totalitarian'; they do not seem to recognize that their advocacy of spending public money on making available concerts, etc., which would not pay for themselves involves exactly this idea. I do not indeed wish to deny that there is a difference between making something 'good' available and preventing something 'bad' from being obtainable (e.g. between the Third Programme and the

[1] See C. A. R. Crosland, 'The Mass Media', *The Conservative Enemy* and Richard Wollheim in *Socialism and Culture* (Fabian Society, 1961).

Reith Sunday) but the difference, important as it is, amounts only to one of the legitimate *methods* of advancing an ideal.

3.C. *The General Welfare.* 'General', unlike 'public' and 'common', has not yet been examined carefully; it seems to me somewhat vaguer than they are, and more of a rhetorical device. For example, though 'general' is the opposite of 'special' there is no commonly used expression 'special welfare' as an antithesis to 'the general welfare'. The main use of 'special' is in the phrase 'special interest' and I have already employed it in that context. But since the ordinary correlate of 'public' is 'private' how can 'public interest' also be contrasted with 'special interest'? I think the answer lies in recognizing that the limits of 'private' are narrower than the limits of 'assignable group'. 'Private interest' tends to be used where the benefit from acting in a way contrary to the public interest redounds to a single person, a family, etc. This does not preclude the possibility that a number of people's private interests may all lie in doing the same thing.

If a politician has the chance of accepting a bribe in return for awarding a defence contract to a more expensive and less effective firm than the lowest bidder, this is only in his own interest or at most that of his family. Similarly, in the examples discussed in XI.3. each person had a private interest in burning soft coal or not clearing the street. These private interests could not be added together to make a special interest contrary to the public interest; on the contrary once a sufficient number of individual house-holders concerted together their common (net) interest would lie in pledging themselves to act in the public interest by burning smokeless fuel or clearing the street.

To get a case where there is a special interest of a group of people distinct from the public interest we have to change the example and suppose that one particular group of householders, perhaps because of some peculiarity of location—upwind of the conurba-tion or possessing a very long frontage—do not find their net interest to lie in burning smokeless fuel or clearing snow from their frontage even if everyone else does likewise. The members of this group now have not merely a private interest similar to each other householder's private interest (in doing the anti-social thing unless restrained along with everyone else) but a *special* interest. In other words they have a common (net) interest among themselves (in opposing legislation making street clearing or the burning of smokeless fuels compulsory) which is contrary to the interest of the rest.[1]

It should be noticed that if we want to contrast 'special interest' with 'public interest' in this case then either 'the public interest' can no longer be equivalent to 'the net interests of the public' or the membership of 'the public' is more restricted than it was before the example was modified to introduce a group with a special interest. If the latter alternative is followed then 'the public' will be all those in the relevant area who are *not* members of the group with a special interest contrary to that of the rest. The group so defined will still be a non-assignable group (since it is the original non-assignable group with a sub-group removed) so it is quite justifiable to refer to it as a 'public'.

The first alternative is more complicated and will not work in all cases. It involves making use once again of the distinction between someone's interests in some particular capacity and his interests in other capacities. If we now define someone's interests 'in his capacity as a member of the public' as the interests which he shares with non-assignable groups, we can then call 'the public interest' those interests which people have in their capacity as members of the public.[2] Such interests may or may not be *net* interests depending on the relative strength of the interests which any particular person has in a particular instance in his other various capacities. Thus, in the case under discussion, we might suppose (though it need not of course be the case) that although the members of the special interest group find their *net* interest lying in opposing legislation they do nevertheless stand to secure some benefit from it. In other words they share with everyone else a benefit from cleared streets and clean air; it is merely that in their particular case (because the cost of clearing is greater and the benefit of clean air less, respectively) the cost is on balance more than the benefit is worth. The interest in cleared streets and clean air which the members of the group share with everyone else is their interest in their capacity as members of the public; and the

[1] This is, of course, always assuming that the advantages of clearing the streets and burning smokeless fuel do outweigh the disadvantages provided everyone does them, in the eyes of the rest of the population.

[2] For an elaboration of this notion and its significance in the theory of 'the public interest' see my paper 'The Public Interest' (1964).

legislation to ensure them is therefore 'in the public interest' in the sense that it is in everyone's interest *qua* member of the public, even though it is contrary to the net interests of one group.

The point of this discussion has been to show that 'public' is well-anchored by the alternative contrasts of 'private' and 'special' and that the vagueness of 'general' in 'general welfare' can be accounted for by its lack of definite opposites. All that one can say about 'general' in the expression is that it tends to convey that everyone within some broad reference-group has been taken into account in formulating the judgement. (It is another illustration of the close association of 'general welfare' with rhetorical flourishes that it does not seem odd when no reference group is specified; but often the entire population of a state is apparently the reference-group.) However, instead of really saying that the welfare of everyone within the reference group has increased or decreased it is sometimes used to say that the *average* welfare of the members of the reference group has increased. This clearly brings it nearer to a maximizing aggregative judgement than any of the other phrases so far examined, the only difference being that 'welfare' itself is narrower than want-satisfaction.[1]

'Welfare', it will be recalled, refers to the physical conditions conducive to health and with this in mind it is easy to see why certain kinds of provision are particularly likely to be justified as being 'for the general welfare': sanitation, open spaces and recreation grounds, adequate supplies of food (especially for children, whose development depends on a correct diet) and medical care. The term 'welfare state' is not altogether illuminating in this respect, since it was apparently coined to express the very general

[1] The analytical advantages of working with averages have been well expressed by Little: 'Most people who consider the welfare of society do not, I am sure, think of it as a logical construction from the welfares of individuals. They think rather in terms of social or economic groups, or in terms of average or representative men. Now it is evident that representative men are very much more like economic men than are real individuals. The tastes of an average man do not change at all rapidly. He does not experiment very much. His life is not subject to any shocks or crises. The average unmarried male cotton operative will not, for instance, suddenly alter the pattern of his consumption by getting married. His position on the social scale will not alter much. The welfare of his friends and relations is unlikely to alter greatly. Much more important, he never dies. Any prediction that a certain change would increase the economic welfare of a real man is always liable to be upset by his death.' (*Critique of Welfare Economics*, 2nd ed., p. 49.)

idea that the state should not confine its activities to order and national defence; and it is very difficult to draw up any list which would be generally accepted of the services which do comprise 'the welfare state'.[1] However, there is some support for my definition of 'welfare' in the fact that the first thing most people apparently think of under the title 'the welfare state' is the National Health Service. Many, indeed, would virtually equate the two; and I think most people would regard such things as retirement pensions or sick pay tied to earnings as going beyond the 'welfare state'. Cash payments on some flat 'subsistence' rate, and family allowances, are in an intermediate position. They are less clearly concerned with 'welfare' than the direct provision of medical care or 'welfare' foods; but inasfar as they are pitched at a level which is no more than enough to keep body and soul together (if that) they can be regarded as providing little over and above 'welfare'.

[1] See R. M. Titmuss, *Essays on 'The Welfare State'* (London, 1958).

XIII

JUSTIFICATIONS OF 'THE PUBLIC INTEREST'

I. GOVERNMENT AS TRUSTEE

IN this chapter I wish to consider some of the reasons there might be for making a special principle out of 'the public interest'. Since those interests which are shared by a non-assignable group ('the public') are no more than a selection from all interests, why should special attention be paid to them? The answer lies, I think, in the peculiar appropriateness of public interests as matters for the concern of the state; but it is not easy to say exactly why this should be so.

I shall begin by taking up an approach which has a distinct plausibility at first sight. The approach in question may be set out in three stages: (1) the government is a trustee for the citizens; (2) the duty of a trustee is to look after his client's interests; therefore (3) the duty of the government is to look after the interests of the citizens, i.e. to do things which are 'in the public interest'. I shall examine the three stages in turn.

(1) *The government is a trustee for the citizens.* This idea has a long history behind it and Locke, in building his theory of government on it, was anything but an innovator. Burke's defence of the idea that the representative is a trustee is also well known ('it is his duty ... to prefer his constituents' interests to his own' but he also owes them his own judgement of what is best). The whole 'trustee' approach is of course incompatible with simple-minded populism, that is, the view that ideally the government should do whatever a majority of the electorate wants done on any given issue—whether it is one on which the majority is competent to judge or not.[1] But

[1] See R. A. Dahl, *A Preface to Democratic Theory*, Chapter II, for the use of 'populistic democracy' as a technical term.

the complexity of modern political issues and the growth of the executive in the modern state with its responsibility for managing the economy and providing the sinews of welfare and coping with the perpetual foreign crisis, has killed this idea stone dead. The government, and especially the lower echelons of the executive, cannot consult the will of the people and is practically forced back on to the conception of itself as a trustee, subject to a blanket retrospective endorsement or rejection at periodic elections. Even if populism is written off there is still some tension between trusteeship and democracy so it is not surprising that the really forthright modern invocations of 'trusteeship' have been in connection with the duties of colonialist powers. The name of the UN 'Trusteeship Council' is a typical manifestation of this; and the whole idea of the 'White Man's Burden' was quite similar in essence.

(2) *A trustee's duty is to look after his clients' interests.* Consider these examples.

'Bloggs and Bloggs, the lawyers, are looking after my interests in the matter.'
'I have appointed Jones to look after my interests while I am away.'
'The architect's fee includes a payment for looking after the client's interests while the house is being built.'
'The customer's interests [sc. of a bank's trustee department] must be safeguarded.'[1]

Why should anyone wish to have a trustee to 'act in his interests'? J. R. Hicks has set out the rationale for this kind of relationship with his usual lucidity:

When a consumer knows that he is ignorant, he may pay for instruction; but he may also pay to have decisions made for him. Doctors and lawyers and architects and stockbrokers may be paid to take certain sorts of economic decisions for their clients. ... [2]

The possibility of the relationship depends on the fact that the concept of interest is such that one can 'look after so-and-so's interests' without knowing anything about his particular likes and dislikes.

[1] Stoughton Bell, *Trustee Ethics* (Kansas City, 1935), p. 134.
[2] 'The Measurement of Real Income', *Oxford Economic Papers* (1958), p. 134.

(3) *The duty of the government is to look after the interests of the public (i.e. to do things that are 'in the public interest').* Consider first the position of the leader of an interest group. An interest group has as its *raison d'être* the furthering of its members' common interests.[1] The leaders of an interest group admittedly act 'in the interests of the members' but they can act only where their members have a *common* interest in getting something done.[2] If the interests of the members diverge, the leaders are paralysed—or if they are not they should be since if they act they can only be advancing the interests of one section of the members over those of another section.[3] An interest group can afford to remain silent on issues where the interests of its members are divided, without disaster to them.[4] But a society politically organized cannot afford the luxury of acting only when the interests of all coincide. Like a family or even a social club a nation must make decisions when interests clash, for its basis of membership is different from that of common interest. It is not enough that those with common interests in a matter organize; there must also be some way of deciding between them.

If the attempt to apply the idea of 'the government as trustee' is nevertheless pressed, it is thus bound to diverge in application from the clear-cut examples of (a) a trustee appointed by an individual

[1] More precisely, an interest group is founded to advance the common interests of ϕ's; the group will then look for support among all those ϕ's who think that policies favouring them as ϕ's will also give them a net balance of advantages, taking all their roles and capacities into account. An interest group is distinguished from a 'cause' group whose members are united by some common aim (other than the advancement of their individual interests), whether this aim be to advance the interests of others or to go beyond interests to change tastes and beliefs. It is also distinguished from a group whose members are not held together by either a common interest as a ϕ or by a common attitude to some matter, for example a family.

[2] At the most they might legitimately act where some of their members were affected in a certain direction and the rest not affected at all. For the resources of the group to be used in all such situations that arose might reasonably be thought in the long run to benefit all the members.

[3] Schattschneider, *Politics, Pressures and the Tariff*, p. 223: 'The perfect vocational constituency is one so formed that its membership is unanimous, acting only on those public questions concerning which it is unanimous, but this makes majority rule anomalous.'

[4] If this happens too often the interest group will of course tend to break up and the elements re-form in combinations which will more often produce unanimity within each group.

or (*b*) a group which acts when its members' interests coincide in some matter and does nothing the rest of the time. And similarly if an attempt is made to continue the analogy with the idea of a trustee 'acting in the interests' of those he represents by saying that the government, as the trustee for 'the public', should pursue 'the public interest', then the concept of 'the public interest' will inevitably get inflated. Given that 'the public interest' has to be applied where interests diverge, the most likely move is to say that 'the public interest' is obtained by summing up all the interests involved, thus making 'the public interest' equivalent to the general aggregative principle.[1] Bentham, it is well known, defined 'the public interest' in this way. Thus, for example, he opens the *Theory of Legislation* with the words '*The Public Good* ought to be the object of the legislator; *General Utility* [understood in the Benthamite way] ought to be the foundation of his reasonings'.[2]

2. HARMONY AND COMMON ENJOYMENT

2.A. *The Principle of Harmony*. That the government should seek the public interest because it is the trustee of the public turns out to be little more than a verbal move. We still need an explanation of why the government should concentrate on advancing *common* interests rather than simply trying to maximize the aggregate amount of want-satisfaction. One possible answer would be that shared interests are, on ideal grounds, preferable to non-shared interests.

[1] In XII.3.C., I said that even where people have opposed net interests they may still share the same interest in their capacity as members of the public. It might perhaps be proposed on the basis of this that where net interests conflict the government should pursue 'the public interest' by pursuing the interests which people have in common *qua* members of the public. This proposal may or may not be a good one—it is the one discussed in the rest of this chapter—but whether it is or is not cannot be established by analogy with the relation of a trustee to his client, for the trustee acts so as to pursue the *net* interest of his client. Moreover, the formula that the state should act so as to pursue the interests shared by the public *qua* members of the public will not give a solution in every case where net interests conflict because there may be no such 'public interest'.

[2] London (1931), p. 1. See also *An Introduction to the Principles of Morals and Legislation* (Hafner, New York, 1948), p. 3. 'The community is a fictitious *body*, composed of the individual persons who are considered as constituting as it were its *members*. The interest of the community then is, what?—the sum of the interests of the several members who compose it.'

The clearest expositor in general terms of this view is L. T. Hobhouse.[1] Hobhouse's 'principle of harmony' is explained as follows:

> The principle of Harmony . . . holds that acts and institutions are good not because they suit a majority, but because they make the nearest possible approach to a good shared by every single person whom they affect.
>
> The common good is simply the total of all the lives that are in mutual harmony. . . . The claim of the individual may be for a mode of life which pleases him, but is not compatible with social service, and it is not for the common good that this claim should be sustained.[2]
>
> Strictly, the Common Good is neither the sum of individual 'goods' as independently determined, nor another kind of good opposed to them. It is the harmony of which each individual good is a constituent.[3]

The difficulty is to see exactly what the 'principle of harmony' would amount to in practice, and about this Hobhouse is tantalizingly silent. But understood literally the principle seems to me somewhat unattractive: the existence of harmless amusements which do not contribute to the well-being of others would seem not without value in any calculation of the relative desirability of two situations. Yet this seems to be suggested by the remark that a 'mode of life . . . not compatible with social service' should not be permitted. A more lenient interpretation of the 'principle of harmony' would make it consist in the denial of value to wants of A which can be satisfied only by frustrating wants of B.[4] Even in the case of clearly anti-social wants this seems to me dubious: the desire to park, say, in a place which obstructs the traffic is certainly an anti-social desire but it is no less real for that and the inconvenience of parking somewhere further away is a real one too. But in addition to anti-social wants the 'principle of harmony' still rules out merely *competing* wants: if I build on a certain site or occupy a certain place in a car park then nobody else can, so the

---

[1] No doubt Hobhouse owes a debt to T. H. Green, but if so the pupil seems to me a good deal clearer than the master.

[2] *The Elements of Social Justice* (New York, 1922), pp. 121, 122.

[3] *The Elements of Social Justice*, p. 25 n.

[4] It is not, I think, impossible that the first, or more stringent, view was really that of Hobhouse. See Note P on page 311.

'good' of my doing it is not 'shared' or 'in harmony' with others' desires.

2.B. *The Case for Common Enjoyment.* The 'principle of harmony' would certainly have the effect of giving a special status to shared wants: but it is a very strong principle and not, it seems to me, an acceptable one. There may be a certain quasi-aesthetic pleasure to be found in contemplating the idea of a world where nobody sought to satisfy wants where this was incompatible with others' satisfying their wants; or even better where all want-satisfying by one person directly helped to satisfy wants of others; but this is surely a frivolous reason for saying that wants other than these should not be counted if people *do* seek to satisfy them.[1]

An alternative which has attracted adherents is to defend as specially worthy one variety of shared wants, namely wants for *common enjoyment.* Opportunities for people to enjoy things together should, according to this argument, be given high priority. 'Common enjoyment' for this purpose means that *A* enjoys something with *B*; it is not satisfied by the condition that *A* enjoys something and *B* enjoys the same thing (i.e. something falling under the same general description). This at any rate seems to be the interpretation suggested by this passage from an article by a recent exponent of the view in question, August Heckscher:

> Money spent on a network of roads is for the purpose of giving the individual with his automobile a chance to move about more rapidly and freely. Money spent on a system of mass transportation, however, is so that the public, *qua* public, can get about. Today, needless to emphasize, the roads are being magnificently developed, while mass transportation languishes. Again, a hospital is built so that individuals can be cared for as individuals, in the loneliest and most personal of ordeals. Parks, on the other hand, are built for the public in its search of common enjoyment.[2]

[1] It is not perhaps necessary to dwell further on the implications of a footnote to the first quotation given in 2.A. from the text of *The Elements of Social Justice*: 'Any person may have within him elements and capacities of harmony with others and also disharmony. What is inharmonious if it cannot be modified must be destroyed. . . . '

[2] August Heckscher, 'Public Works and the Public Happiness,' *Saturday Review*, 4 August 1962, p. 46. See also Heckscher, *The Public Happiness* (London, 1963).

But why should anyone regard *common* enjoyments especially highly? One obvious reason is an aggregative argument: common provision is often simply more efficient as a means of satisfying wants than separate, private provision. To take Heckscher's examples, public transport is more efficient than private where a large number of people have the same journey to make, and the few square feet which everyone could have on his garden in exchange for getting rid of a public park in the neighbourhood would surely be for most people a poor return.

Alternatively, one can take a distributive viewpoint and suggest that the lack of common enjoyments exacerbates the effects of an inequality of property or income.

> We started in the Industrial Revolution to build up a civilization in which everything depended on the possession of money. If you had money, you could see or own good pictures, hear good music, read good literature, and find a generous intellectual enjoyment in your leisure. The poor man's incentive to work lay in the opportunities created by the revolution for becoming rich. So long as he remained poor he had none of these advantages. . . .
> Today we proceed consciously or unconsciously on a different principle. We are trying to build up a civilization in which the want of money shall not cut people off from the pleasures and interests of a civilized society. We no longer regard leisure, music, picture galleries, theatres, good literature, and other amenities as specially reserved for the rich. The line drawn between rich and poor does not separate them sharply as it did a century ago, by the range and character of their pleasures.[1]

These arguments make common enjoyment merely the means to an end. That is to say, no value is ascribed to common enjoyment itself; it is only valuable insofar as it so happens that various ends can be achieved (or most effectively be achieved) only by the

[1] J. L. Hammond, 'The Growth of Common Enjoyment', L. T. Hobhouse Memorial Trust Lecture No. 3 (1933) in *Hobhouse Memorial Lectures 1930–1940* (Oxford, 1948). Cf. p. 28 of the same lecture. To some extent the distinction which Hammond draws in time can be duplicated by a comparison between the USA and Britain. For example, in Britain most areas of beach are open to the public and the only advantage of those with means is that they can go further and stay longer. In the USA, however, much of the best beach is privately owned so that there is a sharp gulf between those who have their own stretch of beach and those who have to take what is left. See generally J. K. Galbraith, *The Affluent Society*.

provision of common facilities. Are there not any arguments in favour of common enjoyment for its own sake? I can find three. One would involve an appeal to the value of 'integration' which I discussed in Chapter VII: if 'integration' as I defined it there is a cause to be furthered then common enjoyment will constitute not merely a *means* to it but a *form* of it. A second is suggested by Heckscher: artefacts intended for common enjoyment, 'works that are truly public,'

> make for neighborliness and a sense of roots . . . remind us we are one with other generations, and . . . give us peace in surroundings that keep the spirit whole. . . . [1]

A third argument, connected with this, would point to the value of having to organize 'common enjoyment'. Norton E. Long has suggested that we should return to the Greek view of citizenship, which 'regards the capacity of a political order to provide significant roles for the realization of the citizens' moral potential as a major criterion of its value'. He writes:

> As we move into an era of greater and greater public consumption, the sustenance of the arts and the refinement of life, as well as the presently burning questions of housing and the conditions of mere existence, will be more and more major functions of urban government. The new city in the terms of Burke may well become a partnership in all art, all science, all culture with a significant concept of the good life as a vital common aspiration. The apostles of metropolitanism are coming to realize that the vision they are seeking is something more than a better means of moving traffic, an improvement in the plumbing, or even an increase in the competitive position of the local economy. It is the possibility of attaining a shared common goal of a better life. The recreated city of the metropolitan area offers the hope of a significant manageable field of civic action in which a warmer sense of fraternity can be realized than in a state or nation. [2]

[1] 'Public Works and the Public Happiness,' p. 46. Heckscher adds: 'The welfare state might be defined as that which seeks by concerted action to increase the private comforts and satisfactions of its citizens. The state as we have been interpreting it . . . seeks through concerted action to lift men above private comforts and to give them some vision of a public happiness.'

[2] 'An Institutional Framework for the Development of Responsible Citizenship,' in *The Polity*, ed. by Charles Press (Chicago, 1962), p. 183.

3. WHY SHOULD THE STATE PROMOTE SHARED INTERESTS?

Even if it is accepted (on the strength of the arguments presented in the last section) that common interests and common enjoyments are especially significant compared with non-shared interests and enjoyments, this would still not prove that their promotion is peculiarly suitable for states. The argument from 'trusteeship' given in Section 1 did indeed purport to show this, but I have suggested that it rests on a verbal play on the expression 'the interests of the public'.

The simplest, and I think strongest, argument in favour of states concerning themselves particularly with shared interests is a simple practical one: unless states promote these interests they will often not be promoted at all. Private individuals or organizations cannot always effectively make sure that widely shared interests are not squeezed out. This can be most easily seen if we recur to the distinction introduced at the beginning of the last chapter between positive and negative actions to secure common interests. The essential characteristics of the matters discussed under 'public policy' was that actions (or, more exactly contracts in connection with actions) had effects on others besides the contracting parties, and since these 'others' might well run into millions it would plainly be impractical to require that they should be brought into the process of negotiating the contract. 'The public' can act, if it is to act at all, only through 'public authorities'.[1] Other examples of 'negative' state action, which can be explained in the same way, are the criminal law and the various safety and planning regulations made by local authorities. Turning to positive state action, the point here is that the benefits bestowed by certain services, such as national defence, law and order, street lighting and others cannot be restricted to those who are willing to pay for them, and in many other cases (such as roads and parks) the cost and inconvenience of collecting money from those who use them would be considerable. In these cases, then, there is a *prima facie* case for a public authority to provide them and collect the necessary revenues by taxation.

Notice that the present argument does not require any assump-

---

[1] Cf. Paul Appleby, *Morality and Administration in Democratic Government*, pp. 18–22; and for an earlier statement, John Dewey's *The Public and Its Problems*.

tion that shared interests are especially valuable; all it claims is that if they are to be promoted at all the state is the only body capable of doing so, and therefore when one is considering what should be done by a state, one should pay particular attention to the requirements of the public interest. Thus, on this view, the often-remarked importance of 'the public interest' *in politics* need not reflect any *general* superiority of 'the public interest' as a value compared with the simple aggregationist criterion. The particular selection of interests involved in the phrase 'the public interest' corresponds to the set of interests which are especially relevant politically.

The promotion of consumer interests provides a good example of both positive and negative state action 'in the public interest'. H. R. Smith, in his book, *Democracy and the Public Interest*, quotes this passage from another writer:

> From an economic standpoint, all citizens have a common interest in a 'living'. Everyone must secure each day some part of the total national stream of real income—such as food, clothing, housing, medical and dental care, automobiles, radios, and furniture, and so forth. The 'consumer interest' is the interest of all citizens in getting more and better goods for consumption at ever lower prices. . . . It follows, therefore, that in so far as government is concerned with promoting the 'common interest' in the economic sphere, its decisions should be guided by the 'consumer interest'. Since every producer is also a consumer, it may be asked why consumers are contrasted with producers? What is wrong about promoting the interests of producers, as such, since they are also consumers? The contrast between the interest of *consumers* and *producers* is made because an organized group of producers usually stands to gain more from a certain policy (such as legalized price fixing, a curtailment of production, an exclusion of competitors, or a protective tariff) than they stand to lose as buyers of the products of others, including their own.[1]

Smith then goes on to comment as follows:

> Is he not, like Rousseau before him, endeavoring to force citizens to be free? Does this passage not clearly mean that the

[1] Vernon A. Mund, *Government and Business* (New York, 1955), 2nd ed., pp. 75–76. Quoted in Howard R. Smith, *Democracy and the Public Interest* (University of Georgia Monographs No. 5, Athens, Georgia, 1960), pp. 148–149.

government is to give priority to the interests of individuals as consumers because, if left to their own preferences, citizens would often choose to give priority to their producer interests instead? (p. 149).

This comment *exactly* misses the point: people do not *prefer* their interests as consumers; they find it more profitable to *promote* their interests as producers. It is precisely in order to promote the equally-preferred consumer interests that the government has to intervene. Indeed, the notion of asking which interest people 'prefer' is rather nonsensical, for if we suppose that people want as much purchasing power as possible then this obviously depends on their money income and the prices they have to pay. The point is that it is easier to act on one's money income by private efforts than on the general price level.

XIV

CONSTITUTIONAL CHOICE AND THE PUBLIC INTEREST (1)

I. THE INSTITUTIONAL PROBLEM

1.A. *Introduction.* The position we have arrived at is this: firstly, 'the public interest' is not a meaningless expression; although (like any words in the political lexicon) it may be abused it has genuine applications too. And secondly, the state, in virtue of its inclusiveness and coercive powers, has an irreplaceable role in the furtherance of these interests of non-assignable groups which make up 'the public interest'. But how to ensure that the force of the state will be applied to the pursuit of the public interest and not to some quite other purpose?—that is the question asked in these last two chapters.

I say 'asked' rather than 'answered' advisedly, since that guileless-looking question sums up one of the central perennial concerns of political theory. Out of this mass of material I shall pick two opposed traditions, which I shall dub the 'power-diffusion' view and the 'power-concentration' view; and I shall conduct my discussion in terms of these two models. Such drastic simplification of a complex tradition of argument carries dangers, I am well aware, but I shall comfort myself with Bacon's dictum that 'truth emerges more readily from error than from confusion'.

1.B. *Two Simple Views.* The easiest way of dealing with the question how one is to ensure that the state power should be used to promote the public interest is to assume that some man or group of men has the ability and the desire to promote it without requiring any further motives. The only problem then is to see that the requisite power is put into their hands. Two possible ways for this to happen, which have been seriously proposed and to some extent put into practice in modern times, are discussed in this section.

The first possibility is as follows: the electorate chooses its representatives for their presumed devotion to 'the public interest' and they then control as far as they can the process by which authoritative determinations are made in particular cases by drawing up rules and laying down policies. (This description is intended to apply equally to a system in which the executive is directly elected, as, in effect, the USA, and to a Cabinet system.) One may number among the supporters of this theory Burke and J. S. Mill. Burke's definition of a party as 'a body of men united for promoting by their joint endeavours the national interest, upon some particular principle in which they are all agreed' clearly fits in with it.[1] Mill elaborated on the role of the electorate by saying that each man should cast his vote as if he were deciding the result of the election by himself, taking the whole country as his reference-group.[2] American presidents, too, have often set themselves up as the guardians of 'the national interest' or 'the public interest' and contrasted themselves, having the whole country as their constituency, with the Congressmen whose horizon is limited to local and sectional affairs and interests.

The alternative theory follows the first one up to the point where the representatives are elected, but at this point it diverges and rather than the representatives themselves controlling (as far as they can) the policies to be pursued they appoint experts who will do the job instead. The locus of responsibility for seeing that the public interest is forwarded is transferred from the politicians to the 'experts' appointed by them (or further appointments of the primary appointees). This has usually been a muted strain both in theory and practice in Britain.[3] But it has found eloquent

[1] 'Thoughts on the Cause of the Present Discontents (1770)', *Works*, I (London, 1899), p. 530.

[2] Whether the party or the man should be the unit of decision is of course one of the points open to dispute within the general setting of the theory.

[3] This should not be exaggerated, however. The Webbs for example wished 'to introduce into politics the qualified expert—to extend the sphere of government by adding to its enormous advantages of wholesale and compulsory management, the advantage of the most skilled entrepreneur'. (Beatrice Webb, *Our Partnership* (London, 1948,) p. 120.) And for practical

defenders in the USA among writers on public administration and has been notably put into practice, particularly in economic affairs, in France since 1945.[1]

1.C. *Criticisms of the Two Theories.* These two theories are open to the objection that their psychological premises are unsound. Neither electors, nor politicians, nor 'experts', it may be said, have the postulated combination of the desire to pursue the public interest and the knowledge of the policies necessary to attain it. Or, to give the objection a slightly more subtle turn, even if *some* do in fact have the required motivation and capacity, it would be foolish to base one's constitutional arrangements on the assumption that all men, or even a majority, will do so.[2] Hume argued for this ingeniously in his essay 'Of the Independence of Parliament'.[3]

> Political writers have established it as a maxim that, in contriving any system of government and fixing the several checks and controls of the constitution, every man ought to be supposed a *knave* and to have no other end, in all his actions, than private interest. By this interest we must govern him and, by means of it, make him, notwithstanding his insatiable avarice and ambition, cooperate to public good. Without this, say they, we shall in vain boast of the advantages of any constitution and shall find in the end that we have no security for our liberties or possessions except the good will of our rulers; that is, we shall have no security at all.
>
> It is, therefore, a just *political* maxim *that every man must be supposed a knave*, though at the same time it appears somewhat strange that a maxim should be true in *politics* which is false in *fact*. But to satisfy us on this head we may consider that men are generally

[1] Glendon O. Schubert's account of his so-called 'Idealists' in *The Public Interest* is unfair, but it does bring together a recognizably similar group of writers.

[2] It should be noticed that the objection does not depend on the assumption that being entrusted with power actually produces degeneration in the character of the power-holder; in other words it does not rest on Acton's well-worn dictum that 'power tends to corrupt'. The point is examined in Note Q on page 311.

[3] *David Hume's Political Essays*, p. 68. Compare the famous Tenth Federalist Paper.

---

examples one has only to think of the so-called 'Morrisonian' boards of the post-war nationalized industries, deliberately designed with the object of letting the 'experts' get on with the job.

more honest in their private than in their public capacity, and will go greater lengths to serve a party than when their own private interest is alone concerned.

To which we may add that every court or senate is determined by the greater number of voices, so that, if self-interest influences only the majority (as it will always do), the whole senate follows the allurements of this separate interest and acts as if it contained not one member who had any regard to public interest and liberty.

If the original optimistic psychological premises are given up at any point, the conclusions as to desirable constitutional arrangements are liable to collapse as well. Why give politicians or 'expert' administrators a free hand if they are merely going to use it to further their own private interests at the expense of the rest of the community?

Even if it is allowed that elected or appointed persons will be conscientious, it may still be argued that a streamlined political system will unavoidably result in many of the opinions and concerns of ordinary citizens being ignored. Thus, Edward C. Banfield in an article on 'The Political Implications of Metropolitan Growth' writes, comparing Britain with the U.S.A.:

The mere absence of dispute, acrimony, unworkable compromise, and stalemate (this, after all, is essentially what the concept 'effectiveness' refers to in this connection) ought not, of course, to be taken as constituting a 'good' political order. Arrogant officials may ignore the needs and wishes of ordinary citizens, and the ordinary citizens may respectfully acquiesce in their doing so, either because they think (as the British lower class does) that the gentleman knows best or (as the American middle class does) that the expert knows best. In such cases there may be great effectiveness —no dispute, no acrimony, no unworkable compromise, no stalemate—but far from signifying that the general welfare is being served, such a state of affairs signifies instead that the needs and wishes with which welfare under ordinary circumstances, especially in matters of local concern, is largely concerned are not being taken into account. To say, then, that our system is becoming somewhat more and the British system somewhat less effective does not by any means imply 'improvement' for us and the opposite for them. It is quite conceivable that dispute, acrimony, unworkable compromise, and stalemate may be conspicuous features of any situation that approximates the idea of general welfare.[1]

[1] *Daedalus* (Winter, 1961): 'The Future Metropolis', pp. 61–78.

A possible reply would be that even if everyone is self-interested, the public interest will still be served by politicians under a simple constitution which gives unlimited power to those elected provided it is made to be in their interests to be returned to office at the next election. For in that case politicians who do not serve the interests of their constituents will not be returned to office; since the constituents are 'the public', politicians will therefore be driven to seek 'the public interest' even if neither they nor their constituents are actuated by any motives except self-interest. But this would only be true if in all matters all the electors had a common net interest in the same policy relatively to any other possible policy.[1] Unless this is so, one must deny that politicians who wish to be returned to office will necessarily find it advantageous to pursue 'the public interest' rather than the interests of a majority in their constituency (or in the case of a party or a President a majority in each of a majority of the constituencies). Especially where there is a clear-cut division along lines of race, colour, religion, nationality, etc., it may obviously be more electorally profitable (if all behave selfishly) to stand for the common interests of the majority bloc rather than the common interests of the whole body of citizens.

1.D. *The Power-Diffusion Thesis.* In order to get the problem presented as quickly as possible I have put forward crudely and uncritically two simple proposals for securing the implementation of public interests and some obvious if exaggerated criticisms. Each of these sides stands in a long tradition of political thought. The tradition underlying the criticisms put forward in 1.C. can be conveniently referred to as the 'power-diffusion' view. On this view, nobody is fit to be trusted with absolute power (whether a single individual or a number large enough to form a majority within a state). It is by checks and balances on those with power rather than by trust in their goodwill that satisfactory results may be achieved in politics. The opposite tradition, which underlies the two theories considered in the earlier parts of this section, may be called the 'power-concentration' view. According to this view, the risks inherent in concentrating power in a certain man or

[1] James Mill, who argues from individual self-interest on all sides to the public interest in his *Essay on Government* apparently makes this assumption of a common net interest among the electorate, perhaps with the exception of certain 'sinister interests' which are, in effect, unjustifiable privileges.

group of men are worth taking because of the advantages this has. In the last half-century the continuing conflict between the two traditions can be traced in discussions of the relative merits of 'planning' and 'pricing' (especially where the merits of 'pricing' have been presented as mainly political) and in the American debate about the desirability of a 'more responsible two-party system'.[1]

1.E. *'The Calculus of Consent.'* The power-concentration view is simple and the possible objections to it are also easy to see and to state. The power-diffusion view is complicated and criticisms of it must be correspondingly complicated. I shall therefore devote the rest of this chapter and most of the next to what seems to me the most sophisticated attempt to state rigorously a version of the power-diffusion theory. This is to be found in a book entitled *The Calculus of Consent.*[2] In this the authors claim to be able to prove that if there were no cost involved in bargaining, everyone would find it in his interest to support a constitutional set-up under which no legislation could be passed and no public expenditures authorized unless there were unanimous agreement on it; or, to put it another way, every citizen would demand a personal veto over any kind of collective action in his society.

Though the book is long and detailed, the essential reasoning

[1] In connection with 'planning' and 'pricing' I am thinking of such writers as Hayek, von Mises and Röpke on the 'power-diffusion' side and Barbara Wootton on the 'power-concentration' side. The expression 'a more responsible two-party system' is taken from the title of the report issued by a committee under the auspices of the American Political Science Association, 'Towards a More Responsible Two-Party System', *American Political Science Review Supplement*, XLIV, No. 3 (September 1950). The best-known recent diffusers have been E. P. Herring and A. Holcombe; the acknowledged leader of the concentrators is E. E. Schattschneider. See especially his article, 'Political Parties and the Public Interest', *Annals of the American Academy of Political and Social Science*, No. 280 (March 1952), 18–26.

[2] J. M. Buchanan and Gordon Tullock, *The Calculus of Consent* (Ann Arbor, 1962). The main elements of the book are accessible in the following three articles: J. M. Buchanan, 'Social Choice, Democracy, and Free Markets,' *Journal of Political Economy*, LXII (1954), 114–123; and 'Positive Economics, Welfare Economics, and Political Economy', *Journal of Law and Economics*, II (1959), 124–138. (Both are reprinted in J. M. Buchanan, *Fiscal Theory and Political Economy*, Chapel Hill, 1960); G. Tullock, 'Problems of Majority Voting', *Journal of Political Economy*, LXVII (1959), 571–579. (See also the controversy arising out of this article: A. Downs, 'In Defense of Majority Voting', *Journal of Political Economy* LXIX (1961), 192; and G. Tullock, 'Reply to a Traditionalist', *Journal of Political Economy*, LXIX (1961), 200.

leading to this conclusion can be simply stated. Let us assume that there is agreement on the initial distribution of property, that contracts are enforced and a minimum of 'human rights' secured by the state. Starting from this initial position let everyone trade who wishes; such trading must make both parties to it better off since otherwise it would not be undertaken. Coercive intervention by the state does not, however, normally carry a similar guarantee of making everyone better off than before since it does not normally require unanimity. Therefore, only if unanimity is required for legislative action can we be sure that nobody loses by the change. The authors consider the possibility that if changes could be made by, say, a simple majority some people might hope to gain more than they lose, but claim to be able to prove that in the long run *everyone* can expect to lose.

Given the existence of bargaining costs, they admit that this ideal must be amended; but they still maintain that it is the benchmark against which actual systems must be measured. The costs of departing from unanimity as a requirement for collective action must be added to the cost of bargaining and that arrangement chosen which will minimize the sum of both.

The argument which Buchanan and Tullock develop can best be considered as composed of two parts; firstly, the assertion that if there were no bargaining costs rational egoists would, and could, operate a system requiring unanimity for changes; and secondly, the assertion that when bargaining costs are allowed for, all that is needed is to reduce the unanimity requirement somewhat. I shall deal with these two stages of their argument in turn, questioning the first in this chapter and the other in the next. Against them, I shall maintain (*a*) that a community of rational egoists could not be (with any institutions) as pleasant to live in as Buchanan and Tullock believe; (*b*) that even rational egoists might do worse than support a simple-majority system; and (*c*) that there is no reason why with only a very moderate capacity for altruism in the electors, a simple majority system should not work quite well.

2. SELF-DEFENCE AND COLLECTIVE PROVISION (i)

2.A. *Introduction.* The authors' construction clearly depends heavily on the existence of some *status quo* on which everyone agrees; otherwise we have no base-line against which to measure the 'changes' which are supposed to require unanimity. According to the authors such a *status quo* is provided by a position where there are no public expenditures and the only laws are concerned with the maintenance of certain 'human rights' and the legal framework of *laissez faire* (enforcement of contracts and perhaps an anti-trust law).

Given this *status quo* the authors argue that it would not be in anybody's interest to allow for alterations without unanimous agreement because this would enable others to 'impose costs' on them. (In Note R (p. 312), I show that their attack on the usual rationale of majority voting is completely dependent on the existence of a unanimous prior agreement on the *status quo*.) This imposing of costs really covers two cases: legislation to prevent people from doing something they would like and the raising by compulsory means (i.e. taxation) of money to pay for collective expenditures. These correspond to my categories of positive and negative applications of 'the public interest' respectively, and I shall take them in turn, dealing with the first in this section and the next; and the second in the last section (4). Before this, however (2.B.), I shall comment briefly on the authors' assumption that everyone might be willing to agree on *laissez faire* and a certain distribution of property as a *status quo* from which changes could be made only by unanimous consent, since it throws some light on their thought processes.

2.B. Laissez faire *and Unanimity*. An obvious objection is that it would be impossible to get unanimous agreement on any particular initial distribution of property; and the authors are not in fact able to deal with it. (They don't even try.) A more interesting point, though, is that even if everyone did agree on some original sharing out of property, this would not entail agreement on whatever income distribution might arise later. The agreement on property might be combined, for example, with an agreement on specific measures of continuous redistribution or on collective provision financed out of a progressive income tax. If so, it would be the post-redistribution position rather than the distribution immediately arising from *laissez faire* which would provide the baseline from which 'gains' and 'losses' would have to be measured, and the baseline from which 'trading' would take place.

There are in fact any number of reasons why at least some

rational egoists would be well advised to balk at underwriting whatever distribution of income arose from *laissez faire*. The authors fail to see this because, I suspect, they are blinded by a picture. This is the picture of the classic bargaining situation in which *A* has a stock of some good (say apples) and *B* has a stock of some other good (say oranges). If they trade they can both gain relatively to their initial position. This picture would be relevant to the present discussion if the only problem were to give out some goods, once for all. It would be sensible for everyone to trade, starting from that initial position; and if everyone accepted the initial position as fair nobody would have any reason for complaining at the final results. But everyone has to eat and this needs a constant outflow of funds. When someone was satisfied with his final trading position he could not simply conserve it; he would have to start using it up. (A few might be provided with a large enough stock at the outset to live on without supplementing it; but this could obviously not be true of all or even most.) A man in a lifeboat with a week's supply of food does not indefinitely remain as well off as he was to start with. He can die without anyone's 'coercing' him by taking his food. Introducing the possibility of trade does not help; the principle of trade is that 'nothing's for nothing' and a man with no money can perfectly well starve in a city. We cannot therefore say that everyone will, if he is reasonable, accept the results of free trade because nobody is coerced and everybody gains. A steady stream of income is needed yet there is no guarantee that there will be work for all who want it at a wage which will be enough to live on. Even with full employment and perfect competition, the net marginal product of some people's most productive work may be very low indeed; and curiously enough, the more technically advanced the economy, the more likely this is. We must also, of course, add that even if all able-bodied people could earn enough to live on, some breadwinners would be mentally or physically incapacitated or handicapped; and there is nothing in *laissez faire* to bring into any relation the size of a wage and the number of people supported by it.

2.C. *The Theory of the Offensive Veto*. The authors' fundamental preconception about a system under which unanimity is needed to make changes in laws or in order to authorize public expenditures is that nobody would use the power to veto except in 'self-defence', i.e. to avoid being made worse off. But a community so self-restrained would not need such elaborate safeguards, whereas one which was composed of ruthless egoists would not find that the use of the veto stopped there. The veto can be used by egoists offensively as well as defensively. If one were concerned only to defend oneself, one would presumably never veto projects which left one entirely unaffected, but it is easy to show that one could in fact benefit from threatening just this. For example, suppose that in an American state which contains a large city the State legislature has to authorize bond issues or the rearrangement of departments by the city. These may not hurt the inhabitants of the rest of the state at all; but they provide a lever by which an 'upstate' or 'downstate' majority in the legislature can extort advantages from the city which might otherwise not be obtainable.

This example can be generalized: if I had a right to veto any expenditure by you, I would be only beginning to use the power given me by this position if I merely used it to veto expenditures harmful to me. Indeed, by threatening to veto all expenditures I could presumably starve you into handing all your earnings over to me except those necessary to your survival. The application of this to the authors' utopia should be plain. If unanimity is required for a piece of legislation or public expenditure a group which is skilful may commit itself to vote against the measure unless it secures almost the entire gain to be expected from the measure itself; and it can do this quite well if it is actually completely unaffected by the proposal. It can also do the same thing if it is favourably affected or indeed if it is adversely affected but not to the extent of the gain which (without side-payments) would accrue to the beneficiaries. It may perhaps be wondered how a group which was unaffected or even benefited by a measure could convince the rest that it would vote against the measure unless it received almost the total net benefit expected to accrue from it. This question can best be answered by taking an example. Suppose that we have a legislature with only two groups in it, and some measure has to be voted on. Each group stands to gain 100 units (say pounds) from the measure's passing.[1] Finally, because of some

---

[1] We may either suppose that the measure is costless to put into operation or that the cost will be allocated in a predetermined way and the two groups stand to gain £100 over and above this cost.

constitutional peculiarity, both groups must vote for the measure in order that it may pass.[1]

Each group has two strategies: it can vote for the measure or it can vote against the measure. There are therefore $2 \times 2 = 4$ possible situations which can arise in connection with the measure. If we call the two groups Row and Column (for reasons that will become apparent) we can describe these possibilities as follows: (1) both vote for; (2) Row votes for, Column against; (3) Row votes against, Column for; and (4) both vote against. Putting this into a more convenient matrix form we have:

	Column	
	Vote For	Vote Against
Vote For	(1)	(2)
Row		
Vote Against	(3)	(4)

Fig. 2

Each of the four situations will have a *pay-off* to the two groups, Row and Column. In the present case the combination of strategies (1) gives each group 100 and the other three combinations give them nothing. We can put this into our matrix, writing Row's pay-off in the lower left corner of each box and Column's pay-off in the upper right corner, as in Fig. 3 overleaf.

Now let us imagine that Row wants to secure not just the 100 shown in the diagram but, say, 90 of Column's gains as well. It must somehow convince Column that it will vote against the proposal unless it receives a side-payment of 90. If we suppose that the figures are net benefits and there is a cost involved, an alternative way of putting it would be that Row insists that it will vote

[1] E.g. a qualified majority is required and neither group has this majority; or there are two houses in each of which the measure has to get a simple majority and each group has a majority in one house.

Column

	Vote For	Vote Against

Vote For		100	o
	100		
		o	
Row			
Vote Against		o	o
	o		o

Fig. 3

against the measure unless Column pays 90 more of the cost. There are two ways in which it can do this: it can either actually lower its pay-off from voting for the measure unless it gets paid; or it can pretend that it stands to lose 90 in the first place. The first may be done for example by taking a bet of more than 100 that it won't vote in favour unless it gets a 90 bribe and won't vote against if it does get a 90 bribe. But for a politician a more practicable way is to stake his reputation. Suppose the reputation of the Row group is worth 1,000 to its members, and they assert publicly that they will not vote for the measure unless they get a side payment of 90, but they will vote for it if they do get 90. Their pay-offs then become:

Column

	Bribe, Vote For	Not Bribe, Vote For

Vote For	10 (Measure passes) 190	100 (Measure passes) —900
Row		
Vote Against	—90 (Measure fails) —910	o (Measure fails) o

Fig. 4[1]

[1] It is assumed that Column will vote Yes under all circumstances since it can never gain by doing otherwise.

The second possibility would be, as I said, for the Row group to pretend that it really disliked the proposal so that its real pay-off in the first matrix was not 100 but —89. It would then be plain to the other side (if they believed this) that they must pay 90 to make it worth while for Row to vote in favour. This is not altogether easy to do where the benefit is an obvious and material one, but it is quite easy where there are matters of principle and preference. Moreover, even where the benefit was clear, one could still say that he disapproved of having the benefit provided collectively and would still vote against it unless paid to overcome his principles.

2.D. *Inefficiency of the Unanimity Principle.* So far, then, I have suggested that the unanimity principle is inequitable in that it enables those not affected by a proposal to claim a ransom in virtue of their power to adopt a dog-in-the-manger attitude and veto it.[1] On ideal grounds, it is offensive in that it puts a premium on dissimulation, obstinacy and cunning. However, I have not yet shown that it is inefficient in the technical sense which interests the authors, viz. that mutually profitable arrangements may fail to be arrived at under it. This I shall now proceed to do, but before that it is necessary to clear up the meaning to be given to the postulate that there are no bargaining costs. Obviously, if the assumption that there are no bargaining costs is taken to mean that all bargains which would benefit both parties are made, inefficiency is impossible by definition. I here mean by the assumption that there are no costs involved in bargaining what would, I think, generally be meant by it: that the communication and consideration of threats, promises and statements of intention (even if there are thousands of them necessary for full bargaining—as there would be with one proposal and a hundred people) does not take effort or expense. Though I here assume perfect knowledge about matters of fact, perfect knowledge of each person's indifference-map (that is, each person's preference as between any possible combination of events) would take us into a fantasy world. Yet even in such a fantasy world one of the sources of 'inefficiency' to be noticed below—incompatible commitments—could still occur.

[1] Buchanan and Tullock suggest at one point that there is no danger of people using their veto to secure positive advantages for themselves since at a pinch those who expect to benefit from common action can always contract together voluntarily to pay for it. This is examined in Note S on page 316.

Generally speaking, inefficiency occurs when the methods just examined for getting more than one's 'fair share' go wrong. Let us then consider a situation in which only one person or group is trying to gain more than its 'fair share'. The person or group may misreckon the amount of surplus there is going. Suppose that Row believed Column's benefit to be 100 as in Fig. 3 and demanded 90 to vote for the measure; if in fact Column's benefit were only 80 Column would refuse to vote for the measure. Row would now like to withdraw the threat, since it has failed; but it cannot do so without sacrificing its reputation for keeping its word. The measure will therefore fail to pass. This is equally clear in the case where Row misrepresents its true preferences and pretends to a loss of 89. It can hardly say 'Well, since you won't pay us we'll change our minds—we really like the bill', without revealing its deception, which, as before, we may take to be more than the measure is worth.

It is important to notice that this is a genuine 'Prisoners' Dilemma' situation in that even if an agreement were made to do the jointly efficient thing (i.e. in this case, be honest) both sides would, if composed of egoists, have an adequate motive for reneging on the agreement. And whereas in most Prisoners' Dilemma situations an enforceable contract with adequate penalties would solve the problem, it is difficult to see how legislators or citizens could get much help from an enforceable agreement to be honest. A change in the rules (e.g. to simple majority voting) would seem more helpful.

3. SELF-DEFENCE AND COLLECTIVE PROVISION (ii)

3.A. *Does Majority Voting Over-Provide Public Goods?* Buchanan and Tullock do not however rest their case on the theoretical advantages of the unanimity principle. They also try to prove that under a system of majority voting public expenditures are inevitably higher than the 'efficient' size (i.e., the size which people would be willing to pay individually), and bring in support of this the 'pork-barrel' phenomenon in Congress. I shall therefore refute this 'proof' in the present sub-section and present an alternative explanation of the 'pork barrel' in Note T on page 317. The authors' basic idea was wittily put by Wicksell when he wrote:

... it is easy for capable but unprincipled politicians to exploit the party constellations of the day for the purpose of swelling public expenditure far beyond the amount corresponding to the collective interest of the people. Then the parties win in turn but in the end they all lose; it is like a game of roulette where the players win and lose in turn but the money finally ends up with the bank.[1]

In Chapter 10 they work out the following example: in a community of 100 farmers each decision to repair one of the roads which lead from the main highway to each group of four or five farms is taken by majority vote. According to the authors, if any large group of the farmers votes egoistically the whole group will be forced into a position where the total expenditure on roads is about double what it would be if each farmer paid for the amount of road repairing he wanted. This comes about as follows: if each farmer simply votes in favour of having the road on which he lives repaired, every proposal to repair a road will be defeated 95–5. Log-rolling must therefore take place if any roads are to be repaired at all; in other words a coalition must form, each of whose members promises to vote for the others' repairs in return for a promise by the others to vote for his own repairs. But under a simple-majority system the size of coalition required to carry out its wishes is only 51. Assuming that the ground-rules lay down in advance that all road-repairs authorized will be paid for by an equal levy on each farmer in the community, this gives any coalition of 51 a chance to have its roads repaired at the cost of the whole community of 100. The members of a coalition of 51 will therefore balance the costs of road repairs *to themselves* against the benefits *to themselves*; and since they only pay half the costs of the road repairs they vote themselves, they will agree to vote for about twice the amount they would be willing to pay for if they had to bear the entire cost between them.

So far so good. Now comes the point where the authors slip in two assumptions which are not defended and which are in fact quite implausible. They suggest that the 49 left out in the cold will find it possible to bribe at least one of the erstwhile majority to

---

[1] R. A. Musgrave and A. T. Peacock, *Classics in the Theory of Public Finance* (London, 1958), p. 87.

defect, by offering him extra good road repairs (side-payments do not seem to be considered in this model; if they were, they would destroy it since the 51 would take money rather than the repairs they didn't want as much as money). But if the 51 had any sense they would make an enforceable contract not to defect later; every member would have a motive for signing it because only one, or at best a few, could gain from defecting, and the rest would lose. Nobody would know in advance whether he would be one of the lucky ones, and so the prospect of being sure nobody would defect, as against that of *either* defecting oneself *or* being double-crossed (depending on one's luck), would be attractive. Moreover, even if some might hope to have above-average chances of defecting, a group of 51 who were willing to agree not to defect would be all that was necessary to produce a contractually-bound majority.

That is the first assumption. The second is even weaker. For some reason which is never so much as hinted at, the authors assume that the new majority will vote itself road-repairs on the same basis as the other group did (i.e. about twice as much expenditure as they would be willing to pay if they had to shoulder the costs themselves) *while leaving intact the appropriation passed by the other group*. Of course, on this assumption it is easy to show that the 'equilibrium position' or 'saddle point' will occur when everyone is getting more road repairs than he would be willing to pay for. But surely the new majority would, at the same time as they passed an authorization for their own roads, reverse the appropriation passed by the other group. There will in fact, be no 'equilibrium position'; the result will depend purely on the rules of the legislative body. If there is some device whereby the legislature packs up for the year on a certain date, whichever group of 51 had the last vote will get its roads repaired and nobody else will; if the session can be closed by the vote of a majority, the first majority to form will do that after passing its own appropriations. Or if neither of these holds, the legislature will simply stay in session reversing one appropriation after another until the farmers are forced by exhaustion to agree on a better method of allocating resources to road building, such as setting up general criteria for a road's being 'repair-worthy' and then delegating to an official the job of applying these criteria.

The authors generalize their conclusion later:

> The analysis of Chapters 10, 11 and 12 demonstrated that the organization of collective action through simple majority voting tends to cause a relative over-investment in the public sector if the standard Paretian criteria are accepted. Note that the effects are always in this direction under the behavioral assumptions employed in our models. This is because the majority voting rule allows the individual in the decisive coalition to secure benefits from collective action without bearing the full marginal costs properly attributable to him. In other words, the divergence between private marginal cost and social marginal cost (the familiar Pigovian variables) is always in the same direction. (p. 201.)

As we have seen this is correct only (a) if majorities do not contract to stick together, and (b) if, when defection does take place, the new majority always leaves intact existing appropriations. The authors' analysis is, however, only alarming because of its claim that the position in which everyone is spending more than he likes is an 'equilibrium' position. Once this is shown as resting on arbitrary and peculiar assumptions, we can look at the problem more clearly. Instead of the results envisaged by the authors we must instead consider one of three possibilities: (a) a determinate bloc of 51 or more persistently vote in their own interests alone, (b) a different and unpredictable coalition will form each session and legislate purely in its own interest or (c) no result will be reached at all, merely an endless series of coalitions each undoing the work of the last. Of these three, the first is a recipe for civil war or secession by the minority and the other two are unsatisfactory to all concerned.

3.B. *'Reasonable' Solutions.* We thus arrive at the significant conclusion that even egoists would be forced, if they were rational, into pursuing the public interest on condition that everyone else did likewise. (The Hobbesian ring of the last phrase is deliberate, for it was Hobbes' point that the best way of reaching self-interested goals is to co-operate with others so long as they are willing to join in.) It would require trust, but hardly altruism, for all concerned to settle on some scheme from which all would benefit compared with the alternatives of deadlock or anarchy. The difference between trust and altruism can be simply illustrated by reference to the basic game-theoretical 'Prisoners' Dilemma' situation. Schematically, this can be represented as follows:

Column

	I	II
	1 2	
i	1 —2	
Row	—2	
ii	2 0	0

Fig. 5

If Row and Column do not trust one another then if they are rational they will both take the second choice (ii, II) thus ending up with 0 apiece. Suppose you are Row. If Column chooses I, you get 2 instead of 1 by choosing ii. If he chooses II you get 0 instead of —2. Thus, either way you gain by choosing ii. Exactly the same analysis applies *mutatis mutandis* to Column. It is worth noticing that if trust is lacking even communication doesn't help (though enforceable contracts would) for whatever you *say* it still pays you (and him) to double cross when it comes to choosing.[1] Surely to say here that in order to score 1 apiece the participants must be *altruistic* would be misleading. Neither has it in his power to get 2 unless the other trusts him, so he can hardly be said to renounce it in taking 1. What they do need is enough trust each to believe that the other 'player' will stick to his agreement to act in the common interest and not double cross. In an infinite number of games between the same players, a player who 'double crosses' can be 'punished' by a non-co-operative response the next time by the other player. In these circumstances rational egoists can be expected to settle down quickly to choosing their first course of action each time, and trust has a positive cash value in terms of *future* plays. Politics is hardly ever a one-shot affair, and there is

[1] Compare Anatol Rapoport, *Fights, Games and Debates* (Ann Arbor, 1960) who claims that bare communication by itself solves the Prisoners' Dilemma (p. 174.)

normally no obvious 'last term' of the series (though an important exception is a US President nearing his eighth year under the Bricker Amendment) so the analogy with a game having an infinite series of plays is close.

The essential point is that where the pursuit of maximum short-run gain makes everyone lose compared with some 'reasonable' solution, it actually becomes a matter of self-interest to aim at the 'reasonable' solution provided everyone else does likewise. 'Reasonableness' here is not meant to cover anything as substantial as a 'sense of justice' or commitment to moral principles (that is, a willingness freely to subordinate one's interests to some principle or set of principles). All I am saying is that without *some* common standards (if only the crude one of 'splitting the difference') rational egoists would be unable to negotiate with one another because there would be no stability in their expectations. Each party *ex hypothesi* wants as much as he can get and there is no way in which the several parties can reach an agreement unless the bare notions of rationality and self-interest are somehow supplemented.

If we could ask how the necessary common standards are to be found, the answer, I think, lies in the idea of an *obvious* solution. But what constitutes 'obviousness'? The only two studies known to me are by Hume and Thomas C. Schelling, both of whom raise the question in much the same context.[1] Both agree that it is some unique and striking feature which provides the 'obvious' solution to problems of co-ordination.

> There seldom is any very precise argument to fix our choice and men must be contented to be guided by a kind of taste or fancy, arising from analogy, and a comparison of similar instances. Thus, in the present case, there are, no doubt, motives of public interest for most of the rules, which determine property; but still I suspect, that these rules are principally fix'd by the imagination, or the most frivolous properties of our thought and perception. (Hume, *Treatise*, p. 504.)

[1] David Hume, *A Treatise of Human Nature*, Bk. III, Part II esp. Section IV; Thomas C. Schelling, *The Strategy of Conflict*, Chapters 3 and 4. Burke's ideas on the value of prejudice are also relevant, but he never seems to have considered anything except the *status quo* as an 'obvious' solution. He was not therefore led to ask what is the general nature of 'obviousness'. See Halévy, *The Growth of Philosophical Radicalism*, p. 159.

Finding the key, or rather finding *a* key—any key that is mutually recognized as the key becomes *the* key—may depend on imagination more than on logic; it may depend on analogy, precedent, accidental arrangement, symmetry, aesthetic or geometric configuration, casuistic reasoning, and who the parties are and what they know about each other. . . . A prime characteristic of most of these 'solutions' to the problems, that is, of the clues or coordinators or focal points, is some kind of prominence or conspicuousness. (Schelling, *The Strategy of Conflict*, p. 57.)

Thus, in the case of the roads, two possible 'obvious' solutions might be to keep all the roads up to some customary standard of repair or to spend an equal amount each year in repairing everyone's road, whether it needed it or not. These solutions would illustrate two of the most common criteria of 'obviousness': the *status quo* and equality.[1]

4. SELF-DEFENCE AND EXTERNAL COSTS

4.A. *The Solution Offered.* It is plain that the grand aim of Buchanan and Tullock is nothing less than the destruction of a whole tradition of political theorizing: the tradition which has seen in the promotion of widely shared common interests—public interests—the most important reason for the existence of public authorities. To the authors, public authorities are merely instruments for enforcing private agreements; and we have seen how they try to force the provision of collective goods into this framework by introducing their principle of unanimity. A 'public authority' which can act only when all those subject to it are agreed is not a *public* authority at all; its 'laws' are simply contracts with a large number of signatories. They are laws only in the sense in which a contract entered into between *A* and *B* might be called a 'law with respect to *A* and *B*'.

So much for the provision of collective goods: what in Chapter XII.1., I called 'positive' applications of 'the public interest'. But I pointed out there that 'the public interest' is also involved in 'negative' applications, where it is generally thought that the state has a duty to intervene on behalf of the community to suppress anti-social conduct. How will Buchanan and Tullock deal with this kind of cue for state action?

[1] Note U is devoted to a further exploration of the *status quo* and equality as 'obvious' solutions. See page 319.

It might be predicted that they will deny any need for explicit intervention on behalf of 'the public' (in fact the entire concept of 'the public' has no place in their world). And it might be guessed that they will attempt to force the usual forms of state action into the mould of private contracts. But the boldness of their proposal is such as to astonish the uncommitted and perhaps even dismay their sympathizers, for it places the onus for ending nuisances squarely on the shoulders of those who suffer from the nuisance. Here is the relevant passage:

> Smoke from an industrial plant fouls the air and imposes external costs on residents in the surrounding areas. If this represents a genuine externality, either voluntary arrangements will emerge to eliminate it or collective action with unanimous support can be implemented. If the externality is real, some collectively imposed scheme through which the damaged property owners are taxed and the firm's owners are subsidized for capital losses incurred in putting in a smoke-abatement machine can command the assent of all parties. If no such compensation scheme is possible (organization costs neglected), the externality is only apparent and not real. The same conclusion applies to the possibility of voluntary arrangements being worked out.[1] (p. 91.)

Before discussing this passage a word should be said about the authors' terminology in it. An 'external cost' is normally understood as a cost which is not borne by the person who imposes it. The authors have an idiosyncratic and misleading definition of 'externality' which equates it with 'inefficiency', an 'inefficient' situation being one where everyone could be made better off by some adjustment. I shall not follow this confusing use, which is analogous to saying that if a firm is using the cheapest combination of inputs for a given output it has no production costs.

4.B. *Objections to the Solution.* What is wrong with the authors' suggestion? It is inefficient and inequitable. It is inefficient in the technical (Paretian) sense that it is liable to lead to an arrangement of resources such that under different rules everyone could be better off. This can be most easily seen from the location of new factories. Under the rules proposed by Buchanan and Tullock nobody looking for a site for his new factory need take any

---

[1] The same solution is propounded by Buchanan in the essay 'Positive Economics, Welfare Economics and Political Economy', *Journal of Law and Economics*, II (1959), p. 114.

account of the external costs which he will impose. He can therefore toss a coin to decide between two locations equally satisfactory to him—regardless of the fact that in one place he would be imposing immense external costs and in the other none at all. Once the factory is built to operate at the most profitable size without having to take account of external costs, the damage is done. The situation is inefficient whether or not the neighbouring householders find it worth paying for smoke-control apparatus to be installed. The authors' view that there is not a 'real externality' (i.e. inefficiency) unless the householders would find it worth while to pay for smoke reduction takes a very short-sighted view of the matter. Once the horse has bolted it may be cheaper to let him go than to chase him; but if we extend our view backward in time we can say that it would have been even better to lock the door in the first place.[1]

The authors' proposed solution is also objectionable on distributive grounds: even leaving aside cases of gratuitous exploitation it is always inequitable for those living near a factory to be, in effect, subsidizing its shareholders and the consumers of its products.[2] (For me, a distributive objection is significant in its own right; but the authors only take distributive considerations into account when they are 'inefficient'. In Note W on page 323 I argue that this kind of inequitability is 'inefficient' on the authors' own terms.)

4.C. *Alternatives to the Solution.* One possible solution would be to write into the constitution that 'no external costs are to be imposed on others without adequate compensation'; and it seems to me odd that the authors do not canvass the idea. The proposal would, however, be unworkable if it were left as vague as this

---

[1] For a more exact statement see Note V on page 322.

[2] R. H. Coase, in an article supporting the same general line as Buchanan and Tullock ('The Problem of Social Cost', *The Journal of Law and Economics*, III (October 1960)) works out an example involving a railway company and shows that it may under some circumstances be more 'efficient' (in the sense that the gainers from the arrangement could overcompensate the losers) for those operating a railway company not to be made responsible for the fires in woods on either side of the line made by sparks from the engine. But this conclusion is merely a special case of the well-known theorem that Paretian efficiency requires concerns whose marginal costs are below their average costs to be subsidized. The question remains: why should the subsidy be provided by those whose property happens to abut the railway line?

because there is no precise criterion of where an 'external cost' starts and where a 'harmless' action leaves off.[1] To build something that shuts out light from others seems an obvious case of the owner imposing costs on other residents; to be compelled to keep a lot vacant for use as a car park or playground without compensation seems clearly going in the opposite extreme and involving the residents' imposing costs on the owner. But there is a vast grey area in between and here the only answer is precise legislative or administrative rules (backed by majority voting), perhaps subject to some vague test of 'reasonableness' in the courts.[2]

It may perhaps be thought that this handing of detailed decision to legislators and administrators could be avoided by writing all the rules into the constitution (which, it will be recalled, requires unanimous assent). But this would be too rigid in at least two ways. First, new ways of behaving in an anti-social manner are constantly being invented; any particular list drawn up at a certain time would soon become incomplete, yet it might be difficult to get unanimous consent for adding new ones to the list without offering compensation to those who saw an especially good chance to make a killing—and this is exactly what, quite apart from new *kinds* of external cost, we want to avoid. And second, the openness of the future militates against drawing up once and for all a code of prohibitions. How, to take an obvious example, could there be a sensible city zoning law to operate in perpetuity, when nothing can be known of future changes in population, work, age distribution, demand for housing, schools or parks?

[1] For a useful discussion with respect to city planning see Alison Dunham, 'City Planning . . . '.

[2] The difficulties of making too much of judicial tests of what is 'reasonable' in this area are amply illustrated in the efforts of the US Supreme Court, especially from the 1880s to the 1930s.

XV

CONSTITUTIONAL CHOICE AND THE PUBLIC INTEREST (2)

1. INTRODUCTION

THE authors' construction, as considered so far, depends on the assumption that there are no bargaining costs and also on the assumption that there are no costs or difficulties involved in acquiring information. The first of these assumptions is explicitly noticed by the authors, and they maintain, as I indicated at the beginning of the last chapter, that if it is relaxed the only change in their constitutional recommendations that is necessary is for the requirement of unanimity for collective action to be replaced by a requirement of a qualified majority. They also recognize that bargaining costs will necessitate representative government rather than direct government, but their analysis of this point is superficial. The second assumption, of non-existent information costs, is not explicitly recognized by Buchanan and Tullock, though perhaps they (erroneously) regard it as included in the first.

I shall maintain in the next two sections that even if the authors' construction were plausible with these two assumptions—in other words, even if my arguments in the previous chapter are without any force at all—a correct analysis shows that once the assumptions are relaxed the construction falls to the ground completely. Then in the last section I shall raise the more general question whether an assumption or universal self-interest is an appropriate psychological foundation upon which to raise a political theory.

2. THE EFFECTS OF BARGAINING COSTS

2.A. *The Theory of Second Best.* By 'relaxing the assumption that there are no bargaining costs' I mean admitting that the communication and consideration of threats, promises, offers, etc., takes time, trouble, money or a combination of these. The authors do relax this assumption in the course of their book (or more exactly they relax an assumption which includes this one) but they do not, in my opinion, realize the full extent to which their theory needs to be modified to take it into account. Their suggested modification is as follows: All decision-making by less than unanimity is inefficient (in their own peculiar terminology, which is different from the normal one, it produces 'external costs').[1] But bargaining also has costs; and since the cost of bargaining *increases* with the size of majority required for a decision, while the so-called external costs *decrease* with the size of majority required for a decision, the 'optimum' majority requirement is given by the point where the sum of the two costs is lowest.

John Stuart Mill put the objection to this method of proceeding well when he wrote:

> They would have applied, and did apply, their principles with innumerable allowances. But it is not allowances that are wanted. There is little chance of making due amends in the superstructure of a theory for the want of sufficient breadth in its foundation. It is unphilosophical to construct a science out of a few of the agencies by which the phenomena are determined, and leave the rest to the routine of practice or the sagacity of conjecture.[2]

The objection can be put more formally by saying that the authors consider only the two variables, external costs and bargaining costs; but a political system involves many variables and if one is disturbed, the 'next best' position of the others may be very different from their original position.[3] For example, the authors

---

[1] As I have pointed out, the authors do appear to admit at one point that if the distribution of income arising under a constitution is very unequal it may be prospectively 'efficient' (in an extended sense) to allow for a measure of redistribution by less-than-unanimous voting. But nothing is made of this point and it is not taken account of at all when the main body of the theory is being worked out. It has therefore seemed to me best to note the admission but to follow the authors in ignoring it in the text so as to represent their arguments faithfully.

[2] *Logic*, Book VI, Chapter 8, section 3, p. 583 (London, 1898).

[3] R. G. Lipsey and R. K. Lancaster, 'The General Theory of Second Best', *The Review of Economic Studies*, XXIV (1956–1957), 11–33: 'The general theorem of the second best states that if one of the Paretian optimum conditions cannot be fulfilled a second best optimum situation is achieved

say that because of bargaining costs unanimity must be departed from. But a less-than-unanimous decision requirement in turn alters the effects of allowing bribery of voters (or, in the delicate language of economics, 'side payments'). Again, bargaining costs make direct government for anything except small groups impossibly time-consuming, and, if every person had to make bargains with every other, inconceivable. The authors say, therefore, that direct government by all those involved must be replaced by representative government. But we must ask once more how this, combined with the bargaining costs that remain, will react on the proposal for an open market in votes.

I shall try to show firstly (2.B. and 2.C.) that the existence of bargaining costs, combined with a requirement of less than unanimity for a collective decision, is enough to make open vote-trading unattractive; and secondly (2.D.) that if this feature of the scheme is eliminated the case for even qualified majorities tends to fall to the ground with it. It is analytically convenient to begin the treatment of the first point by concentrating on direct democracy (2.B.) and then to extend this to the representative government which the authors agree is made necessary by the existence of bargaining costs (2.C.).

2.B. *Open Voting with Bargaining Costs: (i) Voting for Measures.* Let us then consider a fairly large group whose members vote directly on collectively binding decisions and see first what would happen if there were no bargaining costs. We can then introduce bargaining costs and see the changes that would result. Suppose, for example, that in a community of 10,000 there are ten people who stand to gain £1,000 each from a measure (total gain £10,000)

---

only by departing from all other optimum conditions. It is important to note that in general, nothing can be said about the direction or the magnitude of the secondary departures from optimum conditions made necessary by the original non-fulfilment of one condition. . . . It follows from the above that there is no *a priori* way to judge as between various situations in which none of the Paretian optimum conditions are fulfilled. In particular, it is *not* true that a situation in which all departures from the optimum conditions are of the same direction and magnitude is necessarily superior to one in which the deviations vary in direction and magnitude' (p. 12). The truth of this is, I think, intuitively clear. For example, an aeroplane design which depended on the existence of a metal with certain characteristics might require to be scrapped completely if no metal with these characteristics could be found.

while the cost to the rest of the community would be £2 10s. each (total loss nearly £25,000). If there are no bargaining costs it is unlikely that the measure will pass, for the ten bidders cannot buy enough votes to get the measure passed, even if they are willing to pay over almost their entire gains. Take the case most favourable to the syndicate, where only a simple majority is required to authorize collective decisions. Even then the ten bidders could not afford to pay half the voters over £2 10s. to make it worth their voting for their proposal. If they offered less than £2 10s. the only motive for acceptance would be the fear that the measure would be passed by other bribe-acceptors so one might as well take what one could get. But it would obviously be in the interests of all except the bidders for everyone to agree not to accept less than £2 10s. and so this agreement would presumably be reached.[1]

Now introduce bargaining costs. If the cost of making an enforceable universal agreement is high enough (as it surely will be with an electorate of any size) the result will be that the proposal will pass easily. Suppose the ten who want the proposal offer 1s. to the first 5,000 voters who promise to support their proposal. If the voters are egoists, there will be a rush to apply, for each one will be sure that if he doesn't apply others will and the measure will be passed anyway. Better lose £2 9s. than £2 10s.[2] The difference obviously arises because of the weakness of the individual voters facing the united group of ten bidders. If there were no bargaining costs they would agree among themselves how to

---

[1] For completeness, we should analyse the case where the gain of the ten would be sufficient to pay a majority of voters a little over £2 10s. to vote for the measure. Suppose, for example, that the gainers stood to gain £1,500 each instead of £1,000. Here, they could afford to pay each of 5,000 voters up to £3 each and still be in pocket. But if everyone is careful, the measure still will not pass, for the remaining half of the voters can afford to bid anything up to £2 10s. to persuade them *not* to accept the bribe; and since a payment of £3 to vote for them only produces a net benefit of 10s. the opposition should win.

If we go a stage further and rig another example so that the ten bidders *can* beat the opposition, this shows that the total gain is greater than the total losses and the measure is 'efficient' in the sense of '*potentially* Pareto-optimal' though the actual results will not normally be Pareto-optimal since only some voters will be compensated.

[2] The precise limitations on the truth of this analysis are examined in Note X on page 325.

meet the situation and, in effect, bargain collectively with the ten.[1] But, as it is, the only choice before them is to accept the offer or not. A rational egoist can only accept, however poor the offer, and however much he wishes he could make an enforceable contract with his fellow voters not to accept it.

Generalizing this conclusion we can say that if in a direct democracy votes can be bought, then where there are bargaining costs any group which is small enough to concert action among its own members will be able to push through any proposal it wants at small cost to itself, even though everyone except the members of the small group are net losers (that is, even though the payment for their vote in no way compensates for the disadvantages imposed by the measure's being passed.)[2]

2.C. *Open Voting with Bargaining Costs: (ii) Voting for Representatives.* Now let us turn to representative government. The notion of vote-buying here is by no means a clear one, and Buchanan and Tullock do not explain what they have in mind. One possibility would be this: the votes of individual electors in the election of representatives are bought and sold; but once representatives have been elected they are not allowed to accept bribes either from electors or from one another to vote a certain way on a particular bill. Alternatives would be to allow one of these two forms of bribery but not the other; or to allow both. And instead of allowing bribery at the representative-choosing stage this could be prohibited (or simply prevented by making the voting secret). Each permutation of these elements would produce different effects, and each of them would, given the existence of bargaining costs, be undesirable. To show this with tolerable brevity is, however, not easy. I shall therefore concentrate on two models only, and hope that this will be persuasive.

[1] The £2 10s. minimum for accepting a bribe is the most obvious example; but counter-bids from members of the group whose votes are being solicited by the ten can be looked on as a process of bargaining within the group as well.

[2] Notice that this conclusion holds good not just for a simple-majority system but for a qualified-majority system as well. To take an extreme case, suppose that in the above example a 90 per cent majority was needed to initiate legislation. The syndicate of ten would simply say that it would pay 1s. to the first 9,000 voters who promised to vote for their proposal. They would still be well in pocket (£450 paid out for a return of £10,000) and the voters would have exactly the same motive for rushing to accept as before.

(1) In the first, let us suppose that votes for representatives can be bought and sold but all bribery of representatives once elected is prohibited. If office-seekers are motivated by self-interest (and the authors assert that everyone is to be so assumed) then they will promise anything and offer bribes to the electors up to the maximum they can lay their hands on. When elected they will ignore their promises, fill their pockets from the public treasury and emigrate. This is really a way of saying that the self-interest assumption is incompatible with representative government in any shape or form.[1] If we assume instead that office-seekers want to be returned to office again, and that they do not expect to make more than their ordinary pay for the office, then bribes will not be offered to any notable extent by candidates themselves but rather by those who hope to benefit from the return of a particular candidate. Candidates must therefore promise their backers that they will promote various causes if elected; these promises need not be made public. However, if there were no bargaining costs, electors would want to know what their candidates intended to do when elected, for a majority of the electorate in a constituency might well find that the programme of the highest bidder was so much less satisfactory than that of a lower bidder (or even one who was offering no money at all) that on balance they preferred to vote for the lower bidder. It would in such circumstances (which, I suggest, would be the rule) be rational for the group to agree together to vote for this candidate and not accept the higher bribe.

The analogy with direct democracy will no doubt be plain; and this analogy continues to hold when we remove the assumption that there are no bargaining costs. The majority who prefer the lower bidder cannot now concert together to vote for him; each voter is faced with an individual choice and if he chooses selfishly he will take the highest bid for his vote, assuming (correctly, if the other voters are like him) that a majority will choose the highest bidder anyway so he may as well have the bribe

---

[1] The same point may be seen even more clearly if we think of judges. A Buchanan-Tullock constitution would obviously throw an enormous amount of power into the hands of the court which had the job of expounding it; and a decision one way or the other might very often be worth a great deal of money to the parties involved. Yet the authors, who profess themselves so mistrustful of human nature, never once pause and ask themselves whether it would be advisable to entrust such absolute power in so few hands.

himself as a consolation. This is an 'inefficient' result exactly as in the direct democracy example.

(2) Now consider a model where bribery is allowed at every stage. Once again we have to ask how representatives are supposed to be motivated. If they are motivated by self-interest they now have two ways of filling their pockets instead of one: they can either rob the treasury directly or pass legislation favourable to particular groups in return for a monetary *quid pro quo*. If other groups enter the bidding to bribe the politicians *not* to pass the legislation, this simply enriches the politicians still further. It is hard to see why under these conditions there should be a widespread wish for the legalisation of bribery.

If, on the other hand, we are willing to assume that politicians alone are prepared merely to be honest brokers between different groups of citizens, taking nothing for their troubles except their official pay, the situation becomes complex. As before a candidate who wishes to raise money for bribes must give assurances to financial backers that he will vote a certain way on certain issues. But on matters where he has not committed himself to his backers he may now sell his vote in the legislature to the highest bidder. On the present hypothesis the politician is an honest broker, and we must assume that he will not pocket the proceeds himself; so let us suppose instead that he promises to divide any money so gained among those who voted for him at the election. Will this be desirable to egoists? I think not, if there are bargaining costs. Inasfar as the candidate offers bribes to the voters in return for which he has committed himself on certain issues to his backers, the question has already been answered. What we must observe here is that the second element—the selling by the elected representative of his vote on a particular issue, the proceeds being returned to those who elected him—does not mitigate the effects of the first but intensifies them; for here as before only organized special interests will be in a position to pay, yet the majority of the voters in most constituencies might well have been better off if they could have foregone their share of the highest bids, in return for having their representatives vote differently.

2.D. *Qualified Majorities without Bribery.* Now we must see how these conclusions affect the authors' view that even if the requirement of unanimity has to be abandoned it should still be regarded as something to approximate as far as possible. I think the answer must be that without open voting and bribery the entire model breaks down. The case against majority voting for ordinary legislation was that a fairly indifferent majority could, and sometimes would, override a relatively intense minority; but if unanimity were required it would be easy to see that this was inefficient because the majority would be unwilling to pay the minority enough to make it worth their while to withdraw their opposition to the change. Clearly, if side-payments are prohibited the bottom drops out of the case for the unanimity requirement. If unanimity cannot be achieved, this now proves nothing about the relative intensities of the majority and the minority— for all we know (and for all the rational egoist choosing a constitution knows) there may be 90 per cent hotly in favour and 10 per cent weakly against. Nor will any qualified majority escape the difficulty. There seems to be no *a priori* reason for supposing that minorities opposing changes are more intense on the average than majorities favouring them; and if, in the absence of any information to the contrary, we assume that over a period the average intensity of a majority member and of a minority member will be the same we can conclude that more often than not the balance of intensity will lie with the majority rather than the minority. Simple majority voting will therefore be, it would seem, the most 'efficient' in the long run, if side-payments are not allowed.

If we introduce representative government the position is complicated but I do not think the conclusion needs changing. Voting now occurs at two points: the election of representatives by constituencies and the voting on particular measures within the representative assembly. The authors toy with the idea of requiring qualified majorities at the first stage, but it is clear that this could only conceivably work with open voting and bribery. Otherwise there is no possible way in which deadlock could be avoided.[1] If two or more candidates split the vote between them so that neither could get the requisite proportion of the total vote, how could the supporters of one candidate persuade the supporters of the other to switch their allegiance if they could not identify one another and issue threats or promises?

[1] This is indeed true even if only a simple majority of those voting is required to elect, unless the alternative vote is in operation. I should perhaps mention that the authors do not consider multiple-member constituencies.

The case for requiring qualified majorities in the legislature is not ruled out in the same way firstly because the *status quo* is at least a possible solution whereas not getting any representatives elected is not, and secondly because legislatures usually vote openly and are small enough to allow at least some bargaining to take place. But if it is prohibited for the electorate to bribe one another or to bribe candidates or elected representatives, the only thing with which the representatives can bargain is their votes in the legislature, trading an affirmative vote on one subject for a negative vote on another, and so on.

There are several objections to relying on log-rolling to produce qualified majorities, under such circumstances. First, as I have tried to show in Note T on page 317, the inefficient 'pork-barrel' type of log-rolling is especially associated with a requirement of unanimity; and the nearer a system approaches this, the more the 'pork-barrel' is likely to be in evidence. And second, bargaining in a legislature would be an elaborate and time-consuming business if coalitions had to be built up by log-rolling to get anything done; moreover where (as with economic policy or foreign relations) consistency between a number of separate items of policy is necessary a series of majorities each made up differently may fail altogether to provide this consistency.[1]

The third and most serious objection is that so far from producing a closer approximation between the strength of feeling in the electorate and the results of the legislators' efforts, reliance on casual majorities is likely to have just the opposite effect. This last point however depends on one's relaxing the assumption of costless information and I shall therefore now turn to that.

3. THE EFFECTS OF INFORMATION COSTS

3.A. *Information Costs and Casual Majorities.* An extraordinary omission from the authors' analysis is the lack of any reference to costs and difficulties of collecting information. They may perhaps

---

[1] See Schattschneider, 'Political Parties and the Public Interest'; Samuel H. Beer, 'New Structures of Democracy' in William N. Chambers and Robert H. Salisbury (eds.), *Democracy Today* (Collier Books, New York, 1962); and George Kennan, *American Diplomacy 1900–1950* on the United States system of government. A formal requirement of qualified majorities would of course accentuate the distinctive features of Congress.

have intended to include these in their 'bargaining costs' but if so they should have relaxed the assumption that information costs are non-existent at the same time as they relaxed the same assumption about bargaining costs proper. But costs and difficulties in acquiring information are of crucial importance, and a constitution which was satisfactory without them might well be seen as unsatisfactory once they were allowed for. The 'theory of the second best' again applies: even if a complicated 'check-and-balance' constitution were most desirable in the absence of information costs, it does not follow that a *fairly* 'check-and-balance' constitution is most desirable once we allow for information costs. Given the level of information achieved by most voters it may turn out that a very simple constitution visibly putting the power to do things and the responsibility for not doing them into one set of hands is the best solution available.

Consider the kind of information which the ideal constitution of Buchanan and Tullock (even after modification to take account of bargaining costs) requires the individual voter to possess if he is to make the system work. Because each piece of legislation is the result of a separate bargaining process among the elected representatives, and each majority successful in passing a bill has a different composition, an elector who wants to use his vote intelligently must go through a formidable process of study before each election.

First, he must note how his representative has voted in each division since the last election and compare this with how he thinks the incumbent's opponents for election would have voted had they been in the legislature. Or if he prefers promises for the future to (actual or hypothetical) past performance he must find out how the various candidates will vote in the next legislative period on all the questions that will come before them: even to know what these will be (a minor part of the whole performance) would be a remarkable feat of clairvoyance. After these preliminaries each elector must work out what would have been the probable results of each alternative policy on each issue if it had been implemented, and on the strength of all this information decide which candidate is on balance most likely to advance his ideas (or, if he votes selfishly, advance his interests).

Nothing less than all this on the part of each elector is needed to make the system work. If all electors do not take note of all votes by their representative, including those which do not affect them more than any other elector, representatives can ignore the effects of most bills on most of their constituents.[1] This being so we must ask whether these requirements could be or would be fulfilled. The answer on the first count is surely that only someone who had a good deal of native ability, strenuous training, and the opportunity of devoting himself full time to the necessary studies could come anywhere near satisfying the requirements.[2] The answer on the second count is if anything even more serious, for it is easy to show that in a state of any size it would be *irrational* to devote more than an infinitesimal amount of time and effort to keeping oneself informed unless one either contradicted the authors' egoistic assumptions by gathering information out of sheer public spirit or of course unless one actually enjoyed collecting information for its own sake. The reason for this is that for any given person the chances of his vote's being decisive in settling the result of an election are so low that however serious the issues may be it is not worth taking the time and trouble to find out about them.[3]

The conclusion that an egoist will not bother to acquire political information because he has an infinitesimal chance of altering outcomes might be called into question by arguing that it rests on the assumption that an individual has the same chance of influencing outcomes in all systems. But considered realistically the essence

---

[1] Not only *can* a representative do so but he *must*, for there will often be a small but vociferous section of his constituents especially affected by a bill, and if the rest of the constituents are supine on the issue the representative must follow the wishes of the small group since if he doesn't his opponent will be able to do so and get their votes next time without (*ex hypothesi*) losing any votes elsewhere. This, as I pointed out in XIV.3.B., is why minorities do well under a 'check-and-balance' kind of constitution.

[2] Cf. Walter Lippmann, *Public Opinion* (New York, 1922), *passim*, and *The Phantom Public*, (New York, 1927), Chapter 2.

[3] Cf. Joseph Schumpeter, *Capitalism, Socialism and Democracy* (New York, 1950, 3rd ed.), p. 261; and Downs, *An Economic Theory of Democracy* (New York, 1957), pp. 244–245. This technique of discounting the importance of the result by the probability of altering it has already been applied to the question of voluntary contributions to community projects (Note S) and accepting a bribe to vote for a proposal that will be damaging if passed (2.B. and Note X). It is also applied in Note Z to show that on the same psychological assumptions (egoism and not enjoying the thing for its own sake) it is irrational even to take the trouble to cast a vote.

of a power-diffusing system is that it provides many additional points for pressure to be brought to bear on decision-makers besides elections.[1] Therefore, since influence is a function of power-diffusion and information a function of influence, may it not be that although a political system which fragments power *requires* more information on the part of ordinary citizens it at the same time provides a stronger motive for *acquiring* information? This line of approach is one strand in the complex argument which E. C. Banfield develops in the last chapter of his book *Political Influence* (Glencoe, Ill., 1961) in defence of a basically power-diffusing set-up such as that existing in Chicago.

The effort an interested party makes to put its case before the decision-maker will be in proportion to *the advantage to be gained from a favorable outcome multiplied by the probability of influencing the decision.* . . . If the decision-maker is surely going to make the decision on purely public grounds, the possibilities of influencing him are relatively small. . . . If, on the other hand, the official is open to influence by other means than persuasion, the probability of influencing the outcome may be greatly increased. . . . In a system of government in which the possibility of influencing outcomes is great, a vast amount of effort is spent by very able people in the attempt to do so. This expenditure of effort has some socially valuable results. It leads to the production of more information about the various alternatives and to a clarification of the values that are involved. Not only are the officials compelled to take into account more than they otherwise would, but the interests themselves are brought to examine their own and each other's positions with great care. . . . A selection process (or political system) which allows of the exercise of power rather than that of persuasion by affected interests produces a wider canvas of policy alternatives and a more thorough scrutiny of each alternative than does a process which allows the affected interests only the opportunity to persuade. (pp. 333–335).

[1] 'To get through a piece of legislation in Washington—or a state capital—you must win a favourable decision at some half dozen or so critical points: one or more committees in both Houses; the votes of the whole body in both legislative branches; the chief executive, and perhaps more important, his principal advisers in the relevant agencies. . . . On the plane of parties and pressure groups, power in the United States is also fragmented and dispersed.' (Samuel H. Beer, 'New Structures of Democracy'.) Clearly, in the absence of a coherent party controlling all the decisive points, each point is open to separate pressure.

All this seems to me reasonable enough; but suppose we grant that the total amount of information is higher in a power-diffusing system than in a power-concentrating system, does it follow from this that a power-diffusing system will tend to produce the more rational decisions? Not necessarily, I think. One reason against would be that already dealt with in the text: bargaining costs. But even sticking to information we can still suggest that Banfield's argument is not conclusive. It may be, after all, that while a power-diffusing system *generates* more information than a power-concentrating one the additional amount of information it *needs* in order to achieve a comparable level of rationality is even greater. The result would then be that the gap between the requirements of the system and the amount of information generated would be *wider* for a power-diffusing system. If this were the case it would bear out Bryce's comment:

> We may say that if the political education of the average American voter be compared with that of the average voter in Europe, it stands high; but if it be compared with the functions which the theory of the American government lays on him, which its spirit implies, which the methods of its party organization assume, its inadequacy is manifest. . . . [1]

So far I have only been implanting the seeds of doubt: let me now definitely argue that bargaining costs and information costs, reinforcing one another's influence, may be expected to make for greater irrationality in a power-diffusing system than in a power-concentrating one in spite of the greater total amount of information likely to be generated by it. The crux is that the greater total of information will not be evenly distributed among those affected by decisions. Banfield plausibly suggests that people tend to acquire information in proportion to the chances of influencing decisions that affect them and the extent to which they are affected by the decision. The result (intended and actual) of a power-diffusing system is to raise a series of obstacles to changes in the *status quo* or collective expenditures, thus raising the price (in terms of bargaining costs) of getting collective action.

Now when bargaining costs are raised this affects differently the chances of different kinds of group to get decisions in their

---

[1] James Bryce, *The American Commonwealth* (New York, 1910) II, 288; quoted in Robert E. Lane, *Political Ideology* (New York, 1962), p. 364.

favour. (The supporters of power-diffusion agree it will produce different decisions, which means that some gain and some lose.) Small well-defined articulate groups stand to increase their influence because of their low organizing costs (we might call these *internal* bargaining costs'). If a group has a permanent organization in being to advance its interests (e.g. a trade association or a local residents' association) the marginal cost of fighting an extra campaign is quite low. If these groups are the gainers, groups with the opposite characteristics are the losers: large, amorphous, inarticulate groups, especially when they have no permanent organization to promote common interests, have less influence in a power-diffusing system. In other words, public interests lose out to private or special interests.

But because of the connection advanced by Banfield between the chances of influencing a decision and the worthwhileness of collecting information, it follows from what has just been said that whereas those with special interests in some matter will collect more information those with public interests in the matter will collect less. Although, therefore, the *total amount of information brought to the attention of the decision-maker* will probably increase (because there are many special interests and each will find it worth developing its case fully) the content of the information will be strongly biased to the advantage of special interests: the case made for public interests will be weaker absolutely and much weaker relatively than in a power-concentrating system; indeed it may virtually go by default. Similarly, even if the *overall level of political information in the community* goes up as a consequence of increased political activity this overall increase will mask a big increase in information relevant to private interests and a decrease in information relevant to public interests.

A high level of political information, in the hands of either public decision-makers or citizens, is presumably to be desired not for its sake so much as for its presumed contribution to the rationality of political decisions. Yet Banfield's view that in a power-diffusing system the rationality of decisions will increase in the sense that they are likely to be better informed and more responsive to all the relevant claims, seems if anything the reverse of the truth. Pressure for public interests will be far less effective than it would be in a 'perfect' situation (no information costs, no bargaining costs); the case for public interests will be less well presented to the decision-maker; and awareness of public interests among those sharing them will be less. We can supplement these results by bearing in mind that in a power-diffusing system, because a single 'No' anywhere in the series of affirmative decisions required for action (i.e. public expenditure or a change in the *status quo*) is enough to block action, whereas positive action demands a 'Yes' at every point along the line, the system will have a powerful inertial tendency—a strong bias against action. Proposals will thus be discriminated against according to their direction (positive or negative) as well as their source. Proposals for positive action in pursuit of public interests will fare worst, and attempts in the pursuit of private interest to veto action will be most likely to succeed.[1] Negative public efforts and positive private ones will both fall in between: which does better will depend on the precise characteristics of the system.[2]

3.B. *The 'Second Best' with Information Costs.* Even if one's first preference in a 'perfect' world were for a Buchanan and Tullock constitution, information costs reinforce the effects of bargaining costs in making the 'second best' solution to the constitutional problem very different. A power-diffusing system increases information in total among the population and increases the number of ideas and pressures impinging on the decision maker. Yet because it increases the virtually inevitable under-representation of widespread, amorphous, unorganized interests, the final result is liable to be more irrational than in a power-concentrating sys-

[1] 'Despite the current vogue of apologetics for our present contrivance, a vogue which received its most careful statement by Pendleton Herring and its most popular recently at the hands of Herbert Agar, there is no blinking the problem of leadership in American government. This problem is not solved by any modernized version of Calhoun's theory of the concurrent majority. Such a theory places its trust in a Burkean wisdom of the nation operating like Adam Smith's "unseen hand" through the pressure group process. In practice it may mean little more than a fine phrase to cover the politics of drift and log-rolling, harmless enough devices in good times, but fraught with peril in the grim days ahead.' Norton E. Long, 'Party Government in the United States', in *The Polity* (ed. Charles Press; Chicago, 1963), p. 19. See E. Pendleton Herring, *The Politics of Democracy* (New York, 1940); Herbert Agar, *The Price of Union* (Boston, 1950) and also Arthur N. Holcombe, *Our More Perfect Union* (Cambridge, Mass., 1950).

[2] A further argument by Banfield, to the effect that power-diffusing arrangements have majority support where they exist, is examined in Note Y on page 327.

tem. The situation is a bit analogous to a choice between two adding machines for the job of adding a string of three-digit numbers: one only gives the answer to the nearest thousand while the other ignores all even numbers that are fed in.

A power-concentrating system makes up for the shortage of information and effort among citizens by economizing on these scarce commodities: a smaller total amount of information and effort goes further. There are two aspects to this, which I shall call visibility and accountability. A power-concentrating system, with a powerful executive (mayor, President) and/or cohesive disciplined parties, is visible not in the sense that its day-to-day operations are carried out in a blaze of publicity (they probably aren't) but in the sense that the formal, open and easy process of voting plays a fairly important part in determining what is done. In a power-diffusing system elections decide little compared with *ad hoc* bargaining on particular measures, but in a power-concentrating system the result of an election may set the whole line of policy. A power-concentrating system thus concentrates the efforts of the average citizen too: even if he does no more than vote every now and then he will (together with his fellow apathetics) have more influence on political decisions than would reward a similar degree of effort in a power-diffusing system.

Secondly, and more importantly perhaps, a power-concentrating system economizes on information and effort by enabling people to use their influence not for or against certain *policies* but for or against certain *states of affairs*. This is obviously very economical because it is far easier to decide whether or not you like a state of affairs than to decide whether or not a certain policy is likely to lead to a state of affairs that you will like if it occurs.

This can happen because of the existence in a power-concentrating system of a set of 'ins' and a set of 'outs'.[1] In return for power the 'ins' can be saddled with responsibility for what happens. This may of course be rather rough and ready as when a government is held responsible for a slump or inflation caused by

---

[1] Of course, the definition of power-concentration itself requires only that there be a definite set of 'ins'; I am talking about a democratic power-concentrating system in which there is one important set of 'outs' trying to change places with the 'ins'. The disruptive effect on the model of fragmented 'outs' even with power concentrated in the hands of cohesive 'ins' is argued in Long, *The Polity*, Chapter 3.

the world situation rather than its own incompetence; and *vice versa* it enables the government to take credit for windfalls. But at least it forces the government to seek out and pursue public interests, even where the electorate are not aware of or clamant for these interests, because these are a significant contribution to the total well-being of the average elector. (Of course, this does not mean that articulate sectional interests can be slighted unduly —they too carry votes.)

As I said, the key to this economy is the existence of 'ins' and 'outs'.[1] Unless an elector has a clear choice between a down-the-line supporter of the 'ins' and a down-the-line supporter of the 'outs', the thing breaks down. Suppose for example that an elector is faced with several candidates each of which supports certain (different) features of the ins' record and criticizes others. The elector is almost as much at sea as he would be if each piece of legislation were passed by an *ad hoc* majority (indeed, if this sort of choice were offered to many electors it soon would be) for he is back in the position of having to decide what probably were the consequences of each piece of legislation and administrative policy. If, on the other hand, the choice is restricted to 'ins' and 'outs' the elector need only decide whether things have got better or worse since the previous election and follow the simple rule of voting for the 'ins' in case of improvement and the 'outs' in case of deterioration.[2]

Of course there is nothing to stop the elector from voting on actual policies if he wishes, but the point is that even crude 'in' and 'out' voting would be enough to provide a powerful incentive to the group in power to pursue the interests of at least half the electorate, and this would inevitably include many public interests.

3.C. *Information Costs and Marketable Goods.* Even if it is admitted that the existence of information costs adds another objection to the proposal for a deliberately complicated 'check and balance' constitution as the best practical substitute for a unanimity rule, it may still be said that this factor strengthens the case for regarding all state activities as inherently inefficient, just because control over

[1] Cf. Joseph Schumpeter, *Capitalism, Socialism and Democracy*, Chapter XXII, and Anthony Downs, *An Economic Theory of Democracy* (New York, 1957).

[2] More subtly he might establish a 'normal' rate of improvement and vote for the 'outs' unless it had been maintained.

these activities is so limited. Doesn't this clinch the case for using the 'price mechanism' wherever possible?[1]

Suppose that in response to this challenge we say that where a good is marketable (that is, where those who do not pay can be effectively excluded from its benefits) it is better to supply it through the market at a price covering its cost than to subsidize it, provide it free, or make people pay for a certain amount of it whether they wish to or not. Even this statement is open to four qualifications which together add up to a formidable *'ceteris paribus'* clause.

(1) The advantage of pricing must outweigh the cost of collecting the money from users; and where the cost of supplying the good varies little with the demand up to some point the advantage of pricing must outweigh the waste of keeping people from using it who would benefit from using it but would not find it worth paying the price.[2]

(2) It must be a matter of indifference whether the good is supplied by the market or not; if free or subsidized collective provision is desired on ideal grounds for its social implications in giving a common interest to the citizens and widening their identifications, the position is again indeterminate.

(3) The object of free or subsidized provision must be purely the satisfaction of consumer wants as they would be revealed on the market. If instead the object is to influence those wants the results arising from the market cannot be taken as 'optimal' because the

[1] Note that the question I am asking is concerned with whether goods and services should be sold at cost price or not. This is independent of the question whether the state should provide goods and services: the state can sell them (e.g. the nationalized industries) and conversely a private firm could be paid to provide them free (e.g. defence contracts).

[2] The classic case here is of the bridge. Once it is built there is negligible marginal cost involved in an extra unit of traffic, but a toll will reduce the use of the bridge below the 'efficient' level, and marginal cost pricing would require it to be free. Wicksell's proposal that unanimity should be required for public expenditures was based largely on this kind of case since, he said, the only way of finding out whether the thing is worth building in the absence of pricing is whether there is any way of raising taxes to cover the cost to which everyone assents. The unworkability of the proposal itself has by now, I hope, been amply shown, but the possibilities of a gain from collective action remain. See Wicksell, 'A New Theory of Just Taxation', in Musgrave and Peacock, *Classics* . . . ; and Buchanan, 'Knut Wicksell on Marginal Cost Pricing,' *Southern Economic Journal*, XVIII (October 1951), pp. 173–178.

object is different.[1] And where the relevant wants are taken to be those which people *would* have *if* they possessed the best available knowledge, a sophisticated ability to work with probabilities, and enough foresight to take a degree of account for the future which they will not later regret, the actual choice which would be revealed on the market may well be regarded as irrelevant in some cases.[2]

(4) Finally, where the object of free or subsidized collective provision is in effect to redistribute income we again cannot say that it is more 'inefficient' than the market because the object is once more not simply to satisfy existing effective demand.[3]

3.D. *Information Costs and the Supply of Public Goods.* Even with these qualifications the statement that selling a good at cost price is preferable to supplying it free or cheap still only applies where the good in question is of a kind which can be sold on the market. It does not apply to wants which must be satisfied collectively if they

[1] In the terminology of Musgrave, *The Theory of Public Finance* (New York, 1959), pp. 13–14, pricing to cover costs is not best where we are dealing with 'merit wants', that is, wants which political decision makers think should be encouraged. It may be thought that this is ruled out by 'individualistic' assumptions but this is not necessarily so, for a person may decide as a citizen to encourage certain of his wants by law and discourage others. (See the discussion of this point in VI.6.B. and Note F.)

[2] Brian Abel-Smith, 'Whose Welfare State?', in Mackenzie (ed.), *Conviction* (London, 1958), pp. 68–69: 'Free choice works admirably for a housewife buying vegetables. There is the cauliflower. There is the cabbage. Take your choice, dearie. But can you really conclude anything from the choice between a cabbage and a one-in-a-million chance of contracting polio, between a cauliflower today and a cauliflower in the year 2000? How many people know the exact chances of getting ill, or surviving to old age, of breeding a backward child? If they don't know, what conclusions can you draw from the fact that people don't choose to save or pre-insure? When there is delay or risk, free choice proves nothing.'

[3] This can arise in either of two ways. The object may be a general shift in income distribution which cannot for political or administrative reasons be done directly. In this case, unless one of the other three considerations applies it would be more efficient, if it were possible, to redistribute income directly. But alternatively, the whole *point* may be to provide certain things cheap or free (e.g. medical care, drugs, and appliances) not because it is desired to encourage a taste for these items (the 'merit want', ideal-regarding case) but on distributive want-regarding grounds. In other words, the object may be to allow those who have the misfortune to need these things to get them without a diminution of income.

are to be satisfied at all; nor does it apply to the ordinary run of legislation which defines permissible actions by citizens. A possible argument for extension of the conclusion to cover these would be to say that since there are such high costs of information involved in finding out about state activities, these activities should be cut to the bone. But is it a rational response to restrict state action simply because you don't know exactly what the results are? The citizen finds himself in the middle of a web of state activities, some things being provided free, some discouraged by taxes; some actions prohibited, others enjoined. Why should it be assumed that he is going to be better off if these activities are reduced? It seems *a priori* just as likely that he would be better off if they were increased.[1]

As Dahl and Lindblom put it:

> Perhaps what some people mean when they say that collective choice is less rational than market choice is that collective choice is less rational when choice has to be collectivized than market choice is rational when market choice can be employed.
>
> Given the shortcomings of market choice and the impossibility of voting on many kinds of questions, the choices of very foolish leaders will often be much more rational than the badly calculated choices of individuals in the market. . . . *Where the price system is an inappropriate mechanism, market choices are certain to be irrational; but delegation either may or may not be* (pp. 421, 427; italics in original).

4. SELF-INTEREST AND CONSTITUTIONAL CHOICE

4.A. *Introduction*. It is the thesis of Buchanan and Tullock and other power-diffusers that in politics, as in Smithian economics, a 'hidden hand' will lead to safety a society none of whose members ever looks beyond his own private self-interest provided its institutions are well-designed. And the mark of well-designed institutions is that they should provide plenty of 'checks and balances' in the classic phrase—that each person, or at least each minority, should be able to veto any proposed public policy until it has been either amended to suit or sweetened by the addition of some

---

[1] See A. Downs, 'Why the Government Budget in a Democracy is Too Small', *World Politics*, XII, No. 4 (July 1960), pp. 541–563, for an argument to the effect that precisely because citizens *do* tend to underestimate the benefits from activities whose results are uncertain the budget tends to be smaller than it would be if voters had more knowledge—or (*a fortiori* perfect knowledge.

unrelated but attractive *quid pro quo*. I have argued that there are two great faults in this thesis. Firstly, one of the main things politics is *about* is the 'initial conditions' on the basis of which bargaining is supposed to take place. By assuming universal agreement on a once-for-all irrevocable distribution of resources Buchanan and Tullock assume away the central political problem of maintaining a *continuous* working consensus on distribution. And secondly, due both to the advantages it gives to especially shrewd or strategically placed minorities and to the existence of bargaining costs and information costs, the kind of political system espoused by the authors would show a constant bias against (*a*) action as against inaction, and (*b*) public interests as against private and sectional interests.

I have not, however, put forward any detailed positive arguments to show that in the hands of ruthless egoists a power-concentrating system would be preferable to a power-diffusing one. At most I have cast doubt on the authors' proffered 'demonstration' that a power-concentrating system with majority voting inevitably tends to an 'equilibrium' position in which about twice the 'optimum' amount is being spent on public goods. But before asking which set-up would be best for ruthless egoists (when the answer pretty clearly seems to be that any set-up would work very badly) might it not be more sensible to examine with some care the authors' psychological premises? After all, if they had been right in claiming that the kinds of institution advocated by them would produce satisfactory results even with complete egoists one might have agreed happily that the wisest course is to play safe and have such institutions. If people turned out not to be so self-interested this would simply add a further margin for error in the working of the system. But I maintain that the authors' claim is not well founded. If I am right then this comforting course, of preparing for the worst in the expectation that even it will turn out well, is not open to us. It therefore behoves us to ask what psychological premises are really plausible for the countries with which we are concerned.[1]

4.B. *Arguments for the Self-Interest Assumption.* Buchanan and Tullock offer two arguments for their assumption of universal

---

[1] I need hardly say that as it stands this question is exceedingly vague; all the more reason for not extending it to 'human nature'.

self-interest, neither of which is very plausible. One is to point to the existence of interest groups. This is logically on a par with sending someone to the local zoo so as to prove to him all tigers are behind bars. An interest group precisely *is* a group united by nothing except a common interest in some area of public policy. It hires men whose job it is to advance those interests. This does not show that (say) the President of the USA or the average MP is motivated mainly (or, in many cases, at all) by the desire to line his pockets from the spoils of office; nor (which in any case would go outside the simple self-interest assumption) that he is trying purely to advance the economic interests of those who voted for him. Nor does it show that the average voter consults nothing but his own private self-interest in voting. It would certainly be perfectly consistent to vote for a party which would introduce what one considered to be more equitable rules (e.g. a more steeply progressive income tax) even if that were contrary to one's own interest, while at the same time wanting to do well within those rules; just as it is consistent to favour fair trials and fight any case in which one is involved as hard as possible. Indeed, as Downs has shown, a man who was motivated purely by private self-interest would not bother to vote *at all* unless he enjoyed the walk and the process of voting.[1] This follows from the infinitesimal chance any given individual has of changing the result of the election. The argument 'What if everyone did it?' goes outside the frame of reference supplied by the calculus of personal self-interest.[2]

Apart from this, the authors suggest that there is no particular reason to suppose that political behaviour is any different in motivation from economic behaviour and since economists have traditionally done well enough with self-interest axioms they are taking a reasonable line in extending this to politics.[3] But the market might be described as the institutionalization of impersonal ('affectively neutral') selfishness. That is precisely its advantage

[1] Downs, *Economic Theory* . . ., Chapter 14.

[2] Downs himself nods here, saying that even if he didn't expect his vote to make much difference to the result of the election a rational man would nevertheless vote *if* he was afraid that the whole democratic system would collapse as a result of non-voting. But exactly the same argument will normally apply here. One vote (in real life) will make an infinitesimal difference to whether or not the system collapses. (See Note Z on page 328 for further discussion of this point.)

[3] Buchanan and Tullock, *Calculus* . . . , Chapter 3 and p. 306.

as a social invention replacing personal relationships between traders by the 'cash nexus'. The role of 'trader' is stripped of all content except that defined by the market. There is no *a priori* reason for believing, and much evidence for doubting, that people behave the same way in the more richly structured role of organization-member, whether the organization be profit-orientated, religious or social, juryman, party member, citizen, Congressman or President. (See Note F on page 299.)

4.C. *Can Majorities Be Trusted?* In fact, I think the assumption that a majority of the voters in, for example, Britain and the USA suffer from unbounded self-interest is plainly false. Suppose that we take an instance comparatively favourable to the self-interest hypothesis: the general correlation between low income and a desire for equalization of incomes on the one hand and between high income and an opposition to equalization on the other. Surely the most significant thing about this is that the low-income group *only* wants equality and the high-income group *only* resists it. According to Buchanan and Tullock, we should expect some specific group comprising over half the electorate to use the power of the state in order to make themselves rich at the expense of the rest. But this does not happen in democratic countries. It is one thing to demand that everyone should be equal and a very different thing to demand that the rich and poor should change places.[1] Again, the members of an oppressed race such as the American Negroes demand equality, but not the chance to oppress whites to the same degree that they themselves are being oppressed now.

Perhaps the very assumption that there are no bargaining costs encourages the authors to exaggerate the extent to which a majority may use political means to injure the rest. If one considers a sum of money to be divided between three people by majority vote one may expect one pair to form a coalition and divide the money between them.[2] And even in an assembly of a hundred one might not be surprised to find a majority forming for the express purpose of benefiting themselves at the expense of the rest. But

---

[1] Even in the French and Russian Revolutions, I think it is correct to say that there was no deliberate policy of making those who had been privileged *worse* off than the rest of the population, and that it was only inasfar as they resisted equalization that they finished up worse off than the rest.

[2] See Buchanan and Tullock, *Calculus* . . . , Chapter 11. Compare Rapoport, *Fights, Games and Debates*. Chapter 12.

in a great modern state, *ad hoc* coalitions of this kind are scarcely feasible, and if there is a division it must turn on some simple distributive disagreement, such as the *status quo* versus greater equality.[1] The kind of very precise and complete exploitation of minority by majority found in the artificially simple situation of three people dividing a sum of money by majority vote is barely practicable among a homogeneous finely differentiated population of many millions.[2] Unless interests were highly polarized (as in some Latin American states, for example), any platform that could appeal to a majority would inevitably have to rely largely on widely-shared interests.[3] Combined with the minimal sense of justice to which I have already alluded (e.g. the tendency to press politically for equality rather than a reversal of positions) this may well be enough to enable the 'majority tyranny', the fear of which is the stock in trade of the opponents of simple constitutions, to be avoided.[4]

This is obviously a very superficial treatment of a vast subject but it does perhaps allow the tentative conclusion that whereas the disadvantages of a power-diffusing constitution are palpable and unavoidable, the dangers of a power-concentrating constitution may be escaped provided first that there is not an extreme degree of polarization of interests among the population, and second, that

---

[1] There is an article to be written about the political functions (as against the disfunctions, which we all know about) of information costs and bargaining costs.

[2] Moreover a two-party system where all the candidates of a party stand on the same platform already rules out sectional interests which individual candidates left to their own devices might find it profitable to support or necessary to submit to. See Norton Long, 'Patriotism for Partisans: a Responsible Opposition', in *The Polity*, pp. 41–49, and V. O. Key, 'Public Opinion and the Decay of Democracy', *The Virginia Quarterly Review*, XXXVII, No. 4 (Autumn 1961), pp. 481–494.

[3] See Schattschneider, *Party Government* (Holt-Rinehart-Winston Book, 1960), Chapter 2.

[4] Of course, if one regards moves towards equality as an example of this 'tyranny' the answer must be quite different, for the long-run equalizing effects of majority rule seem incontrovertible. Madison, for example, in the tenth Federalist paper, mentions 'an equal division of property' as one of the 'improper and wicked projects' which a majority may want and which must be guarded against. (Everyman edition, p. 47.) If this is one's view there is probably no alternative to entrenching the privileged minority constitutionally—either specifically or in a more roundabout way by giving veto power to all minorities.

there is a certain amount of moderation among the governed and of responsibility among the governors. Whether or not these conditions exist in any given society cannot be determined by *a priori* reasoning. One must look and see.

4.D. *Conclusion.* In Chapter XIII I tried to show that there are a number of separate reasons for giving the state a large responsibility for securing and advancing the common interests of its citizens. In the last two chapters I have been asking whether it is possible to make any general statements about the kind of constitutional machinery best calculated to ensure that the state's efforts will be bent in that direction. I contrasted two general approaches. The first, which is very common in Britain, is also to be found among many writers on public administration in the USA. Starting from the necessity for creating an apparatus which is capable of doing the work, the adherents of this approach take the problem of preventing the apparatus from running amok in their stride, and assume that putting popularly elected persons at the head of it will take care of any difficulties on this score.

The other approach underlies the American constitution and is still strong in the USA. It is more sceptical about power, even if it is put into the hands of popularly elected persons, and tends to demand a complicated and power-diffusing constitution. If the first approach can appeal to Plato, Aquinas, Hobbes, Rousseau, the philosophers of the Enlightenment, and the Benthamites, the second has behind it the weight of what James Harrington called 'ancient prudence' as well as such moderns as Locke, Paine, Montesquieu and the writers of the Federalist Papers. In this chapter and the preceding one I have been examining a recent statement of the second position. Its essential point is that if collective action is genuinely beneficial it should presumably be able to secure unanimous approval; and even if the existence of 'bargaining costs' makes it impractical to demand that nothing be done without unanimous consent, this still represents the ideal from which deviations will be allowed reluctantly. (For the precise formula see above XIV.1.D.)

I have argued that a Buchanan/Tullock constitution, even if it could be set up, would not work in the way that their theory leads them to anticipate. On the other side: self-interest in politics may be less intense and less universal than they suppose; while technical limitations reinforce moral sentiments in making it less likely that majorities will oppress minorities under a power-concentrating set-up than that minorities will exploit majorities under a power-diffusing set-up.

It would be surprising if a question which has exercised many of the best minds that have been applied to the study of politics in over two thousand years could be settled by a handful of axioms and formulae; but these may at least help us to identify the areas of disagreement and perhaps even to reduce them.

CONCLUSION

THE end of a book of this nature marks the limits either of the author's own stamina or that which he (no doubt optimistically) attributes to his possible readers. It plainly does not mark the limits of the subject. Any of the topics here might easily have been treated at greater length and the list of topics might easily have been added to. The reader has here a selection from the things that might have been written (and, he will be thankful to learn, less than half the length of what *was* written in earlier drafts) so it is perhaps more than usually incumbent on the author at this point to make some attempt to say what his object has been and why he chose these particular means to it.

What I have been attempting to do in the central part of this book (Chapters VI to XIII inclusive) is to substantiate certain general theses about political principles by means of selected examples. These general theses might be summarized as follows:

(1) The political principles commonly employed in contemporary Britain and the USA cannot be regarded as subsumable under one principle or as different means to a single end. But it does not follow from this that political evaluation cannot be 'rational'. The kind of analysis of consumers' choice given by J. R. Hicks in *Value and Capital* can be sensibly applied to one making a political evaluation. A consumer choosing between a little more of good X and a little less of good Y on the one hand, and a little more of good Y and a little less of good X on the other, can be regarded as making a rational choice provided his choice forms a part of a pattern satisfying certain simple criteria of consistency. There is no need to imagine him as trying to maximize some homogeneous quantity ('utility' or 'satisfaction'). In just the same way, one may conceive rational political decisions as being concerned with the question whether (say) a given reduction in 'equity' more than counterbalances an associated increase in 'efficiency'.

Instances have been noted frequently in the text where each of a number of different principles, applied exclusively to a particular

286

matter, would lead to policy recommendations widely divergent from any of the other principles similarly applied. And in various places I have concluded that conflicting views as to the right policy to be pursued in some matter commonly turn on the disputants' assigning different trade-off relationships among the values that are agreed on all sides to be relevant to the case. I have also suggested that considerations whose importance is widely agreed on, such as fulfilling 'reasonable' expectations and respecting certain 'negative freedoms', derive their importance from their strategic position at the confluence, so to speak, of a number of different ultimate principles. On my view these are not *alternative* supports but *mutually reinforcing* supports.

(2) Though the principles currently in use are not reducible to one, they can nevertheless be classified into certain broad groups. The most fundamental distinction to be drawn is that between on the one side 'want-regarding' principles which take wants as given and take account of only the amount and distribution of want-satisfaction, and on the other side 'ideal-regarding' principles which rank the satisfaction of some wants higher than the satisfaction of others even if the preferences of the person whose wants are in question are different. Within the former category of 'want-regarding' principles, a distinction is to be made between 'aggregative' principles which concentrate on the amount of want-satisfaction and 'distributive' principles which take into account the rationale and proportions of its distribution.

The thread of the discussion in Chapters VI to XIII is provided by want-regarding concepts: VI to IX are concerned mainly with distributive concepts and X to XIII with aggregative ones. But within this framework I have quite deliberately introduced considerations of different kinds within a single chapter where they seemed relevant. For example, the chapter on 'Freedom' contains a discussion of aggregative want-regarding justifications and ideal-regarding justifications as well as aggregative want-regarding ones; the chapter on 'Equality' is largely devoted to trying to show that distributive considerations are *not* sufficient to justify commonly held anti-segregation positions; and so on through all the chapters.

(3) The third contention which the discussions in Chapters VI to XIII seek to substantiate (and the last I shall mention here) is that the content of a principle varies according to the institutional

context in which it is applied. The criteria of a fair trial, a fair race, and a fair lottery, cannot be understood unless one has a good grasp of the rationale of trials, races and lotteries, as social decision-making procedures; justice in a trial and a football match have different criteria stemming from the difference between the objects of trials and football matches; and so on. I have tried to make these contentions persuasive by detailed analysis, which is surely the only way that they ever can be made persuasive.

The rest of the book can now be put into perspective. If Chapters VI to XIII are concerned with exemplifying certain theses in action, then the first six chapters are concerned by and large with setting out those theses and laying the groundwork for the rest of the book. (Chapters II and IV engage in the sort of negative groundwork-laying which consists in clearing away ideas that would block later developments. Chapters XIV and XV, on the other hand, lie at the opposite extreme of generality. They constitute an attempt to examine, in a more analytical and less discursive way than has been customary in the past, the most appropriate institutional embodiment of just one value: the public interest.)

Having stated my objects I must now try to defend the means chosen, and in particular to justify the selection made in Chapters VI to XIII. It follows from what I have already said that in discussing a particular principle or particular applications of that principle my ulterior purpose has been to bear out my claim that certain general conceptions about political principles and their application are true and illuminating. Now of course since the claim that these conceptions are useful can only be substantiated by showing their usefulness in action, the discussion of particular principles or particular applications must take much the same form as it would if my object were simply to throw light on the principles for their own sakes. The difference comes in the selection of cases. If the object is purely to throw light on as many principles as possible, then one can say that six cases discussed are six times better than one case discussed, and so on *pro rata*. If, however, one's object is to show that discussion is aided by the use of certain general conceptions, one case is hardly any good at all, for a set of conceptions would have to be quite extraordinarily hopeless not to be fitted by at least one handpicked case. The compensation for this is that beyond a certain point the search for further confirming cases can be regarded as tending to yield diminishing returns. There is a close connection, methodologically speaking, between the validation of general conceptions about principles and general conceptions about flowers or stars: beyond a certain point the sheer number of supporting cases is less significant than the range from which they are drawn and their including what are *prima facie* the most difficult cases. I have tried to make this my guide-line in choosing cases for discussion: I have aimed at including a broad range of principles and at dealing with *prima facie* awkward ones especially. (See III.5.) Whether I have followed the guide-line well and whether the actual examples do support my claims are, of course, things that the reader must judge for himself.

So far I have been looking back. I would prefer to end by looking forward, and asking what lines of future development seem most promising. Unfortunately programmes for other people (or even oneself!) to carry out have a nasty habit of coming unstuck but it is hard to see how we could do without them entirely. Let me begin with a negative point already foreshadowed: I doubt whether *for the purposes I have outlined* there is very much to be gained from doing more of the same thing as is done here in Chapters VI to XIII. If these examples work and *pro tanto* substantiate the theses they are intended to substantiate, the degree of support they provide would not be materially increased by showing that other examples work too. If, on the other hand, the main theses are not well founded then it should be possible to show this by demonstrating either that everything I say about my chosen concepts is wrong or (I hope, more plausibly) that even where I do happen to say something true this is achieved in the teeth of the false directions suggested by my general theses. Obviously if I could see at the moment how to make this criticism stick I would have written a different book; but I am quite prepared to concede that it may be possible to do it.

Assuming, however, that refinement and extention rather than demolition is called for where the main theses are concerned, the next step that suggests itself to me is the extention of the enterprise attempted in the last two chapters to other concepts and other institutions. In Chapters XIV and XV I concentrated on one concept—the public interest—and on one kind of institution (admittedly an important one) namely government. Although I was

helped here by the existence of a long-standing controversy conducted at a fairly high level of generality with carefully articulated
positions on each side, I do not see why the same general method
could not be applied elsewhere in an attempt to determine, with a
certain degree of analytical rigour, the form of institutions best
calculated to advance other values.

Of course, one could quite truly say that the characteristic
'political philosophy' of the past, from Plato's *Republic* on, has
been concerned with just that problem: matching institutions with
values. To meet this I must point to the phrase 'a certain degree of
analytical rigour' which I slipped into my definition of the 'method'
which I am advocating. And at the risk of falling into what has
sometimes been called 'temporal chauvinism' let me say that I
would hope to see this 'rigour' arising from the marriage of two
modern techniques: analytical philosophy and analytical politics.[1]

By 'analytical philosophy' I mean to refer to the movement
associated especially with the name of J. L. Austin which has made
it respectable to seek fidelity to the actual uses of words rather than
trying to clamp down verbal equivalences on them. So far applications to political principles are not very thick on the ground
but the last few years have witnessed an increase.[2] By 'analytical
politics' I mean the attempt to simplify the complex reality of a
situation by picking out certain aspects of it and then building a
model relating these aspects.[3] This kind of thing is a commonplace

---

[1] Is the risk such a grave one anyway? I doubt if much has ever been
achieved in the sphere of intellectual production (as distinct from connois-
seurship) without a touch of it. To spend one's working life rolling the classics
round the tongue like old brandy (as advocated by Leo Strauss and disciples)
hardly seems likely to advance the sum of human knowledge. If we really
want to imitate the Greeks the first thing to do is stop looking over our
shoulders all the time.

[2] The best work is, in my view, being done in the USA: for example,
Joel Feinberg's 'Justice as Desert' (mentioned in Chapter VI) and the articles
by Gregory Vlastos and Alan Gewirth in *Social Justice* (ed. R. Brandt; Englewood Cliffs, N.J., 1962). It is unfortunate that the common impression (even
among some philosophers) of the way in which 'analytic philosophy' is
relevant to politics has been set by T. D. Weldon's *The Vocabulary of Politics*
(Penguin, 1953) which in spite of its title is an application of unreconstructed
logical positivist criteria of meaning to traditional political thought rather
than a detailed analysis of concepts.

[3] Buchanan and Tullock's, *The Calculus of Consent*; Schelling's, *The Strategy
of Conflict*; Downs', *An Economic Theory of Democracy* and Part III of Banfield's

in economics but fairly new outside it; most of the best work has in fact been done by former, or still practising, economists.

Analytical philosophy and analytical politics have tended to be carried on in separate compartments, yet each needs the other. The analysis of concepts becomes beyond a certain point tedious logic-chopping; even more, the attempt to draw practical conclusions from political models can only too easily come to grief on excessively crude (or—even worse—vague and evasive) value premises.[1]

If the two modes of analysis can be brought together to form a new discipline, which will pursue the traditional concerns of political theory with new tools, the rough and ready efforts of the preceding pages should soon be obsolete.

---

[1] One of the main criticisms of Buchanan and Tullock is that—quite apart from the way they abuse it—their principle of Pareto-optimality simply will not do as a unique political principle; nor is it (as they seem to believe) any more 'value free' to espouse it than it is to espouse, say, the principle of equality.

Political Influence have already been mentioned in the text or in the notes. Let me add to this list Herbert Simon's *Models of Man* (New York, 1957) and William Riker's *The Theory of Political Coalitions* (New Haven, 1962).

NOTES

BOOKS of this nature sometimes fall into one of two classes, which I shall (unfairly, of course) dub the British and American kinds. The first, or British, kind rests on the assumption that provided one is original and interesting there is no need to mention (or perhaps even to have read) any other books on the subject. The second, or American, kind rests on the assumption that if one provides a critical survey of everything that has ever been written on one's subject one has done all that is needful. The simplest alternative to either of these extremes is to follow a few paragraphs written on the British method by a few written on the American method throughout the book; but this tends to be rather disconcerting to the reader. I have tried to avoid this difficulty by a variation on the above method (a variation which of course brings its own difficulties) namely that of being mainly 'British' in the text and mainly 'American' in the notes collected here at the back. By and large, then, these notes provide comments on alternative or supplementary views to those put forward in the text; though I have also taken the opportunity in a few cases to put into a note some further discussion of a point dealt with more cursorily in the text.

(A) ROUSSEAU AND MAJORITARIANISM (See IV.3.B., page 59)

Rousseau's statement in *The Social Contract*, that if I am in the minority then I must have been mistaken in my opinion, may sound reminiscent at this point, but it is quite different. On the 'majoritarian principle' to be in the minority is, by definition, to be wrong—what ought to be done simply *is* what the majority wishes to be done. Rousseau, however, believes that the answer to the question 'What ought to be done?' is independent of what anybody thinks; it is whatever is for the common good. It is a contingent fact, according to Rousseau, that under certain conditions (equality, simplicity and virtue) the majority, provided its members ask themselves the right question (viz: is this for the common good?) are more likely than not to arrive at the correct answer because the individual biases of the voters will tend to balance out.

Rousseau's thought has, I think, been so badly misunderstood because (apart from the confusing terminology) we are not used to thinking that there is a 'right answer' in politics. If we replace the political context with one of, say, a group whose members are set a problem in arithmetic, we can see more clearly what he is getting at. Suppose then that the group is set an arithmetical problem of some complexity. Not everyone will get the right answer, but those who go wrong are just as likely to be too high as too low in their answer; and the right answer is more likely to get a majority than a single wrong answer.

A theorem which Condorcet worked out in connection originally with juries (and which is treated in Duncan Black's *Theory of Committees and Elections* (Cambridge, 1958), pp. 164–165) is relevant here. Provided every voter has an (equal) above fifty-fifty chance of getting the right answer, the majority opinion of the group will be right more often than that of any single member of the group voting.

More precisely, if each member of the group is right in proportion v of the cases dealt with, and wrong in a proportion e, where $v + e = 1$, then if in a given instance h members of the group give one answer and k members the other answer $(h > k)$, the probability that the h members are right is:

$$\frac{v^{h-k}}{v^{h-k} + e^{h-k}}$$

See further on this pages 9–14 of my paper 'The Public Interest'.

(B) WOLLHEIM'S 'PARADOX' (See IV.3.B., page 59)

In his article 'A Paradox in the Theory of Democracy' (*Philosophy, Politics and Society*, 2nd series, ed. P. Laslett and W. G. Runciman (Oxford, 1962) pp. 71–87), Richard Wollheim identifies the 'paradox' as follows: an adherent of the principle of 'Democracy' who is in the minority on an issue may appear to find himself committed to saying both 'A ought to be done' (because I think so) and 'B ought to be done' (because a majority wishes it to be done). But his 'solution' simply consists in denying that there really is a contradiction between the two. He distinguishes 'direct' principles from 'oblique' principles:

> Examples of direct principles would be *Murder is wrong, Birth-control is permissible.* Examples of oblique principles would be *What is commanded by the sovereign ought to be done,* or *What is willed by the people is right.*
>
> Now, my suggestion is that two judgements of the form 'A ought to be the case' and 'B ought to be the case' are not incompatible even though A and B cannot be simultaneously realized *if* one of these judgements is asserted as a direct principle whereas the other is asserted as a derivation from an oblique principle—provided that the direct and the oblique

principle are not themselves incompatible. Now, I am aware that the proviso might give rise to some difficulty, for it might be natural to think that A ought to be enacted was incompatible with any oblique principle from which B ought to be enacted could be derived, *ipso facto*. For my principle to have any area of operation, it is of course important to exclude incompatibility of this kind and to permit as relevant only incompatibility of a more immediate kind. (p. 85.)

I must confess myself baffled by the notion that if the 'immediacy' of an incompatibility falls below a certain value the incompatibility somehow disappears, and my bafflement is not reduced by any of Wollheim's further arguments. To assert 'A ought to be done' and 'B ought to be done' (where A and B are incompatible) simply *is* to make two inconsistent assertions. If, then, it is true that 'either the two assertions *are* compatible, or else Democracy is inconsistent' (p. 84) one can only reply: 'So much the worse for Democracy.' Or, to put it less drastically, the notion of 'Democracy' will have to be reformulated so as to avoid the inconsistency. This reformulation I have attempted to supply in the text through my apparatus of primary and corrected wishes.

(C) SINCERITY AND STRATEGY FOR A MAJORITARIAN
(See IV.3.B., page 61)

Farquarson, in his unpublished study of voting, always contrasts two types of voter: the 'sincere' voter, who votes for whatever measure comes highest in terms of his own values, and the 'strategic' voter, who votes in such a way as to bring about a final result as high as possible in terms of his own values. The 'strategic' voter, for example, may vote against his first preference in order to make sure that in the subsequent vote his second preference will win over the (third) possibility he likes least; but the 'sincere' voter will at each stage vote for the most preferred measure available, even though by voting for his first preference he brings about a win for the possibility he least likes.

Now take the case of an adherent of the majoritarian principle. To decide which side of a certain motion is preferable according to his own values he must make a corrected judgement. (If he merely voted 'sincerely' on the basis of his primary judgement he would not necessarily be voting in favour of the motion which, in the light of *all* his principles, came highest in his estimation.) But in order to make a corrected judgement he must work out what result would be most in accordance with his majoritarian principles and then vote on whichever side will approximate this result most closely. Is this 'sincere' or 'strategic'? If it is 'strategic' then it is certainly very different from strategic voting aimed at furthering one's own *primary* purposes. You may, for example, hold the principle that the results should come out as they would if everyone adopted the optimal strategy. In either case, if some vote 'sincerely' and some 'strategically', your own corrected judgement may require you to vote differently from the requirements of either sincere or strategic voting on the basis of your primary judgement.

(D) HARE ON WANTS AND IDEALS (See IV.6.A., page 72)

In *Freedom and Reason* Hare employs a conceptual apparatus of interests, ideals and moral principles. Moral principles are principles which apply where interests conflict; 'ideals of human excellence' are prescriptions which need not involve a reference to more than one person. An interest is the ability to satisfy one's desires now and in the future. Hare allows that ideals can be treated as desires, and therefore as components of interests (e.g., on page 157 he speaks of 'that interest which consists in the freedom to pursue varying ideals', and on page 160 he says 'to have an ideal is *eo ipso* to have an interest in not being frustrated in pursuit of it'.) The desire to have a moral principle put into effect can also be included as a component of interest: '. . . any evaluation, just because it is prescriptive, incorporates the desire to have or do something rather than something else' (page 170).

Hare now asks: 'What happens when interests conflict with ideals?' (p. 156) and supplies the answer in Chapter 9. It should perhaps be noticed at the outset that the question is rather infelicitously put inasmuch as ideals are *components* of interests. Let us therefore reformulate the question as: what happens when interests arising from ideal desires conflict with interests arising from non-ideal desires (i.e., mere 'brute' desires)?

Hare's answer to this question is that interests of all kinds should be treated on all fours in applying the 'golden rule' calculus and arriving at a morally principled judgement to cover the situation.

> [A liberal (as opposed to a fanatic)] will be in favour of allowing anybody to pursue his own ideals and interests except in so far as their pursuit interferes with other people's pursuit of theirs. When this point is reached, he will, in arbitrating between people's interests and ideals, give as much weight to each person's as to any other's; he will not give his own ideals and interests precedence because they are his own. (p. 178).

The extremely *il*liberal implications of this solution become apparent when one appreciates the range covered by Hare's 'ideals'. They include, for example, both the judgement 'I would be a better man if I ran a mile before breakfast each day' (see p. 154) and the judgement 'The world would be a better place with no Jews in it' (see p. 161).

Now from the point of view of a want-regarding judgement taking everyone's wants into account (Hare's morally principled judgement) it seems completely unexceptionable to include the first ideal as a want. It makes no significant difference, in terms of the man's claim to have his want catered for if possible, whether he wants to run a mile because it conduces to his ideal of human excellence or because he thinks it would be fun.

The second ideal however, that the world would be a better place with no Jews in it, is an ideal of a very different kind, and if we regard it as a want then it is also a want of a very different kind. Hare, noticing the difference, calls it a 'universal' desire, because it is a desire for anyone having certain characteristics to be exterminated (p. 170). In my terminology it would be a publicly-oriented want; and I suggest in the text that such wants should not be counted when one is making a want-regarding publicly-oriented judgement. I give, in the text and also in Note E, my reasons for suggesting this step. All I want to do here is substantiate my charge that Hare's proposal for counting 'universal' ideals as desires (for the purpose of making morally principled judgements) has highly illiberal implications.

Let us suppose then that those whose ideal is that all Jews should be dead, or all homosexuals behind bars, enormously outnumber the Jews and homosexuals themselves (who, we can safely assume, will take a contrary view). It seems very hard to explain, if wants are to be matched against wants (counting ideals as wants, of course) why the majority should not prevail. Certainly on an aggregative calculation one might quite conceivably get the answer that the majority has the greater 'mass' of wanting on its side. (John Stuart Mill's view, in *On Liberty*, that as an empirical matter this couldn't happen does not seem plausible to me as a universal proposition though it no doubt holds most of the time.)

Moreover, Hare is not confined to admitting only those universal desires which arise from ideals: there can be universal 'brute' desires too, and unless they are explicitly ruled out they too must be counted. Thus, instead of saying 'An ideal society would have all homosexuals behind bars', someone might simply say 'I hate and detest the very thought of any homosexuals not being behind bars'. The effect on the 'utilitarian' calculus would be the same.

As a result of these considerations I would suggest that what Hare styles 'fanaticism', namely, the belief that it is justifiable to pursue ideals for their own sake, because of their good content, may actually be less illiberal than counting in publicly-oriented wants for the purpose of the 'utilitarian' (want-regarding) calculus. Of course, the most 'liberal' approach would be to rule out both; but my own view is that liberalism carried to this point ceases to be a virtue.

(E) KINDS OF WANT (See IV.6.A., page 72)

It seems worth while trying to clarify at this point the different kinds of want with which we are concerned. The diagram below gives the basic relationships at a glance.

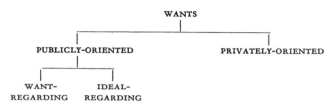

The distinction between publicly-oriented and privately-oriented wants has already been introduced in I.3.C. and elaborated in IV.3.C. I shall not therefore discuss it further. What I am concerned with here is eluci-dating the division I have made among publicly-oriented wants into want-regarding and ideal-regarding.

Want-regarding publicly-oriented wants are those which can be expressed without mentioning anything other than totals and distribu-tions of privately-oriented want-satisfaction; ideal-regarding publicly-oriented wants are those which require in their statement the mention of certain *kinds* of privately-oriented want being satisfied or dis-satisfied.

When one is trying to combine different people's wants into a political judgement there is a standing temptation to lump all prefer-ences together as 'wants' and then apply some (aggregative or distribu-tive) principles to these 'wants'. In this way what is at one level a publicly-oriented (want-regarding or ideal-regarding) judgement be-comes, at the next level of judgement, another 'want' to be taken account of. Thus, at the first level we have A's (privately-oriented) want for state S_u of A, B's (privately-oriented) want for state S_v of B . . . and so on for C, D, E. . . . At the second level we have A's judge-ment that state S_w of A, B . . . (etc.) would be desirable, taking account of A's want for A_u, B's want for B_v . . . (etc.); we have B's judgement that state S_x of A, B . . . (etc.) would be desirable, taking account of A's want for A_u, B's want for B_v . . . (etc.) and so on for C, D, E. . . . (These are publicly-oriented judgements which are based on privately-oriented wants.)

At the third level, we can get (unless of course we rule it out—which is what I am proposing we do) the process outlined in the previous para-graph, where the judgement based on privately-oriented wants becomes a further (publicly-oriented) 'want' to be taken into account. Thus, at this third level, if we allow it to take place, A judges that state S_y of A, B . . . (etc.) would be desirable, taking into account A's want for A_u and his 'want' for A_w, B's want for B_v and his 'want' for B_x . . . (etc.); and B judges that state S_z of A and B, etc., would be desirable, taking account of the same things as A did; and so on for C, D, E . . . (etc.).

One obvious objection to allowing this process to go beyond the second stage is that once it does there seems no way that is not completely arbitrary of cutting off the series so as to prevent an infinite regress. Thus, in our example, A and B take account in the next round of A_y and B_z as well as all the previous items, and so on *ad infinitum*. I am rather disinclined to rest the case on this technical point, which is why I do not use it in the text. I suspect that anyone who was really determined to save the idea of treating publicly-oriented judgements as 'wants' in successive publicly-oriented judgements could do so with the exercise of some ingenuity. For example, it might be argued that each successive member of the series would represent a weaker 'want' so that the limit of the series could be approached sufficiently closely in a limited number of moves.

I prefer, therefore, to stick to the argument used in the text, even though I have to confess that it is less an argument than a flat statement and that I can see no way of increasing its plausibility to anyone whom it does not strike on reflection as plausible. In IV.3.C., then, I suggest that 'what I have called "publicly-oriented wants" are not actually put forward as wants at all. To treat them as wants is to degrade them and to fall into absurdity'. This seems to apply equally well to want-regarding publicly-oriented wants and ideal-regarding publicly-oriented wants. In order to avoid raising too many problems at once the examples given in IV.3.C. were of want-regarding cases; and the force of my argument is perhaps more easily apparent here. If I believe that an injustice has been done to someone the fact that it would make me feel better to believe that the wrong had been righted would not, it seems to me, add an extra reason for righting it. However, I think the argument applies equally well to the ideal-regarding case with which I am concerned exclusively in IV.6.A. If I think people would get more out of life if they went to the theatre more it seems to me just as out of place as in the previous example to adduce as an extra reason for encouraging people to become theatre-goers the fact that I would get pleasure from the thought of other people (whom I don't even know) getting more out of life.

When we assent to the proposition (if we do) that other things being equal it is a good thing for wants to be satisfied I simply do not think that we have in mind these publicly-oriented wants. And when the problem they present is brought to our attention I suggest that we should avoid the apparently neat and tidy solution of assimilating them to the other wants while retaining the form of the proposition unchanged.

(F) THE EFFECT OF PARTICIPATING IN A COLLECTIVE DECISION (See IV.6.B., page 74)

'The whole process of choosing has itself an influence on one's identifications, therefore on the self, and therefore on the goals one seeks to maximize. On the whole, the process of making market choices tends to narrow one's identifications to the individual or, at the most, to the family. The process of voting, on the other hand, with all that it presupposes in the way of discussion and techniques of reciprocity, tends to broaden one's identifications beyond the individual and the family.' (Dahl and Lindblom, p. 422.)

'A man's opinion as to the desirable size of a normal family might be totally different, on the one hand, when he faces the problem as a citizen taking a stand on the population issue if this is brought to the political forefront, and, on the other hand, when he faces his own family limitation problem.' (Gunnar Myrdal, *Value in Social Theory* (London, 1958), pp. 86–87.)

'A person may have a "general attitude" of dislike toward Negroes. And, under certain circumstances, in his role as "property owner", he may join with others to use violence in preventing a Negro from moving into his neighbourhood. However, the same person may be mobilized and disciplined at his job by his labor union's definition of the situation. In his role as a 'union steward' he may even be sympathetic with a Negro who had been insulted by the refusal of a white girl to dance with him at a union dance.' (Joseph D. Lohman and Dietrich C. Reitzes, 'Note on Race Relations in Mass Society', *American Journal of Sociology*, LV, No. 3 (November 1952), 242.)

For a clear statement of the idea that political action may elicit wider sympathies than the market, see Reinhold Niebuhr's contribution to *The Organizational Revolution* by Kenneth E. Boulding (New York, 1953). Compare also A. D. Lindsay in *The Essentials of Democracy* (London, 1935), p. 67: '... educational endowment and licensing laws may perfectly well be passed by the votes of ordinary people who would not make the necessary effort to get education or deny themselves liquor in their individual action, but who have a higher standard of values for themselves and others as members of the community.'

(G) LIBERAL SOCIETY AND MASS SOCIETY
(See IV.6.D., page 83)

A kind of society in which there is a general unwillingness among people to allow others to act on publicly-oriented ideals with the object or effect of changing those people's tastes has been variously defined, either in its totality or in particular aspects. Plato, in the *Republic*, held that Athens was such a society, and called the phenomenon 'democracy' (clearly meaning to refer to a social phenomenon rather than a purely political one). Matthew Arnold, observing the same tendencies in Victorian England, called it 'anarchy' (referring explicitly to the lack of standards). Numerous other writers have isolated the economic aspect of the phenomenon, laying the blame for the plight of the producer on capitalism or more generally the commercial mentality. Thus, we find Marx, Ruskin, William Morris and Veblen all arguing that work is not inherently painful, but work directed solely by what will sell most profitably is; the 'instinct of workmanship' should be allowed to set its own standards for what is produced. Veblen applied the same conception to the 'higher learning', claiming that it should be directed by 'idle curiosity' (one might say: the standards of the person doing the work) rather than the requirements of the university for prestige and funds.

More recently, and especially since 1945, what is basically the same phenomenon (with new technological refinements) has been commonly regarded as constituting (or at least forming an important aspect of) 'mass society'. However, I think that William Kornhauser, in his book *The Politics of Mass Society* (London, 1960) tends to misrepresent the grounds on which 'mass society' has been criticized. This may possibly be because, as a liberal American scholar, he finds it difficult to take seriously the idea of a critic of mass society wishing to make the ideal-regarding judgement that the 'elite' should try to implement *their* ideal-regarding judgements. Thus, in Part I of his book, Kornhauser classifies criticism of 'mass society' into two kinds. The first, which he calls the 'democratic' criticism, complains that the 'masses' are cynically manipulated by the 'elite' through advertising and propaganda into condoning and increasing the latters' wealth and power. The second, which he calls the 'aristocratic' criticism of mass society, complains that the 'masses' attempt to impose their own vulgar and commonplace tastes on the cultured 'elite'; and Kornhauser then suggests that the way to satisfy both sets of critics is to have a 'pluralistic' society such that the 'elite' and the 'mass' are insulated from each other. But, in my view, this would hardly satisfy *any* of the critics.

The main weight of the criticisms of 'mass society' bears on the *un-*

worthiness of the relations between groups rather than the *existence* of such relations. The 'democrats' complain that people of ability prostitute their talents by selling them to the highest bidder and producing whatever is asked of them. In other words, it is manipulation—the misuse of talent in the interests of power or money—rather than influence as such, which is the target of the 'democratic' critics. (At most, one can say that some—e.g., C. Wright Mills in *The Power Elite* (New York, 1959) and J. K. Galbraith in *The Affluent Society* (London, 1958) —confine themselves so much to criticism of manipulation that they do not specifically contrast it with influence exerted with integrity; but even then neither do they explicitly condemn it.) The 'aristocrats' are even more flagrantly misrepresented: their objection is not that the talented are not left alone, but that they are not allowed to influence *others*. Possibly de Tocqueville, on whom Kornhauser leans so heavily as an 'aristocratic' example, does emphasize the attempts of the 'mass' actually to restrict the 'elite' as well as the lack of influence of those with superior culture. But in this he was an exception. Ortega y Gasset's *Revolt of the Masses* (London, 1951) is far more typical.

Kornhauser is quite right in noting that the 'aristocratic' and 'democratic' positions are consistent with one another; but not by advocating 'pluralism'. That would be like saying that if a conversation is not going well the best way to improve it is to lock the participants in separate rooms. The reconciling proposition is that influence should be exerted by the competent openly (no depth-psychology) and with integrity (in accordance with the highest standards of which they are capable). Indeed, so compatible are the two sides that they may fuse in a single writer and make any attempt to separate them out artificial. A recent example is provided by R. Williams, *The Long Revolution* (London, 1961).

(H) THE 'PRICE MECHANISM' (See V.2(2)., page 87)

One often sees 'the price mechanism' mentioned as a social decision procedure, especially by economists of a *laissez faire* tendency. Dahl and Lindblom also treat 'the price mechanism' as a procedure in their survey. However, I have not included it in my classification because it seems to me that it is not a procedure itself but a device which may be used in connection with any procedure. To include 'the price mechanism' as a procedure would be like making a classification of shops into fish shops, bread shops, butchers' shops . . . and shops that stay open on Wednesday afternoons.

A price mechanism is in operation wherever there is a common unit in which the values of more than one commodity can be expressed and anyone with a certain number of units can spread them among the commodities in any way he chooses. The relative values of the commodities and the total number of points each person has may be fixed by authority (as with the British points rationing scheme during the Second World War) or they may be determined by perfect competition, or by bargaining in other conditions, and so on.

To confine the term 'price mechanism' to a complete *laissez faire* economy and nothing less is highly misleading since it implies that in any other sort of economy choice among commodities is impossible. Inasfar, however, as 'the price mechanism' is treated as synonymous with either perfect competition or *laissez faire* it is a sub-class of the 'bargaining' category, i.e. that where certain forms of duress are ruled out.

(I) COMPROMISE (See V.2(3) page 88)

It is of some interest to ask what is the status of 'compromise'. The answer seems to be that it covers both certain cases of bargaining and certain cases of discussion on merits. The line between the two tends to be hardest to draw exactly in those cases which one is inclined to call compromises. The difficulty in classification arises because compromise is in effect a way of circumventing the necessity for further discussion; it is therefore difficult or perhaps even impossible to determine in some instances whether it has operated as a substitute for bargaining or as a substitute for discussion on merits.

Suppose that I ask £50, you offer £40 and we 'split the difference' so as to agree on £45; or that you demand two air bases, I refuse to consider having any and we agree on one: there may be two motives at work. We may each realize that our initial positions are unreasonable and that splitting the difference would be a 'fair' result. In this case the compromise is really a substitute for discussion on merits: each side recognizes that the other has a good case but instead of arguing it out they take a short cut. Alternatively, we may each realize that our power to inflict damage on one another, our resources and our wits are well matched and decide that since the result of amoral bargaining is likely to be a midway position we may as well move directly to this position and avoid the trouble of bargaining and the risk of taking up irreconcilable positions for bargaining purposes from which we cannot back down and thus both miss a deal we would like. Here the compromise is a short-cut to the most favourable result either of us could sensibly hope for if we bargained as hard as we could.

As I point out in the text, though, it may be quite unclear which of these motives is at work, and quite often both may be operative in a rather confused way. (The word 'reasonable' plays an important role here in slurring over the difference between the two. To say that someone is asking an unreasonable price means both that he won't get it and that he ought not to get it. If he gets his price the concept becomes unglued: you may either say that the price must have been reasonable after all or that all it shows that there's one born every minute.)

For example, if compromise involves 'splitting the difference' between two initial positions, how are the initial positions arrived at? An initial position for the purpose of difference-splitting does not become one merely by assertion. If that were so, the buyer would always offer nothing at all (or even demand payment for taking the thing away) while the seller would ask an unlimited price. The series of figures between which the difference is split are in a quite narrow range, and this range is defined almost interchangeably as the most the seller can expect to get and the most he ought to get, and *vice versa* for the buyer. (I take the example of a buyer and seller for simplicity but this is not essential to the point.)

John Hallowell's statement in Chapter II of *The Moral Foundation of Democracy* (Chicago, 1954) that anyone who extols compromise must be equating might with right, is surely too sweeping. A compromise may simply embody the predicted outcome of bargaining, but it is also possible to recognize in the demand of another party a claim which one *ought* to recognize, and here compromise may embody instead the predicted outcome of discussion on merits.

(J) COUNTERVAILING POWER AND FAIRNESS
(See VI.3.B., page 105)

The question whether fairness can be defined for a bargaining situation is raised conveniently by John Kenneth Galbraith in his book *American Capitalism: The Concept of Countervailing Power* (London, 1958); see also Gunnar Myrdal, *Beyond the Welfare State* (New Haven, 1960). In this book, Galbraith proposes that the state should act on the bargaining power of business and labour by, for example, manipulating the unemployment rate and altering the trade union law so as to make it easier or harder to unionize employees, conduct strikes, etc.

Whatever may be the merits of this proposal I think that any suggestion that by so acting the state would be making bargaining between business and labour 'fair' ought to be resisted; though it would be acceptable to say that the state would be trying to secure a just outcome to the bargaining process (in a sense of 'just' other than the rule-based one). To say that intervention in the initial strengths of the opponents would be making bargaining 'fair' (or 'fairer') would be assimilating the case to one of contest. But the analogy breaks down at the crucial point, for the idea of a contest is to test the competitors for the possession of some quality or qualities, so that one can define 'fairness' in a contest as that which makes it more likely that the competitor with the greater amount of the quality which is being tested will win. Bargaining is *not* like a contest in this respect. There is no 'relevant quality' to be tested so one cannot define 'fairness' in terms of raising the likelihood that the possession of more of the relevant quality will produce success. If the Galbraith proposal has any analogy in contests then it is to someone's deciding that Jones 'ought' to win the race (because, say, he needs the prize-money most) and then giving sleeping pills to the other competitors and pep pills to Jones himself.

'Parity of bargaining power' is a myth in a way in which 'equality of opportunity' is not, because it cannot be specified independently of the desired result. If the *status quo* in labour relations is desirable, the 'parity' must plainly consist in the existing relative strengths in bargaining power; if it is desirable for wages and conditions to improve then 'parity' will occur only after the balance has been tilted; and *vice versa*. The Galbraith proposal is perfectly defensible on the grounds that manipulating bargaining-power can bring about a more just outcome of bargaining and I do not believe that Galbraith himself places much emphasis on other considerations. But in the hands of less cautious (and, often, more interested) people it can easily be suggested that 'fair' relative bargaining power can somehow be defined independently of its anticipated results; and this, I claim, is to rely on a false analogy with contests.

Mr Plamenatz has commented at this point:

> Surely, *parity of bargaining power* can be defined independently of the result just as much as *equality of opportunity* can. True, the conditions constituting parity can't be defined without reference to the interests at stake—but then the conditions constituting equality of opportunity can't be defined without reference to what the opportunity is for.
>
> Isn't parity of bargaining power one kind of equality of opportunity?

It seems to me that the difference between contest and bargaining lies not in the interests involved—which might sometimes in both cases be money, for example—but in the way that the 'right result' is to be specified. In the case of contest the 'right result' is for the side with most of the quality *which the contest is supposed to be testing* to win. But the 'right result' of bargaining is *not* for the side with the most bargaining power to win (or if it is this is an accident—the *criterion* of a 'right result' is different). 'Equality of opportunity' is the elimination of 'irrelevant' factors from having any influence on the result of a contest; but since there are no 'relevant' factors in the case of bargaining I do not see how there can be any question of 'equality of opportunity' or anything at all closely analogous to it.

(K) PETERSON AND VAIZEY ON 'TEACHER FAMINE'
(See VII.2.C., page 131)

Curiously enough the very dubious argument about 'teacher famine' has been more popular of late among critics of the English public schools than the far better founded straight distributive one (which certainly works against English public schools as they now are, even if not against all private education as such). Thus A. D. C. Peterson wrote in an article 'Teachers for the Sixth Form' (*The Guardian*, 18 December 1962, p. 6) as follows:

> We are in fact entering a period of teacher famine and already teachers are the one commodity rationed in this country. A local authority may not (but an independent school may) employ more than the nationally agreed quota. It is quite unrealistic to suppose that we could ever in this generation halve the teacher/pupil ratio of maintained secondary schools. Yet until we do this they will not achieve parity with their independent rivals.
>
> But the obverse of this is surely that one does not in famine conditions allow the rich to buy more than their share, whether of food or education.

And a few weeks earlier John Vaizey (reported in *The Guardian*, 22 November 1962, p. 4) said:

> To the objection that any decision to prevent expansion in the private sector would interfere with the basic right to have one's children educated as one wanted, the Labour Party could have the legitimate response that the exercise of this right was only at the expense of the children of the great mass of people. 'Some public schools have 12 or more mathematics masters with good degrees; many maintained grammar schools have one; most secondary modern schools have none.'

Both of these passages build on the assumption that there is a fixed supply of teachers and the only question is how they are to be divided up among schools of different kinds. How do we know that the graduates in the public schools would stay in school-teaching if they ceased to teach in public schools? How, for that matter, do we know that the Ministry of Education's quota scheme distributes a fixed pool of teachers within the state system rather than reducing the total size of the pool? It is certainly possible to conceive a situation in which public and private sectors, and local authorities within the public sector, were competing for a fixed pool of teachers; but it seems far more likely that the size of the pool is determined by the attractiveness of withdrawal from the employment market altogether (married women) and alternative occupations. If so it would be far more to the point to raise teachers' pay (especially in the more unpopular areas) and/or curb the amount alternative employers can pay.

(L) ARBITRARINESS (See IX.3.D., page 171)

Saying an arrangement is arbitrary is not always a criticism of it: as I pointed out in VI.3.B. (p. 104) the essence of a fairly carried out chance procedure is that the result should be arbitrary, which for this purpose means that it should be unconnected with any personal qualities of those participating in the lottery or whatever it may be. However, an arrangement may be criticized as 'arbitrary' either where it is thought that some procedure which *does* take account of personal qualities ought to be used or where the arbitrary procedure is not thought to have the property of 'randomness'. For example: suppose that *n* men are needed in the armed services and any able-bodied men will do equally well. Then, from a simple aggregative point of view, it doesn't matter how these *n* men are selected so long as those who could make special contributions to the general welfare as civilians and those for whom military service would be a special hardship are exempted. Apart from these exceptions any way of choosing the required number would do —*e.g.*, starting at the beginning of the alphabet and working through, starting with the tallest and working down; and so on. But these would be generally thought of as 'arbitrary' in an objectionable way; and a solution avoiding this criticism would involve either calling up all those of a certain age not exempted on special grounds or introducing random arbitrariness by a lottery as in the USA. The point becomes clearer still if we suppose that there are a million men aged 18, that a million trained man-years are needed and that it takes a year to train a man. The million trained man-years can either be obtained (among other ways) by calling up the whole million for two years or half of them for three years. The second is obviously far more efficient, but it may well be thought less equitable.

The general form of the problem is that a certain number can (or must) participate in something good (or bad), and from an aggregative standpoint it doesn't matter much how the selection from a larger group is carried out (except of course inasfar as feelings of being a victim of inequity rankle and must be counted in the calculation, and this depends on equity being a principle independent of the aggregationist principle).

(M) LAMONT ON 'GOOD FOR YOU' AND 'GOOD FOR ME'
(See X.3.B., page 180)

In *Principles of Moral Judgement* (Oxford, 1946) Lamont gives a number of quotations containing the word 'good' and then says:

> They make or imply a distinction between 'good for you' and 'good for me'. A year which is good for me is not necessarily good for everyone. The welfare of the native population is not necessarily the same as the welfare of humanity at large. European institutions may promote the best development for us, but not for Africans. We can distinguish between what is good for the empire and what is good for the Irish nation, though the same thing may promote both. Monarchy may be good for one people, but not for another (pp. 101–102).

But this conclusion must be handled with care. All that has been shown is that a *policy* which affects me favourably may not affect you favourably; it has not been shown (though it may, of course, still be true) that the criteria for 'being affected favourably' are different as between you and me. The adherent of the so-called 'universalizability principle' is not committed to the absurdity that if an action or policy has good results for one person it must have good results for everyone. All he must maintain is that if a certain result is to count as making the policy that produces it 'good for x' while the same kind of result is not to count as making that policy 'good for y' this must be explained by reference to some 'relevant difference' between x and y.

In the case of 'interest', the only 'relevant difference', I have suggested, is whether or not someone will so grossly misuse increased opportunities to get what he wants that it is 'in his best interests' not to get increased opportunities. Subject to this the criteria of something's being in a person's interest do not vary according to the person and it is precisely this which makes it possible to ask someone to look after or represent one's interests. Compare the utility of having sufficiently rigid public criteria for 'a good cut of meat' or 'a good sherry' to enable one simply to ask someone to get these without having to specify further what is wanted.

(N) 'CORRUPTION' AND THE WOLFENDEN REPORT
(See XII.2.C., page 213)

Lord Devlin points out in *The Enforcement of Morals* (Proceedings of the British Academy, 1959) that the Wolfenden report

> has to define or describe its special circumstances [justifying state intervention in 'private' immorality] so widely that they can be supported only if it is accepted that the law *is* concerned with immorality as such.

. . . If prostitution is private immorality and not the law's business, what concern has the law with the ponce or the brothel-keeper or the householder who permits habitual prostitution ?'

Again

> if society is not prepared to say that homosexuality is morally wrong, there would be no basis for a law protecting youth from 'corruption' or punishing a man for living on the 'immoral' earnings of a homosexual prostitute, as the Report recommends. (pp. 10–13.)

In my terminology the point here is that talk of 'corruption' must involve reference to an ideal of human development (in this context in a heterosexual rather than a homosexual direction) and that even if the Report's recommendation were restricted to minors in conditions of dependence this would still involve an intervention on purely ideal grounds; for 'corruption' is surely the creation of *bad* character.

I believe that the consistency of the Wolfenden recommendations can be defended but only if they are regarded as being the results of weighing the 'immorality' (or, less question-begging, the undesirability of a larger as against a smaller incidence) of homosexuality and prostitution against the value of freedom to do what you want. An application of Mill's criteria would give different results, especially with regard to prostitution, so I think Devlin's point is well taken. On homosexuality the prohibition of 'corruption' might be defended on Mill's grounds if homosexuality were equated with drug addiction, i.e. a condition which a person may later wish to change but is then powerless to. But isn't heterosexuality also fairly irreversible by the age of 21 ? Somewhere a judgement that it's better to be heterosexual has to be smuggled in; and since the context is one of deciding what the law is to be, one can't say that homosexuality is not in a person's interests because his desires will lead him to break the law.

(O) DEVLIN ON PUBLIC CONSCIENCE AND PUBLIC INTEREST
(See XII.2.C., page 213)

Lord Devlin, in *The Enforcement of Morals* calls into question the possibility of treating behaviour widely thought to be immoral as falling under the 'public conscience' category rather than the 'public interest' category. He does not apparently deny that a meaningful distinction can be drawn in principle between those actions which affect a non-assignable group and those which do not. He simply denies that as a matter of fact any actions which are generally thought in a community to be 'immoral' can properly be included in the category of actions which do not affect others, at any rate so long as the feelings aroused by the thought of the action are sufficiently intense.

This view of Devlin's should be distinguished from one (for which there is some good historical evidence) to the effect that institutions which start as instruments of the public conscience may develop into instruments of a developing conception of public interest. Thus, according to the American sociologist E. A. Ross

> Pristine justice is dispensed for the benefit of the wronged man, and only slowly does there arise the idea of a paramount social interest in the repression of crime. But the time comes when it is the district attorney who prosecutes the law-breaker and not his victim, when it is the public peace that has suffered and not A or B, and when the taking of a composition is punished as 'the compounding of a felony'. (*Social Control*, p. 120.)

And Baroness Wootton, analysing a parallel modern process of development suggests that the 'moralising trend' in wage bargains shows two distinct phases. First,

> the wage bargain is ... regarded as the private concern of the parties directly involved and of the organizations acting on their behalf, in which the community is concerned only to enforce fair play on both sides. Then it becomes a three-cornered transaction, in which the public at large has its own interest, no less deserving of consideration than the interests of the employers and the workers directly concerned. Justice must now be done as much to those who are not parties to the immediate bargain as to those who are. (*Social Foundations of Wage Policy*, pp. 102–103.)

In the first phase the public is 'interested', which can here be replaced by 'concerned'; only in the second phase does the public press 'its own interest'.

Devlin's argument is that by merely *being thought* immoral an action necessarily becomes affected with a public interest. The nub of the argument is put in this passage:

> If men and women try to create a society in which there is no fundamental agreement about good and evil they will fail; if having based it on common agreement, the agreement goes, the society will disintegrate. For society is not something that is kept together physically; it is held by the invisible bonds of common thought. If the bonds were too far relaxed the members would drift apart. A common morality is part of the bondage. The bondage is part of the price of society; and mankind, which needs society, must pay its price. (*The Enforcement of Morals*, p. 12.)

This argument must be distinguished (as Devlin fails to distinguish it) from that dealt with in XII.2.B. according to which certain specific institutions such as marriage are held to be 'good for' people and therefore protected. But this is to make things too easy for himself.

He writes:

Marriage is part of the structure of our society and is also the basis of a moral code which condemns fornication and adultery. The institution of marriage would be gravely threatened if individual judgements were permitted about the morality of adultery; on these points there must be a public morality. But public morality is not to be confined to those moral principles which support institutions such as marriage. People do not think of monogamy as something which has to be supported because our society has chosen to organize itself upon it; they think of it as something that is good in itself and offering a good way of life and that it is for that reason that our society has adopted it. (p. 11.)

But what Devlin has to show is that even where there is no institution such as marriage at stake there is a public interest in suppressing immorality because there is a public interest in maintaining a like-thinking community. Or to put it another way, he has to show that over and above particular institutions there is the institution of 'public morality' which is as worthy of protection on grounds of public interest as the institution of the state. As far as I can see Devlin offers no evidence for this beyond his repeated assertion of it, and it seems to me a good deal more plausible to suggest that the Mill–Wolfenden criteria offer a guide to the matters about which the members of a community *can* safely agree to differ without threatening the dissolution of the community as a going concern. (Or perhaps one might amend this to say that any community that did require for its cohesion the persecution of scapegoats (Jews, homosexuals or whatever it might be) would be to that degree a bad kind of community on both want-regarding and ideal-regarding criteria.)

Of course, even if it happened to be true that a 'public morality' aimed at conduct with no immediate repercussions on others were a necessity for the subsistence of a society the question would still remain whether implementing that public morality with legislation or embodying its contents in 'public policy' would do much to preserve it. Much that Devlin says appears to suggest that even in his view the law is carried by the 'public morality' in these matters rather than the 'public morality' being buttressed by the law. The same question may of course be raised in connection with legal prohibitions and the voiding of contracts where this is supposed to support the 'public good'. It must surely be a serious embarrassment to any theory which assigns to the law a large place in the 'protection' of the institution of marriage that fornication and adultery are *not* crimes.

(P) HOBHOUSE'S 'PRINCIPLE OF HARMONY'
(See XIII.2.A., p. 230)

Mr Plamenatz writes: 'Isn't it fairer to Hobhouse, and also more sensible, to take him as meaning that a man's satisfaction is valueless if it is incompatible with a common interest or good?' Mr Plamenatz's views on this must obviously carry weight but I should at least like to suggest that there is some external evidence which makes it possible that Hobhouse intended the stronger version. Firstly, T. H. Green, an acknowledged influence, seems to have held the doctrine that 'rights are based on functions' with a clear recognition of its (I would say) detestable implications. For example, on page 158 of the *Lectures on the Principles of Political Obligation* he solemnly discusses the question why should we not kill all those who cannot fulfil 'some function in the social organism' and argues that the only reason is that such people do after all fulfil a function—namely that of providing suitable objects for the exercise of virtuous qualities by the rest of the community. Secondly, Harold Laski, writing at about the same time as Hobhouse and under many of the same influences, apparently held a similar doctrine.

> My rights are built always upon the relation my function has to the well being of society; and the claims I make must, clearly enough, be claims that are necessary to the proper performance of my function. My demands upon society, in this view, are demands which ought to achieve recognition because a recognisable public interest is involved in their recognition. (*The Grammar of Politics*, 4th ed., London, 1937, p. 95.)

There is no 'right' to enjoy oneself unless there is a 'recognisable public interest' involved: this is obviously a statement of the 'strong' thesis, and the note of Puritanism displaced from God on to 'society' is very reminiscent of Hobhouse.

(Q) CORRUPTION AND TRUSTWORTHINESS
(See XIV.1.C., page 239)

In Chapter 2 of their book, *Power, Corruption and Rectitude* (Englewood Cliffs, N.J., 1963) A. A. Rogow and H. D. Lasswell argue (in a somewhat casual and anecdotal way) that the Acton thesis is not in general borne out in US experience: power may corrupt, ennoble or do nothing at all to a person's character. But it does not follow from this, as they appear to believe, that what I define in XIV.1.D. as the 'power-diffusion' view is thereby refuted. In Chapter 1 they suggest that the Acton dictum (or more exactly its forerunners) is responsible for the fragmentation of governmental power in the USA whose results they deplore. Whatever may have been the case historically, the 'power corrupts' view is not a necessary presupposition of the 'power-diffusion' view. For example one might argue, against the desirability of concentrating power, that the kind of people who seek power tend to have pathological characteristics to start with, so that even if they don't deteriorate as a result of achieving power (or even if they improve a bit) they still won't be very trustworthy. (This is a view with which Lasswell himself has been associated; and Robert E. Lane seems to lean towards it in *Political Life* [Glencoe, Ill., 1959]). Or, alternatively, one might merely claim that power-wielders are a fair sample in respect of rectitude of the general population. Since the general population contains some pretty untrustworthy people one might still maintain that there was a significant *risk* of getting undesirable people in positions of great power unless you make sure that *nobody* is in a position of great power. I do not want to suggest that these considerations are sufficient to establish the 'power-diffusion' view and I do not think they are, as will become apparent later. But they are enough, surely, to show that the view rests on more secure foundations than the Actonian dictum that 'power tends to corrupt'.

(R) BUCHANAN AND TULLOCK ON 'MAJORITY RULE'
(See XIV.2.A., page 244)

Whenever a choice has to be made by voting between two mutually exclusive policies x and y (y may of course simply be 'not to do x') the common-sense view, with which I agree, is that only decision by a simple majority will ensure that more are satisfied by the result than are frustrated. Suppose there are five people in a railway compartment which the railway operator has omitted to label either 'smoking' or 'no smoking' (let us assume that no presumption either way is to be drawn from the mere absence of labelling). Each of them either wants to smoke or objects to others smoking in his vicinity and there is at least one representative of each school present. Is there any reason why, if the matter is to be settled by voting, three out of five should *not* be a sufficient majority to decide? Only, it seems to me, if they had already agreed that there was a presumption in favour of settling the matter one way which should be decisive *unless* some special majority could be achieved. Concretely: they might all agree that *prima facie* there was a strong case for allowing smoking and that this should only be overruled by a four-fifths majority. But if they are unable to agree on the merits of the case even as far as saying that there is a presumption one way or the other, then if they are to settle it by voting at all they must surely abide by a simple majority. It seems to me that it is the point about 'no presumptions as to merits' which contains the heart of the case for majority voting; and none of the authors' arguments touches it.

The first occasion on which they attack the uniqueness of simple majority decision is after they have just introduced two curves representing 'external costs' and 'bargaining costs'; as the size of the majority (as a proportion of the total) required for a decision rises, 'external costs' fall and 'bargaining costs' rise. A curve representing the sum of these two curves is then constructed and the 'optimum' majority requirement is said to lie at the lowest point of this curve. The authors point out that there is no special reason to suppose that this will occur at the 50 per cent mark. But it is evident that the only reason here for diverging from unanimity as a requirement for valid decisions is the cost of bargaining. In other words, the assumption underlying the construction of the 'total cost curve' is that each person has explicitly accepted the *status quo*. It has no relevance to the normal situation (and that of our hypothetical railway travellers) where there is no pre-existing agreement on a *status quo*.

Later on, the authors complain that political choices are too often looked on as 'zero sum' conflicts, where one man's gain is another's loss, and urge us to look instead to trading as our model. Here, they argue, there is 'mutuality of gain'. Neither coerces the other, neither gains at the expense of the other (p. 252). But a *political* situation is precisely one that arises when the parties are arguing not about mutually useful trades but about the legitimacy of one another's initial position. If Crusoe has a legal title to the island, Friday would sooner work for him than starve, and Crusoe would sooner have Friday work for him than not. There is therefore 'mutuality of gain': 'gains from trade' are possible. But suppose Friday raises the political question: should Crusoe own all the island? Here at once we get a conflict of interest; it is absurd to say that Friday should here make it worth while for Crusoe to accept this change by offering a *quid pro quo*, for it is precisely the legitimacy of their relative positions which Friday is calling into question. Again, the authors beg the significant questions by assuming an agreement which all parties allow to cover the present case already in existence. This makes their conclusions trivial.

It is worth while noticing in this connection that Wicksell insisted that the principle of unanimity only applied where the initial distribution of income and property was accepted as fair by all concerned:

> It is clear that justice in taxation presupposes justice in the existing distribution of property and income. . . . The principle of the veto right of the minority which has been defended in this essay, equally rests on the premise that the property status of each individual is fully acknowledged

by the State and must in justice be so acknowledged. . . . If, however, this presupposition does not correspond to the facts, if there are within the existing property and income structure certain titles and privileges of doubtful legality or in open contradiction with modern concepts of law and equity, then society has both the right and the duty to revise the existing property structure. It would obviously be asking too much to expect such revision ever to be carried out if it were to be made dependent on the agreement of the persons primarily concerned. ('A New Principle of Just Taxation', p. 108. See also Carl G. Uhr, *Economic Doctrines of Knut Wicksell* (Berkeley, 1960), Chapters 8 and 12; and the discussion between Buchanan and Uhr: Buchanan, 'Wicksell on Fiscal Reform: Comment', *American Economic Review*, XLII (September 1952), pp. 599–602; and Uhr, 'Wicksell on Fiscal Reform: Further Comment', *American Economic Review* (June 1953, pp. 366–368).

Their remaining argument, in spite of a few turns into the byways, rests just as squarely on the assumption of a prior agreement covering the case in hand, as the previous ones. They suppose someone to argue that if a number less than half can block proposed action this amounts to minority rule, and reply that 'minority rule' should be applied only to situations in which a minority can *carry* proposed action. Now clearly it is true that it is one thing for any permanent member of the Security Council to be able to veto a resolution, and quite a different thing for any permanent member to be able to pass by itself a resolution in the name of the Security Council. In fact, the latter would not result in a 'Council' at all since each permanent member could simply head its ordinary diplomatic communications 'Resolutions of the Security Council'.

The whole idea of 'minority rule' in the sense of minority power to authorize action is absurd since there is nothing to stop different minorities passing conflicting laws within a few minutes of each other. Indeed it is significant that the authors never elaborate their concept of 'minority rule' into a workable (or, indeed, conceivable) institution, and I suspect the whole idea is simply thrown in to discredit the 'orthodox' view that 50 per cent and 50 per cent + 1 are opposite sides of an important line. For example, in order to reduce confusion to a minimum let us suppose that once a law on some subject had been passed by the requisite minority (say 40 per cent) no law inconsistent with it could be passed for a year. Clearly, under this arrangement any group of 40 per cent which also had control over the order-paper together with the body which decided what constituted 'inconsistency' would be quite literally a determinate group of 'minority rulers' exactly as much as if they were a majority under ordinary procedures elected from gerrymandered constituencies.

I should perhaps mention here that although 50 per cent + 1 is the smallest number which ensures that directly contradictory motions will not both be carried by the same assembly without any change in any-one's voting record, I am well aware of the difficulty which may arise from 'cyclical majorities' where there are more than two competing measures before an assembly. But this does not destroy the uniqueness of simple majority voting because there is no higher majority require-ment which guarantees freedom from the difficulty. Even the stock 3-man-3-proposal presentation obviously works against anything up to and including a two-thirds majority requirement; and, more important, if more than a two-thirds majority is required to carry any proposal and one of the proposals is to do nothing this represents just as arbitrary a victory for one as does pairing off the proposals in a random order and voting on them.

Let us then not talk about 'minority rule' if this suggests the power to initiate changes in the *status quo*. It is still disingenuous of Buchanan and Tullock to deny that in many cases requiring a qualified majority for changes in the *status quo* the result is that the minority gets what it wants and the majority doesn't. Whether or not we call this 'ruling' (or 'coercing') is indifferent so long as we understand the nature of the position. (See Duncan Black, 'Wicksell's Theory in the Distribution of Taxation', in J. K. Eastham (ed.), *Economic Essays in Commemoration of the Dundee School of Economics* 1931–1955 (Dundee, 1955), pp. 7–23, esp. pp. 17–19.)

They give this example (p. 257): there are a hundred persons on a hayride and a fork in the road looms ahead; 74 want to go right and 26 left. With a simple majority rule they will go right, but with a three-quarters majority rule they will stop. This does not, they say, represent a 'victory' for the 26 over the 74 because the 26 don't get what they want either. But now let us imagine a slight change in the set-up. Suppose that they are going along the road and come to a river; 26 want to stop for a bathe while the other 74 want to go on. If as before the rule says that 75 are needed before the cart goes on, this does represent 'victory' for the 26, who have got precisely what they want. Which of these examples is most similar to modern politics? I am willing to allow that one might have two groups in a society which wanted to go equally far in opposite directions ('forward' and 'back-ward') and especially if they were of approximately equal size one might consider it only fair that they should split the difference and stay where they are (the Third Republic rested on much this sort of com-promise). But the more usual situation is surely where one group wants changes and the other is by and large quite satisfied with things as they are. If the former group is larger than the latter and a qualified majority is required for changes then the smaller group gets its way and the larger group does not—it is as simple as that.

For example, during the Eisenhower period the Congressional

Republicans had a slogan: 'A third plus one.' When they achieved this figure and thus prevented the President's veto from being overridden had they won or hadn't they? (To avoid complications one should think of an automatic two-thirds requirement for change rather than an optional veto.) An even more flagrant example was the power of the British House of Lords before 1911 to hamstring any reforming majority in the House of Commons. It was wisely said that 'no matter who wins elections the Conservatives are always in power'. (Again, a rule requiring a qualified majority for change would have produced much the same effect.)

The authors' only reply to all this is, as I stated earlier, to repeat that they assume that all the parties have agreed to the procedure in question. Thus, in connection with their own example of the people on a hayride, they say:

> The argument may be advanced that, in such hypothetical situations as this, the interests of the greater number should be counted more heavily; but this, presumably, is a question that is appropriately answered only at the time when the decision-making rules are chosen. (pp. 257–258.)

The interesting question, namely: what happens if there is no prior agreement on decision-making rules? is not asked.

(S) VOLUNTARY PROVISION OF PUBLIC GOODS
(See XIV.2.D., page 249)

The instinct of the man in the street is to suspect that if something of general benefit is left to voluntary agreement it will not get done; and this instinct is sound. Even if there were not, in the ordinary sense of the word, bargaining costs, dissimulation would still be a good move for someone intent on dodging his share of the cost. The only form of bargaining which would get egoists to contribute is for each person to say: 'I will contribute if and only if everyone else does.' But in any large group there will quite likely be some who are genuinely indifferent to the project; if so, this form of combined threat and promise will result in the scheme's falling through, for the indifferent will not care if it does even if they are the cause. But once 'conscientious objection' is allowed, so that those who are in favour of the scheme merely say that they won't contribute unless everyone *who will benefit* does, this leaves the way open for cheating by those who will in fact benefit but say they won't.

For convenience I shall deal here with the question of what happens to voluntary contributions if we relax the assumption that there are no bargaining costs. The answer is, I think, that once bargaining costs are allowed for, voluntary methods will only work inasfar as those concerned are *not* egoists. If some of the beneficiaries are egoists and some are not, public provision will be less than the 'efficient' size, and the non-egoists will have to share the entire cost. In any large group threats and promises will be out of the question for most people; all they have to decide is whether to promise to contribute or not. An egoist will, if he is rational, decide this by guessing the probability that his contribution will be decisive in getting the scheme adopted, multiplying this probability by the net benefit he expects if the scheme is adopted, and comparing it with the cost of a contribution. The answer will almost invariably be that it is rational not to offer to contribute. If, say, ten thousand offers are needed before some scheme for a public amenity becomes viable, the chance that without your offer it will get exactly 9,999 is obviously remote. The argument 'What if everyone did that?' will not move an egoist because, where costs of bargaining exist, he cannot make his offer conditional upon payment being made by all those who benefit—quite apart from the fact that there are, as we have shown, difficulties even with that.

(T) THE EXPLANATION OF THE 'PORK BARREL'
(See XIV.3.A., page 250)

There is an undeniable tendency for the US Congress (and perhaps other elected bodies) to vote for dams, harbours, bases and other local benefits in excess of what is justifiable. Even if it were true that the 'pork barrel' is associated with majority voting this would not prove the authors' theory to be correct, since these might be alternative explanations of the connection. (To deny this is to commit the fallacy of 'affirming the consequent'.) But if there is no such connection, this does conclusively prove their theory wrong. I wish to suggest that the phenomenon is connected not with majority voting but with a requirement of unanimity. The nearer a system comes to requiring unanimity for decisions, the more prevalent we may expect to find the 'pork barrel' phenomenon. The United States comes nearer to a 'unanimity system' than any other Western democracy; it also suffers most from the 'pork barrel' problem; compare it for example with Britain which is formally a pure simple majority system. (See, for the national level, Dahl and Lindblom, *Politics, Economics and Welfare*, pp. 335–348; and Rogow and Lasswell, *Power, Corruption and Rectitude*, pp. 15–25; and for Chicago, E. C. Banfield, *Political Influence* (Glencoe, Ill., 1961), p. 235.)

The tendency of systems requiring something approaching unanimity for a decision to be most prone to the 'pork barrel' phenomenon can be explained in two ways, which supplement one another. Firstly, we can use the analytical apparatus developed in XIV.2.D. We saw there that without bargaining costs and with perfect knowledge (leaving telepathy out of account) rational egoists would, under a unanimity system, misrepresent their preferences and commit themselves to vote against things they really wanted in order to get a bribe as well. If we replace straight payments by dams, harbours, bases and defence contracts we are immediately in the world of the pork barrel, the world of Congress. Suppose that a bill will, if passed, benefit the bulk of each Congressman's constituents; why should not a Congressman who is (by himself or with a group of others) able to hold up the bill by his strategic position along the legislative pipeline, threaten to do just that unless he gets another base in his constituency? On this theory the most 'pork' will go to the constituents of those Congressmen who are in the best position to hold the Administration and the rest of Congress to ransom by threatening to block legislation and appropriations of national importance. That this seems to fit the facts well may be verified by anyone who cares to count the number of bases in Georgia.

The second explanation of the 'pork barrel', which as I said supplements the first, introduces imperfect information. I discuss the general consequences of imperfect information in XV.3. but it is perhaps easy to guess that log-rolling under conditions of imperfect information will tend to produce over-investment in projects which yield specific benefits to determinate groups, because such benefits are highly visible to the beneficiaries whereas costs are not so visible to the general taxpayer. The Veterans' Bonus, which was vetoed by every President between the wars, and passed over his veto, is an excellent example of this process though it is strictly a transfer of income rather than a public good. (See E. E. Schattschneider, *Party Government*, pp. 194–196.) It clearly cannot be explained as a case of a majority of constituencies filling their pockets at the expense of the rest; on the contrary the strength of the Veterans was (and is) precisely that they are present in about equal proportions in every constituency. Tariffs are another example where the cost to the rest of the community was ignored and only the benefit to the protected producer noticed. As Schattschneider pointed out in his study of the tariff revision of 1929–30:

Apparently equal stakes do not produce equal pressures. The protective tariff is well established because large areas of adverse interests are too inert and sluggish to find political expression while an overwhelming proportion of the active interests have been given a stake in maintaining the system. (*Politics, Pressures and the Tariff*, p. 163.)

(U) THE *STATUS QUO* AND EQUALITY AS 'OBVIOUS' SOLUTIONS (See XIV.3.B., page 256)

Both Hume and Schelling, whom I quoted on 'obvious ness', recognize the continuation of the *status quo* as an 'obvious' solution to disagreements; and it is surely a familiar experience to find that even if nearly all the members of a group are dissatisfied with an existing rule or practice it is impossible to get even rough consensus on any single alternative. Hume's own example is property.

> 'Tis evident, then, that their first difficulty, in this situation, after the general convention for the establishment of society, and for the constancy of possession, is, how to separate their possessions, and assign to each his particular portion, which he must for the future inalterably enjoy. This difficulty will not detain them long; but it must immediately occur to them, as the most natural expedient, that every one continue to enjoy what he is at present master of, and that property or constant possession be conjoin'd to the immediate possession. Such is the effect of custom, that it not only reconciles us to any thing we have long enjoy'd, but even gives us an affection for it, and makes us prefer it to other objects, which may be more valuable, but are less known to us. What has long lain under our eye, and has often been employ'd to our advantage, *that* we are always the most unwilling to part with; but can easily live without possessions, which we never have enjoy'd, and are not accustom'd to. 'Tis evident, therefore, that men wou'd easily acquiesce in this expedient, *that every one continue to enjoy what he is at present possess'd of;* and this is the reason why they wou'd so naturally agree in preferring it. (*A Treatise of Human Nature*, pp. 503–4.)

But this example illustrates the limitations of the *status quo* as a solution. First, there must *be* a *status quo*: the rule to do what has been done before is no use if one is in a new situation (e.g. colonizing an empty continent). And, second, the *status quo* has very little persuasive power in itself when once people start to question the basis of a traditional arrangement; and this is more likely to happen the more difference it makes precisely *what* the arrangement is (i.e. the less true it is to say: 'It doesn't matter much what the arrangement is so long as we have *some* arrangement').

If something more immediately 'obvious' is called for, 'equality' is probably the strongest candidate. Schelling notes:

> ... the remarkable frequency with which long negotiations over complicated quantitative formulas or *ad hoc* shares in some costs or benefits converge on something as crudely simple as equal shares, shares proportionate to some common magnitude (gross national product, population, foreign-exchange deficit, and so forth), or the shares agreed on in some previous but logically irrelevant negotiation. (*The Strategy of Conflict*, p. 67.)

As Berlin puts it:

> The assumption is that equality needs no reasons, only inequality does. . . .
> If I have a cake and there are ten persons among whom I wish to divide
> it, then if I give exactly one tenth to each, this will not, at any rate auto-
> matically, call for justification; whereas if I depart from this principle of
> equal division I am expected to produce a special reason. ('Equality',
> in Olafson (ed.), p. 131.)

Moreover, the magnetic power of equality is evidenced by the fact that
so many different ideological starting points have led to equality as an
ideal. Rational self-interested citizens need not hold any of these
ideologies, but they could hardly fail to be impressed by the 'natural-
ness' of equality. For example, there is a natural law/natural right
tradition which claims the natural equality of all men; sometimes the
claim has a religious basis. Kant treated equality as an 'ideal of reason';
and in our own time many people would simply say that equality is
'right' or 'fair' without offering a metaphysical underpinning. In a quite
different tradition, utilitarians from Hume and Bentham to F. Y. Edgeworth and Pigou held that, since money has a diminishing marginal
utility, equal distribution will tend to maximize the utility derived
from any given sum. (For Hume, see *An Enquiry Concerning the Principles
of Morals* (Open Court Books, 1960), Section III, Part II. There is no
corresponding passage in the *Treatise*. For Bentham, see for an exhaustive discussion, Halévy, *Growth of Philosophical Radicalism*, Chapter
2. Edgeworth's views may be found in 'The Pure Theory of Taxation'
and Pigou's in *The Economics of Welfare* (London, 1948).) And on a
different tack, John Rawls, in his paper 'Justice as Fairness', derives
this 'original equality' directly from an assumption that the participants in a practice 'are sufficiently equal in power and ability to
guarantee that in normal circumstances none is able to dominate the
others' (p. 86). C. B. MacPherson brings out an analogous feature of
Hobbes' theory when he says:

> Hobbes takes it that an equality of fact sets up an equality of right,
> without bringing in any outside value judgement or moral premisses.
> He does not prove that fact entails right, he simply assumes that it does
> because there is no reason why it should not. There is no reason why any
> man *should* conceive himself above others; hence it is self-evident that he
> should not. (*The Political Theory of Possessive Individualism* (Oxford, 1962),
> p. 75. The equality of fact in question is the ability any man has to kill
> any other.)

However, equality too is not without its difficulties. Where there is
a fixed amount of something (good or bad) to be shared out, equal
shares may well be a workable solution. But what if the way in which
things are shared in period *t* affects the amount available for sharing in

period $t + 1$? For example, what if equal incomes, by removing incentive, would reduce the total amount to be divided? Rawls suggests that in this sort of case equality should be taken as the baseline from which proposed deviations are to be measured.

> ... an inequality is allowed only if there is reason to believe that the practice with the inequality, or resulting from it, will work for the advantage of *every* party engaging in it. Here it is important to stress that *every* party must gain from the inequality. Since the principle applies to practices, it implies that the representative man in every office or position defined by a practice, when he views it as a going concern, must find it reasonable to prefer his condition and prospects with the inequality to what they would be under the practice without it. The principle excludes, therefore, the justification of inequalities on the grounds that the disadvantages of those in one position are outweighed by the greater advantages of those in another position. (p. 83.)

(Incidentally, on p. 84 n. 6, Rawls claims Hume as a predecessor, in virtue of the *Treatise*, Book III, Part II, section II. Since I have already used exactly the same passages in a different context I should perhaps explain the difference in interpretation. There is no doubt that Hume says that 'every single person must find himself a gainer in balancing the account'. But the question is: what is each person to compare with the results of enforced and stable rules, in deciding whether he is 'a gainer' from them? Rawls implies that the relevant comparison is with a set of rules which prescribe equality, but I do not find this idea anywhere in the *Treatise*. All that Hume seems to require is that each participant in the practice should be a net gainer *compared to a situation with no enforced rules at all*. And, as I said earlier, Hume's only contribution (in the *Treatise*) to specifying what particular rules should be chosen is that the set-up already in existence should be continued, or failing that, any rule which impresses itself on the imagination should be chosen.)

The snag with the Rawlsian solution from the present point of view is that it reintroduces all the opportunities for deadlock which the rule of 'equality' was intended to remove, since there is infinite room for disagreement as to the overall effects of any particular inequality. Moreover, the question whether a particular incentive will be 'sufficient' to elicit the desired redirection of effort can only be regarded as a factual question at all when the numbers of people involved is large and they cannot concert their actions. If these conditions are not met the people concerned can *say* how much they will require to alter their behaviour; and this is not a prediction but a statement of intention. Asking the representatives of an industry what concessions they would 'need' to meet a certain investment or export target is in fact to open negotiations with them, even if the process is called 'consultation'. (Professor Beer has expressed the point by saying that if a psychologist could ask his laboratory rat how much cheese he would require to make him run through the maze he would no doubt reply: 'A great big lump.' That is the position when industrialists (or any other organized groups) are asked to name their own incentives.)

(V) EXTERNAL COSTS AND INEFFICIENCY
(See XIV.4.B., page 258)

The solution to the problem of external costs (understanding the expression in its usual sense) which is put forward by Buchanan and Tullock violates the standard conditions for a Pareto-optimal position. (These are given, for example, in Little's *A Critique of Welfare Economics*, Chapters 8 and 9; and in W. J. Baumol, *Welfare Economics and the Theory of the State* (Harvard, 1952), Chapters 3 and 4.) Because external costs are not represented in the costs of a firm the costs taken into account by the firm are not the total costs involved in production. Firms will therefore be located so as to minimize only that part of the cost of production which will be borne by them, rather than to minimize the *sum* of their own costs and those imposed on the local residents. It is important to see that this basic inefficiency is in no way mitigated by the fact that it may sometimes be worth while for the residents in the neighbourhood to pay the firm to suppress its external costs. The factory will always be located wherever it is most profitable when making smoke, because the owners know that they do not have to accept an offer from the residents in the area for suppressing the smoke unless it is even more profitable than letting the smoke continue.

It may be said that this inefficiency could be avoided if residents always bought off prospective factory builders before the factory was built. There are two answers to this. Firstly, in many cases the external cost would not be so high nor the cost of smoke abatement so low as to make it profitable to buy off the firm. Nevertheless, output would be compared to the optimal position 'too large' and prices 'too low'. Secondly, a willingness to buy off everyone who threatened to make a nuisance in the neighbourhood would be rash. It would put a premium on antisocial conduct. If air pollution is to be a source of profit, why should not an enterprising rascal buy up vacant lots all over the country and threaten nearby residents that he will put up some noisome factory unless he is bought off? The householders would presumably be glad to reach for their cheque books when the letter came. A factory already in operation could be equally unscrupulous at great profit to itself. If it can either make smoke (noise, smell, etc.) or not make it, what is to stop it threatening to make smoke unless it is bought off? This is a perfectly possible move even if making smoke does not involve a saving in production cost itself. Or, if a more domestic example is preferred, a man who knows he would have to be paid for *not* keeping pigs in his backyard, *not* running a pneumatic drill all night, etc. would be able to make quite a fortune before some neighbour, wisely taking the law into his own hands, shot him dead.

(W) INEQUITY AS INEFFICIENCY (See XIV.4.B., page 258)

Although Buchanan and Tullock do not accept the validity of any ethical consideration except that of inefficiency, they do nevertheless admit that not even a rational egoist could avoid looking at the distribution of the pie as well as its size. Indeed they have to admit this in order to save their theory; for if the only criterion of an 'efficient' set-up (that is, one acceptable in prospect to a rational egoist) is that no further bargains are possible which will make everyone better off, there is no point in insisting on unanimity for distributive changes. If fifty-one per cent (or for that matter one per cent) of a group propose to kill the rest and have the power to, this is only a straightforwardly 'inefficient' outcome if there is some alternative which would make everyone better off. For example, the prospective victims might be able to persuade the others that they would be more useful to them alive as slaves. If so, though, we have to say that then slavery would be 'efficient'. And of course the oppressors might (like the Nazis *vis-à-vis* the Jews) still prefer the luxury of killing their victims to the sordid utilitarianism of enslaving them.

Faced with this result Buchanan and Tullock decide to extend the notion of efficiency (Pareto-optimality). They now say (Chapter 13) that someone who is deciding what constitution to support should consider the distribution of welfare which is likely to occur under any given constitution. If income has a diminishing marginal utility, a more equal distribution within a society of a given total income should be preferred to a less equal one—unless of course you expect to get one of the high incomes. The authors are, however, extremely nebulous about the institutions a rational egoist should favour as a means to 'efficient distribution' and immediately say (p. 194) that the redistribution would be likely to go 'too far' if thrown open to majority vote. Nevertheless the admission that a rational egoist would be concerned with distribution is an extremely significant breach in the authors' position and it is rather surprising that so little is made of it. For in this admission they allow that, even without taking the costs of bargaining into consideration at all, a rational egoist might throw open income distribution, however hesitantly, to less than unanimous voting.

I raise the general question whether redistribution under majority voting may be expected to 'go too far' in XV.4.C. Here I want only to argue that having external costs imposed on one by others, or having to pay for the removal of an external cost imposed on one by others, is a gratuitous loss which a rational egoist might well seek to avoid. The fact that such costs, as far as anyone can tell in advance, are likely to be distributed in a random way and are also likely to be heavy for particular individuals, shows that all the elements which make it rational to support intervention are present. The reason why the authors do not accept that it would be rational to support the suppression of external costs without compensation appears to be a confused amalgam of two factors. The first is their obsession with the idea of gains from trade; but this has no relevance to the present issue. The case for allowing compensation payments is independent of the question: who should be compensating whom? Suppose it is worth £10 to you not to have to clear the weeds from your yard and it is worth £9 to me to have you clear them; nobody else is involved. Clearly the efficient solution is for the weeds to remain. But this will occur equally well whether the rule is that you can let the weeds grow unless I can persuade you to remove them or whether it is that you have to clear them unless you can persuade me to let you off. The only difference—and it is not a small one—is that in the second case you have to pay me £9 to withdraw my opposition whereas in the first case you can cause me £9 of damage with impunity. And, conversely, if it is worth £10 to me to have you clear the weeds and only worth £9 to you not to clear them, the weeds will be cleared either way; but in one case you have to do it for nothing while in the other I have to bribe you £9 to do it. In short, all the authors have established is that it is better to allow people the choice of suppressing external costs or paying compensation than to insist that they always suppress the external costs. But they have not established the inefficiency of a 'suppress or compensate' system.

The second factor is a curiously limited idea of coercion which virtually confines it to the penalties of the law; but if we take a broader view and say that it is coercion when you are made to do something you don't want to by the threat of something worse unless you do, we can surely say that someone who has to pay a sum of money to avoid being made even worse off by smoke or some other nuisance, is being coerced into paying the money. (Substitute 'loss of reputation' for 'smoke' and you have a precise definition of blackmail.)

It is of course true that someone who is prevented from or made to pay compensation for imposing costs on others is thereby made worse off than he would have been without these restrictions. According to Buchanan and Tullock, being made worse off without one's own permission is exactly what is meant by an external cost—at least on their definition. A blackmailer might thus say that 'external costs' are imposed on him by a law which forbids him to ply his trade; but once we realize that any suppression of anti-social activities is included in this vastly extended use of 'external cost' we can avoid being impressed.

(X) BRIBERY WITH BARGAINING COSTS
(See XV.2.B., page 263)

The first limitation on the analysis of the text is the one already mentioned: the cost of bargaining must be greater than the loss resultant on the measure's passing (in this case £2. 10s. or £2. 9s., depending on whether or not one is among those who get the bribe). When one thinks of the amount of organization needed to induce enough people to sign a form saying they agree (under pain of some penalty) not to vote for the measure provided a sufficient number of others do likewise to block the measure, and then to publicize the fact that enough signatures had been obtained, this hardly seems a strong condition. It is a particularly weak condition in that all those who stand to lose from the measure's being passed stand to lose an equal small amount, for this means that even if the total cost of organizing resistance were lower than the total loss, resistance would still not take place (among egoists) unless those who organized the resistance were reimbursed for their time, effort and expense by all the rest. Where there are a few large losers we generally find them taking the lead in organizing opposition, because it may well then pay them to do so even without reimbursement from those less affected.

Let us suppose, then, that the cost of organizing collective resistance is too high. Each person is now thrown back on himself: he must decide what to do, making the best guess he can about what others will do, but not supposing that anything *he* does will alter anything *they* do. How, if he is a rational egoist, will he go about the calculation? First he must estimate the chance that his own vote, if switched by the bribe from adding a vote against the harmful proposal to adding one in favour of it, would be decisive in altering the result of the referendum or election. Then he must multiply this probability by the amount he stands to lose if the measure is passed, and compare the resultant amount with the size of the bribe. If the first is larger he should refuse the bribe and vote against the measure; if the second is larger he should take the bribe. This is also the method by which a rational self-interested person would decide whether to contribute to some communal provision, as was pointed out in Note S.

On the formula just given it will be rational to take a bribe which is only a tenth of the damage one anticipates from the measure if it is passed, unless one believes that one has more than a one in ten chance of casting the deciding vote. It is difficult to imagine that one could often be confident of this in a group of, say, a thousand voters; in a group of a hundred thousand the probability that one will swing the result by voting one way or the other must surely be tiny unless one has special knowledge that the result of the vote will be close. And how could this happen when everyone is calculating on the same lines as oneself, and everyone knows that everyone is doing so, and . . . ?

Mr Plamenatz has asked at this point: 'Why, if voters stand to lose 50s., should an offer of 1s. cause them to rush to apply? Are you assuming that each voter knows only that he stands to lose? Or that the cost of finding out what others stand to lose exceeds 50s.?' I do not assume either of these things, though they might of course sometimes be true. All I assume is that nobody believes that his own decision will alter the decisions of others. (His own decision may indeed alter the *result* of the vote; but I have argued that the probability of one's own vote swinging the result single-handed is very low.) Once the point is conceded that one voter's decision does not influence another voter's decision and that there is a very low probability of his vote's changing the outcome, we have a classical 'Prisoners' Dilemma' situation:

	Column Measure Passes	Measure Fails
Accept Bribe, Vote For	— 49s.	+ 1s.
Row Refuse Bribe, Vote Against	— 50s.	0

Fig. 6

Here we consider one voter, Row, and his payoffs. Disregarding any effect his own vote might have on whether the measure passes it is plain that he is better off accepting the bribe whether the measure passes or not. Either way he stands to gain a shilling. Now cease to disregard the chance that his own vote may be decisive for the result of the referendum. (In technical terms, cease to regard 'Column' as 'Nature' with autonomous probabilities of 'choosing' one strategy rather than the other.) The situation is still not altered unless the chance of Row's vote being decisive is high enough to make it worth risking

the loss of the shilling (o instead of 1s. or −50s. instead of −49s.);
and I have suggested that this is unlikely to happen.

(Y) POWER-DIFFUSION AND MAJORITY APPROVAL
(See XV.3.A., page 274)

Banfield argues that where a power-diffusing system is established it
can't be too bad because a majority could always change it.

> The distribution of influence may be viewed as the outcome (as of a given
> moment) of a continuing 'game' which has been going on under rules
> that a majority of the players have been free to change at any time. That
> the rules are as they are implies that they seem fair, over the long run,
> to most of the players. Accordingly, the outcome at any particular time
> is also fair, even though some players are losing. (*Political Influence*, p. 331.)

But this is dubious, for in a system where substantive decisions can
normally be blocked by any determined minority it is likely that constitutional changes and informal political changes (e.g. in party structure) affecting the distribution of power will also be capable of being
blocked by a minority. If there is a minority which finds a *net interest*
in a power-diffusing system (as distinct from gaining sometimes and
losing sometimes with the gains and losses either cancelling out or
leaving a net debit) then the existence of such a minority would be
enough to explain the continued existence of a power-diffusing system,
once established. Schattschneider has argued forcefully in *The Semisovereign People* (New York, 1960) that there is such a minority which
benefits from the fragmentation of decision-making power.

> Special-interest organizations are most easily formed when they deal with
> small numbers of individuals who are actually aware of their exclusive
> interests. To describe the conditions of pressure-group politics in this way
> is, however, to say that it is primarily a business phenomenon. (p. 35.)
> The bias of the [pressure] system is shown by the fact that even non-
> business organizations reflect an upper-class tendency. (p. 33.)
> The flaw in the pluralist heaven is that the heavenly chorus sings with
> a strong upper-class accent. Probably about 90 per cent of the people
> cannot get into the pressure system. (p. 35.)

And Norton Long has drawn the conclusion from this in *The Polity*:

> As long as the control of strong points in state and national legislatures,
> the weakness of party organization, and the effectiveness of pressure
> group action offer ample means to the business classes in the community
> to protect their short run vested interests, it is doubtful indeed that they

will leave their well prepared defensive positions for the open field of party warfare. (p. 26.)

There is no more reason to believe that the beneficiaries of this system would part with it voluntarily than that those sectors of the community enjoying the advantages of gross over-representation would willingly part with their entrenched vested interest. (p. 32.)

(Z) WOULD AN EGOIST VOTE? (See XV.4.B., page 281)

Mr Plamenatz has commented on my criticism of Downs: 'Why isn't it worth [someone's] while to vote, if he's afraid of the system collapsing as a result of people failing to vote?' The trouble here lies, I would suggest, in the transition from discussing *one* man's decision as to whether or not he will vote to mentioning his belief that the system will collapse as a result of *people* failing to vote. It is true, of course, that our individual voter trying to make up his mind is one of the relevant 'people' but he is *only* one. From an egoistic point of view it is only worth his while to vote if the system will collapse if *he* doesn't vote (not if *people* don't vote). Or, more exactly, it is only worth his while to vote if the cost of voting (time, trouble, shoe-leather, etc.) is exceeded by the expected value of the unpleasantness of the system's collapsing multiplied by the probability that his vote will single-handedly stave off such a collapse. Remember that since he is an egoist there is no point in saying to him 'What would happen if everyone thought like you?', for this is irrelevant unless you can show that how he thinks will have a significant effect on how others think (and act).

Mr Plamenatz also writes:

> Your argument, if it applies at all, must apply to rational altruists as much as to rational egoists. It is an argument about what it is worth one man's while to do where consequences depend on the actions of thousands.

But it is not clear to me that this is so. If someone were willing to adopt the whole community as his reference-group one could put both distributive and aggregative arguments of considerable plausibility to him. On distributive grounds one could argue (on the Kantian, anti-'free-rider' principle) that it is unfair not to vote when others are taking the trouble to do so. (Notice this does not introduce the invalid assumption that one's voting will somehow *make* others vote.) And on aggregative grounds one could argue that nothing else one could do with the half hour needed to vote would be more conducive to the *general* welfare, of which one's own welfare is, of course, only a tiny constituent part.

The reason why it may pay every member of a group (each taking himself only as reference-group) to do something which, if they all do it, leads to common disaster, is not that 'consequences depend on the actions of thousands' but rather that the consequences of the individual act affect thousands as much as they affect the agent. Suppose (disregarding all consequences) I would rather have 5s. than vote. (For example, I would slightly sooner work for the half hour it takes to vote and I would make 5s. in the time.) Then, taking only myself into consideration, it is not worth my voting unless the expected (negative) value of the consequences of not voting is greater than 5s. (For example, if I put the loss to me represented by the overthrow of the system at £10,000 there must be over one chance in 40,000 that my not voting will single-handedly produce that outcome.) It may well be, on this calculation, that the expected (negative) value of not voting is less than 5s., so it isn't worth my while to vote. But it may well be worth my voting if I am concerned with maximizing well-being in the community as a whole. For example, say that the expected (negative) value of my not voting is a halfpenny to me; from *my* selfish viewpoint I lose 4s. 11½d. by voting; but if the rest of the community consists of 48 million people and they all rate the cost of the regime's collapse as I do, the total cost to the community of my own not voting is £100,000! On almost any basis, I would surely vote if I were altruistically inclined, even though it cost me 4s. 11½d.

A community faced with this 'Prisoners' Dilemma' situation in real life could, of course, prevent collapse even if the whole population were egoists by rigging the incentives, i.e. fining non-voters or paying voters. Provided the incentive were sufficient to make voting attractive to an adequate proportion of the electorate the problem would be solved. In practice, however, the practical problem is averted by the fact that many people either think they have a duty to vote and act on it or take a positive satisfaction in voting. Almond and Verba, in *The Civic Culture*, report that in their sample, the following percentages of those who had voted in the last three national elections or in recent local elections said that they 'feel satisfaction in going to the polls' (p. 146):

USA	..	..	..	71
UK	..	..	..	43
Germany	..	..	35
Italy	..	..	..	30
Mexico	..	..	..	34

So long as an adequate proportion of the electorate either think they have a duty to vote or feel satisfaction in voting as a symbolic or expressive function it is not necessary to introduce incentives. Nor, incidentally, it is either necessary *or possible* to say that people have a duty to vote if the number who enjoy voting is large enough by itself; for in that case neither the aggregative nor the distributive argument works. The aggregative argument doesn't work because there is *no* probability of the system's collapsing without your vote; and the distributive argument doesn't work because you can perfectly well will everyone to act on the maxim: 'Only vote if you enjoy it (so long as you happen to know enough people enjoy it to keep the system afloat).'

BIBLIOGRAPHY

ABEL-SMITH, BRIAN. 'Whose Welfare State?' in Norman MacKenzie (ed.), *Conviction*, London, 1958.

ABRAMS, MARK. 'The *Socialist Commentary* Survey' in Mark Abrams and Richard Rose, *Must Labour Lose?* Penguin Books, Ltd., 1960, pp. 11–58.

AGAR, H. *The Price of Union*, Boston, 1950.

ALBU, AUSTEN. 'The Organisation of Industry' in R. H. S. Crossman (ed.), *New Fabian Essays*, London, 1952, pp. 121–142.

ALCHIAN, A. A. 'The Meaning of Utility Measurement', *American Economic Review*, XLIII (March 1953), pp. 26–50.

ALLEN, WALTER. *All in a Lifetime*, London, 1959.

ALMOND, G. and VERBA, S. *The Civic Culture*, Princeton, 1963.

American Political Science Association. 'Towards a More Responsible Two-Party System', *American Political Science Review* (Supplement), XLIV, No. 3 (September 1950).

APPLEBY, PAUL H. *Morality and Administration in Democratic Government*, Baton Rouge, 1952.

ARNOLD, THURMAN. *The Folklore of Capitalism*, New Haven, 1937.

ARROW, KENNETH. *Social Choice and Individual Values*, New York, 1951.

BANFIELD, EDWARD C. 'A Critique of Foreign Aid Doctrines' in C. J. Friedrich (ed.), *Public Policy*, Cambridge, Mass., 1962.

—— 'The Future Metropolis', *Daedalus* (Winter, 1961), pp. 61–78.

—— *Political Influence*, Glencoe, Ill., 1961.

BARRY, BRIAN M. 'Justice and the Common Good', *Analysis*, XXI, No. 4 n.s. (March 1961), pp. 86–91.

—— 'The Public Interest', *Proceedings of the Aristotelian Society*, Supplementary Volume XXXVIII (1964), pp. 1–18.

BAUMOL, W. J. *Welfare Economics and the Theory of the State*, Cambridge, Mass., 1952.

BEARD, CHARLES A. *The Idea of National Interest*, New York, 1934.

BEDFORD, SYBILLE. *The Faces of Justice*, London, 1961.

BEER, SAMUEL H. 'New Structures of Democracy' in W. N. Chambers and R. H. Salisbury (eds.), *Democracy Today*, Collier Books, New York, 1962.

BELL, STOUGHTON. *Trustee Ethics*, Kansas City, 1935.

BENN, S. I. and PETERS, R. S. *Social Principles and the Democratic State*, London, 1959.

BENN, S. I. 'Interests in Politics', *Proceedings of the Aristotelian Society*, LX (1959–1960).

BENTHAM, JEREMY. *The Theory of Legislation*, London, 1931.

BENTLEY, ARTHUR F. *The Process of Government*, Indiana, 1949.

BERLE, ADOLF A., JR. *The 20th Century Capitalist Revolution*, Harvest Books, 1954.

BERLIN, SIR ISAIAH. 'Equality', *Proceedings of the Aristotelian Society*, Supplementary Volume, LVI (1955–1956). Reprinted in Frederick A. Olafson (ed.), *Justice and Social Policy*, Spectrum Books, 1961.

—— *Two Concepts of Liberty*, Oxford, 1958.

BLACK, DUNCAN. 'Wicksell's Theory in the Distribution of Taxation' in J. K. Eastham (ed.), *Economic Essays in Commemoration of the Dundee School of Economics 1931–1955*, Dundee, 1955.

—— *The Theory of Committees and Elections*, Cambridge, 1958.

BLOOMFIELD, LEONARD. *Language*, New York, 1933.

BOULDING, KENNETH. *The Organizational Revolution*, New York, 1953.

BRAITHWAITE, M. 'Words', *Proceedings of the Aristotelian Society*, LIV (1953–1954), pp. 209–232.

BRAITHWAITE, R. B. *The Theory of Games as a Tool for the Moral Philosopher*. Cambridge, 1955.

BROAD, C. D. *Five Types of Ethical Theory*. London, 1930.

BRYCE, JAMES. *The American Commonwealth*, New York, 1910.

BUCHANAN, JAMES M. 'Knut Wicksell on Marginal Cost Pricing', *Southern Economic Journal* XVIII (October 1951), pp. 173–178.

—— 'Wicksell on Fiscal Reform: Comment', *American Economic Review*, XLII (September 1952), pp. 599–602.

—— 'Social Choice, Democracy and Free Markets', *Journal of Political Economy*, LXII (1954), pp. 114–123.

—— 'Positive Economics, Welfare Economics, and Political Economy', *Journal of Law and Economics*, II (1959), pp. 124–138. Also in J. M. Buchanan, *Fiscal Theory and Political Economy*, Chapel Hill, 1960.

—— and TULLOCK, GORDON. *The Calculus of Consent*, Ann Arbor, 1962.

BULLITT, STIMSON. *To Be A Politician*, Anchor Books, 1961.

BUTLER, JOSEPH (BISHOP). *Sermons*, edited W. R. Matthews, London, 1914.

CANNAN, E. [essay] in American Economic Association, *Readings in the Economics of Taxation*, London, 1959.

CARTER, A. 'Too Many People', *Fabian Society*, (1963).

CHAMBERLAIN, N. W. *A General Theory of Economic Process*, New York, 1955.

COASE, R. H. 'The Problem of Social Cost', *Journal of Law and Economics*, III (October 1960).

COLE, LAMONT C. Review of Rachel Carson, *Silent Spring*. *Scientific American* (November 1962), pp. 173–180.

CRANSTON, M. *Human Rights Today*, Ampersand Books, 1962.

CROSLAND, C. A. R. *The Future of Socialism*, London, 1956.

—— *The Conservative Enemy*, London, 1962.

CROSSMAN, R. H. S. 'The Ultimate Conservative—Professor Michael Oakeshott' in R. H. S. Crossman, *The Charm of Politics*, London, 1958, pp. 134–138.

DAHL, ROBERT A. *A Preface to Democratic Theory*, Chicago, 1956.

—— and LINDBLOM, CHARLES E. *Politics, Economics and Welfare*, New York, 1953.

DEVLIN, LORD PATRICK. *The Enforcement of Morals*. Proceedings of the British Academy, 1959.

DOWNS, ANTHONY. *An Economic Theory of Democracy*, New York, 1957.

—— 'Why the Government Budget in a Democracy is Too Small', *World Politics*, XII, No. 4 (July 1960), pp. 541–563.

—— 'In Defense of Majority Voting', *Journal of Political Economy*, LXIX (1961), pp. 192 ff.

DUNHAM, ALISON. 'City Planning: An Analysis of the Content of the Master Plan', *Journal of Law and Economics*, I (October 1958), pp. 170–186.

EDGEWORTH, F. Y. 'The Pure Theory of Taxation' in R. A. Musgrave and A. T. Peacock, *Classics in the Theory of Public Finance*, London, 1958.

EDWARDS, PAUL. *The Logic of Moral Discourse*, Glencoe, Ill., 1955.

EYSENCK, H. J. *Uses and Abuses of Psychology*, Penguin Books, Ltd., 1954.

FAGAN, ELMER D. 'Recent and Contemporary Theories of Progressive Taxation' in American Economic Association, *Readings in the Economics of Taxation*, London, 1959. pp. 19–53.

FEINBERG, J. 'Justice and Personal Desert' in J. W. Chapman and C. J. Friedrich (eds.), *Nomos VI: Justice*, New York, 1963.

FITZGERALD, P. J. 'Voluntary and Involuntary Acts' in A. G. Guest (ed.), *Oxford Essays in Jurisprudence*. Oxford, 1961. pp. 1–28.

FRANK, JOHN P. *Mr Justice Black: The Man and His Opinions*, New York, 1949.

'Franks Report'. Report of the Committee on Administrative Tribunals and Enquiries. Cmnd. 218 (1957).

FRIEDMAN, MILTON. 'The Role of Government in Education' in Robert A. Solo (ed.), *Economics and the Public Interest*, New Brunswick, N.J., 1955.

FULLER, LON. *The Forms and Limits of Adjudication* (mimeographed).

GALBRAITH, J. K. *The Affluent Society*, London, 1958.

GALBRAITH, J. K. *American Capitalism: The Concept of Countervailing Power*, London, 1958.

GEWIRTH, A. 'Political Justice' in R. Brandt, ed., *Social Justice*, Englewood Cliffs, 1962.

GINSBERG, M. 'On the Diversity of Morals' in Ginsberg, *Essays in Sociology and Social Philosophy*, I, Mercury Books, 1962.

GODWIN, WILLIAM. *An Enquiry Concerning Political Justice*, edited by R. A. Preston, 1926.

GREEN, T. H. *Lectures on the Principles of Political Obligation*, London, 1960.

GRICE, H. P. 'Meaning', *Philosophical Review*, LXVI (1957), pp. 377–388.

GUTHRIE, TYRONE. Article in *The Observer* (12 March 1961).

HAGAN, C. B. 'The Group in Political Science' in Roland Young (ed.), *Approaches to the Study of Politics*, London, 1958.

HALÉVY, ELIE. *The Growth of Philosophical Radicalism*, Beacon Books, 1955.

HALLOWELL, JOHN. *The Moral Foundation of Democracy*, Chicago, 1954.

HAMMOND, J. L. 'The Growth of Common Enjoyment' (L. T. Hobhouse Memorial Lecture No. 3, 1933) in *Hobhouse Memorial Lectures 1930–1940*, Oxford, 1948.

HARE, R. M. *The Language of Morals*, Oxford, 1952.

—— 'Universalizability', *Aristotelian Society*, LV (1954–1955).

—— *Freedom and Reason*, Oxford, 1963.

HART, H. L. A. 'Negligence, *Mens Rea* and Criminal Responsibility' in A. G. Guest (ed.), *Oxford Essays in Jurisprudence*, Oxford, 1961, pp. 29–49.

HAYEK, FRIEDRICH AUGUST VON. *The Road to Serfdom*, Phoenix Books, 1954.

—— *The Constitution of Liberty*, London, 1960.

HECKSCHER, AUGUST. 'Public Works and Public Happiness', *Saturday Review* (4 August 1962).

HERRING, E. PENDLETON. *Public Administration and the Public Interest*, New York, 1936.

—— *The Politics of Democracy*, New York, 1940

HICKS, J. R. 'The Rehabilitation of Consumers' Surplus', *Review of Economic Studies*, VIII, No. 2 (February 1941).

—— *Value and Capital*, Oxford, 1946.

—— *A Revision of Demand Theory*, Oxford, 1956.

—— 'The Measurement of Real Income', *Oxford Economic Papers* (1958).

HITCH, CHARLES J. and MCKEAN, ROLAND N. *The Economics of Defense in the Nuclear Age*, Cambridge, Mass., 1960.

HOBHOUSE, L. T. *Elements of Social Justice*, London, 1922.

HOLCOMBE, A. N. *Our More Perfect Union*, Cambridge, Mass., 1950.

HOLMES, OLIVER WENDELL, JR. 'The Path of the Law' in Perry Miller (ed.), *American Thought from the Civil War to the First World War*, New York, 1954.

HOMANS, GEORGE C. *The Human Group*, New York, 1950.

HUME, DAVID. *An Enquiry Concerning the Principles of Morals*, Open Court Books, 1960.

—— 'Of the Dignity or Meanness of Human Nature' and 'Of the Independence of Parliament' in Charles Hendel (ed.), *David Hume's Political Essays*, New York, 1953.

—— *A Treatise of Human Nature*, edited by L. A. Selby-Bigge, Oxford (1st edition), 1888.

JOUVENEL, BERTRAND DE. *Sovereignty: An Enquiry into Political Goal*, Cambridge, 1957.

KARIEL, HENRY S. *The Decline of American Pluralism*, Stanford, 1961.

KENNAN, GEORGE F. *American Diplomacy 1900–1950*, Mentor Books, 1952.

KEY, V. O. 'Public Opinion and the Decay of Democracy', *The Virginia Quarterly Review*, XXXVII, No. 4 (Autumn, 1961), pp. 481–494.

KNIGHT, F. H. *Freedom and Reform: Essays in Economics and Social Philosophy*, New York, 1947.

KORNHAUSER, WILLIAM. *The Politics of Mass Society*, London, 1960.

LAMONT, W. D. *Principles of Moral Judgement*, Oxford, 1946.

—— *The Value Judgement*, Edinburgh, 1955.

LANE, ROBERT E. 'The Fear of Equality', *American Political Science Review*, LIII (1959).

LANGER, SUSANNE K. *Philosophy in a New Key*, Mentor Books, 1948.

LASKI, H. J. *The Grammar of Politics*, 4th edition, London, 1937.

LEWIS, SIR GEORGE CORNEWALL. *Remarks on the Use and Abuse of Some Political Terms*, London, 1832.

LEYDEN, W. VON. 'On Justifying Inequality', *Political Studies*, XI, No. 1 (February, 1963), pp. 56–70.

LEYS, WAYNE A. R. *Ethics for Policy Decisions*, New York, 1952.

LIEBLING, A. J. *The Press*, Ballantine Books, New York, 1961.

LINDSAY, A. D. *The Essentials of Democracy*, London, 1935.

—— *The Modern Democratic State*, Oxford, 1943.

LIPPMANN, WALTER. *Public Opinion*, New York, 1922.

—— *The Phantom Public*, New York, 1927.

LIPSET, S. and GLAZIER, N. 'The Polls on Communism and Conformity' in Daniel Bell (ed.), *The New American Right*, New York, 1955.

LIPSEY, R. G. and LANCASTER, R. K. 'The General Theory of Second Best', *Review of Economic Studies*, XXIV (1956–1957), pp. 11–33.

LITTLE, I. M. D. 'Social Choice and Individual Values', *Journal of Political Economy*, LX, No. 5 (October 1952), pp. 422–432.

—— *A Critique of Welfare Economics*, 2nd edition. Oxford, 1957.

LLOYD, DENNIS. *Public Policy*, London, 1953.

LOCKE, JOHN. *The Second Treatise on Civil Government* and *A Letter Concerning Toleration*, edited by J. W. Gough. Oxford, 1948.

LOHMAN, JOSEPH D. and REITZES, DIETRICH C. 'Note on Race Relations in Mass Society', *American Journal of Sociology*, LV, No. 3 (November 1952).

LONG, NORTON E. *The Polity*, ed. Charles Press, Chicago, 1962.

LOVEJOY, A. O. *The Great Chain of Being*, Cambridge, Mass., 1948.

MABBOTT, JOHN. *The State and the Citizen*, Grey Arrow Books, 1958.

MCCARTHY, MARY. 'The Contagion of Ideas' in *On the Contrary*, New York, 1961.

MACK, MARY P. *Jeremy Bentham: An Odyssey of Ideas, 1748–1792*, London, 1962.

MACPHERSON, C. B. *The Political Theory of Possessive Individualism*, Oxford, 1962.

MADISON, JAMES. Federalist Paper Number Ten. *The Federalist*, Everyman's Library No. 519, London, 1948.

MAINE, SIR HENRY. *Lectures on the Early History of Institutions*, London, 1914.

MARSCHAK, JACOB. 'Towards an Economic Theory of Organization and Information' in R. M. Thrall, C. H. Coombs and R. L. Davis (eds.), *Decision Processes*, New York, 1954, pp. 187–220.

MARSH, NORMAN S. 'The Rule of Law as a Supra-National Concept' in A. G. Guest (ed.), *Oxford Essays in Jurisprudence*, Oxford, 1961. pp. 223–264.

MARX, KARL and ENGELS, FRIEDRICH. 'Critique of the Gotha Programme', *Selected Works*, II, Moscow, 1962.

MILL, JAMES. *Essay on Government*, Cambridge, 1937.

MILL, JOHN STUART. *Autobiography, On Liberty* and *Utilitarianism* in Max Lerner (ed.), *Essential Works of John Stuart Mill*, Bantam Classic, 1961.

—— *A System of Logic*, London, 1898.

MILLER, J. D. B. *The Nature of Politics* London, 1962.

MILLS, C. WRIGHT. *The Power Elite*, Galaxy Books, 1959.

MINOW, NEWTON N. 'Television and the Public Interest', *Etc.* XVIII, No. 2.

MISES, LUDWIG, EDLER VON. *Human Action: A Treatise on Economics*, London, 1949.

MOORE, G. E. *Principia Ethica*, Cambridge, 1903.

MORRIS, CHARLES W. *Signs, Language and Behavior*, New York, 1946.

MUND, VERNON A. *Government and Business*, 2nd edition, New York, 1955.

MUSGRAVE, R. A. *The Theory of Public Finance*, New York, 1959.

MYRDAL, GUNNAR. *The Political Element in the Development of Economic Theory*, Translated by Paul Streeten, London, 1953.

MYRDAL, GUNNAR. *Value in Social Theory*, Translated by Paul Streeten, London, 1958.

—— *Beyond the Welfare State*, New Haven, 1960.

NAMIER, SIR LEWIS B. 'Human Nature in Politics' in Fritz Stern (ed.), *The Varieties of History*, Meridian Books, 1956.

NEUMANN, J. VON and MORGENSTERN, O. *The Theory of Games and Economic Behavior*, 2nd edition, Princeton, 1947.

NICOLSON, NIGEL. *People and Parliament*, London, 1958.

NISBET, ROBERT ALEXANDER. *The Quest for Community: A Study in the Ethics of Order and Freedom*, New York, 1953.

OAKESHOTT, MICHAEL, 'Political Education' in P. Laslett (ed.), *Philosophy, Politics and Society*, First Series, Oxford, 1956.

—— *Rationalism in Politics*, Methuen Books, 1962.

ORTEGA Y GASSET, J. *The Revolt of the Masses*, London, 1951.

PARETO, VILFREDO. *The Mind and Society* (Trattato di sociologia generale), edited by Arthur Livingston, New York, 1935.

PARSONS, TALCOTT. *The Structure of Social Action*, Glencoe, Ill., 1949.

PETERSON, A. D. C. 'Teachers for the Sixth Form', *The Guardian* (18 December 1962).

PICKLES, WILLIAM. *Not With Europe: The Political Case for Staying Out*, Fabian International Bureau, Tract 336 (April 1962).

PIGOU, A. C. *The Economics of Welfare*, London, 1948.

PLAMENATZ, JOHN. 'Interests', *Political Studies*, II (1954).

POUND, ROSCOE. *Social Control Through Law*, New Haven, 1942.

PRICHARD, HAROLD ARTHUR. 'Does Moral Philosophy Rest on a Mistake?' in Prichard, *Moral Obligation: Essays and Lectures*, Oxford, 1949.

RAPOPORT, ANATOL. *Fights, Games and Debates*, Ann Arbor, 1960.

RAWLS, JOHN B. 'Two Concepts of Rules', *Philosophical Review*, LXIV (1955), pp. 3–32.

—— 'Justice as Fairness', *Philosophical Review*, LXVII (1958), reprinted in Frederick A. Olafson (ed.), *Justice and Social Policy*, Spectrum Books, 1961; and in Peter Laslett and W. G. Runciman (eds.), *Philosophy, Politics and Society*, Second Series, Oxford, 1962.

REDFORD, EMMETTE S. *Ideal and Practice in Public Administration*, University of Alabama, 1958.

RIESMAN, DAVID. *The Lonely Crowd*, Anchor Books, 1950.

RIKER, W. *The Theory of Political Coalitions*, New Haven, 1962.

RITCHIE, D. G. *Natural Rights*, London, 1924.

ROBBINS, LIONEL. *An Essay on the Nature and Significance of Economic Science*, London, 1948.

ROGOW, A. A. and LASSWELL, H. D. *Power, Corruption and Rectitude*, Englewood Cliffs, 1963.

ROLPH, C. H. (ed.). *The Trial of Lady Chatterley*, Penguin Books, Ltd., 1961.

ROSS, E. A. *Social Control: A Survey of the Foundations of Order*, New York, 1922.

ROSS, SIR WILLIAM DAVID. *The Right and the Good*, Oxford, 1930.

—— *Foundations of Ethics*, Oxford, 1939.

ROTHENBERG, JEROME. 'Conditions for a Social Welfare Function', *Journal of Political Economy* (1953).

—— *The Measurement of Social Welfare*, Englewood Cliffs, 1961.

ROUSSEAU, JEAN-JACQUES. *The Social Contract.*

RUSSELL, BERTRAND. 'Freedom and Government' in Ruth Nanda Anshen (ed.), *Freedom, Its Meaning*, New York, 1940. pp. 249–264.

RYLE, GILBERT. *The Concept of Mind*, London, 1949.

SAMUELSON, PAUL A. *Foundations of Economic Analysis*, Cambridge, Mass., 1948.

SCHATTSCHNEIDER, E. E. *Politics, Pressures and the Tariff: A Study of Free Private Enterprise in Pressure Politics, as Shown in the 1929–1930 Revision of the Tariff*, New York, 1935.

—— 'Political Parties and the Public Interest', *Annals of the American Academy of Political and Social Science*, No. 280 (March 1952), pp. 18–26.

—— *The Semisovereign People*, Holt-Rinehart-Winston Books, 1960.

—— *Party Government*, Holt-Rinehart-Winston Books, 1960.

SCHELLING, THOMAS C. *The Strategy of Conflict*, Cambridge, Mass., 1960.

—— 'Reciprocal Measures for Arms Stabilization' in Donald G. Brennan (ed.), *Arms Control, Disarmament and National Security*, New York, 1961.

SCHLESINGER, A. M. JR. *The Coming of the New Deal*, Vol. II of *The Age of Roosevelt*, Cambridge, Mass., 1959.

SCHNEIDER, HERBERT W. *Three Dimensions of Public Morality*, Bloomington, Ind., 1956.

SCHUBERT, GLENDON. 'The Public Interest in Administrative Decision-Making', *American Political Science Review*, LI (June 1957), pp. 346 ff.

—— 'The Theory of the Public Interest in Judicial Decision-Making', *Midwest Journal of Political Science*, II (February 1958), pp. 1 ff.

—— *The Public Interest: A Critique of a Concept*, Illinois, 1961.

—— 'Is There a Public Interest Theory?' in C. J. Friedrich (ed.), *Nomos V: The Public Interest*, New York, 1962. pp. 162–176.

SCHUMPETER, JOSEPH. *Capitalism, Socialism and Democracy*, 3rd edition. New York, 1950.

SCHWARTZ, BERNARD. *The Professor and the Commissions*, New York, 1959.

SCITOVSKY, TIBOR. 'A Note on Welfare Propositions in Economics', *Review of Economic Studies*, IX, No. 2 (1942).

—— 'What Price Economic Progress?' *Yale Review* (1960).

SELF, PETER. *Cities in Flood: The Problems of Urban Growth*, London, 1961.

SHAW, GEORGE BERNARD. *The Intelligent Woman's Guide to Capitalism and Socialism* in *Complete Works*, London, 1949.

SHIRER, WILLIAM L. *The Rise and Fall of the Third Reich*, Crest Reprint, 1962.

SIDGWICK, HENRY. *Lectures on the Ethics of T. H. Green, Mr Herbert Spencer and J. Martineau*, London, 1902.

—— *The Methods of Ethics*, 7th edition, London, 1930.

SIMON, H. A. *Models of Man*, New York, 1957.

SIMON, YVES R. *The Philosophy of Democratic Government*, Chicago, 1951.

SMART, J. J. C. *An Outline of a System of Utilitarian Ethics*, Melbourne, 1961.

SMITH, HOWARD R. *Democracy and the Public Interest*, Athens, Georgia, 1960.

SORAUF, FRANK J. 'The Public Interest Reconsidered,' *Journal of Politics*, XIX (November 1957), pp. 616 ff.

STEFANSSON, VILHJALMUR. 'Was Liberty Invented?' in Ruth Nanda Anshen (ed.), *Freedom, Its Meaning*, New York, 1940.

STEPHEN, SIR LESLIE. *John Stuart Mill*, Vol. III in *The English Utilitarians*, London, 1900.

STEVENSON, C. L. *Ethics and Language*, New Haven, 1944.

STONE, JULIUS. *The Province and Function of Law*, Sydney, 1946.

STONIER, ALFRED and HAGUE, DOUGLAS C. *A Textbook of Economic Theory*, London, 1953.

STOUFFER, SAMUEL. *Communism, Conformity and Civil Liberties*, New York, 1955.

STRAWSON, P. F. *Introduction to Logical Theory*, London, 1952.

SUMNER, W. G. 'The Absurd Effort to Make the World Over' in Perry Miller (ed.), *American Thought: Civil War to World War I*, Rinehart Editions, 1961.

TITMUSS, R. M. *Essays on 'The Welfare State'*, London, 1958.

TOWNSEND, PETER. 'A Society for People' in Norman MacKenzie (ed.), *Conviction*, London, 1958, pp. 93–120.

—— Article in *The Observer* (24 February 1963).

TRUMAN, DAVID B. *The Governmental Process*, New York, 1951.

TUGWELL, REXFORD G. *The Economic Basis of Public Interest*, Wisconsin, 1922.

TULLOCK, GORDON. 'Problems of Majority Voting', *Journal of Political Economy*, LXVII (1959), pp. 571–579.

—— 'Reply to a Traditionalist,' *Journal of Political Economy*, LXIX (1961), pp. 200 ff.

UHR, CARL G. *Economic Doctrines of Knut Wicksell*, Berkeley, 1960.

—— 'Wicksell on Fiscal Reform: Further Comment', *American Economic Review* (June 1953), pp. 366–368.

VAIZEY, JOHN. *The Economics of Education*, London, 1962.

—— Report of a lecture (*The Guardian*, 22 November 1962).

VICKREY, WILLIAM. 'Utility, Strategy and Social Decision Rules,' *The Quarterly Journal of Economics*, LXXIV (1960), pp. 507–536.

VINER, JACOB. 'The Intellectual History of Laissez-Faire', *The Journal of Law and Economics*, III (October 1960).

VLASTOS, G. 'Justice and Equality' in R. Brandt, ed., *Social Justice*, Englewood Cliffs, 1962.

WALLAS, GRAHAM. *Our Social Heritage*, London, 1929.

WEBB, BEATRICE. *Our Partnership*, London, 1948.

WEBB, SIDNEY. *Towards Social Democracy*, Westminster, 1916.

WECHSLER, H. 'Toward Neutral Principles of Constitutional Law', 73 *Harvard Law Review* 1 (1959), pp. 26–35.

WELDON, T. D. 'The Justification of Political Attitudes', *Aristotelian Society Supplement*, XXIX (1955), pp. 115–130.

—— 'Political Principles' in P. Laslett (ed.), *Philosophy, Politics and Society*, First Series, Oxford, 1956, pp. 22–34.

WICKSELL, KNUT. 'A New Principle of Just Taxation' in R. A. Musgrave and A. T. Peacock, (eds.), *Classics in the Theory of Public Finance*, London, 1958, pp. 72–118.

WICKSTEED, PHILIP. *The Common Sense of Political Economy*, London, 1910.

WILLIAMS, RAYMOND. *The Long Revolution*, London, 1961.

WILLOUGHBY, W. W. *Social Justice: A Critical Essay*, New York, 1900.

WILSON, JAMES Q. *Negro Politics: The Search for Leadership*, Glencoe, Ill., 1960.

WITTGENSTEIN, LUDWIG. *Philosophical Investigations*, 2nd edition, Oxford, 1958.

'Wolfenden Report'. Report of the Committee on Homosexual Offences and Prostitution, Cmnd. 247, 1957.

WOLFF, ROBERT PAUL. 'Reflections on Game Theory and the Nature of Value', *Ethics*, LXXII (April 1962), pp. 171–179.

WOLLHEIM, RICHARD. *Socialism and Culture*, Fabian Society, 1961.

—— 'A Paradox in the Theory of Democracy' in Peter Laslett and W. G. Runciman (eds.), *Philosophy, Politics and Society*, Second Series, Oxford, 1962.

WOOTTON, BARBARA. *Social Foundations of Wage Policy*, London, 1958.

YOUNG, MICHAEL. *The Rise of the Meritocracy*, Penguin Books, Ltd., 1961.

ZIFF, PAUL. *Semantic Analysis*, Ithaca, N.Y., 1960.

INDEX

majoritarianism (*contd.*):
— privately oriented wants and, 62–6
— Rousseau and, 292–3
— rule of majority and, 312–16
— sincere and strategic voting and, 294–5
— Wollheim and, 293–4
majority:
— *ad hoc*, 268–74, 276
— interest of, 241, 276, 283
— and offensive use of veto, 246
— power-diffusing system and, 327–8
— qualified, *see* qualified majority voting
— rule of, 312–16
— simple, *see* simple majority voting
— trustworthiness of, 282–3
— *see also* majoritarianism
manipulation of wants, 70–1
marginal cost pricing, 277n
marginal rate of substitution, 7–8
market prices:
— and desert, 112–13
— and public interest, 33–4
— use of, limits on, 277–8
— *see also* price mechanism; subsidy by state
marketable goods, 277–8; *see also* price mechanism
marriage, 211, 310
Marschak, Jacob, 46n
Marsh, N. S., 149n
Marshall, Alfred, 77, 78n
Marx, Karl, 55n, 114, 300
Mason, David T., lviiin
mass society, and liberalism, 83n; 300–1
material interest, concept of, 187n; *see also* interest(s)
material welfare, concept of, 187–8
meaning:
— causal theory of, 17–18
— conventional element in, 20–1
— conventional intention theory of, 22–6
— evaluation and, 27–31
— intention theory of, 18–19
— *see also* normal content of utterance or of form of utterance
medical care, public provision of, 127, 128–32, 134n
merits, discussion on (social decision procedure), *see* discussion on merits (social decision procedure)

Mill, James, 241n
Mill, John Stuart:
— on citizen's role, 78n, 238
— as humanist, 77n
— on equity, 156
— on freedom, 42, 67, 71n, 141n, 142, 144n, 145
— on impartiality, 97n
— on incentives, 114n
— on legislator's job, 81, 238
— on limits of state action, 71n, 142, 213n, 308, 310
— on plurality of values, 4
— on scientific method, 261
— on self-regarding actions, 13n, 71n, 142n
— on utilitarianism, 40n, 296
Miller, David:
— on desert, lvi–lvii, lix–lxii, lxiv, lxi–lxii, lxiv
— on interpretation of texts, xxxi
— on needs, lxv–lxvi, lxviii–lxix
— on social justice, liv, lvi–lvii
— on value pluralism, xl
Miller, J. D. B., 207n
Mills, C. Wright, 301
minority:
— intense, 62, 267
— rule of, 314–15
Minow, Newton N., 217
Mises, Ludwig von, 52n, 86n, 242n
Monckton, Walter, 160n
money, diminishing marginal utility of, 102, 156n, 167, 200n
Montesquieu, Charles Louis de Secondat, 284
Moore, G. E., 39n
moral principles, 37n, 295–6
morality:
— personal, and conflicts of loyalties, 13
— public, institution of, 308–10
— *see also* immorality; moral principles
Morgenstern, Oskar, 5n
Morris, Charles W., 17n
Morris, William (1834–1896), 300
Morrison, Herbert, 239n
Mund, Vernon A., 235n
Musgrave, R. A., 278n
Myrdal, Gunnar, 46–7, 201n, 299, 303

Namier, Sir Lewis B., 56

welfare state (*contd.*):
— and want-satisfaction, 42
— and welfare, concept of, 188,
224–5
Wellbank, J. H., lviiin
Wicksell, Knut, 157n, 250–1, 313–14
Wicksteed, Philip H., 176n
Wiggins, David, lxv, lxvi, lxvii,
lxviii–lxix
Williams, Bernard, xxix
Williams, Raymond, 301
Willoughby, W. W., 14n, 15n, 119n
wills, spontaneous coincidence of, 86n,
87
Wilson, Charles E. (General Motors),
189
Wilson, James Q., 121n, 123n, 128n

wishes, primary and corrected, 59–61,
294–5
Wittgenstein, Ludwig, xxxii, xxxiv, 57n
*Wolfenden Report on Homosexual
Offences and Prostitution*, 42n, 67–9,
213n, 307–8, 310
Wolff, Robert Paul, 144n
Wollheim, Richard A. 59n, 221n, 293–4
Wootton, Barbara, 159–61, 167n, 242n,
309
words, 22–3, 28–31; *see also* language
workmen's compensation, and desert,
113
writers, *see* arts; speech, freedom of

Young, Michael,, 104n, 134n

Ziff, Paul, 9, 29